# 1 MONTH OF
# FREE
# READING

## at

## www.ForgottenBooks.com

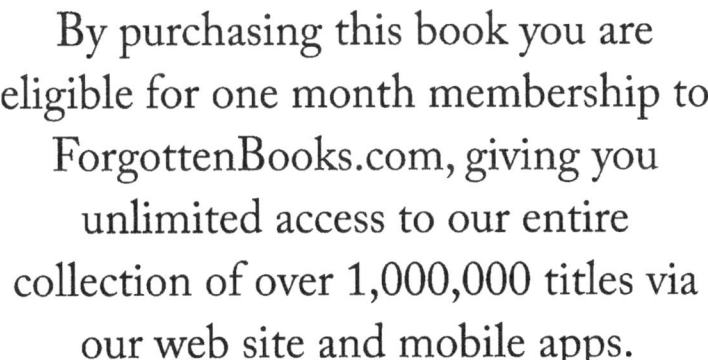

By purchasing this book you are eligible for one month membership to ForgottenBooks.com, giving you unlimited access to our entire collection of over 1,000,000 titles via our web site and mobile apps.

To claim your free month visit:

www.forgottenbooks.com/free912332

ISBN 978-0-266-93603-9
PIBN 10912332

This book is a reproduction of an important historical work. Forgotten Books uses state-of-the-art technology to digitally reconstruct the work, preserving the original format whilst repairing imperfections present in the aged copy. In rare cases, an imperfection in the original, such as a blemish or missing page, may be replicated in our edition. We do, however, repair the vast majority of imperfections successfully; any imperfections that remain are intentionally left to preserve the state of such historical works.

**UNIVERSITY OF ILLINOIS
AT URBANA-CHAMPAIGN**

# 47th annual HONORS DAY

Friday Afternoon, April 30, 1971, at 1:30

**ASSEMBLY HALL**

## HONORS DAY

HONORS DAY is observed annually as an occasion upon which the University of Illinois at Urbana-Champaign gives public recognition to those students who excel in scholarship.

Each undergraduate student receives Honors Day Recognition and has his name recorded in the Honors Day Book if he has placed on the Dean's List of his college since the last preceding Honors Convocation. "Honors Day Recognition (year)" is recorded on the student's official University record.

The students whose names appear in this program are in two categories: those who have won recognition by having qualified for the Dean's List, thus winning honors recognition, and those who have qualified for University Honors (Bronze Tablet).

The general Senate rules for recognition of honors students and the rules of procedure by which such students are selected appear on the last pages of this program.

## UNIVERSITY FACULTY HONORS COUNCIL
## COMMITTEE ON HONORS DAY RECOGNITION

RICHARD R. MARSH, Chairman
WILLIAM FEYERHARM
KARL E. GARDNER
KENNETH B. HENDERSON
ALAN K. LAING
NELSON I. LEONARD
A. C. MOORE
JAMES R. PAYNE
ROGER R. YOEGER

*Student Member*
DONALD A. SHAPIRO

Members of the following honorary societies
are serving as ushers:
ALPHA LAMBDA DELTA
PHI ETA SIGMA
TORCH

Dr. Richard R. Marsh, Director of University
Honors Program at the Urbana-Champaign Campus,
is serving as Marshal.

# CONVOCATION PROGRAM

JACK W. PELTASON, *Presiding*
Chancellor of the University of Illinois at Urbana-Champaign

## PROCESSIONAL*

"March Romaine".................................*Charles Gounod*

THE FIRST REGIMENTAL BAND
EVERETT KISINGER, Conducting
Assistant Director of University Bands

## INVOCATION

RABBI EDWARD FELD
Hillel Foundation

## RECOGNITION OF HONOR STUDENTS

DEAN ROBERT B. DOWNS
Dean of Library Administration

## GREETINGS FROM THE BOARD OF TRUSTEES

EARL M. HUGHES
President of the Board of Trustees

## INTRODUCTION OF THE HONORS DAY SPEAKER

JACK W. PELTASON
Chancellor

## HONORS DAY ADDRESS

LYLE H. LANIER
Executive Vice-President and Provost of the
University of Illinois

## BENEDICTION

RABBI EDWARD FELD

## RECESSIONAL*

"March Moderato" from "Trois Grandes Marches"......*Joseph Hummel*

* The audience is requested to remain seated during the processional, and during the recessional until the academic procession has left the Assembly Hall.

## UNIVERSITY HONORS (BRONZE TABLET)

The following students were awarded University Honors in February, 1971, or are to be awarded University Honors in June, 1971. As a general rule, they have ranked in the upper three per cent of all the students in their college in their cumulative grade-point average based on all credits earned at the University. Annually these names are inscribed on the Bronze Tablet which hangs permanently in the south corridor of the University Library. Other information on eligibility may be found on the last pages of this program. An asterisk appears beside the names of those students who have performed successfully as Edmund J. James Scholars.

ANDERSON, ROSS BYRON
*BALKE, NELSON EDWARD
*BARDELMEIER, DENNIS GENE
*BARTON, JAMES MICHAEL
BELSLEY, KATHRYN GENE
BERGER, JOEL EMANUEL
*BERMAN, RONALD CHARLES
*BERTOGLIO, MARK RAYMOND
BIOLCHINI, RITA JEAN
*BLOM, BERNHARD EMILE
*BOWEN, EVELYN ROSE
BREEZE, CYNTHIA MASSANARI
BRIGGS, LAURA E.
*BRIGHT, PEGGY RENEE
*BROTMAN, ERICA
*BROWN, JEFFREY PAUL
*BROWN, ROGER MARK
*BUSHMAN, MARY ANN
*CHAN, WAI KUNG
*CHESLEY, PATRICK JOHN
*DARKEN, PATRICIA MILLER
*DAVIS, LAURA REBECCA
*DIEHL, RANDY LEE
*DOUGLAS, DAVID JOSEPH
*DOWLING, GLORIA VALBORG
*EISEL, JOHN LESLIE
*ELLIS, JEFFREY JAMES
*EPPLIN, JEROME JOSEPH
*FULLER, DANIEL LEROY
*FULLER, KIM FRANCIS
*FUNK, JAMES LORAINE
*GILES, JOHN EDWIN

GINDER, GORDON DEAN
*GOBEN, BETTY ANN
*GODAR, MARY KATHRYN
*GULLANG, DEBORAH JEAN
*HAAS, DANIEL DILLON
HANES, RICHARD ARTHUR
*HIGGINS, BRYON MARK
*HOLADAY, ALLAN SCOTT
*HUBER, BRUCE ALAN
*JECMEN, ROBERT MILTON
*KATZ, VICKI SIEGELMAN
*KENDRICK, LAURA JEAN
*KERR, STANLEY PAUL
*KESLER, JAMES L.
*KLEIN, CHARLES ALLEN
*KLEISS, ALICE JOAN
*KOONCE, WAYNE ALLAN
KROLAK, LUCY ANN
LANCASTER, DAVID RUSSELL
LANE, CHARLES RAY
LARSON, DALE BRADLEY
*LARSON, KRISTINE GARMAYER
*LEOPOLD, WILBUR RICHARD, III
*LERITZ, JAMES PETER
*LINDQUIST, KENNETH WILLIAM
LINDQUIST, WILLIAM CARL
*LITTLE, DANIEL EASTMAN
*LUBIN, STUART FREDRIC
LUNDE, PAULA ANN
MARSHALL, PAUL EDWARD
*MASSINGILL, MARSHA ELAINE
*MASTERS, MARJORIE LUESE

4

*MATTHEWS, SHELDON HAROLD
MENG, BONNIE KAY
MENG, CONNIE FAY
*MILLER, GARY J.
*MOORE, DIANE ELAINE
MUELLER, MARY LOU
*MUNZ, JOHN HARTZELL
*MYERS, JOHN RILEY
*NOSEK, RICHARD DOUGLAS
*O'HARE, RANDALL SCOTT
*OHMAN, SANDRA MAE
*PARKS, DAVID MOORE
*PATINKIN, TERRY ALLAN
PERINO, KATHLEEN ANN
*PETERSON, GEORGE ALLEN
*PETERSON, LARRY DEAN
*PETERSON, ROBERT THOMAS
PETERSON, ROY ASBERG
*PLONDKE, JAMES CHARLES
*REEM, DENISE ELAINE
*REINER, DAVID LAWRENCE
*REULER, PEGGY ROSE
*RICHARDS, LAUREL ANN
RICKERT, CLAUDIA RAE
RITCHER, GARY KIPP
ROSBOROUGH, TERRILL KENT
*ROSZKOWSKI, MARK EDWARD
*ROTTMAN, DAVID BRUCE
*RUDDELL, BRIAN WAYNE
*RUNDELL, KATHRYN LUTZ
*RUTLEDGE, JAMES EDWARD

*SAFFORD, SHARON ANN
*SCHALLER, MICHAEL JAY
*SCHOENBERG, DANIEL ROBERT
SHEREY, BRENDA LEE
*SLUTKIN, GARY
*SONNEMAKER, MICHAEL WILLIAM
*SOUTHON, EDWARD HENRY
SPANGLER, SUZANNE PAMELA
*STANLEY, BONNIE BRADY
STEFFEN, RONALD WAYNE
*STOLLER, JAMES JOSEPH
*STRANG, AUDREY LYNN
*SUDLOW, WILLIAM JOSEPH
*SWAIN, PAULA C.
TAYLOR, WILLIAM MICHAEL
*TRIGGER, JOYCE STARR
*UBELL, FRANKLIN DAVID
VASELESKI, RAYMOND CHARLES
WATSON, LAURA LEE
WEBER, PENNY SUE
*WEIL, MARGARET SUE
*WEISEL, REBECCA LYNN
*WEISHAR, MICHAEL CHARLES
*WINTER, DOUGLAS EARL
*WISS, JAMES ERNEST
*WORSHAM, PATRICK MICHAEL
*YESINOWSKI, JAMES PAUL
*ZACK, GREGORY WILLIAM
*ZANCHO, DEBORAH HARTMAN
*ZOELLICK, MARILYN MARTHA

# HONORS DAY RECOGNITION

The following students are recognized for their academic excellence as demonstrated by their having had their names appear on the Dean's List of their college since the preceding Honors Convocation. An asterisk appears beside the names of those students who have performed successfully as Edmund J. James Scholars for one year. The requirements for placing on the Dean's List are found on the last pages of this program.

## COLLEGE OF AGRICULTURE

ABELL, HELEN LOUISE
*ADAMI, PAUL EDWARD
AHERN, KATHLEEN ANN
AKERS, DEANNA LINN
ALBIN, PERRY SANFORD
ALESSANDRI, KATHRYN HABES
ALISON, SUSAN CHARLOTTE
*ALLEN, MARK EATON
ALLERS, KENNETH WAYNE
*ALLHANDS, RODGER VERNON
AMLING, ROBERT MARTIN
AMSTUTZ, PAUL EDWARD
ANDERSON, CLYDE RAY
ANDERSON, DALE HENRY
ANDERSON, MARILYN MCCURDY
ANDERSON, RICHARD FRANKLIN
ANDERSON, ROSS BYRON
ANDRIS, MARVIN RUSSELL
ARMON, WILLIAM JOHN, JR.
ARMSTRONG, CHERYL JORENE
ARNE, BARBARA RUTH
ARNOLD, KENNETH RAY
ASSELBORN, DONNA MARIE
AUGSBURGER, BRUCE EUGENE
AUGUSTINE, WILLIAM LOWELL
AUL, JERRY STEVEN
AULT, MARTHA JANE
AUPPERLE, DAVID ALLEN
AURIENE, BARBARA GRACE
AUSTMAN, JERRY PAUL
AYERS, STEPHEN ROBERT
BACH, JANICE ANN
BAJJALIEH, NICHOLI LLOYD
BAKER, KAREN CHRISTINE
BAKER, TIMOTHY GUY
*BALKE, NELSON EDWARD
*BALSTERS, KENNETH EDWARD
*BANE, DAVID PAUL
BARISH, ROBIN ILANA
BARNARD, DENNIS L.
BARNES, DEBORAH KAY
BARTLEY, JOHN LESLIE
BAUGHER, KENNETH DEAN
BAUGHMAN, DAVID EDWIN

BAUGHMAN, JAMES EDWIN
BAUMAN, DOREEN ANN
*BAUMGARTNER, FREDERICK LYLE
BAXTER, JAMES RICKARD
BEACH, CYNTHIA JEANNE
BEAM, CAROL LYNN
BECK, DONNA MARIE
BECK, JULIE FRANCES
BECKES, PATRICIA LOU
BEEM, RICHARD STINE
*BEND, DONALD DUANE
BENITZ, PETER
*BENSON, JAMES EDWARDS
BENSON, ROBERT KENT
BERBAUM, SHIRLEY RAYBURN
BERG, CRAIG PEMBERTON
BEST, DAVID ALAN
BESWICK, DONALD DEWITT
BEYERS, THOMAS GERARD
*BIDNER, MARILYN JEAN
BIDNER, MARLYS MCCLELLAND
BIDNER, ROBERT GENE
BIEBER, JUDITH ANNE
BIELBY, DENISE DEL VINTO
BIGGS, JACKIE WALTER
BINCH, BARBARA ALLYN
BIRD, JERRY LEE
BISCHOFF, THOMAS ARTHUR
BLACK, LYNN ERVIN
BLAIR, TERRY MONTAIGNE
BLAKE, GARY LEE
*BLANK, RUTH ELLEN
BLAUERT, GARY THOMAS
BLOUNT, DALE ROBERT
BLUCK, ELLEN MARIE
BLUNIER, LARRY GENE
BOCK, ROGER WAYNE
BOEHNE, CURTIS WILLIAM
BOGNER, LORAINE ELIZABETH
BOHNHOFF, ROBERT JOHN
BOLL, ROBERTA JANE
*BOLLINGER, DEAN HERMAN
BORAH, GARY LYNN
BOSKE, GARY J.

*Bowen, Sandra Lynn
Bowler, Kathleen Ann
Bowles, Marlin Lynn
Bowman, David Bruce
Boyer, Barbara Jean
Boyle, Walter Durley
Bozic, Carole Susan
Braatz, Dana John
Bracey, Roy Wayne
*Bradbury, Peter James
Bradley, James Philip
Brandt, Mary Elizabeth
Brar, Sharon Kaur
Bremer, David Lee
Brenne, Lynda Elizabeth
Brenner, Diane Cecelia
Brewer, Kenneth Charles
Bridges, David Earl
Bridson, Randy George
*Brinkmann, Carl Ernest
*Brinkmann, Kenneth Gene
Britt, William Roland
Brooks, Sandra Miller
Brown, Charles Gerard
Brown, Frances Susan
Brown, Herbert Michael
Brown, Robert Joseph
Brunton, Byrle Barron
*Buck, James William
*Bugos, David James
Builta, Steven Stimpert
*Bundy, Linda Sue
Burgener, Donna Lyn
Burns, Connie Lou
Burns, Richard Laurence
*Burns, Thomas Paul
Burrow, Daniel Carl
Busse, Donald Frederick
Butler, Roberta Lee
Byers, Randy Eugene
*Callahan, Colleen Rae
Campbell, John Alan
Cannell, Sheva Renee
Canterbury, Sarah Elizabeth
Cantlin, John Lawrence
Cardoni, Robert L.
Cariens, Gary Lynn
Carlson, Cheryl Lynn
Carlson, Donald Lawrence
Carter, Carol Ann
Carter, Larry Lee
Carter, Olivia L.
Carvalho, Celia Napierala
Cassel, Georgia Ellen
Caudle, Norman Earl
Ceglinski, Eugene William
Chappel, William Ernest
Charleston, David Albert
*Cheever, Matthew Alan
Chirolas, Darlene Jean
Christ, Ruth Ann
Christensen, Dana Kent
Christiansen, Linda Ruth
Clack, Robert Meadows
Clark, Nancy Jean

Clary, Dale Allan
Cline, Robert Lee
Cochran, Stuart Allan
Cogswell, Janice Corrine
Colby, Carol Jean
*Colgan, Constance Kay
Collier, James Franklin
*Collins, Katherine May
Connor, Beth Kathleen
Connor, Joseph Francis
Conover, Mindy Lou
*Constantine, Adriann Gail
Cook, Jo Rana Waterbury
Cooley, Glen Dale
Corbin, Ruth Ann
*Cornelius, Steven Gregory
Corum, Larry James
*Covert, Donna Joyce
Craddock, Leigh Howard
Craft, Andrea Adel
Cramsey, Richard Gerard
Crane, Carol Ann
Cristy, Larry William
Crockett, Jerry Lloyd
Cromlich, Kathleene Diana
Cross, Greg William
Cudmore, Byron Glen
Cumpata, James Alan
Cusick, Patricia Hull
Dallas, Edward D.
*Damery, Darrell Rodney
Damhorst, Mary Lynn
Daniel, Karen Joyce
Dann, Barbara Jo
Davidson, Richard John
Davis, Alice Marie
Davis, Georgiana Jean
Davis, Margery Salisbury
Davis, Michael Allen
Davis, Paula Marie
Davis, Phyllis Ann
Davis, Susan Elaine
Dawson, Susan Herich
*Dazey, Dennis Dean
Deakin, Gregory Alan
Deason, Debra Ann
Dedecker, Mark Lon
Deets, Alan Le Roy
Dehart, David Gordon
*Deiss, Donald Dean
Demick, Richard James
Derrig, Robert George
Devries, Larry Allen
Dewitt, Roger Merle
Deyoung, Wayne Wilfred
Dickey, Steven L.
Dickinson, Richard William
Dicks, Orville William, Jr.
Diel, Steven Lynn
Dierker, Donald Eugene
Dierks, Patricia Ellen
*Dierolf, Gary Michael
*Dierstein, Julie Jene
Dillon, Cynthia Marie
Dipietro, Joseph Anthony

8

DOLL, STEVEN JOSEPH
*DONAHUE, FRANCES LEE
DONILE, DONNA MARIE
DONOVAN, MARGO RUTH
DONOVAN, MICHAEL FRANCIS
DONOVAN, SUSAN JEAN
DOWNEY, TIMOTHY WILL
DOYLE, RONALD WAYNE
DRAKE, MARGARET RUTH
DUCHETTE, EDWIN SCOTT
DUIS, ROBERT GENE
DUNCAN, WILLIAM KELLOGG
DUNKER, ROBERT ELDON
DURCHHOLZ, DALE LEROY
DWYER, JAMES FRANCIS
DYER, LEROY WILLIAM
EARLEY, DAVID EUGENE
EAST, PATRICIA JOY
EATON, KATHRYN ANN
EBERS, LARRY GENE
EBERT, ROGER RAY
EISENBERG, CHERI FRAN
EKSTROM, PAULA KUSY
ELIAS, CATHERINE SYPHERD
ELLIOTT, NANCY JUNE
ELMQUIST, CHRISTINE LEE
*ELSON, STANLEY EARL
ENLOE, STUART EDWIN
EPPSTEIN, ROBERTA LARSON
ERNAT, JOHN ROBERT
ESPE, RICHARD ARVID
ETHERTON, TERRY DEAN
ETHRIDGE, JAMES IVAN
FADDEN, WILLIAM DAVID
FAHR, STEPHEN CHARLES
FALKENTHAL, SUSAN MAE
FARISS, SUSAN LYNNE
FARK, JANET SUE
FARRIS, MICHAEL RAY
FAY, RICHARD BRIAN
FELDMANN, LINDA LUCILLE
FELTES, RICHARD JOHN
FERGUSON, JEFFREY JON
FERRE, PAULA KAY
FERRIS, CHRISTINE ANN
FESSER, DALE JOHN
FEWELL, THOMAS WILLIAM
FINCK, JANANNE
FINKLE, KENNETH DAROL
FISHER, JOHN ALBERT
FLACK, ALAN LEONARD
*FLANIGAN, JAMES ROY
FLEISHER, HOMER LUTHER, III
*FLENNIKEN, JOHN MICHAEL
FLOECKHER, JAMES MONROE
FLOWERS, JEANENE SUE
FOGLE, JANE LESLIE
FOIT, NANCY JOYCE
FOLEY, STANLEY EDWIN
FOSTER, JAMES STANHOPE
FRANCIS, ROGER WILLIAM
*FRANCIS, WILLIAM ARTHUR
FRANK, PHILLIP HENRY
FREDERICK, ALLAN WAYNE
FREDRICKSON, JANE MARIE

FREISE, WAYNE HOWARD
FRITZ, DARRELL ROY
FRUIN, RANDALL LOUIE
FULGENZI, GEORGIA LYNN
*FULLER, DANIEL LEROY
FULMER, ANTHONY TOLEN
*FUNK, JAMES LORAINE
*FUNK, MELBA ROLF
GALLAGHER, BRIDGET VICTORIA
GALLAGHER, MICHAEL TERRENCE
GALLOWAY, SAMUEL HARDIN
GAMSU, LYNN EVE
*GANTZERT, GORDON MAURICE
GARDNER, VICKIE LUHR
GAREN, WENDY SUE
GARLISCH, LARRY ALLEN
GARWOOD, GREGORY FRAN
GASS, JEROME HENRY
GASSMAN, MARSHA ANN
GATS, ROBERT JOHN
GEIGER, GARREL EVAN
*GERDES, LARRY GENE
GERDES, LELA MAE
GETZELMAN, A. ROBERT
GILL, RONALD EUGENE
*GINNETTI, ANDREA ANNE
GLAENZER, DAVID LEE
GLAZER, CAROL HAUSHEER
GLECKLER, LARRY WINFRED
GLOVER, TERESA DONNE
GOEDDE, PAUL ALLEN
GOEKE, JOSEPH CONRAD
GOODWIN, AMY LEE
GORSKI, ALANA MARIE
GRABBE, VERN RUAL
GRAFF, DOUGLAS JOSEPH
*GRAFF, LAWRENCE EDWARD
GRAMM, CYNTHIA LOUISE
GRAMM, MICHAEL LEE
GRANDT, LESTER LYN
GRAY, KATHERINE PERIN
GRAY, RONALD LYNN
GREENE, JERRY ALAN
GREENE, THOMAS LEE
GREGG, DAVID WILLIAM
GRENNAN, MICHAEL JOHN
GRIMES, COLLEEN EVONNE
GROSS, ROGER ALLEN
GRUBE, DENNIS ARTHUR
GVILLO, FREDERICK HENRY
HAAKE, ROBERT PAUL
HABERMAN, KATHRYN BARBER
*HADRABA, BARBARA JO
HAFENRICHTER, MARY JEAN
*HAGEN, DANIEL RUSSELL
HAGENBUCH, DAVID GLEN
HALEY, DIANNE ELSIE
HANE, RICHARD DOUGLAS
HANES, RICHARD ARTHUR
HANFLAND, LINDA LOUIS
HANOVER, LAREN MARK
HANSON, PATRICIA LOU
HARMS, CLIFFORD HERBERT
HARMS, DANIEL WARREN
HARSHBARGER, WARREN FRANCIS

9

HARTSTIRN, RANDALL ROY
HAWTHORNE, STEVEN ROBERT
HEALY, EILEEN MARY
HEATON, TED DE WAYNE
HEDRICK, LINDA JEAN
HEINRICH, TOM DALE
HEISNER, BERNARD MELVIN
*HELLMICH, JANET MARIE
HENDERSON, S. HUNT
HENDRIX, GARY GAYLORD
HENRIKS, BRUCE WILLIAM
*HEPPERLY, PAUL REED
*HERBERT, CARL EUGENE
HERRIMAN, ROGER DALE
HERRIOTT, LESLIE ANN
HEUER, MARY JANE
*HEUSEL, MARY HOWALD
HICKS, JERRY RAY
HIGGINS, STEPHEN KEITH
HILDEBRAND, KAY ELAINE
HILER, GEORGE MYERS
HILER, STEVEN EDWARD
HILL, ELEANOR ANN
HINKEN, JOHN R., JR.
HINRICHS, KEITH EDWARD
*HINTON, MARY BETH
HODEL, CHARLES ALAN
HODEL, LARRY JAMES
HOFFMAN, DANIEL RICHARD
HOFFMEISTER, ROBERT ALAN
HOGAN, JOSEPH W.
*HOLADAY, ALLAN SCOTT
HOLCOMB, SUSAN ROCHELLE
*HOLDSWORTH, ANNE HOLSTINE
*HOLFORD, BARBARA JEAN
HOLMES, THOMAS ROBERT
HOLMSTROM, ROGER KENNETH
HOOKS, DAVID ARTHUR
HORN, CHARLES SAMUEL
*HORTIN, MARY JANE
HOSKINS, JAMES R.
*HOSKINS, THOMAS HENRY
HOUSEHOLTER, ELDO DEAN
HOWARD, THOMAS CHARLES
HUBBARD, ROBERT KINGSLEY
HUDSON, LINDA JEAN
HUDSON, MARK EDWARD
HULDER, ELIZABETH ANN
*HUNLEY, HEATHER VALERIE
HUNT, PRISCILLA EWING
HUNTER, JANET CAROL
HURT, CHRISTOPHER ALLAN
HUTCHINSON, ROBERT HAMILTON
IEHL, WAYNE RICHARD
INSKEEP, LEROY GENE
ISAAC, SUZANNE EMILY
JABLONSKI, BEVERLY JEAN
JACOBS, JAMES EDWIN
JAKES, KATHRYN ANGELA
JAMES, RICHARD ALLAN
JANOVIC, SANDRA LEE
*JANSSEN, RACHEL LOUISE
JAY, WILLIAM EDWARD
JENNINGS, LEE ROBERT
JENSEN, EDWARD CHARLES

JERABEK, JAMES SCOTT
JOHNSON, CARL PHILLIP
JOHNSON, GUY HENRY
JOHNSON, JANET SUE
JOHNSON, JILL MARIE
JOHNSON, KEVIN MICHAEL
JOHNSON, LARRY LAVERN
JOHNSON, MARGO ANN
JOHNSON, NANCY JO
*JOHNSON, PAUL CURTIS
JOHNSON, SUSAN ESTHER
JOHNSON, WILLIAM MICHAEL
JONES, DANA ELAINE
JONES, JAMES SCOTT
JONES, RONALD DEAN
*JOYCE, JAMES EDWARD
KAHN, WILLIAM MICHAEL
KAISER, EDDIE HOWARD
KALINOWSKI, JUDITH GAIL
KALLAL, HENRY JOSEPH
KALLAL, MARY JOSEPHINE
*KALLAL, THERESA MARY
KAPPES, ROSEMARY KAY
KARI, FRANK WALTER
KAY, DARLA IRENE
KEISTER, MARK QUINN
KELLY, JOHN JOSEPH
KEMMIS, TIMOTHY JOE
KENDRICK, KATHRYN SUE
*KENNEDY, LARRY RALPH
KERR, ALICE ANN
KILLEY, JAMES DANIEL
*KING, E. RAY, III
KINGDON, DUANE ALAN
*KINNEY, DIANE SUE
KINNEY, DONNA LEE
KIPER, MARSHA ANN
KIRBY, EDWARD J.
KIRK, JENNIFER JILL
*KLECKLER, DANNY RAY
KLEHM, ARNOLD J.
*KLEISS, ALICE JOAN
KLOZA, CHRISTINE JOANNE
KLUTE, SALLY
KNAB, JOHN WILLIAM
KNAUTH, KENNETH ALAN
KNOX, HELEN SUSAN
KNUDSON, CHARLES ELBERT
KOGAL, JAMES THOMAS
*KOCH, BEVERLY ANN
KOCH, MYRON WILLIAM
KOEUNE, EUGENE NICHOLAS, III
KOHRING, KATHLEEN RUTH
KOLTVEIT, DAVID EUGENE
KOMANETSKY, RUTH ANN
*KORSMEYER, STANLEY JOEL
KRAHL, MARCIA THERESA
KRAMER, SANDRA LEE
KREIMEIER, VICTORIA LOUISE
KRUEGER, KARL ALBERT
KRUG, SUSAN KAY
KRUM, FAYE EILEEN
KUENSTLER, WILLIAM FRANK
KUHNS, GARY LEE
KUHNS, SHARON DODD

10

KUMMEROW, KAY LOUISE
KUNKLE, GEORGE LYNN
KUNKLE, JAMES EUGENE
KUSNERZ, RAYMOND LEE
KUSTES, JOHN THOMAS
LAESCH, JOHN HERBERT
LAESCH, PHILIP THEADORE
LAGER, MARTHA LYNN
LAMAR, SUSANNE
LAMBERT, KATHY JULINE
LAMOREUX, MARILYN ZWICKER
LANCASTER, TERRY DWENE
LANDERS, CHARLES ALBERT
*LANG, RITA ANN
LANSFORD, CLAUDIA LARSEN
LARSON, ARTHUR BRYCE
*LARSON, ROBERTA JEANE
LARSON, SUZANNE
*LAW, DALE ALLEN
LEAF, CHRISTINE ANNE
LEE, GREGORY JAMES
LEEPER, RANDALL ARTHUR
LEHMANN, JOHN DANIEL
LEICK, THOMAS JOHN
LEIDER, DAVID JOHN
LEMAN, HOWARD DEAN
LEMAN, RUSSELL A.
LESAGE, DAVID BERNARD
LESSLEY, JAMES VERNON
LEVAN, HOLLIS CAROL
LEVERENZ, AMY LOUISE
LEVINE, BRUCE STEVEN
LEWIS, GEORGE WILLIAM
LEWIS, KAREN DIANNE
LIBBIN, JAMES DAVID
LIBBRA, ALAN GENE
LOCK, CAROLYN JANE
LOMAX, LARRY GENE
LORESCH, PAMELA SUE
LOY, HAROLD MARVIN
LUDWIG, PAUL SINCLAIR
LUKAS, VIRGINIA KAYE
LURIE, MARILYN ELAINE
LUTH, GARY EDWARD
LUTH, LARRY DALE
LUTTRELL, WILLIAM REED
LUTZ, DONALD HOWARD
LY, SANCHEZ FRANCISCO
MABRY, JEAN MARIE
*MACK, TOM EUGENE
MACKEY, ANN L.
MALLICOAT, OREN DUANE
MARCHETTA, MARILYN FRANCES
*MARCINIAK, PATRICIA ROSE
MARCOOT, ROGER EARL
MARINICH, JOSEPH STEPHEN
MARSHALL, PAUL EDWARD
MARTEN, RANDY ALLAN
MARTIN, KEVIN ELI
MASSIE, DUANE KEITH
MAUTZ, KRISTIN BARBARA
MAWSON, STEVEN DALE
*MAYNARD, JOHN CLIFTON
McCARTHY, RICHARD THOMAS
McCAULEY, TERRY ROLAND

McCRACKEN, THOMAS RAYMOND
McCULLOUGH, STEPHEN LEON
McDERMOTT, KATHRYN FAYE
*McGEE, DAVID ALLEN
McINTYRE, CAROLYN SCHWARTZ
McKEE, PATRICIA ELAINE
McLAUGHLIN, MICHAEL DEAN
McLAUGHLIN, STEPHEN JOHN
McMILLAN, JUDITH SCHAUFELBERGER
*McMULLEN, PATRICK JOHN
McNUTT, FRANK FOREST
McTAGGART, TERESA LOUISE
MEALIFF, DAVID FRANK
MEERS, EDWARD WILLIAM
MEIER, JERRY BERNARD
MEINHOLD, VAUN HAROLD
MELTON, RICHARD ROBERT
MEYER, CHRISTINE LYNN
MIKKILA, SUSAN MARIE
MILLER, DALE RAY
MILLER, JAMES JONATHAN
MILLER, JAMES RANDOLPH
MILLER, JUDITH LYNN
MILLER, SCOTT C.
*MILTON, PENNY MARIE
MITCHELL, VICKI LYNN
MOHR, DAVID ROLLA
MOISAN, LAWRENCE GEORGE
MOLITORIS, BRUCE ALBERT
MONROE, RONALD LEE
MONROE, SHARON DAVENPORT
MOORE, EDWIN GRANVILLE
MOORE, LARRY DAVID
MOORE, ROLLAND DALE
MOOSE, PAULA ANN
MORGAN, FRANCES AIRDO
MORGAN, KEITH WARREN
*MORRISON, JANICE ELAINE
MORRISON, MARGARET ELLEN
MORRISON, RONALD STEPHEN
MUELLER, ARTHUR HARRY
MUELLER, CONSTANCE GEIGER
*MUELLER, JAMES F.
MUELLER, MARY JEANNETTE
MUELLER, THOMAS EDWARD
MUIR, WILLIAM MARTIN
MURPHY, GLENN EDWARD
MURRAY, MARY FRANCES
MUZZY, PAMELA JEAN
NACHENBERG, CARON LYNN
NELSON, CYNTHIA CHRISTINE
*NELSON, RICHARD ALAN
NELSON, ROGER WILLIAM
NELSON, WILLIAM GREGORY
NESLADEK, NANCY KATHRYN
NESLER, GARY ANDREW
NESSLER, FREDERIC WILLIAM
NEWCOMER, ANNE LOUISE
NICHOLAS, JOSEPH COLLIN
NICOLAY, DONNA SIMER
NIEHAUS, MARTIN GREGOR
NIGHTINGALE, FRED MARVIN
NILES, LESLIE RAYMOND
NOGGLE, REX ARLEY
NOLTE, THOMAS

11

NOR, ARTHUR GEORGE
*NOSBISCH, MARLENE MARY
NUSBAUM, MARK EDWARD
O'BRYAN, PAULA LOY
O'BRYAN, PHILIP BRANSON
OCHS, JOHN DAVID
OCIEPKA, MARY ROSE
OETTING, VICKI RAE
OLSON, E. LOUISE
OLSON, GAYLORD LEE
*OLSON, GREGORY LYNN
OLSON, JOHN MYRON
*OLSON, MARILYN SUE
*OLTMAN, GREGORY RAY
ONEILL, EDWARD WILLIAM
ORRIS, MARY DIANE GIFFIN
OSBORN, RICHARD ALAN
OTTE, JOHN ALVIN
OUART, DAVID LESTER
*OYER, VERLE CURTIS
PAARLBERG, RICHARD MARLIN
PALEY, DEBORAH KAY
PALLARDY, STEPHEN GERARD
*PALMER, BARBARA JANE
PALMGREN, PAUL WARREN
PAPKE, WILLIAM WALTER
PARISH, DARREL FORNY
*PARK, ALYN SEYMOUR
PARRETT, DOUGLAS FREDERICK
PARTRIDGE, EUGENIA JOAN
PASTROVICH, JAMES EDWARD
PECHMAN, IRENE SCHMITT
PEHLKE, ROBERT ERVIN
PENNER, VIVI HELANA
*PERCIACH, SUSAN JANE
PERKINSON, GARY LYNN
PETERS, CHRISTINE RAE
PETGES, RICHARD KEITH
PETTY, DONNA KAY
PFEIFFER, RICHARD H.
PIEKARSKI, JOHN RAYMOND
PILGER, THEODORE ROBERT
PIPER, KENNETH MELVIN
PITZEN, TRACY JAMES
PLUMER, MICHAEL DEAN
POEHLER, JANE ELLEN
POLETTI, PETER JOSEPH
*POLZIN, DAVID JAMES
POPE, TERRY ALLEN
POWELL, THOMAS JAMES
POWERS, WILLIAM WARREN
PRATT, CANDACE GAIL
PRENTICE, GAIL PATRICIA
PRICE, CAROL ANN
PRICE, CONNIE KNAPP
PRICE, DEBORAH SUE
*PRICE, JILL MICHAELINE
PROBST, CARL S.
PROBST, DENNIS ANTHONY
PULLIN, ETHEL ANN
QUANSTROM, CARL MARTIN
QUINTON, JAMES ERIC
RAFFE, MARC ROYCE
RALSTON, ROBERT WALLACE
RANEY, CYNTHIA ANN

*RATHGEBER, TERRANCE WILLIAM
RAY, DEBORAH ANNE
*REA, MARY ELLEN
REEDER, GERALD WILLIAM
REEP, JOHN DOUGLAS
REES, WILLIAM M.
REEVE, STEWART ANGUS
REGAL, DIANE ADELE
REICHART, VICKI SUZANNE
REINHART, TERRY EUGENE
REISS, WILLIAM LOGAN
REPULSKI, EDWARD FRANCIS, JR.
REVELL, JOSEPH LAWRENCE
RHEINWALD, JOHN GEORGE
RICE, THOMAS GLENN
RICHARD, KRISTINA MARIE
RICHARDS, GARY LEE
RICHARDS, ROSS L.
RICHARDSON, ROBERT OWEN
RIEKER, KEITH EDWARD
RINCKER, HARRY GENE
RINCKER, JAMES DARRELL
RINGGER, EARL EDWIN
RINGHOFER, STEPHEN MICHAEL
*RINKENBERGER, KENNETH
RINKENBERGER, RONALD DEAN
*RITTER, JACQUELINE KAYE
RITTER, WILLIAM ALLEN
ROBERTS, DAVID BRYANT
ROBERTS, SHARON KAY
*ROBINSON, BRENDA FAY
ROE, REBECCA JANE
ROETTGER, LARRY WAYNE
ROGERS, MICHAEL LEE
ROHRBACK, STEVEN JOSEPH
ROLF, JAMES K.
ROSBOROUGH, BRUCE DAVID
ROSENBLOOM, GAIL JOAN
ROSER, DOYLE WAYNE
ROULAND, SHARON LEE
ROWELL, RONALD LEE
ROWLAND, VIRGINIA ANN
*RUCH, PHILLIP LEE
RUDOLPHI, ADOLPH LEO
RUDOLPHI, JOSEPH PAUL
RUPPRECHT, JEAN ANN
RUTHERFORD, ROGER LYN
*RUTLEDGE, DEBORAH ANN
RUTLEDGE, WILLIAM ALLEN
SAGER, BRIAN PETER
*SAILER, LOU ELLEN
SALINE, GARY DUANE
SALRIN, THOMAS RICHARD
SALZMAN, MARJORIE ELAINE
SANDERS, KATHLEEN ANN
SANDERS, ROGER RAY
SANDFORD, SUZANNE MARIE
SANDIFER, BETTY RUTH
SAUDER, RICHARD ALAN
SAUDER, STEVE EARL
SAUER, ANDREW HUNTER
SCARFO, STEPHEN RAYMOND
SCHERER, DAVID LEE
SCHERER, ROBERT RUSSELL
SCHETTLER, THOMAS KELSO

12

SCHILLING, STEPHEN ROGERS
SCHLAPP, GARY DEAN
SCHLUETER, WAYNE ANTHONY
*SCHMID, BENJAMIN DAVID
SCHMIDT, GARY RANDALL
SCHMIDT, KEITH DOUGLAS
SCHMIDT, LAURA EILEEN
SCHRAUT, BARBARA ANN
SCHROCK, JUDITH LUKINS
SCHULZE, HOLLY ELIZABETH
*SCHUMAKER, CAROL ANN
SCHUPBACH, WILLIAM EUGENE
SCHUWERK, ANDREW BURNETT
SCHWOERER, THOMAS LEE
SCRIBNER, KATHY ANN
SEABOLD, TERRY RAYE
SEBENS, GARY RAY
SEIBERT, TOM FOX
*SEPP, PAUL EDWIN
SHAPIRO, LETTY ANN
SHEARER, GEORGE FREDERICK
SHEARER, HAROLD W.
SHEARER, PAUL SCOTT
SHELTON, STEVEN MICHAEL
SHIMEL, DENNIS WYLIE
SHIMMIN, LYNN ROBERT
SHOCKLEY, ELOISE HOFFMAN
SHOLLENBERGER, DEBORAH LYNN
SHULL, JEANNE CAROL
SHUMATE, JANICE LEE
SIEMERS, ROGER LEE
SILVA, GAIL ROBIN
SIMMONS, BRENDA LOU
SIMMS, DAVID ALLEN
SIMONINI, ANN ELIZABETH
SIMPSON, JAMES ROBERT
SIMS, PATRICIA ANNE
SIMS, WAYNE RICK
SINGLER, RONALD EUGENE
SISLER, ROBERT E.
SISSON, VERNE ALLEN
SKRHA, SHERRY LYNN
SLATER, DAVID WILMER
SLAYMAKER, ROBERT GEORGE
SLAYTON, JERRY PAUL
*SMITH, DANIEL SHEPHERD
*SMITH, GARY EDWARDS
SMITH, GEORGE KENT
SMITH, JOHN BRUCE
SMITH, MARK STEVEN
SMITH, RUSSEL EUGENE
SMITH, WILLIAM EUGENE
SOLON, BART JAMES
SOLON, EDWIN GEORGE
SOSTRIN, CAROL LYNN
SPANGLER, DOUGLAS RAYMOND
SPEAR, MICHAEL OLAN
SPECHT, CHARLES W.
SPELTER, HENRY NICHOLAS
*SPILKER, GAYLORD JOHN
SPRECHER, DAVID JOE
SPRINGER, PATRICIA JEAN
SPROULS, MARK WARREN
STAHLMAN, STEVE WILLIAM
STAUDER, MELANIE ANN

STEFFEN, JAMES R.
STEINER, FERN C.
STENGER, DAVID MICHAEL
STEPANCZUK, PAUL PHILLIP
STEPHEN, BARBARA JEAN
STERN, MARY CHARLOTTE
STEVENS, JANET GETTINGS
STEVENSON, CRAIG ALLEN
*STEVENSON, TERESA GALE
STOCK, DUANE RICHARD
STODDARD, JAMES ALAN
STOLL, JOHN ELDON
*STOLLER, JAMES JOSEPH
STONER, DAVID JAMES
STORZ, STEVEN EUGENE
STRADER, CARTER ALLEN
STRAYHORN, EARLENE EDWINA
STREID, PETER JOSEPH
STRINGER, BARBARA TAYLOR
STROTHMANN, PATRICIA LOU
STUEHM, HARRIET CROWLEY
STUMPF, ALAN EDMUND
STURM, TIMOTHY DWAIN
SUCHAN, RICHARD ANTON
SUS, CAROL ROSE
SUTTON, JAMES WESLEY
SVEAN, KENNETH RAYMOND
*SVOBODA, WAYNE ETNYRE
SWAGER, PATRICIA DICKS
SWEARINGEN, WALTER SPENCER
SWOBODA, RODNEY EDWARD
SYDOW, JEANINE WILMA
*TALLON, LYLE DUANE
TAMMEN, DALE RYLAND
TANTON, RICHARD WILLIAM
TARTER, WILLIAM RODELL, JR.
TAYLOR, CHESLEA CHARLES, II
TAYLOR, DEBORAH ANN
*TAYLOR, DOROTHY ANN
TAYLOR, GREGORY SCOTT
TAYLOR, PAMELA ANN
TEBUSSEK, CHARLES DAVID
*TEGELER, JAMES JOSEPH
TEIJIDO, JOSEPH ALBERT
TEMPLE, CAROL KAY
*TENHOUSE, ARTHUR ROBERT
THOMAN, BRUCE JEFFERY
THOMAS, BARBARA JEAN
*THOMPSON, JAMES STANLEY
TIVNAN, TERESA MARIE
TOLAN, JAMES LYLE
TOM, ROSALIE
*TOMBAUGH, LARRY WILLIAM
TONSOR, SHARON KAY
TOTSCH, JAMES PAUL
TRACY, JOHN STEPHAN
TRANQUILLI, RITA MARIE
TREECE, EDDIE JOE
*TREES, SCOTT CLYDE
TRENT, DAVID ALAN
TREWARTHA, JOHN RICHARD
TRONC, JANICE KENNEDY
TUCKER, CAROL PATRICIA
TUNNICLIFF, BROCK MATHEW
TWENHAFEL, CALVIN E.

13

UNDERWOOD, GERALD LEE
URISH, PATRICIA DIANE
*VAIL, JANE ELLEN
VALENTINE, DEBORAH ANN
VAN BUSKIRK, JAMES HOWARD, JR.
*VANDER JAGHT, GAIL
VAN ORMAN, DAVID MARC
VAN RHEEDEN, CONNIE JO (KLEIN)
VAN WERINGH, JANET
*VELDE, WILLIAM KENT
VIALL, PETER LESLIE
VITALI, ALBERT LOUIS
VOIGT, CHARLES EDWARD
VOLK, LEON WILLIAM
*VOLK, RHEA MARIE
VOREIS, RICHARD LEE
VROOM, JAY JOHN
*WAGHER, BONNIE NELSON
WALKER, DUANE DAVID
WALKER, MICHAEL BRIAN
WALKER, ROBERT EDWARD
WALLACE, JERRY LEE
WALLACE, JOHN WILLIAM
*WALSH, LINDA ELIZABETH
WASHBURN, ANNA ELIZABETH
WATKINS, JOHN WINTER
WATSON, BARBARA LEE
WATSON, LAWRENCE LEON
WAX, JOHN ERVIN
WAX, MARTHA MARIE
WEBER, KIMBERLY JANE
*WEBER, MICHAEL ROBERT
WEBER, WAYNE EUGENE
WEIDNER, LENORA ANN
WENDE, GAIL ANN
WENDTE, LEON WILLIAM
*WENZEL, DUANE EDWARD
WENZEL, FRANCES LEA
WENZEL, SHARON ELIZABETH
WERNER, LYNDON ANDREW
WESSON, GREGORY DONALD
WHALEN, COLEEN ANN

WHEAT, LEONARD GEORGE
WHITMAN, ANN MARIE
WHITTLES, EDANA LOUVISA
WHORTON, NANCY JANE
WIDHOLM, BETH ANN
WIENRANK, GEORGE DAVID
WIERSEMA, SUSAN OSTROWSKI
WILLIAMS, DALE DOUGLAS
WILLIAMS, JOANN ELAINE
WILLIS, RICHARD OWEN
WILLIS, WILLIAM JOSEPH
WILLITS, STEVEN LAWRENCE
WILLOUGHBY, KENNETH CHARLES
WINDHORN, ROGER DEAN
WINKELMANN, ROBERT EUGENE
WINTER, BARBARA A.
WIPERT, MARCIA GEN
WISLOW, NANCY LOUISE
WISSMILLER, JAMES ELWOOD
WOGNUM, BARBARA SCOTT
WOLF, JON ROBERT
WOLF, ROBERT EUGENE
WOLFF, DALE FRANKLIN
WOLLEK, ELLEN KAY
WOOLEVER, MAX LEE
WORMLEY, RICHARD BUDD
WORTHEM, DENNIS WAYNE
WURMNEST, JAMES VAL
WYLLIE, JAMES PRICE
YAEGER, LINDA RAE
YAGOW, DANNY ROGER
YAHNKE, GAYLE
YORK, TIMOTHY FLANN
YURKOVICH, DAVID PAUL
ZAHOS, SALLY WORZ
ZARKO, MARCIA ELEANOR
ZEGART, LESLEY ROBERT
ZELLER, RICHARD LEE
ZMUDKA, JAMES FRANCIS
ZUBER, JOHN CHARLES
ZUBER, KRISTNA SUZANNE
ZWILLING, KENNETH WILLIAM

## INSTITUTE OF AVIATION

ADKINS, CLIFTON RAY
ANDERBERG, STEPHEN JOSEPH
ANDREWS, MICHAEL JOHN
BEALS, DENNIS MELVIN
BECHER, KENNETH ROY
BEDOWS, ROBERT LAURENCE
BIGGOTT, ROBERT BRIAN
BOHBRINK, CLARK GILBERT
BOWEN, STEPHEN JAMES
BRANER, DENNIS RICHARD
BRESLIN, STEPHEN JOSEPH
BROWN, LEASON HOWARD
BUCK, JOHN E.
BUEHLER, WILLIAM BENET
BURNS, JAMES JOHN
BYLINA, DENNIS THOMAS
COSGROVE, JOHN ROBERT
DALLMAN, CHRIS ALLEN
DAVISSON, GLENN ROBERT
DEMARIA, JAMES LOUIS

DEMIAN, DAVID RONALD
*DREW, TODD SCOTT
EARLE, WILLIAM ROBERT
FODOR, MICHAEL ALAN
FRANCIS, HARRY FREDERICK
FREEMON, JAMES PAUL
FULLERTON, DAVID ALAN
GEORGE, DENNIS ALLEN
GIBFRIED, PAUL ROBERT
GILGER, DALE RAY
GREEN, HAROLD ALAN
HALLS, JOHN THOMAS
HARDIN, LARRY LAVERNE
HARMON, TROY LEE
HARTSHORNE, JOHN WARREN
HELLE, DUANE VERLE
HEROD, MICHAEL DAVID
HUGHES, MICHAEL THOMAS
JOHNSEN, CARL BRADLEY
JUNKER, GARY RAY

14

KAPPEL, BRUCE ROBERT
KENNEDY, PATRICK CHARLES
KINTZLE, DARRELL JOSEPH
KIRKMAN, JAMES EDWARD
KLASSEN, ALAN FRANCIS
KLECKA, EDWARD JOHN
KLING, RICHARD JACK
KLINT, RONALD EUGENE
KNIERIEM, DAVID WILLIAM
KNIGHT, CHARLES FRANKLIN
KRAUS, MICHAEL MARTIN
KROES, MICHAEL JOSEPH
KRUMPOCH, FRANK JOSEPH
KUHNKEY, PHILIP GEORGE
LANDIS, RICHARD CLAIR
LARSON, LAWRENCE HOWARD
LEEPER, LARRY ALLEN
LEGGANS, STEPHEN EARL
MANNING, RICHARD PATRICK
MANNING, ROBERT GEORGE
MARINANGEL, RICHARD MARTIN
MARTIN, KEVIN O.
MAST, TERRY LEE
MEIER, STUART ALLEN
MELLETTE, ROBERT RAY
MICHELSON, PAUL NORMAN
MILLS, ROBERT DOUGLAS
MONSON, DANA MORGAN
MORRELL, JOHN HILLARD
MULCAHEY, TOM L.
NOELKE, THOMAS ROBERT
NORTHCUTT, KENNETH A.
PATTERSON, GREG RICHARD

PEUCKER, WALTER CONRAD
RAGEL, STEPHEN WILLIAM
RIEDEL, PETER WILLIAM
ROTHERMEL, DONALD MARK
RUSSELL, DAVID ERIC
*SAMPSON, ROBERT HAROLD
SAUDER, HOWARD G.
SCHEUNEMAN, KURT EDWARD
SCHWAB, FRANK
SHIRE, AARON DAVID
SHOOK, BRUCE ALAN
SIMEK, STANLEY MICHAEL
SIMTH, DENNIS CHARLES
SOMMER, VINCENT H., JR.
SPECHT, DONALD ALBERT
SPINA, RONALD LEE
SPOETH, STEPHEN ALLEN
STALCUP, STANLEY FRANK
STEPPIG, BRUCE ALLEN
SUNDELL, RONALD CHARLES
SUTTON, MICHAEL ROBERT
TYNDALL, NORMAN BRUCE
VANCE, WILLIAM FORREST
VILLANO, JAMES NICHOLAS
WASHOW, DONALD RAYMOND
WEBER, GLENN KENNETH
WEGRZYN, LAWRENCE MICHAEL
WEST, DENNIS JOSEPH
WHITWORTH, THOMAS W.
WISNIEWSKI, FREDERICK JOHN
WOJTENA, JOSEPH STANLEY
ZIENTARA, GARY STEVEN
ZIMMERMAN, FRANK

## COLLEGE OF COMMERCE AND BUSINESS ADMINISTRATION

*ABATE, MARK ROBERT
ABELL, DARRYL GENE
ABRAMS, RICHARD NELSON
ACKLAM, CHARLES ROBERT
ACKLAND, GARY ALLEN
ADAMCZYK, RICHARD STEPHEN
ADAMS, LAWRENCE JOEL
ADAMS, MARY LOU
AGOCS, ENORE JOAN
ALDRICH, DAVID OLIVER
ALLEN, MICHAEL BURTON
AMBERG, STEPHEN CHARLES
ANDERSEN, RUSSELL MARTIN, JR.
ANDERSON, CRAIG LEONARD
ANDERSON, DENNIS CHARLES
*ANDERSON, GREGORY CHARLES
ANDERSON, THOMAS EDWARD
ANTOS, JOHN JEFFREY
*APPENZELLER, BILLIE KAY
ARMBRUST, RITA KENTNER
*ARMSTRONG, BENTON LEROY
ASHBY, FRANKLIN EUGENE
ASHEIM, PAUL WILLIAM
ASHER, LOUIS TOPPY
ATKINSON, JAMES WILLIAM
AYERS, JAMES RICHARD
AYERS, JAMES RODNEY
BAKER, FELIX JOHN
BANNER, JOHN GEORGE

BANUL, ROBIN
BARBER, JERRY GAIL
BARON, LOUIS PHILIP
BARR, JOHN ROBERT
BARTELSON, DARYL GENE
BARTELSTEIN, RONALD ALAN
*BARTHOLOMEW, DEBRA KAY
BASINGER, DAVID PAUL
BAST, KENNETH LENZ
BATES, JOHN BRADLEY
BEATTY, DALE LEE
BEAURLINE, ANDREW GARY
BECK, BRUCE ALLEN
BECKHART, PAUL ERIC
BEITMAN, HARTFORD
BEJROWSKI, JAMES JOSE
*BEKOWSKY, IRA BARRY
BELL, BRADLEY JOHN
BELL, MARVIN LEE, JR.
*BELL, WILLIAM DOUGLAS
BENJAMIN, JAMES COVER
BEREGSASI, ADALBERT
*BERG, ALLEN CURTIS
BERGE, JAMES JOHN
BERMAN, CHARLES H.
*BERMAN, RONALD CHARLES
BICISTE, DONALD CHARLES
BIELAWA, DANIEL WALTER
BIGGINS, JOHN PATRICK

15

BILL, JOHN RICHARD
BINENFELD, MARC LOEL
BLAIR, BRADLEY JAMES
BLAIR, EDWARD ALLEN
BLAKEMORE, THOMAS FREDERICK
BLANKENSHIP, MICHAEL
BLOCK, RICHARD NORMAN
BODEE, RICHARD LOUIS
BOLDT, KENNETH ALAN
BOLEN, GARY LEE
*BOLLMAN, TERRY LEE
*BONNELL, LESLIE DENNIS
BOWER, PETER O'CONNELL
BOWMAN, ROBERT, III
BRACKETT, JERRY RAY
BRESLIN, RICHARD JEROME
*BRIGHTBILL, FREDERICK
BRINEGAR, GEORGE BARLOW
BRINKMANN, WILLIAM JAMES
BROCKETT, JERRY KEITH
BROEKER, STEVEN LOUIS
BROWAR, JOHN LAWRENCE
BROWN, DALE WOODROW
BROWN, DAVID HAROLD
BROWN, DENNIS VARNER
BROWN, GLENN CHARLES
BROWN, JOSEPH NATHAN
*BROWN, RANDALL SCOTT
BROWN, RANDI MEREDITH
*BROWN, RAYMON MICHAEL
BROWN, ROBERT BRADLEY
BROWN, WARREN CAMPBELL
*BUCKLIN, ROBERT SCOTT
BUIKEMA, ROBERT WILLIAM
BULLIS, GRANT MARCUS
BURGWALD, ROBERT ARTHUR
BURNS, THOMAS EDGAR
BURRUSS, LINDA FAITH
BUSCH, DAVID CARL
BUSH, DOUGLAS JAN
BUSSA, ROBERT GENE
*BUTLER, JAMES MICHAEL
*BYERS, FRANKLIN HAYS, II
CAGLIUSO, KENNETH JOSEPH
CAHILL, W. ROBERT
CAIRO, STEVEN
*CALDERWOOD, TERRY JOAN
*CALLAGHAN, PATRICK FRANCIS
CALZA, THOMAS JOSEPH
CAMPBELL, JAMES EMERSON
CAMPBELL, LEE ROBIN
CAMPBELL, RAND ALAN
CARGILE, MICHELE MITCHELL
CARLSON, DAVID HENRY
CARLSON, PHILIP CARL
CARPENTER, ROBERT EDWARD
CARTER, HENRY EDWARD
CARY, JOHN HOWARD
CASTAN, ALLAN HILLARD
CASTELLANI, JERRY ALAN
CASTLEMAN, DAVID GALE
CATALANO, JOHN GEORGE
*CATLETT, STEVEN TILTON
CHALWICK, JEROME THOMAS
*CHAN, JAMES LAP-CHI

CHAPMAN, WILLIAM CARL
CHAPUIS, LARRY EDWARD
CHARLES, MICHAEL LEONARD
CHENAULT, ORA BRACKETT
CHERO, THOMAS HANKINS
CHERRY, DAVID RAY
CHOMKO, DANIEL STEPHEN
CLANCY, MICHAEL JOHN
CLARK, DONALD GEOFFREY
CLEWORTH, THOMAS FRANK
CODD, JOHN EDWARD
COHEN, NEAL IAN
COHEN, SHELDON BRUCE
COLLINS, DANIEL JOHN
CONAGHAN, THOMAS MICHAEL
*CONDON, SUSAN JOANNE
*CONROY, JOHN ALEXANDER
CONWAY, WALTER
COOK, JAMES CARL
COONEY, KENT HERBERT
COOPER, DIANE MICHELLE
CORNELIUS, WILLIAM THEODORE
CORRY, FRANCIS EDWARD
COSTELLO, GAYLE MURRILLE
COUGHENOUR, GREGORY ALAN
COUGHLIN, RICHARD TODD
COVER, DAVID LEE
CRAIG, TIM EDWARD
*CRANE, RICHARD ALAN
*CRISTY, DEBORAH ANN
*CROUCH, JOHN MICHAEL
CULLODEN, CHARLES ANDREW
CULUMBER, THOMAS EMIT
CUMPSTONE, ROBERT LLOYD
CUNNINGHAM, ANDREW PEARCE
*CUTRIGHT, KAY LYNNE
*CZWORNOG, MICHAEL
DABROSKI, CRAIG ADAM
DAILEY, MICHAEL JOSEPH
DAIZOVI, ROBERT
*DALBANI, THOMAS LAWRENCE
DALTON, GERALD REID
DAMICO, JOSEPH LAWRENCE
*DAUPHINAIS, JAY P.
DAVENPORT, KENT WHEATLEY
DAVIS, CHARLES JOSEPH
DAVIS, GARY LEE
*DAVIS, HOWARD JAY
DAVIS, JAMES MICHAEL
DAVIS, JEFFREY JUDE
DAVIS, STEVEN LEROY
DAWSON, MICHAEL RAYMOND
DAWSON, PHILLIP
DAWSON, WILLIAM EDWARD
DAY, MICHAEL STEVEN
DECKER, PAUL OSBURN
DECKER, STEVEN R.
DEITZ, ROBERT GALLATIN
DELONG, DEBORAH LYNN
DENAP, FRANK ANTHONY
DETRICH, JEFFREY JAMES
DEZORT, TOMMY EDWARD
DIAMOND, DAVID LAWRENCE
DIAMOND, JEFFREY BRYCE
DICKMAN, DAVID MARTIN

16

*DIFONZO, KENNETH WAYNE
DIX, RONALD LEE
DOAK, ROBERT FREDRICK
DONAHUE, PATRIC MCKINNEY
DONNELLY, JOHN J., JR.
DORSETT, DAVID MERRIMAN
*DOYLE, THOMAS EDWARD
DRESHAR, KAREN LEE
DUBBS, JOHN WILLIAM, III
DUCHARME, TOM PAUL
DUFFY, THOMAS JOSEPH
*DUGGAN, TIMOTHY ERIN
DULSKI, ROY JOSEPH
DUNBAR, GLEN BERRY
DUNCAN, BRUCE CARL
DUPONT, JOHN RICHARD
DYER, LYNDELL EUGENE
DYREK, EDWARD LEWIS
EDELSON, STEVEN DAVID
EDLEY, WILLIAM FORNERIS
*EDWARDS, JAMES LOUIS
*EISEL, JOHN LESLIE
EISENBERG, MARTIN LOUIS
*EISENSTEIN, MARTIN IRWIN
EISSFELDT, THEODORE LOUIS
ELDRIDGE, WILLIAM FRANKLIN
EMERSON, JAMES COLBY
*ENGLE, HOWARD STUART
ENZINGER, RICHARD SMITH
EPSTEEN, RALPH HOWARD
EPSTEIN, CHARLES BENTON
ERDMAN, RICHARD ALAN
ERNST, ROBERT MICHAEL
ERVIN, STANLEY CALVIN, JR.
*ERWIN, THOMAS KEITH
ETSCHEID, WYLIE EDGAR, JR.
*EVANS, ARTHUR HAROLD
EVANS, BRUCE DAVID
FAAS, CURTIS GENE
FABER, TERRANCE ALLEN
FARMER, DAVID KENNEDY
FAULDS, DOUGLAS ROBERT
FEDER, STEVEN LORRY
FEICHTER, MELANIE LYNN
FEINBERG, RONALD CHARLES
FELSENTHAL, ALAN DAVID
FELTES, TERRENCE ROWLEY
FERGUSON, THOMAS CHESTER
FERRETTE, DOUGLAS ROY
FERRO, PETER ANTHONY, JR.
FICHTER, JOHN KENNETH
*FISHER, DEBORAH ANN
FLATT, PHYLLIS KAY
FLORA, WARE BAKER
FON, GERALD LEE
FORNANGO, MARK ALAN
FOSTER, FRANKLIN JAY
FRADKIN, STEVEN GLENN
FRANKEL, JOHN HERMAN
FRAZER, BEATRICE CHRISTINE
FREGEAU, JOHN CHARLES
FRIEDLINE, JAMES RAY
FRIEDMAN, JOEL MARK
FRIEDMAN, ROBERT SAM
FRITSCHER, KURT WILLIAM

FRYE, DAVID CHARLES
FUCHS, MARC ELDON
FULTON, ROBERT FULLARTON
GAAR, GEOFFREY ALLAN
*GAHLON, JAMES MAURITZ
GALLAGHER, MICHAEL MARK
GAMAGE, ALDEN EUGENE
GAMAGE, MARK LEE
GANGE, RICHARD JOHN
GARDNER, DANIEL SIDNE
GARDNER, GERALD WAYNE
GARDNER, TERRY JOHN
GARLITS, JOHN RICHARD
GARVIN, STEPHEN DONALD
GASKILL, WARREN CHASE
GASPARO, JAMES THOMAS
*GASS, JOANNE MARIE
*GEHRS, RONALD FERDINA
GEISS, ALBERT EDWARD
*GERSHENZON, BRUCE WILLIAM
GIAMPOLI, JOHN JOSEPH
GIANOPOULOS, ANTHONY
GIBALA, NICHOLAS JOHN
GIBLIN, WILLIAM THOMAS
GILLESPIE, GENE EDWARD
GIMPEL, ALLEN BERNARD
GIRARD, DAVID RODERICK
GLASSBERG, BUDD STANLEY
GLAZER, IRWIN
GLICKMAN, ARON JEFFREY
*GOHR, DONALD LAWRENCE
GOLDBERG, DAVID A.
GOLDBERG, MICHAEL BARRY
GOLDBERG, MICHAEL LEE
GOLDMAN, DONALD LEE
GOLDMAN, PEGGY JEAN
GOODMAN, GARY MARC
*GOODZEY, JOHN ROBERT
GORAN, MARK HOWARD
GORENSTEIN, STEVEN
GOSS, RICHARD MATHEW
GOVERNILE, DANIEL FRANK
GRAESSER, KENNETH ANDREW
GRAHAM, MICHAEL PAUL
GRAN, GREGORY JOHN
GRANDONE, EUGENE
GRANDYS, ALVIN KRYST
GRANT, CHERYL KAY
GREEN, JAMES EDWARD
GREEN, SOL
GREINER, JOHN ADRIAN
GRIESHABER, GARY HERMAN
*GROSS, ALLEN FRANK
GROSS, NATHAN IRVIN
GUDGEON, JOHN WILLIAM
GUENTHER, JAMES ALBERT
*GUSSIS, ALAN HARVEY
GUTSHALL, ARTHUR ROBERT
GYENES, LAWRENCE ANDREW
GYNAC, GERALD C.
HACKETT, SUSAN IRENE
HAGEN, CHARLES ROBERT
HAHN, CHARLES ANTHONY
HAIGHT, CHARLENE ELLEN
HAKES, HARRY WARD

17

HALL, BEVERLY KAY
*HALL, MARY JANE
*HAM, ELDON LEE
HAMBOURGER, ALAN CHARLES
HAMEISTER, EUGENE LOUIS
HAMER, RICHARD EDWIN
*HAMILTON, CHARLES THOMAS
HAMPTON, VERN JAMES, III
HANDY, DELMAR JOSEPH
*HANEY, FORREST LEON
HANNON, JOHN PAUL
HANSEN, GLENN FRED
HANSON, KEVIN T.
HARASEK, LYNN LOUISE
HARMS, ROBERT WADE
*HARMS, TED E.
HARRIS, ROBERT DEAN
HARRIS, ROBERT WADE
HARRISON, WILLIAM HALE
*HART, DOUGLAS L.
HARTIGAN, JOHN FRANCIS
HARWIG, THOMAS WILLIAM
HASBROUCK, LAWRENCE FREDERICK
HASKINS, LUTHER G., III
*HATTENDORF, TERRY DON
HAYES, HOWARD ANTHONY
HEARL, RAYMOND EDWARD
*HEDRICK, JOHN RUSSELL
*HEGSTAD, SVEN OLAF
HEIDENREICH, ROGER LEE
HEITZ, MICHAEL GEORGE
*HELFAND, CORY MENDEL
HELFAND, MITCHELL J.
HELFER, MICHAEL THOMAS
HENDERSON, JAMES EDWARD
*HENSEL, DONALD DEXTER
HENSON, DAVID ALLAN
HENWOOD, HARRY JAMES
HERTEL, DONALD PAUL
HERTZ, JED BURTON
HERZMANN, FRANK JUERG
HINDMAN, STEPHEN PHILLIP
HITZEMANN, JERALD DALE
HLAVNA, DEBORAH PRUDENCE
HOEPPER, CHARLES THOMAS
HOFFMANN, STEPHEN EDWARD
HOGAN, MARK T.
HOGAN, STEPHEN JAMES
HOLMAN, TERRY LINN
HOLMEN, NEIL ERIK
HOLMES, ROGER WILLIAM
HOPKINS, JAMES PHILIP
HORWITZ, JEROME RAOPH
HOTZE, JOHN KEITH
HOUGH, THOMAS WRIGHT
HOUGHAM, ROBERT GREGORY
HOWAT, CLAUDE RICHARD
HUDSON, SUSAN ANN
HUDZIK, ALBERT GEORGE
*HUMPHREVILLE, JUDITH ANNE
*HUNTOON, HARRY KARL
HURD, THOMAS ROGER
*HUSTON, JOHN MATHEW
HYDZIK, PAUL JOSEPH
HYMAN, JAMES CRAIG

INGRAM, SCOTT LINDSEY
INMAN, DAVID MARSHALL
ISRINGHAUSEN, PAUL EDWARD
ITAMI, RICHARD JOSEPH
ITTERSAGEN, JOHN MARK
JACKOWIAK, THOMAS EDWARD
JACOBS, JOHN RAYMOND
JARED, THOMAS BRYAN
JENEN, PAUL RAYMOND
JENNINGS, JERRY WAYNE
*JENSEN, DAVID MARTIN
JESKE, MARC RICHARD
JOHNS, GREGORY ALAN
JOHNSEN, DAVID RAYMOND
JOHNSON, BRUCE PHILLIP
JOHNSON, DAVID STANLEY
JOHNSON, DAVID WALTER
*JOHNSON, LARRY CHARLEE
JOHNSON, LARRY FRANCIS
*JOHNSON, RANDALL DUANE
JOHNSON, RANDALL JOHN
JOHNSON, RAYMOND FRANCIS
*JOHNSON, RICHARD PAUL
JOHNSON, ROBERT HOWARD
*JOHNSON, RONALD WAYNE
JONES, CHARLES HUNTER
*JONES, DANA RAY
JUDSON, KEITH GARRY
JUENGER, BRUCE EDWARD
JULIUS, JOSEPH ROBERT
KAHLER, LAWRENCE MARTIN
KAMIN, WILLIAM BOTH
KAMINSKI, MICHAEL WALTER
*KANE, DAVID ARTHUR
*KAPLAN, STEVEN JAY
KASS, DAVID ARTHUR
*KASS, IRWIN LEE
KATEIVA, ANTHONY JAMES, JR.
KATZ, JORDON RICH
KATZ, STEVEN MARTIN
KATZENBACH, MICHAEL JAMES
KAVENEY, GEORGE JOSEPH, JR.
KAYE, RONALD KENNETH
*KEACH, KELVIN GRAY
KEENAN, ROLAND PATRICK
KELLER, WILLIAM GRIMM
KELLMAN, JEFFREY ALOY
*KELLY, JOHN PAUL
KELLY, WILLIAM DANIEL
KELMAN, KEITH NATHAN
*KENDRICK, MARGARET ANN
KENNEDY, KENNETH FRANCIS
KERNER, JEROME PAUL
KEROFF, STEVEN ROBERT
KERRINS, JOHN MICHAEL
KESSLER, SAMUEL LOUIS
KEYSOR, GLEN THOMAS
KILLION, DAVID PAUL
KINDORF, WILLIAM, III
KING, DIANE MARIE
KING, JAMES EDWARD
*KING, NANCY JUNE
KISS, JOHN MICHAEL
KISSANE, CHRISTINE
KLAAS, PALMER VERN

KLEIN, DONALD JAMES
KLIEN, RAYMOND EUGENE
KOENIG, STEVEN MARK
KOEPKE, DAVID ALLEN
KOKALBLAS, RONALD CLAUDE
*KOLLER, JAMES OSSIAN
KOPF, KEITH ARLIN
KOPRIVA, ROBERT STEVEN
KORNFEIND, JOHN GLENN
KOURIS, PAUL ANDREW, JR.
KRANZ, MICHAEL FRANCIS
KRCHAK, DAN WARREN
KREDA, LARRY ALAN
KRESL, STEPHEN GLEN
*KRUSE, STEPHEN KENT
KUBIK, PHILIP MICHAEL
KUCERA, GEORGE THOMAS, JR.
*KUNTZ, JANICE ANN
KURKOWSKI, RICHARD MICHAEL
KURLAND, JEFFREY MARK
KUSNIR, RICHARD
*KWIECINSKI, RICHARD ADAM
LAGER, MICHAEL LEE
*LACY, STEPHEN RICHARD
LAMB, DENNIS JAMES
LAMM, GARY LAWRENCE
LAMPERTZ, DALE ELLIOTT
LAMPINEN, JOHN ALFRED
LANDE, ROBERT JAY
LAUBE, BRUCE ANDREW
*LAVINE, RONALD MARK
LAWSER, WILLIAM HOWARD
LAZARUS, JOEL DAVID
LEARY, JAMES KEITH
LEE, JEROME EDWIN
LEGEL, DONALD ALAN
LEONARD, DAVID EUGENE
LEONE, PAUL MATTHEW
LEPLEY, JOHN ALAN
LESNIAK, JERRY PAUL
LEVINE, SIDNEY MARK
*LEWIS, DAVID JOHN
LEWIS, HERMAN PHILIP
*LEWIS, ROBERT WATKINS
LIEBERMAN, MARK C.
LINDBERG, CHARLES ALLEN
LINK, JACQUELYN LOUISE
LISS, GENE ANTHONY
LIVESAY, JAMES RAY, II
LLOYD, EDWARD GENE
LOEWENSTEIN, DAVID HARRY
LOOS, DAVID ERVIN
LOOSLI, GREGORY PAUL
LOOSLI, RONALD EUGENE
LOUER, CRAIG RAY
LOW, CLIFTON LEONARD
LUDVIGSON, DAVID GERALD
LUKEHART, GORDON CAMERON, JR.
LULLO, THOMAS ALAN
LUNDGREN, JAMES COLIN
*LUSCOMBE, MARK ALAN
LYNCH, JOHN FRANCIS
LYNN, MICHAEL WILLIAM
LYNN, NORMAN STUART
LYTLE, MICHAEL JAMES

MACHENS, GEORGE MICHAEL
MACKEY, JAMES JOSEPH
MADISON, LARRY M.
MAGGIO, DONALD EUGENE
MAGILL, MICHAEL KENNETH
MAINZER, JAMES MICHAEL
MAKI, PATRICIA CAROLINE
*MALLICOAT, HERMAN ALLEN
*MALLORY, ROBERT MARK
MANNY, CLYDE VICTOR, II
*MARCO, GAIL DIANE
MARCOTT, RICHARD JAMES
MARCUS, HARVEY STEVEN
MARRS, MICHAEL RICHARD
MARTINEK, RUSSELL GEORGE
MASCOTTI, EDWARD CHARLES
*MASKEY, REBECCA SUZAN
MASLOV, EDWARD IRA
*MASTERS, CURTIS BRIAN
*MASTERS, MARJORIE LUESE
MASTERS, RICHARD EARL, JR.
*MATTHEW, CAROLYN JEAN
MATTINGLEY, GREGORY ALEN
MAUCK, LAWRENCE MERLE
MAURER, JAMES HOWARD
*MAUTZ, CARL DAVID
MAXHEIMER, FREDERICK
MAXWELL, BARRY SCOTT
MAY, DEAN KENT
MAY, DONALD WILLIAM
*McCAMY, RAYMOND WINFIELD
McCARTNEY, JAMES WOODROW
McCAULLEY, ALLEN ROBERT
*McCLAYTON, THOMAS ROBERT
*McCUMBER, DOUGLAS RAY
*McDANIEL, MARK ORA
*McDERMOTT, PATRICK WILLIAM
McEVOY, MARTIN BATES
*McFARLAND, PATRICK ARTHUR
McGILL, ALAN JAMES
McGRANE, JAMES BERNARD
McGRATH, GARY MICHAEL
*McGRATH, THOMAS JOHN
McLAIN, PETER REED
McNICHOLS, PHILIP OEHM
McVEY, MICHAEL RODNEY
McVOY, TIMOTHY JAMES
McWILLIAMS, MICHAEL DAVID
MEECE, MELISSA JEAN
MEEKS, JOEY LEE
MEHOCHKO, KENNETH EUGENE
MENONI, MICHAEL ROBERT
*MERRION, PAUL ROBERT
METZGER, DENNIS WILLIAM
MEYER, CARLTON ERNEST
*MEYER, DONALD JOHN
MEYER, RANDY R.
MEYER, ROGER FRED
MEYERING, WILLIAM ALBERT, JR.
MICKEY, MARK JOHN
MIKSTA, DANIEL LESLIE
*MILES, DOUGLAS ELLIS
MILLER, MICHAEL EUGENE
*MILLIGAN, STUART CARROLL
MINOTT, BRUCE CRAIG

19

MOEHRING, WILLIAM LEE
MOELLER, LEWIS MICHAEL
MONTERASTELLI, STEVEN
MOODY, HUNTER COURTLAND, JR.
MOORE, DAVID WALTER
*MOORE, MARY ANTOINETTE
MOORE, SALLY KATHARINE
MOREHART, ANNE MARIE
MORGAN, IRVING JACK
MORRISON, EDWARD WILLIAM
MORRISON, KEVIN PATRICK
*MORROW, DWIGHT WAYNE
*MOSHER, KEVIN LEE
MOSS, JONATHAN YOST
*MOYE, CHARLES EDWARD
MOYER, JAMES EARL
MROZOWICZ, MICHAEL EDMUND
MUCH, PAUL JAY
MUCK, LEON GENE
*MUDORE, JOHN LAWRENCE
MUELLER, MELINDA MAE
*MULCRONE, KEVIN JOSEPH
MULLEN, JOHN GRANT
MULLIGAN, CHRISTOPHER KEVIN
*MUNZ, JOHN HARTZELL
MURPHY, JAMES MICHAEL
MURPHY, JOAN MARY
MURPHY, JOHN JOSEPH
MURPHY, MICHAEL EDWARD
MURPHY, PAUL JUSTIN
MURTAUGH, MICHAEL EDWARD
MUSSMAN, CRAIG LEE
MUSTAIN, DOUGLAS DEE
NAATZ, KENNETH ALLEN
NAATZ, ROBERT WARREN
NAFT, BARBARA
NAGEL, MARC
*NASH, ROBERT NELSON
NATKER, ANDREW JAY
NAUMAN, DANIEL LEE
NEATHAMMER, VALERIA JENE
NEBECK, JOHN HOWARD
NEBEN, MICHAEL ELLIOTT
NELSON, ADRIANE LYNN
NELSON, BRIAN TERRILL
NELSON, KEITH RUSSELL
NEMEYER, DAVID LANCE
NERI, THOMAS JOSEPH
*NESTA, WILLIAM ARTHUR
NEUBECK, TERRENCE JOHN
NEVELL, PATRICK LEO
NEWHOUSE, SHERRILL LOUISE
NICHOLS, JOHN HOWARD
NICHTER, MARK STEVEN
NICKERSON, THOMAS JAMES
NIZIOLEK, PAMELA JOYCE
NOLTE, WILLIAM JOHN
NORDQUIST, STEVEN LEE
NOVAK, ROBERT ANTON
NOWAK, RALPH GEORGE
NUNEMAKER, RICHARD ALAN
NUNN, LARRY EUGENE
*NUSINOW, ALAN IRA
NUSS, WILLIAM EDGAR, III
NYSTROM, DONNA KAY

OBENAUF, RONALD STEPHEN
*OBERROTMAN, ALAN MAURICE
O'BRIEN, M. KATHLEEN
O'BRIEN, MARTIN CYRIL
O'BRIEN, MICHAEL RAY
OCKER, WILLIAM EUGENE
O'CONNELL, DAVID JOSEPH
OFTEDAHL, GLEN FRANK
O'HARA, EUGENE JOSEPH
*O'HARE, RANDALL SCOTT
OHM, LAWRENCE KENNETH
OLSON, DAVID RICHARD
OLSON, DAVID WILLIAM
OLSON, KAREN MARIE
OLT, THOMAS SCOTT
OQUINN, JANICE MARIE
ORLOWSKY, ALAN GEORGE
OSSOLA, KENNETH JOSEPH
OSTROWSKI, CHARLES JOSEPH
OTTO, MERLYN WILLIAM
PACEK, JAMES LEE
PACER, ALAN FRANKLIN
PAGE, ROGER L.
PALMER, HUGH HEGELER
*PALMIERI, VINCENT LEO
PANCOAST, ROBERT EDWARD
*PANTHER, MICHAEL JOHN
PARKER, HARLEY WILLIAM, JR.
*PARKS, JOHN ROBERT
PATTERSON, DAVID WILLIAM
PEARLMAN, ANDREA KAY
PEARSON, GREGORY EDWIN
PESSIN, BRUCE SHERWIN
PETERIK, DONALD
PETERSON, RICHARD FRANK
*PETERSON, ROBERT THOMAS
PETTY, RANDOLPH ALLEN
PFEFFERLE, DANIEL ARNOLD
*PIANO, LAWRENCE J.
PICHMAN, THOMAS PHILLIP
PICKENS, SCOTT EDWARD
PICKRELL, WILLIAM HOKE
PIERSON, ROBERT BENNETT
PISZ, KAREN ANN
PITTS, HOWARD JAMES
PLACK, JAMES ALAN
*PODOLSKY, BARRY MICHAEL
*PODOLSKY, BONNIE LYNN
POHLMANN, JAMES ALAN
POLIVKA, TERRY GEORGE
*POLLACK, MICHAEL DORN
POPPER, ALLAN ROBERT
PORTES, NANCY BRAZIE
*POTTER, PATRICIA LYNN
POWERS, DAVID WILLIAM
*POWLESS, JAMES KENNETH
POYNTER, RICHARD ELLIS
PRAZEN, RAYMOND
PRENDERGAST, JAMES ROBERT
PRESS, JEFFREY MAURICE
PRZETACZNIK, THOMAS MITCHELL
PUGH, MARK CHRISTOPHER
RAFTÉRY, TIMOTHY MICHAEL
*RALSTON, ALAN LYNN
RAMP, MEREDITH CARLYLE

RASMUSSEN, MICHAEL CLYDE
RAUCH, PETER JOHN
RAY, RUTH ANNE
REDMAN, ARNOLD LEONARD
REED, RONALD OWEN
REID, ROBERT WILLIAM
REINEBACH, LEE ROBERT
REINER, GLENN BERT
REISMAN, CARY STEVEN
RENKES, DEAN ARNOLD
REUTER, EDWARD CARL
REYLER, FANNY ADELA
REYNOLDS, DOUGLAS IRVING
*RHOTON, JUNE ELIZABETH
RICHARD, DAVID PAUL
RICHARDSON, WILLIAM FAIRBANKS
RICKERT, MICHAEL THOMAS
RIDER, STEVEN WAYNE
RIEGER, BRIAN LOUIS
RILEY, THOMAS ROY
RINDLER, MICHAEL EDWARD
RITTER, RANDALL EUGENE
ROBERTSON, WILLIAM FITZGERALD, III
ROBINSON, SCOTT DOUGLAS
ROCKOFF, MICHAEL IRWIN
RODENBURG, JOHN ROBERT, JR.
*RODGERS, JANICE ELAINE
ROGAL, IRA ALAN
ROGERS, STEVEN MICHAEL
ROMACK, CHARLES MICHAEL
ROOSEVELT, GREG EDWARD
ROSEN, BARRY I.
ROSEN, LESLIE JEAN
ROSEN, MICHAEL ABRAM
ROSENBLOOM, MICHAEL HOWARD
ROSENGREN, RICHARD IRVING
ROSS, CARL ARTHUR
*ROSS, DONNA JEAN
*ROSZKOWSKI, MARK EDWARD
ROTH, WILLIAM JAMES, JR.
ROTH, WILLIAM PETER
ROTHSTEIN, RICHARD
ROY, KENNETH EUGENE
RUBENACKER, JEROME MICHAEL
RUBIN, RONALD TYLER
*RUBINSTEIN, CHARLOTTE
*RUDDELL, BRIAN WAYNE
RUSSIN, GERALD ROBERT
RUTHER, JOHN GRAY
RYDEN, JAMES ROBERT
SABIN, ROBERT LEONARD
*SACKETT, VERNON PAUL
SAGO, DORIS JEAN
*SAKOL, BARRE MARC
SALTZMAN, MICHAEL ALAN
SANDLER, PHILIP WAYNE
SANFORD, JEFFERY ALAN
SANTAGATO, LOUIS ROGER
SANTUCCI, CARLO
SASAKI, LYNNE TOYOKO
*SAYLES, MELANIE SUSAN
*SCHALLER, MICHAEL JAY
SCHAUB, RICHARD LEE
SCHECHTMAN, DAVID BRIAN
*SCHECHTMAN, PERRY BRUCE

SCHEIBEL, CLETA ANNE
SCHELL, BARBARA ZIMMER
SCHELLING, ELMER MICHAEL, JR.,
SCHERER, DAN GENE
SCHERER, STEPHEN EUGENE
*SCHIFF, MARK HOWARD
SCHINDEL, RICHARD HENRY
SCHINDLER, BARBARA MARIE
SCHLAX, JAMES ALAN
SCHMITT, DONALD JOHN
SCHULGASSER, HENRY W.
SCHWARZ, MARILYN ANN
SCHWIERJOHN, ROGER GERARD
SCOTT, MELVIN LEONARD
SCOTT, ROBERT JOHN
SCREMENTI, ANTHONY CARL
SERGEANT, RAYMOND FRANCIS
SEYMOUR, ROBERT ROLAND
SHACTER, STEWART MORRIS
SHANE, PHILIP BARRY
SHANER, JEFFREY LEE
SHANLEY, JOHN B.
SHAPIRO, DEBRA ARLENE
SHARP, ROBERT DOUGLASS
SHEARER, JOHN WESLEY, III
SHEFFER, STEVEN JOSEPH
SHEPARD, TRENT ALLEN, JR.
SHERMAN, RONALD WARREN
SHIVERS, GLORIA ANN
SHLOSBERG, JEFFREY LEWIS
SHMIKLER, DAVID JOEL
SHOTLIFF, STANLEY GROSS
SHOWTIS, WILLIAM JOHN
SHURMAN, LINDA KATHLEEN
*SHUTA, JAMES MICHAEL
*SIEBERT, CATHERINE ROSE
SIEBURG, EUGENE JAMES
SIEGEL, STEVEN PAUL
SIKORA, GEORGE RICHARD
SILBERMAN, RICHARD GELEERD
SILVER, MICHAEL LEONARD
SIMMS, JAMES MICHAEL
SIMON, HOWARD SAUL
SINDEWALD, WALTER FRANK, JR.
SINGER, MARC LAWRENCE
SKADDEN, JOHN DONALD
SKIBBE, JEFFREY
SKOOG, CHARLES ARTHUR
SKORBURG, JOHN WILLIAM
SLEDZ, HENRY WALTER
SLEEP, RICHARD ALLEN
SLENTZ, ROBERT JAMES
SLIVKEN, EDWARD CHARLES
SLOTT, DONN RICHARD
SMEJKAL, DONNA MARIE
SMITH, CHARLES LEE, JR.
*SMITH, JAMES LEE
SMOLEN, DAVID JOHN
SMOLEN, ROBERT STANLEY
SNIDER, WILLIAM THOMAS, II
SNYDER, JERRY LYNN
SNYDER, KOERT LESLIE
*SNYDER, TERRY LEE
SOBOL, GARY DUDLEY
SOCOL, ROBERT SCOTT

21

*Soderberg, Robin Mae
Soldwedel, Steve Alan
Sorensen, Larry Roger
*Sorkin, Samuel Maurice
Spaniol, Michael Alan
Speer, David Joseph
Speer, Douglas Rick
Speer, Michael Craig
Springer, Victor Otto
Sproat, David Arthur
Sprock, Frederick Evans, Jr.
Staat, Larry George
Stafford, Mary Ford
Stafseth, David Robert
Stanczak, Stanley Lawrence
Stansil, Douglas Bruce
Stanton, Joseph Edward
Starks, Linda Jean
Stasik, Mark Gregory
Stauber, Joseph William
Stazzone, Peter
Stegmann, James Lee
Stephenitch, Paul Donald
Stephens, Harry Bennett
*Stepnicka, Craig Douglas
*Stern, Gary Michael
*Stern, Robert Steven
Stewart, Connie Ann
Stewart, Glen Paul
Stewart, Robert Douglas
Stillwell, Henry Sheldon, II
Stilts, Ronald George
Stisser, Marcella Rhea
Stock, Richard Michael
*Stoffel, H. Ronald
Stokes, Larry David
Stokvis, Eugene W.
Stone, Daniel Lawrence
Stone, James Michael
Strater, Donald Brook
Striblen, Scott Richard
Stromberg, Frank Russel
St. Thomas, Stephen Field
Stuckemeyer, Roy Dean
Stuebe, John Walter
Sturhan, William Lee
Subeck, Bruce Arthur
Sugar, David Samuel
*Sugarman, Barrett
Sunkel, Morris Arthur
Susin, James Anthony
*Susina, Lawrence Milan
*Sutton, John Timothy
Sutton, Robert Lee, Jr.
Sutton, Thomas Henry
Swabowski, Thomas John
*Swanson, Kurt Robert
Sweeney, Patricia Marie
Swindells, William Edward
*Tanenberg, Ellyn Resser
Tankersley, Joseph Olliver
Taylor, Diana (Murphy)
Taylor, James Nichols
Taylor, John Robert
Taylor, Russell Harvey

Tayman, Martin Edward
Theesfeld, Timothy Lyn
Thetford, James Charles
Thilmony, Martin Anthony
Thomas, Daniel Alfred
Thompson, James Matthew
Thompson, Lawrence Richard
*Thompson, Norma Josephine
Thonn, David John
Thonn, William Eugene
Tibbs, Marvin Ray
Tice, Richard William
Tikalsky, Jerome Rudolph
Toedter, Dennis Lee
Tolian, John Robert
Tolley, Larry Dean
Tortorello, Robert Joseph
Traicoff, James Tripp
Trone, Thomas Neil
Tuck, Hazen Henry
Tucker, Thomas Joseph
Turim, Richard Steven
Turner, Dale Roy
Turner, Jill Elaine
Twyning, James Vernon
Uchida, Kenneth Robert
Udolph, Michael Eparaim
Unger, Lloyd George, Jr.
Unti, David Louis
Upton, Jerry Dean
Uzuanis, Richard Andrew
Vallejo, Richard
Van Arsdell, Stephen Cottrell
Van Deusen, Derek Lee
Vecchio, Steven George
Vieregg, James Robert
Vignocchi, Madalena Joan
Vinkler, Paul Stanley
Viskniskki, Thomas Powell
Vobornik, Frederick Carl
Wade, Martin Louis
Wade, Roger Orville
Wagner, Francis Michael
Wagner, Judith Ann
Wagner, Robert Alan
Wahls, Richard Streid
Waide, Michael Joseph
Walker, George Warren
Walker, James Bancroft
Wallace, Charles Robert
Wallace, David Charles
Wallace, Joseph Mearle
Waller, Charles Sidney
Waller, William Gregory
Waller, William Stites
Walsh, Daniel Joseph, Jr.
Walsh, Thomas Allan
Walsh, Thomas Harry
Walters, Paul David
Wangles, Paul Bruce
Ward, Darrell Thomas
Ware, William Clay
Wasz, Donald George
Watkins, Dennis Keith
Watson, Richard Charles

22

WATTS, THOMAS RAY
WEAVER, STANLEY BLAKE, JR.
*WEBER, CHARLES RICHARD
WEBER, GLENN CHARLES
WEIL, RONALD ALAN
*WEINSTEIN, ANDREA JEAN
WEINSTEIN, JERRALD
WEINSTEIN, PAUL EVAN
WEISER, RONALD ALAN
WEISS, MITCHELL ALAN
WELCH, BRADFORD MERL
WELCH, MICHAEL THOMAS
WELSCH, ERIC DANIEL
WELSCH, THOMAS RICHARD
WENCEL, PATRICIA ELLEN
WESCOTT, GREGORY TODD
*WEST, ROBERT THOMAS
WESTENBERGER, GEORGE LEONARD, IV
WESTON, MARK HERBERT
WESTPHAL, ROGER ALLEN
WHALEN, WILLIAM HARRIS
WHITE, LAVERN ALLEN
WIEMAN, RUSSELL GORDON
WILKINSON, MICHAEL C.
WILL, RICHARD ERIC
WILLARD, JOHN WILLIAM
WILLIAMS, JERRY LEE
WILLIAMS, JOHN ANDREW
WILLIAMS, KENNETH LEE
WILLIAMS, ROBERT JOSEPH
WILLIAMSON, JAMES J.
WILLIAMSON, STEPHEN MICHAEL
WILLIS, STEPHEN I.
WILLMAN, CHARLES HENRY
WILSON, ALAN GEORGE
WILSON, JAMES MICHAEL
WILSON, MARTIN STANLEY
WILSON, RAY ALLARD

WILSON, STEPHEN DOUGLAS
WINER, RICHARD EDWARD
*WINHOLD, LARRY MELVIN
*WINTER, LARRY ALAN
WINTER, THOMAS ALLEN
WISCHNOWSKI, HARVEY ROBERT
*WITLIN, JACK LAWRENCE
*WITSCHY, CARL EDWARD
WOESSNER, DAVID CARL
WOJCIECHOWSKI, JAMES
WOLDORF, JAY JEFFREY
WOLF, CRAIG VAN DYKE
WOLFE, DAVID LOUIS
WOLFE, JOHN HENRY
WOLFF, IRA F.
WOLFSON, MARK ALAN
WOLINSKY, SHELDON JAY
WOLTERS, BRUCE DALE
WOODRING, RICHARD CLARE
WOODWARD, PAMELA ANN
WOOLRIDGE, CECIL, JR.
*WORSHAM, PATRICK MICHAEL
WRIGHT, CHRISTOPHER WARE
WRIGHT, DAVID JONATHAN
WSZOLEK, DANIEL
WULF, DAVID ELDOR
YARNALL, TERRENCE GUY
YAXLEY, THOMAS EDWARD
YOPP, STEVEN EDWARD
YOUNGMAN, GRANT EDWARD
YOUNT, RICHARD CARLTON
ZARA, GARY MARION
ZBOROWSKI, CHESTER ALVIN
*ZELL, WILLIAM BRIAN
ZIFF, HOWARD DAVID
ZIMBLER, IRA
*ZUKOR, PAUL RONALD
ZUKOSKY, WILLIAM CURTIS

## COLLEGE OF COMMUNICATIONS

ABRAHAMSON, TERRY ALAN
ADAMS, DANNY EUGENE
ADERHOLD, GAIL LESLEY
ALEXANDER, NANCY KAY
ALTMIX, AMY LOUISE
AMADON, CYNTHIA
ARENTZ, JOAN MARIE
ARNOFF, HOWARD JOEL
AUGUSTINE, BARBARA ANN
BAILEN, DENNIS MARC
BAIN, HOWARD M.
*BAITS, KATHY DIAN
BAKER, LYNDA K.
*BARBER, DOROTHY LEE
BARRA, JOHN ANTHONY
BATES, WILLIAM RUSSELL
*BAUERNFEIND, DEBANEY ANN
BEALS, CAIRN MARIE
BEAUMONT, GARY LANE
BELTRAMINI, RICHARD FRANCIS
BENDER, CAROLYN AMELIA
BERG, JEAN CAROL
*BERMAN, DAVID ELIOT
BERROYER, BARBARA MCDONALD

BIESIADECKI, KATHRYN VON RUDEN
BINGENHEIMER, ROBERT
BISPLINGHOFF, RONALD
BLANKENSHIP, BONNIE LEE
BLANKENSHIP, WILLIAM
BLOOM, ELLYN JOY
BLUCK, JOHN GEORGE
BLUM, MARADANA
BOLLERO, PAULA JEAN
BONAVIA, NANCY EILEEN
*BOWEN, EVELYN ROSE
BRACKEN, MICHAEL LEE
BRENNECKE, JANE A.
BRINKMAN, ROBERT TODD
BROOM, WILLARD LESLIE
*BROTINE, BRENT ABRAHAM
*BROTMAN, ERICA
BRUSH, JAMES RICHARD
BRUSHABER, PHILIP WILLIAM
CADWELL, RALPH CHARLES
CAMPBELL, SAMUEL WHITNAH
CHADWELL, PHYLIS R.
CHAZIN, MICHAEL FRANK
*CLOUGH, JEAN ANN

23

COCKBILL, THOMAS WILLIAM
COHEN, ARNOLD
COHEN, LINDA LEE
COHEN, SUSAN A.
CONNELLY, SHANNON MARIE
COOK, GAY
*CORNER, BELINDA FRUCHTL
CRAMES, LIZABETH GAIL
CURRIE, JEFFREY SCOTT
*CUTLER, LEONARD IRA
DALKOFF, MALCOLM
*DALLY, EDWIN PAUL
*DANN, MICHAEL HARLEY
DARO, DEBORAH ANN
DEFOREST, LEE ALLEN
DELGIUDICE, CARMEN JOHN
DENENBERG, JEFFREY EDWARD
DERUS, MICHELE LORRAINE
DEUTSCH, HELEN
DROLEN, RANDALL BERNARD
DUDLEY, MARIAN PRICE
DURKEE, THOMAS EDWARD
DYBA, FRED
EATON, FREDERICK
*EDWARDS, JOANNA
EISENSTEIN, ALAN H.
ELBOW, VALERIE ANN
ELLIS, STUART HALL
ENNENBACH, JOSEPH PETER
*ERIN, PAT
FALLS, KAREN LOUISE
*FASSLER, CYNTHIA BIVINS
FAVUS, PHYLLIS INET
FERRIS, JOHN PETER
FERROLI, MARGARET ROSE
FIDELER, LOUIS EUGENE, III
FILES, JAMES LINCOLN
FINE, STEVEN JOEL
FINK, BETTY ANN
FINKEL, LINDA FERNE
*FITZHENRY, SUSAN
FLEISHER, JANICE MORENE
FOX, KATHRYN MARY
FRANK, NANCY JANE
FRENCH, DAVID ALLEN
FRIEDMAN, ROSS MICHAEL
FROMME, BARRIE FRANK
GAMM, IRA I.
GANT, PHILLIP MARSHALL
*GARRITY, KIM ALLISON
GAUGER, GREGG AMES
GAYE, BARBARA ANN
*GESKEY, MARILYN ELFRIENDA
GOAD, GAIL FRANCES
GOLDSCHMIDT, JONA
GRAHAM, KATHLEEN EDDA
*GRIFFARD, ROBERT PAUL
GRIFFEY, JOHN JAY
GRIMM, GRETCHEN MARY
GRYGA, MARILYN ANN
*HALICKI, ROBERT RAY
*HAMENDE, VICKI LARAYNE
*HAMMER, CHARLES RUSH
HANSON, MARGARET ANN
HARBUZIUK, ALEX DAVID

HARMS, MARCIA MENG
HASSIEPEN, GAY LYNN
HAURI, CHRISTINE GAIL
HAUTER, SARA DOERING
HEAD, CAROLYN ANN
HEALY, REBECCA SUE
HECK, STEVEN MICHAEL
HEINZEL, JAMES THOMAS
HEINZEROTH, LOREN RICHARD
HETKE, RICHARD BRIAN
HILFRINK, MICHAEL BRUCE
HILLMAN, GLENN ROBERT
HIRSEN, STEVEN ALFRED
HOFF, DAVID HILTON
HOGAN, ELIZABETH ANNE
HOLTSBERG, WARREN EUGENE, JR.
HOPKINS, STEPHEN PETER
HOPPER, JEFFREY ALAN
*INGRASSIA, PAUL JOSEPH
IRMO, STEPHEN GREGORY
IRWIN, STACEY LYN
JACKSON, LINDA SUSAN
JARVIS, JUDITH KUREK
JERN, DAVID R.
*JERUTIS, CYNTHIA ANNE
JOFFE, GLEN CHARLES
JOHNSON, DAVID CARL
JOHNSON, WARREN ALBERT
*JOHNSTON, BARBARA FRANCES
JONES, WILLIAM MICHAEL
JORDAN, MARGARET ALICE
JUNGER, DENNIS ALBERT
KAHN, PAULA RAE
KAISER, JOHN
KAISER, JOHN
*KALAN, JONATHAN RUSSEL
KANES, ROBERT JEFFERY
*KAPLAN, BRUCE SCOTT
KASPER, KATHY LYNNE
KEEN, JAMES PATRICK
KELLY, KATHLEEN JANET
KELLY, MARY LUCILLE
KESSLER, DAVID BRUCE
KIDWELL, REBECCA SUE
KIES, GERARD CHARLES
KITA, DENNIS MICHAEL
KLEIN, MICHELE FRANCES
KLOTWOG, PATRICIA LYNN
KOCH, LOIS JEAN
KOPECKY, VIRGINIA BLANCHE
KRACEN, LAUREL RAUSCHENBERGER
KUHN, BRENT DEWITT
KULINSKI, MARY BETH
KUTTNER, JILL
KUYKENDALL, RONALD CHARLES
LAMB, BARTON MARSHALL
LAMPE, RUSSELL WILLIAM, JR.
LANGNER, THOMAS JAMES
LARSON, DALE BRADLEY
LASTOVICKA, JOHN LADDIE
LAUE, THOMAS EDWARD
LEMNA, JOHN EDWARD
LESPERANCE, KATHLEEN
LINDEMAN, LENORE HELEN
LIPSCHULTZ, PAMELA ANN

24

*Litman, Neal Howard
Long, Jane Elizabeth
Lotman, Loretta
Luczaj, Gregory John
Manoyan, Daniel Franklin
Margolis, Elizabeth
Mariani, Jeanne Celeste
Marovitz, Mitchell Evan
Masek, Terrence James
McCallum, John Field
McCormick, Mary Ann
McManaway, Marc Lane
McMillion, Kathleen Joyce
Meadors, Linda Lee
Medoff, Norman Jeffrey
Meilach, Susan Ellen
Melo, Niels Samuel
Melvin, Linda Mae
Mendelson, Donald Lee
Messett, Jane Anne
Migon, Nancy Sue
Miller, Marsha Lee
Mitchell, Linda Sue
Mitchell, Phyllis Ann
Moore, Robert Allan
*Morita, Stirling Paul
Morris, David Shepherd
Mutter, Alan Daniel
Naylor, Denis Lee
Nelson, Christina Aileen
Nelson, Janet Ann
*Neustadtl, Sara Jane
Neville, Gary Michael
Nicksic, Beverly Jayne
Nielsen, Jill Vivian
Nielsen, Michael Charles
Nilson, Nancy Ann
Norton, Thomas Carter
Novak, Edward E.
O'Brien, Terrence Eugene
O'Connell, John Patrick
O'Connor, Kim Lee
Oczkowski, Philip John
Oliver, Gail
Oscarson, Denise Carol
Ostrowski, Christina Marie
Palmer, Kathleen Carroll
Paluska, Annette Sue
Patton, Richard Frost
Pava, Enid Gail
Pearl, Barton Lee
Perlman, Mark Alan
Petersen, Bruce Lester
Petersen, Jurgen, III
Peterson, Mark Alan
Pfordresher, William
*Ping, Marjorie Ann
Poletti, Patricia Ann
Politis, Harry Mike
Politsch, Kent Eugene
Price, Jeffrey Lawrence
Pritikin, Nancy Kunz
Radosavlyev, Anne
Rapp, James Anthony
Rappaport, Ilene Rona

Rathman, Cynthia S.
*Reinhart, Carol Louise
Reithel, Dawn Cheryl
Rescho, Richard Farrell
Ricchio, Dawn
Richards, Margaret Elizabeth
Robinson, James Michael
Robinson, Robert George
Rodin, Curt Norman
Rogas, James Lynn
*Rogers, Donald Douglas
Rook, Renee Rae
Rubenstein, Shelley Elaine
Rubin, Michael Richard
Rudich, Roger David
*Rugen, Karen Ann
Rundell, Edward Normal
Russ, Bonnie Marie
*Sallinger, Richard Joseph
Saltz, Irwin Jay
Scalise, Libby Wolf
Schaub, Gunter Rudolph
*Schiefelbein, Susan Elizabeth
Schindel, Linda Marie
Schroader, Jon Lee
Schroeder, Gene Roger
Schwarberg, Jan Alinda
Seaberg, Robert John
Seebold, Bonnie Jean
Shapiro, Sherry Arlene
*Sheehy, Stephanie Fiske
Sherman, Steven Marc
Shifrin, Harvey Saul
Shmikler, Carla Emil
Siatt, Wayne Joel
Siehr, Steven Frederick
Siles, Madonna Margaret
Sims, Norman Howard
Slocum, Thomas James
Snyder, Katherine Michelle
Soden, David Thomas
Solomon, Jerry S.
Spaskos, Athina
Spatz, Diane Lea
Stamm, Gary Melvin
*Start, Patricia Pasdiora
Stec, Paula
Stefani, John David
Stein, Andrea Kay
Steiner, David Ward
Stephens, Nancy Jane
Stinton, Cynthia Lou
Stone, Phillip Douglas
*Stottler, Marcia Ann
Stungis, Elaine C.
Sudalnik, James
Suffrin, Edward Steve
Sullivan, Patricia Anne
Sullivan, Ralph Lewis
Summer, Joel Sherwood
Tabor, William Thomas
Talley, Randall Craig
Taylor, Nancy Jane
Teal, Mary Caroline
Thomann, Allan Michael

25

THORPE, BARBARA ANN
*TINDILL, JANIS LEE
TOBEY, LINDA SUE
TOMASKA, DONALD JOHN
TOWLES, GREGORY THOMAS
URBAN, FRANCES ANN
VARYU, DONALD LESLIE
VIRNICH, CHRISTINE JACQUELINE
VITEK, FRANK JOHN
*VOREIS, PAMELA WHITING
WALKER, RUTH ELLEN
WALLACE, CAROL HARRIET
WARMA, AMY MARIE
WESOLOWSKI, JAMES JOSEPH
WHEELER, STEPHEN MONROE
WHIPPLE, MALCOLM MONTRITH, JR.

WHITE, BARBARA JEAN
WIEGAND, RICHARD EARL
WILCOX, DONALD WAYNE, JR.
*WILLIAMS, ANNE CELESTE
*WILLIAMS, ROBERT KIM
WINEFIELD, RICHARD MORRIS, JR.
*WINTER, DOUGLAS EARL
*WINTERBAUER, NANCY VIRGINIA
WOLF, LOUIS MARC
WOLFE, LYNN MARY
WOLLOCK, ANDREA JOY
WONDOLOWSKI, MICHELE
WUNDERLICH, RODGER CARL
*ZAIDEMAN, BARBARA JO
ZIFF, SANDRA JOY
*ZIV, JAMES KENNETH

## COLLEGE OF EDUCATION

ABRAMSON, NANCY MYRA
ACKERMAN, MARCIA LYNN
ACKINS, VIVIAN
ADAMSON, SUSAN KAY
ADEN, VELVI GIGLIO
ADES, TRUDY SUSAN
AGES, KAREN MARIE
AGRE, GARY LEE
AHNGER, SUSAN ELIZABETH
AIDEM, DIANE MARIAN
AIELS, MARTHA JO
AKERS, LINDA SUSAN
ALLEN, CATHERINE SUE
ALLEN, GERALD WAYNE
ALLEN, JAMES RICHARD
ALMON, GEORGIE LYNNE
ANDERSON, HOLLY SUE
ANDERSON, LYNN ADELE
ANDERSON, MARGARET GRACE
*ANDERSON, PATRICIA LYNNE
*ANDRES, SUSAN CLAIRE
ANDREWS, DAVID JOHN
ANDREWS, JENNIFER
ANTICOL, BONNIE DALE
ANTMAN, FAYE
ARMSTRONG, CHRISTINE ANN
ARTHUR, BARBARA ALICE
ATKENSON, LINDA ANN
AVRUCH, SUSAN
BADNER, HOLLY SUZANNE
BAIR, KATHLEEN LOUISE
BAKER, TERRY LYNN
BANDY, BETH RAE
BARANOV, DAVIDA ALINE
*BARBAKOFF, ADRIENNE JOYCE
BARBER, CARLA SUE
BARBER, JULIE ANN
BARBER, PAULA JEAN
*BARKER, BARBARA
BARKER, MARSHA LYNN
BARRY, JOAN CATHERINE
BARSHEFSKY, NITA SIMON
BARTH, RODNEY JOSEPH
BASS, MARY KAYE
BATES, RANDALL EUGENE
*BATTERMAN, KAREN SUE

BAUKERT, EMIL EDWARD
BAUMRUCKER, JANICE MARIE
BEATY, CATHERINE
BEAUMONT, JOYCE LYNN
*BECKER, BARBARA SHARON
*BECKER, ETHEL ANN
BELL, KRISTINE ROWLAND
BELL, SUSAN KAREN
BELL, SUSAN LEE
BENDER, CAROL JANE
BENSEN, LINDA LOU
BENSON, CONSTANCE CORSON
BENTLEY, THOMAS IRWIN
BERG, LINDA ANN
BERGDOLT, ANITA LOUISE
*BERGER, ELLEN ROSE
BERGER, SUSAN JO
BERGLUND, DAVID CRAVER, JR.
BERKENSTADT, DEBBIE SUE
BERMAN, LINDA FAYE
BERNOVER, ROSANNE H.
BERRY, BONNIE JEAN
BICKLER, MELINDA KAY
BIERIG, JUDITH PEGGY
BIERZYCHUDEK, CHERYL LYNN
BIEWENGA, DAVID MICHAEL
BINGHAM, JERRY WAYNE
BIOLCHINI, RITA JEAN
BIRDSONG, GAIL ELLEN
BIRNEY, ADRIENNE MARCIA
BIRTIC, SUSAN LYNN
BITRAN, JANE
BITTERLING, CONNIE LONG
BIZAR, JANET SUSAN
*BLACK, JANE OLSEN
*BLACK, JEAN BAKER
BLACK, NANCY SUE
BLAKELY, NORA BROOKS
*BLATH, BARBARA ANN
BLINSKI, ADRIENNE JOY
BLITSTIEN, LORI SUE
BLOCK, PATRICIA LYNN
BLOOM, BARBARA LYNN
BLOOM, JANET LOUISE
BLUM, SHARYL LYNN
BLUMBERG, FRED ARTHUR

26

BLUME, VERNA CLAUDIA
BODENSTEIN, ANNE HELENE
*BOGORAD, PHYLLIS LYNN
BOLKE, RICHARD GALE, JR.
BOOS, SHEILA KAY
BOROWY, EDWARD ANTHONY
BORTZ, TRUDY LYNN
BOURNE, ALICE MARIE
BOWMAN, JEANNE ANN
*BOYSEN, JEAN LOUISE
BRANDT, LINDA RUTH
BRAY, LINDA JEANNE
BRAZELTON, DAN ALLEN
BRENNER, ROGER JOHN
BRESKOVICH, KAREN JEAN
*BRESSLER, SHARRI GAIL
BREWE, JOYCE EVELYN
BREWER, KAREN SUE
BRIELER, SARAH CRAY
*BRIGGS, MARTHA LUELLA
*BRISKMAN, RANDY JOYCE
*BRODY, BARBARA DAWN
BROEREN, CECILE CREATH
BROERS, SHARON KAY
BROOKS, RITA MAY
BROWN, GENIE AILSON
BROWN, KENNETH DEMPSIE
BROWN, SHERRY B.
BROWN, SUSAN MERRILL
BRUBAKER, NANCY
BRYANT, SUSAN JEAN
*BUCHSBAUM, MARGALIT CLARA
BUDKOWSKI, CAROL SUE
BUFFEN, JUDITH LYNN
BULANDA, ROBERT JOHN
BULLOCK, GREGORY HERB
BURGER, KATHERINE SHARI
*BURMAN, LUAN
BURROUGHS, JUDY LANIE
BURTEN, JANET GAIL
*BURTNESS, KATHRYN GRACE
BUSCH, REBECCA BROWN
*BUSCHBACH, SUSAN KAY
*BUSH, GAIL LYNN
BUSHMEYER, GAIL ELIZABETH
BUTLER, GLORIA HELEN
BUYSSE, BARBARA ANN
BYLENOK, BARBARA ANN
BYRAM, DONALD ROY
CABIN, SHARON RUTH
CABLE, ANN ELIZABETH
CADEK, CAROL MARIE
CADWELL, GARY REGINALD
CALVI, DIANE VIOLA
CAMPBELL, CATHY FAIRWEATHER
CARLSON, JOAN MARIE
CARMICHAEL, CATHY JAYNE
CARMICHAEL, JANIS ELLEN
CARPENTER, ROGER STEVEN
CARROLL, CHRISTINE
CARTER, SARA JANE
CASTLE, ARLENE JOY
CESAK, LINDA LEE
*CESARONE, ROBERT JOHN
CHABOT, RONALD THOMAS

CHANEY, KAREN LYNN
CHAPLICK, ROSE LYNN
CHAPMAN, LESLIE BARBARA
CHELSETH, ROBERT STEVEN
CHERTKOW, FERN JOY
CHILDS, CONSTANCE RENA
CHRISMAN, RICHARD
CHRISTOPHER, GUY THOMAS
*CIESLA, GAIL
CLARK, JERRY EDWIN
CLARK, MARCIA JANE
CLATT, CHRISTINE
*COE, PATRICIA ANN
COFFIN, LINDA ANN
COHEN, ANNE LOUISE
COHEN, LARRY ALAN
COHEN, MARLENE ELAYNE
*COHEN, PATTI KATE
COHN, JUDY
*COHN, PAULA BETH
COLBERG, JANICE MAYNARD
*COLBERT, NANCY LYNN
COLE, ELYNE JOHNSON
COLE, GWENDOLYN DELORES
COLE, KIM ELLEN
COLEMAN, LYNNE ROZELL
*COLEMAN, SHELLEY JEAN
COLOSKY, EVELYN MARGRET
CONRAD, PENNY LOUISE
COOK, KATHARINE MARIE
COOK, KATHRYN JEANETTE
COOK, MARILYN KAY
COOK, SANDRA KAY
COOKS, EILEEN NANCY
COOPER, KAREN JOY
COOPER, MARJORIE RHEA
CORCORAN, JANET SCHUH
CORRIGAN, MARY FRANCES
*COURT, MARCIA LOUISE
COX, DIANE MARGARET
COX, KATHLEEN RAE
CRANE, JULIE FRANCES
CRAWFORD, JAN
CREMENS, ANN MARIE
*CRESCENZO, MICHAEL
CRESPI, PAMELA LYNN
CROKE, LILLIAN JOAN
CROOK, SHARON KAY
CROW, CYNTHIA LOUISE
CRUZ, CARMEN AIDA
CULLEN, JEANIE LUCY
*CULLOTTA, CAROLYN DOROTHY
CUMMINGS, ROBERT CLYDE
CUNNINGHAM, KATY ANN
CUSHING, G. M.
CUSTER, TERRY REED
CYBORSKI, MYRA LESLIE
CYGAN, JOLENE BERNICE
CZAJA, FRANK WILLIAM
DAFFERNER, CAROL McCALLISTER
*DALLEY, CAROLYN A.
DALY, BONITA LAW
DAMKO, KAREN ANNE
DANIELS, BELINDA SUSAN
DANNER, MERRY ANN

27

*Darken, Wendy Kay
Davis, Anna Jane
Davis, Jacqueline Diane
*Davis, Marilyn Deborah
Dawson, Carlee Eulene
Daynard, Leslie Marie
Deboice, Mary Lucile
Debord, Barbara Mary
Decaluwe, Mary Catherine
Dechene, Gail Susan
Decho, Joann Marie
Degraw, Larry Dean
Dehen, Katharine Leigh
Deitch, Margaret Helen
Deninno, Mary Ann
Dennis, Susan Lois
*Depke, Kathleen Ellen
Dettmering, Diane Amelia
Diamond, Robert
Diestelmeier, Joan Evelyn
*Dietz, Kathryn Gail
Dinges, Judy Lynn
D'Inverno, Nancy Carmela
Dishkin, Sharon Mae
Dixon, Carol Kathryn
Dixon, Susan Lynn
Dobryman, Frieda
Dohrn, Roberta Marie
Donahoe, Theresa Mary
Downs, Benjamin Elisha
Dragich, Mary Susan
Drago, John Lawrence
*Dreifuss, Susan Helen
Drew, Robert Nolan
Drinkall, Anita Paydon
Drone, Gary Charles
Drummond, Nancy Georgia
Dudley, Marilyn Kay
Dunnan, Theresa Colleen
Dunseth, Max Allen
Duppert, Kathryn Jean
Eash, Merline Rosanne
Eckerling, Sally Ellen
Edelman, Linda Sue
Edwards, Cynthia Ann
Eggemeyer, Byron Alfred
Eggert, Judith Lee
Eisen, Marilyn Evelyn
Elkin, Janis
*Ellis, Sandra Paula
Endelman, Sue Ellen
*Endicott, Sheryn Elaine
Engelking, Johna Deanne
Engerman, Gloria Caryl
Epstein, Judith Marilyn
Erb, Bruce John
*Erickson, Karen Jane
Erwin, Meredith Kay
Esenther, Barbara Ellen
Eubank, Alice Roberta
Evans, Cindy Ann
Exner, Bonnie Rose
Faber, Patricia Sue
*Fagerburg, Charlotte
Falconer, Patti Jo

Fandler, Frederick Ernest
Fearneyhough, Sharen Renee
Feingold, Bari Joyce
Feinner, Elyse Bonnie
*Feldman, Jill Leslie
Feldman, Marilyn Pearl
Fels, Eileen Susan
Fenchel, Roberta Jeanne
Ferrell, Elmer Dale
Fetman, Linda Jill
Fettig, Judith Anne
Fey, Jeanne Terese
Ficken, Janet Louise
Fiebelkorn, Barbara Charlotte
Filbey, Melissa Ann
*Fine, Carole Sue
Finkley, Jane Hill
Firestone, Glenda Susan
Fischer, Mary Margaret
Fisdel, Sandra Faye
*Fisher, Joyce Margaret
Fisher, Lauren Iris
Fisher, Thomas Scott
Fishman, Janet Sue
Fitch, Joanne Stoller
*Fleming, Mary Therese
Fleming, Nadine Yvonne
Flynn, Judy Vinecore
Flynn, Kathleen Elizabeth
Flynn, Michaela Ann
Foley, Jane Elizabeth
Ford, Deborah Ann
Fornell, Paul David
Fortna, David Eugene
*Foss, Catherine Marie
Foster, Susan Kathleen
Franzen, Elaine Caroline
Freedman, Beth Gail
French, Catherine Lynn
French, William Gregg
Frick, Mary Taliaferro
Fricke, Barbara Jean
Friedman, Joann Marilyn
Friedman, Shelia Karen
Fritz, Cheryl Marie
Froehlich, Dorla Rae
Froehlich, Paula Joyce
Frowein, Karen Louise
Fuchsen, Mary Judine
Fullett, Sandra Ellen
Fulton, Nancy Joan
*Fulton, Susan Marie
Furlong, Terri Margaret
*Galuska, Denise Rae
Gambles, Larry
*Gams, Linda
Gano, Catherine Ann
Garinger, Cynthia Shaw
Garry, Constance Irene
Gass, Geraldine Lisbeth
Gerber, Nancy Lynn
Gerber, Richarde Christine
Gerstein, Judith Michelle
Ghere, David Lynn
Gibbs, Joyce Kay

GILCHRIST, JANE MARIA
GILL, VIRGINIA ELIZABETH
GILMAN, SUSAN BABNARD
GINGERICH, MARY TERESA
GIUFFRE, MARY LYNNE
GLAZE, LAUREL ANN
GLENNER, LINDA CAROL
GLODY, MEREDITH
GLYNN, ANN
GOLD, ILYSE KAREN
GOLD, MARJORIE LYNN
*GOLDBERG, MYRA BERNICE
GOLDEN, BARBARA JEAN
GOLDENBERG, GAIL ANN
*GOLDMAN, DIANE PHYLLIS
GOLDMAN, JULIE RAE
GOLDMAN, LINDA
GOLDMAN, LYNN KARON
GOLDSHOLL, JUDITH LYNN
GOLDSMITH, MARLENE JOY
GOLDSMITH, SANDRA SUE
GOOD, ANN
GOODMAN, JUDITH SUSAN
GOODMAN, SANDRA HELENE
GORDON, FRANCINE ELLEN
*GORDON, MARCIA ANN
GORENSTEIN, MELANIE
GORMLEY, CAROL JANET
GRAHAM, MARY BETH
GRAHAM, MARY JANE
*GRANDT, KATHLEEN RUTH
GRAVES, BARBARA LANE
GRAVES, SUSAN PATRICIA
*GRAY, CHARLES HODGES
GREAVES, NANCY LYNNE
GREEN, DIANE MARIE
GREENE, JOAN MARIS
*GREENSTEIN, NANCY ANN
*GREENSTEIN, SANDRA JUNE
*GREENWALD, CATHY JO
GREVE, JANE
GRIPPANDO, ANNE MARIE
GRISWOLD, PAULA RAE
GROTHENDICK, LINDA LEE
GUDERLEY, SUSAN GAIL
GUNDERSEN, LEE KAREN
GUSTAFSON, ELAINE MARIE
GUSTAFSON, KAREN FRANCES
GUTEN, SHARON EILEEN
GUTHRIE, ROGER ALAN
*GUTIERREZ, MARIA LISA
GUYSENIR, DEBORAH MERLE
GYURA, KAREN LYNN
HAAS, PAMELA BUCHANAN
*HAAS, THERESE COLLOTON
HABERLEN, MARGITA MURIN
HALPERIN, DEBRA SUE
HALPIN, THOMAS JAMES, JR.
HAMMER, RONALD RUSSELL
HANNON, ROBERT J.
HANOVER, NANCY RITTER
HANSEN, BARBARA JEAN
HANSEN, CAROL DIANNE
*HANSEN, JOAN CAROLE
HANSON, ELANA LEE

HARBOUR, IRL D., JR.
*HARDUVEL, MARIA CHRIST
HARDWICK, JILL WHITE
HARRINGTON, CLAIRE SUZANNE
HARRIS, LUEDELLA
*HARSHBARGER, JANICE ACKEBERG
*HARTLEY, SONDRA LOY
HARTRICK, PAULA DOREEN
HARTWEGER, ROSALIE MARIE
HASS, JUDITH
HATCH, DIANE JANE
HATTIS, CYNTHIA EILEEN
HAUFE, LORRAINE MARIE
HAUPTFUEHRER, PATTI JO
HAVLIK, SANDRA JEAN
HAWES, MARILYN FREY
HAY, CARL MARTIN
HAYDEL, JUDITH FISCHER
HAYDEN, JAMIE ELLEN
HEAPS, RICHARD WAYNE
HECHT, RONALD ALLAN
HEDRICK, DIANNE SOPHIA
*HEFFLEY, GAY JEAN
HEIDORN, BARBARA ANN
HEILBRUNN, JANICE HOPE
HELD, CAROL HOFBAUER
HELFER, SHERRY CREININ
HELM, CAROL JEAN
HELMAN, SUSAN ELAINE
HEMPE, LINDA LOU
HENDERSON, JERRY WAYNE
*HENDRICKSON, DIANE WYNNE
HENDRY, DENISE F.
HENEK, JUDITH ANN
HENNESSY, LINDA KAY
*HENRIKSON, DIANE ELIZABETH
HENRY, JOHN REEVES
HERMAN, MARJORIE ANN
HERMELE, GRETTA LUCILLE
HERMSMEIER, MARILYN S.
HERRIOTT, MARILYN KAY
HERRIOTT, MARSHA ANN
HERRON, KATHLEEN JANET
*HESTAD, MARSHA ANNE
HIATT, CATHY SHEETS
HICKLE, MARY LYNN
HICKMAN, DONALD GAFFORD
HIGHLEY, JUDITH ANN
HILL, DONNA LESLIE
HILLS, HEATHER GLORIA
HINNERICHS, MARILYNN
HITZEMAN, BARBARA ANN
HOBBS, DOLORES ANN
*HOCHBERG, GAIL EILEEN
HOCHBERG, SUSAN MYRA
HOCKENYOS, KAREN
HOEKENDORF, SHARON JANICE
HOERR, DIANNE MARIE
HOFFMAN, ANITA ROSE
HOFFMAN, BARBARA KAY
HOFFMAN, LEE
HOFFMAN, LINDA SUE
HOFFMAN, PAUL EDWARD
HOLLINGSWORTH, JOY KAY
HOMAN, PAMELA LOUISE

29

HORTON, MARCIA DIANE
HOUGHTON, LINDA ANN
HOUSER, SARAH ELIZABETH
HOUSTON, ELOISE NORMA
*HOWELL, SHARON SUE
HUBBARD, KAY FRANCES
HUGHES, SUSAN KAY
HULL, SUSAN ELIZABETH
HUNDLEY, SALLY HENSOLD
HURST, PATRICIA LOUISE
*HUTTER, LINDA ANNE
HUTTON, MARIGENE RUMBAUGH
*IFFT, NANCY JEAN
INFUSINO, CATHY ANN
INGRAM, GAYLYNN FARR
ISAACSON, LINDA SUE
*ISHIDA, LYNN CHERIE
ITO, DONNA SHIGEKO
JACKSON, RUTH LYNN
*JACOBS, DEBRA LYNNE
*JAEGER, ROBERTA LYNN
JERDEN, BARBARA JO
JOHANSEN, SHERI PATRICIA
JOHNSEN, JOANNA
JOHNSON, BARBARA LYNN
JOHNSON, BETH SUSAN
JOHNSON, BONITA SUE
*JOHNSON, CHRISTINA KAY
JOHNSON, JANICE LYNN
JOHNSON, JOANN
JOHNSON, JUDITH LEE
JOHNSON, KAREN JOYCE
JOHNSON, LINDA HOHMANN
JOHNSON, LINDA JEAN
JOHNSON, NANCY MARIE
JOHNSON, REGINALD L.
JOHNSON, VALERIE ANNE
JOHNSTON, DEBRA LYNN
*JOHNSTON, SUSAN DUVALL
JONES, JULIE ANN
JONES, NANCY PHYLLIS
JORGENSEN, JAMES EDWIN
JOYCE, JANET ELIZABETH
JOYNER, JULIE ANN
*KACSH, JUDITH ELLYN
KAGAN, JOYCE ELLEN
*KAGAN, ROSALYN H.
KAHN, JUDITH DEBORAH
*KAHN, MAUREEN E.
KALIN, MARY KATHARINE
KALKANIAN, GEORGETTE LEE
KAMM, RICHARD WALTER
KANE, CHERYL ELLEN
KANTOR, CHARLENE JOY
*KAPLAN, ADALYNN
KASCH, MARJORIE ANN
KATZ, GERALDINE RENEE
KATZ, IONE EVE
KATZ, SHARON ELAINE
KAUFMAN, SHEILA LYNN
KAWABATA, KAREN MARIE
KAY ANNE, THERESE
KAY, CAROL JEANNE
KAYHS, REBECCA ANN
KELLER, LAURA CHANCE

KELLY, MARIE ROESLER
KERR, LESLIE ANN
KESLER, CHRISTINE DIANE
KILKENNY, SHARON LEE
*KIMMEL, LESLIE ERVIN
KING, MARYANN
KIRINCICH, MARLENE K.
*KIRK, ELEANOR LYNN
KIRSINAS, LORETTA STELLA
KISS, SHARON SEARIGHT
*KLAUKE, DIANE MARIE
KLEIN, SUSAN BETH
KNIGHT, MYTRLE UNDERWOOD
KNOLL, GERALDINE CAROL
KOEHLER, SUSAN LYNN
KOEPKE, NANCY JEAN
KOERNER, SANDRA SUE
KOHN, SUSAN BETH
*KOLBER, SUSAN LYNNE
*KOMIE, CYNTHIA ANN
KONIG, PATRICIA LYNN
KOREY, RICKI SUSAN
KORRY, MICHELLE
KOSZCZUK, JANET ANN
KOTARBA, ANITA MARY
KOUROUPAS, GEORGIA ANN
*KOVAC, PATRICIA ELIZABETH
KRACHER, KAREN KRISTINA
KRAUSE, KAREN MARY
*KREIMEIER, VIRGINIA EDNA
KROLAK, LUCY ANN
KUFLICK, LESLIE ANNE
KULWIN, JILL LESLIE
KUNTZ, DONNA JEAN
KURTZ, RONNA M.
*LABELLARTE, LYNN MARIE
LACE, ANNE WHITNEY
LAESCH, RUTH ELSA
LAIRD, DOLORES GOETZE
LAKE, ANDREA JAN
LAMZ, TERRY ANNE
LANDOLT, SHERYL SUE
LANG, JUDITH LYNN
LANGE, RICHARD FRANK
LANGLEY, DEBORAH ANN
LARSON, KATHLENE ANDERSON
*LARSON, KRISTINE GARMAGER
*LASKY, MARSHA IONE
*LAUBAUGH, RACHEL ANN
*LAUGAL, PATTI LEE
LAWLYES, LAIRD DEAN
LAWRENCE, HELEN VICTORIA
LAWRENCE, LINDA FERN
LEACH, TERESE ANN
*LEAHY, KATHRYN MARY
LEDUC, BARBARA WILLIAMS
LEE, BARBARA ANN
LEE, FRANK SELBY
LEE, PATRICIA ANN
LEE, REBECCA ANN
LEEDS, MARCY KAY
LEESMAN, MARIANNE
LEHNER, NANCY CAROLE
LEHRNER, LINDA SUE
LEICHTI, JEAN BETH

LEITNER, RONA KARAN  
LERMOND, MARGARET VERONICA  
LESHNER, HELEN MICHELLE  
*LESKE, DEBORAH ANN  
LESMEISTER, JOAN  
LETNER, TAMMY LEE  
LEVICK, LINDA HASKELL  
LEWIS, JEAN TRANGUILLI  
LEWIS, MADELINE  
LEWKE, BARBARA DARL  
LIBERMAN, DEBRA ANN  
LIBERT, ALVA IRIS  
LINDEN, ELIZABETH ANN  
LINSKY, JEAN FRANCES  
LINSKY, NANCY CAROL  
LINSKY, SALLY ANN  
LINZ, WENDY KAY  
LIPPINCOTT, PETER WARD  
LIPSCHULTZ, SUSAN FAYE  
LIPSKY, IRIS JAN  
LIPSON, SHELLEY MERLE  
*LITTLE, MARY ELIZABETH  
LOGAN, KATHLYN HOPE  
*LOGAN, LISA RUTH  
LOMAX, PEGGY ANN  
*LONDON, DEBORAH  
LOPEZ-COLES, CARLOS MANUEL.  
LORBER, GERI GAIL  
*LUCK, JULIE ANN  
LUST, NANCY LYNN  
*LUTZ, PATRICIA DIANE  
LYNK, MARY JANE  
LYNN, SALLEE DEE  
LYONS, BETTY JO  
MABREY, FRANCES SHIRLEY  
MACLENNAN, PATRICIA MATUSZAK  
MADDEN, DONALD EUGENE  
MADDOX, MARTHA MARIE  
MADISON, LOREN JAMES  
MADSEN, MICHAEL ALAN  
MAHACHEK, DIANE LYNN SCHEFFNER  
MAHER, LOIS CUNDIFF  
MAIER, DEBRA KAY  
MALKIEWICZ, KAYE LAMAR  
MALMGREN, HELEN ANNE  
MANDEL, MIRIAM SHARON  
MANDLER, CATHY BUCHBINDER  
MANIRE, DAWN LAVON  
MANN, MARY LOU  
*MARCUS, LINDA ELLEN  
MARINE, MURIEL NANETTE  
*MARKSTAHLER, ELIZABETH LINDELL  
*MARKWELL, PATRICIA LYNN  
MARSH, PATRICIA L.  
MARTIN, DANNY KAY  
*MARTIN, MICHAEL KEMP  
MARTIN, NANCY ROSE BRADLEY  
MARTIN, PAMELA LEE  
*MARTIN, SUSAN PATRICE  
*MASEK, DAWN MARIE  
MASSIE, BARRIE JOAN  
MASSIE, LAURA DIANE  
MATSON, JON EDWARD  
MATTHEWS, PAIGE ELAINE  
MATTSON, JOAN ELLEN  

*MAY, REBECCA JEAN  
MAYER, ARLETTE FLORINE  
MCATEE, ELEANOR ANN  
MCCALL, FREDERICK CLANCY  
MCCARREN, KATHLEEN ANN  
MCCAW, ELEANOR ANN  
MCCLELLAND, ROBERTA PLUTH  
MCCONNELL, GAIL SUZANNE  
MCCORD, GLORIA ANN  
MCCORMICK, EDITH MARGARET  
MCDANIEL, CATHY JAYNE  
MCDOWELL, BEVERLY JEAN  
MCGOWEN, DAWN KAREN  
MCINTOSH, PATRICIA DORIS  
MCNAB, BARBARA LORRAINE  
MCNEELY, MARY ANN  
MCNEIL, DEBORAH KAY  
*MEACHUM, JANET RAE  
*MEADE, CYNTHIA ANN  
MEDE, SHARON MARIE  
MELLOW, KAREN RICKY  
MELVIN, JUDITH ANN  
MENG, BONNIE KAY  
MENG, CONNIE FAY  
MERDIAN, JO ANN  
MERKIN, JACALYN NITA  
MERRICK, LYNN KAREN  
MERSCH, LOIS JEAN  
METALLO, SHARON MARIE  
MEYER, BARBARA ANNE  
MEYER, SUSAN LYNN  
MICHALSKI, PHYLLIS MARIE  
MICLOW, SUSAN MARY  
MIES, VERA JEAN  
MIKES, JUDITH LYNN  
MILGROM, ARLENE JOYCE  
MILKOWSKI, GEORGE EDWARD  
MILLER, JANICE BARBARA  
MILLER, MARY LINDA  
MILLER, NELSON CONWAY  
MINOR, BRENDA ANN  
MISEK, MARGARET SICHTA  
MISKOVIC, LINDA SUSAN  
MITCHELL, PAMELA SUE  
MITCHELL, SHARON ELIZABETH  
MIZOCK, DEBRA LYNN  
*MNISZEWSKI, MALVINA THERESA  
MOHR, MARILYN WILCOXON  
MOKATE, RITA LORENE  
MOLINE, MICHELE SUSAN  
MONFREDINI, JAMES LYNDELL  
MOODY, JILL ELIZABETH  
*MOORE, FRANCES MAIN  
MOORE, GLORIA DARLEEN  
MOORE, LINDA GUDGEL  
MOORE, MARY ANN  
MORRIS, LINDA MAE  
MORROW, MARCIA ELIZABETH  
MOSER, CYNTHIA LOUISE  
MOSKOWITZ, MARILYN  
MOSKOWITZ, SUSAN MYRA  
MOWERY, DOROTHY JUNE  
*MOY, AUDREY LYNN  
MOY, ROSE C.  
MUELLER, BECKY RAE  

31

MUELLER, MARY LOU  
*MULLER, RICKI SUE  
MUNNO, MARY LOU  
MURPHY, EVA KATHLEEN  
MURPHY, JULIE ANN  
MUSCHEWSKE, LYNN MARIE  
MUSICK, LYLA LEA  
MYERS, DONNA LYNNE  
MYLIN, COSETTE CARLYON  
MYLIN, THOMAS EDWARD  
*NADEL, JAN LESLIE  
NAUYALIS, MADELON LOUISE  
NAVARA, BEVERLY CHRISTINE  
NEDZA, JENNIFER EILEEN  
NELSON, BRUCE GORDON  
NELSON, ELLEN PATRICIA  
NEWELL, JOHN EDWARD  
NEWMAN, DENISE LYNN  
NIANICK, CHERI LEE  
NICHOLS, JOHN CURTIS  
*NICKESON, HOLLY KAY  
NICKUM, LYNNETTE EIPERS  
NIRULA, RANJANA  
*NISHIMOTO, BARBARA JANIE  
NOREM, ROXANNE KAY  
NORTON, ANITA GAY BADGER  
NOURSE, SHERRY RAE  
*NOVAK, BARBARA ANN  
OAKES, SALLY LIVENGOOD  
O'BRYAN, NANCY SUSAN  
*O'GEARY, MARY ALICE  
O'HARE, COLLEEN LYNCH  
OHLSEN, BARBARA JEAN  
O'LEARY, AILEEN  
O'LEARY, MAUREEN  
OLIC, BARBARA FRANCES  
*OLLENQUIST, KRISTINE  
OLSON, MOIRA DELAROSA  
OLSON, NANCY PARKS  
O'MEARA, ELIZABETH MOORE  
OSTRIHON, CHERYL ANN  
OVITT, DORIS TOMB  
*OWEN, JANICE RUTH  
PAETZHOLD, GEOFFREY LYNN  
PAHLKE, BARBARA JEAN  
PALUCCI, ROBERTA JEAN  
PAMPE, SHARON AILEEN  
PANZER, JAMES ANTHONY  
PARAS, RUTH ELIZABETH  
PARIS, JAN ARLENE  
PARISI, MARIA SYLVIA  
PARKER, GLORIA MARIE  
PARYS, BARBARA ROSE  
PASCO, SHELLEY LOWREY  
*PATINKIN, MARSHA GAIL  
*PATTERSON, GWENDOLYN  
PAVILONIS, BARBARA  
*PAVIS, VALERIE ANN  
PAWLAK, RENEE  
PAWLOWSKI, DIANE JOSEPHINE  
PEARSE, ROBERT BERNHARD  
PECHTER, DEBORAH JEAN  
PECHTER, MARILYN RAE  
*PEMBERTON, SARA RHOPES  
PERINO, KATHLEEN ANN  

*PERISHO, KATHLEEN OLSON  
PERKINS, KIMBARK  
PERLIK, SUSAN ELYSE  
PERRY, KENNETH RAY  
*PETERSEN, NANCY MARIAN  
PETERSON, JOHN ERIC  
PETERSON, ROY ASBERG  
PETR, JOHN JAMES  
PETROFF, DIANE VIRGINIA  
PETROFF, LINDA CONSTANCE  
PETRYK, MARILYN ROSE  
PETRYSHYN, KATHLEEN E.  
PETTERSON, ANN MARIE  
PHELAN, RAYMOND JOSEPH  
PHELPS, MARGARET LOUISE  
PICKARD, JOANNE MERLE  
PIENKOS, BARBARA LOUISE  
PILOTTE, DIANA MARIE  
*PODELL, JUDITH SUE  
PODJASEK, ANNE MARIE  
PODLISKA, SHARON DOLORES  
PODOLSKY, SHARON RUTH  
POLLACK, WENDY JOYCE  
POMERANZ, FERN  
POMERENKE, JUDITH KATHRYN  
*PONOROFF, CAROL RUTH  
POPA, SHARON KAYE  
PORTER, MARY ELIZABETH  
PORTER, PENNY ANN  
POWE, BRENDA JOYCE  
POWELL, LENORA ANN  
POWELL, LINDA LOUISE  
PRATHER, CHERYL LYNN  
PREDICK, CHRISTINE TYLER  
PROCTOR, BETTY LYNN  
PUTERBAUGH, GERALD DUANE  
PUTERBAUGH, NORMA HEISE  
QUANSTROM, NANCY LEE  
QUICKSTAD, CAROL JEAN  
QUINN, JAMES STEPHEN  
QUIRIN, YVONNE CECILIA  
*RABIN, DONNA LEE  
*RAGINS, MARCY BERYL  
RANDALL, ANNE CAMELIA  
RAPAPORT, DIANE SYLVIA  
RAVER, FRANK LEWIS  
REAY, ROSEMARY ANN  
REDMAN, JUDITH BEAIRD  
REED, CHERYL BODINE  
REES, SUSAN HARLEY  
REID, LINDA ANNE  
RENFRO, CYNTHIA MARIE  
RESNICK, VICKIE MAE  
*RHOADES, CATHY ANNE  
RHODES, KANDA DRUANNE  
RICHARDSON, JANE ALICE  
RICHMOND, SUSAN L.  
RIDLEN, BARBARA JO  
RIEGER, JUDY ELLEN  
RIGGINS, JANET KATHLEEN  
*RITHOLZ, MARCIA BETH  
ROADRUCK, SUSAN MARY  
ROBERTS, CAROL JEAN  
ROBINSON, BEVERLY MCNEIL  
ROBINSON, MARGARET TERESA

ROBNETT, CONSTANCE LEACH
ROETTGER, CINDY KAY
ROKOS, KATHLEEN JO
*ROOF, JULIA GENE
ROOMBOS, JAMES RICHARD
ROSE, ANDREA DAWN
ROSEMONT, JOANN BARR
ROSEN, JOANN TOBY
ROSENFELD, MARLA JOY
*ROSENTHAL, JUDITH ILENE
ROSS, JOYCE LEE
*ROSS, MARGARET ELIZABETH
ROURKE, NANCY BETH
ROVETTO, JUDITH HYDE
RUBENACKER, KATHLEEN ANN
RUBENKING, MARLA KIM
*RUBIN, CAROL JANE
RUBIN, GLORIA M.
RUDOLPH, BUNNIE ZIEGLER
*RUNKLE, TERESA NAN
RUSH, KARMA LEE
RUSSELL, CAROL ANN
RUSSELL, GAYLE BETH
RYPSKI, JOHN
RZECHULA, CASEY SCOTT
SABIN, PHILIP DANIEL
SAFARCYK, DIANE MARIE
*SAGAN, CAROLE
SALTIEL, DEBORAH NANCY
SAMS, REBECCA JANE
SAMUEL, REBECCA JANE
SANDERS, KATHLEEN MARIE
SANDMAN, SUSAN CAROL
*SANDROLINI, LAURA
SANES, FRANCINE SHEILA
*SAPORA, JEANNE ELAINE
SAPORITO, FRED JOSEPH
*SATTER, SHARON
SAUCEDO, JARITA DARNELL
SAUER, CATHLEEN MARIE
SAUTTER, DIANNE LEE
SAVAGE, HELENE SUSAN
SAVITT, JANICE VIVIAN
SAXMAN, NANCY JANE
SCHAADT, PAMELA LEE
SCHAEFFER, JENNIFER ANN
SCHECHTMAN, MERRILEE SUE
SCHINDLES, LAUREN RAE
*SCHLAPP, GAIL JOYCE
SCHLIPPER, DONNA MARY
*SCHMIDT, CHERYL LYNN
SCHNITZ, KAREN LYNNE
SCHOEN, DELORES BAYLIFF
SCHOOLEY, ELIZABETH JUNE
SCHOTT, KRISTINE MARGUERITE
SCHOUSBOE, VIBEKE NOKENTVED
*SCHRINER, MARILYN GEORGIA
*SCHROEDER, JILL SUSANN
SCHULMAN, ELISSA
SCHULTZ, DANA CAROLAN
SCHULTZ, RHONDA BETH
SCHWARTZ, EILEEN DONNA
*SCHWARTZ, MERLE LYNN
SCHWEITZER, KEITH EUGENE

SCHWENDEMAN, SUSAN MARIE
SCOTT, BARBARA JOANNE
SCOTT, SHARON ANN
SECEMSKY, REBECCA REGINA
SEDLACEK, CAROL ANN
*SEGAL, JORY HINDE
SEIDEL, AVA FAITH
SEIFERT, GAYLENE LUCILLE
SELLS, CRAIG LAMONTE
SENSENBRENNER, RUTH ELLYN
SERGOTT, PAULETTE ANN
SERPE, ROGER ANTON
SHANK, PATRICIA LOUISE
SHAPIRO, PAULA HOPE
SHAYMAN, CAROLYN GAY
SHEADE, EUDICE
SHEFFIELD, ALFRED MARTIN
SHELLEY, DOROTHY VICKERS
*SHER, JUDITH RENEE
SHERE, CAROLYN LEE
SHERMAN, PATRICIA MARIE
SHERMAN, VIVIAN ADELE
*SHIMOJIMA, ANNE LANI
SHINNER, SUSAN MERLE
SHOGREN, JANET CAROL
SHUTT, JANICE KAY
SIADAK, JOHN WILLIAM
SIDRAN, DEBORAH LOIS
SIEGEL, CATHY ROSE
SIEGEL, LINDA FAYE
*SIEGEL, MICHELLE JOY
SIEGEL, SHERRY JO
*SIEGELMAN, VICKI LYNN
SIEVERS, GLORIA KAY
SIEVERS, MARY ANN
SILVERMAN, JUDITH LOUISE
SILVERMAN, TERI ELLEN
SIMONINI, NANCY JEANNE
SINCLAIR, JOAN ELLEN
SINGER, SHARON LYNN
SINOPOLI, JACQUELINE ANNE
*SKARZYNSKI, CAROL ANN
SKUDRNA, LYNN MARSHA
SLAVIN, SUSAN TERI
SLOCUM, SUZANNE MARIE
SLOTNICK, SHERRILL
*SMELCER, WILMA JEAN
SMITH, BARBARA ELIZABETH
SMITH, CAMILLA ANN
SMITH, CATHRYN SUTHERS
SMITH, DAVID JAMES
SMITH, KATHLYN KLING
SMITH, LINDA SUE
*SNEARLY, CYNTHIA LEE
SODER, CHERYLL MARIE
SONNI, STEPHEN JOSEPH
SPAK, SUE ELLEN (COHN)
SPEARMAN, WILLIAM NEWTON
*SPIEGEL, SUZANNE
SPRINGS, STEPHANIE SUSAN
STAMBACH, SALLY ANN
STAMMER, BARBARA ANN
STANEK, PAULETTE HELEN
STANGE, CAROL SYLVIA

*Starr, Joyce Ann
Starrick, Kathi Sue
Stedman, Patricia Ann
Steinbrink, Elizabeth Ann
Steinholtz, Susan Beth
*Stern, Francine
Stewart, Keith LaVerne
Stoffel, Marilyn Christina
Stolarik, Michele Marie
*Stomper, Connie Marie
*Strang, Audrey Lynn
*Strauss, James Bartley
Stromberg, Susan Marie
Strube, Paul Douglas
Suberkropp, Sharon Ann
Sulkin, Rosalyn
Sullivan, Mary Donnelly
*Sutter, Kathleen Rinkenberger
*Swain, Paula C.
*Swanson, Barbara Jean
Swanson, Paul Walter
Swiatowiec, Sandra Joan
Szot, Barbara Ann
*Szymanski, Catherine Lingane
Takiff, Lois Terri
Tanaka, Judith Marie
Tankersley, Sharon Kay
Tanquary, Mary Jane
Tatelbame, Ileane Faye
Taylor, Cheryl Radabaugh
Taylor, Jan Paulette
*Templeton, Helena Lenore
Thelin, Virginia Poole
Thomas, Julia Butler
Thomas, Karen Nancy
Thomas, Katherine
*Thomas, Madalyn Lenore
Tighe, Carolyn Claudia
*Tilton, Priscilla Ann
Tinkham, Marilyn Rene
Tognarelli, Annette Marie
Togtman, Mary Ellen
Tomlin, Carol Sue
Toporek, Helen
Torii, Diane Osako
Treadman, Valerie Ann
*Trevillian, Carol Ann
Turnbull, Joy Suzanne
Turner, Jacquelyn Jeanette
Ueno, Emi
Uhl, Roseann Cecilia
Ulmer, Edwin Lawrence
Unatin, Janice Ellen
Unverzagt, Neil Gerald
Urick, Ronald Stephen
Vangilder, Kay Louise
Van Hoesen, Susan Helen
Van Osdell, Mary Patricia
Verbin, Helaine Zandra
Verbin, Jacqueline Lewis
Vician, Joanne Marie
Vinson, Mary Ann
Vitt, Barbara Ann
Vogel, Kathy Rauser

Vokac, William Beran
Wade, Willie Nell
Wagner, Michele Irene
Walchirk, Susan Hanna
Wales, Sheryl Eileen
Walker, Veronica Ziska
Wallingford, Constance B.
Walter, Joan Elizabeth
Walton, Lamont
Ward, Barbara Elin
Ward, Deanne Kay
Warman, Robin Sheryl
Warsaski, Debra Ann
Wassel, Lynn Gail
Wassel, Tina Jean
Watne, Christine Ann
Weber, Shari Vicki
*Weigel, Barbara Meredith
Weinberg, Ricky Arthur
Weiner, Lynn Lipson
Weinstein, Lynn Gail
Weinthaler, Diane Louise
Weinthaler, Jeanne Marie
Weisman, Cindy
Weiss, Margo Kay
*Weissman, Sandra Thea
Welch, Pamela Jane
Wells, Catheryn Ellen
*Wende, Karen Jill
Wendell, Deborah Badendick
Wengerhoff, Susan Michelle
Werner, Barbara Ruth
Wessel, Jananne Rae
Wessels, Barbara Ann
*White, Carol Sue
White, Cherryl Vaunda
Whiting, Dixie Lou
Whitney, Kathie Lynn
Wijas, Marcia Irene
Wilker, Ellen Lee
*Wilkus, Janice Ann
Williams, Patricia Kay
Wilson, Barbara Lynn
Winston, Michelle
Wiseman, Glenna Mae
Wold, Gary Robert
*Wolff, Merle Sue
Wolff, Sandralee Ann
Wolgel, Sari Linda
*Wolinetz, Miriam Lynn
Woods, Ruby Carolyn
Woolen, Linda Darlene
Yellen, Marlo Ann
Young, Linda Ruth
*Young, Norma Eilene
Zeiters, Barbara Jean
Zelent, Cynthia Kay
Zeretzke, David Lance
Zibman, Diantha
Zikmund, Larry Paul
Zirkle, Kay Taylor
Zlotnik, Irene Barbara
Zubak, Barbara Ann
Zumpf, Joseph Edward

34

# COLLEGE OF ENGINEERING

ABBOTT, STEPHEN CHARLES
ABENDROTH, JOHNNIE RAY
ABERLE, LINDA MARIE
ABRAJANO, ROBERT FRANCIS
ADAMS, MICHAEL JOHN
ADELT, RICHARD ALLEN
ADKINS, CHARLES DONALD
ADKINS, MICHAEL DOUGLAS
ADKINS, RUSSELL LAWRENCE
AIKUS, ALBERT JOSEPH
ALBRECHT, PETER DANIEL
ALI, SAIYED MOHAMMED
*ALLEMONG, JOHN JAY
ALLEN, DANIEL MARK
ALLINGTON, KENNETH JOHN
ALLISON, CECIL WARREN
ALLMAN, MICHAEL ERNEST
ALMQUIST, EDWARD QUINTON
*ALPERN, MICHAEL
*ALTON, GUY RICHARD
ANDERSON, CARL VICTOR
ANDERSON, DAVID WILLIAM
*ANDERSON, DONALD WAYNE
ANDERSON, GARY EARL
*ANDERSON, JOHN HOMER, JR.
ANDERSON, PAUL DOUGLAS
ANDRES, ROBERT JOSEPH
ANDREWS, DALE RUSSELL
ANDREWS, ROBERT JAY
ANTHONY, PAUL JOHN
APPLEMAN, JOHN STANLEY
ARMBRUST, RONALD ORAN
ASH, THOMAS MICHAEL
*ASHTON, JAMES BARRY
ASSELBORN, DEAN EDWARD
*ATHERTON, JAMES HAROLD
*ATKINSON, RUSSELL ROGER
AUTH, PHILIP ALBERT
*AWKER, RANDAL WILLIAM
BABLER, ROBERT BOYD
BACHTA, JOSEPH K.
*BAECHLE, ROBERT LOUIS
BAKER, JONATHAN READ
BAKER, PAUL ALLEN
*BALAZS, RONALD MICHAEL
BALDACCI, JOHN WILLIAM
BALDWIN, STEPHEN ERIC
BALKEY, JACK THOMAS
*BALLOU, ALAN ERRETT
*BALSAN, JOHN RENNE
BANDERA, CHARLES FRANCIS
BARAN, SANFORD BRUCE
BARBARO, ANTHONY JOSEPH
BARENFANGER, CHARLES WILLIAM
BARNHART, JON RONALD
*BARR, KENNETH HARRY
BARTIK, STEVEN RUSSELL
BARTLETT, DONALD LARRY
BARTO, KENNETH VERN
BATEMAN, PHILIP LESTER
BATES, CHARLES MILTON
BAUDINO, RODNEY JAY
BAUER, DARRYLL RAYMOND

*BEAMS, DAVID MICHAEL
BEAUCHAMP, RICHARD ALLEN
BEAUMONT, JAMES ALAN
BEAUPRIE, SCOTT EDWIN
*BEAVERS, JOHN ALVIN
BECHEM, ANTHONY JOSEPH
BECK, DAVID ANDREW
*BECK, STEPHEN CHARLES
BECKEMEYER, RONALD EDWARD
*BECKER, BRUCE CARL, II
BECKER, JAMES KALEV
BECKERLE, MICHAEL JOHN
*BEELER, JOSEPH KENT
BEGLEY, THOMAS REID
*BELDEN, JOHN PHILLIP
BELL, THOMAS HUGH
*BELTZ, WILLIAM FOARD
BENASSI, JOHN MARIO
BENJAMIN, RANDALL HAROLD
BENNETT, GREGORY ROBERT
*BENTEN, JAMES SMITH
*BENTON, MARK CAMERON
BENWAY, RALPH BRUCE
BENZULY, ROBERT DARREL
BERG, KENNETH DAVID
*BERGER, MICHAEL F.
BERGMAN, ROBERT ALLEN
BERGSTROM, ERIC KENNETH
*BERGSTROM, RICHARD LEE
*BERNDT, WAYNE EDWARD
BERNSEE, FREDERICK RICHARD
BERRY, HENRY THOMAS, JR.
BERRY, MICHAEL GRAYDON
*BEST, LARRY VERNON
*BETTNER, ALLEN WAYNE
BEUTLER, CARL EMIL
BEVER, JOSEPH FRANK
BEVERIDGE, JAMES ROBERT
BEYER, ANTHONY THOMAS
*BEYERS, JOSEPH WAYNE
*BILLING, MICHAEL GERARD
BIRTCHER, WILLIAM ALAN
BISCEGLIE, FRANK THOMAS
BISHAF, PHILLIP CHARLES
BISHOP, CORDELL MARION
BISHOP, DENNIS RAY
BISHOP, THEODORE ANDREW
BISPLINGHOFF, ROSS LEE
*BITZ, DONALD MICHAEL
BLACK, JOHN WILLIAM
BLANAR, GEORGE JERRY
BLANDFORD, JAMES BERNARD
BLES, JOHN SCOTT
BLESSIN, ROBERT ALLEN
BLEVINS, JACK LOUIS
BLOSS, DONALD RUSSELL
*BLUMBERG, RICHARD PAUL
BLUMENTHAL, MICHAEL EVAN
BLYLY, DON ALAN
*BOEKHAUS, KENNETH LEROY
BOGARD, WILLIAM TERRY
BOHL, KENNETH ROBERT
*BOI, MARTIN THOMAS

35

Boirum, Ralph Neil
Bonomi, William John
Borczak, Richard Paul
*Born, Christopher Paul
*Borth, David Edward
Boruta, Nicholas
Bossert, Ralph Orland
Bosy, George Stephen
*Boudreau, James Karle
Bounkeopraseuth, Boun Houa
Bouslog, Lyle Eugene
Bouxsein, Francis Remy, II
Bowman, John William
Boyles, Dave Alan
Boysen, Gregory Paul
Brabets, Timothy Patrick
*Bracken, Robert Michale
Bracy, Lorenzo Emanuel
Bradbury, Phillip James
Bralley, James Alexander, III
Bramhall, Jason Candia V.
*Brash, Douglas E.
Braun, Gordon Paul
Braun, Kurt
Brennan, Patrick Paul
Brenner, Mark Alan
*Bretzlaff, Robert Stewart
Brian, Jack Hughes
Bridgham, Larry Edward
Brierley, Thomas William
Brockmeyer, Jerry Wayne
Broderick, Thomas Steven
Brodnick, Gregory Roy
Brooks, Peter Dennis
*Brown, David Mark
Brown, Michael Allan
Brown, Randall Hale
Brown, Richard Allen
Brown, Richard Lynn
*Brown, Richard Wallace
Brown, Thomas Glenn
Bruce, Dennis Michael
Bruce, Robert William
Brull, John Jay
Brunkow, David Allan
Brunner, Harold W., Jr.
Bruss, Robert Herman
*Budzinski, Robert Lucius
Buehler, Martin Giles
Buehring, Arthur William
*Buescher, Melvin Henry
Buford, Robert John
Buhr, Marvin Dean
*Bullard, Marshall Elsworth
Bunger, Aubrey Dean
Buns, Robert Michael
*Burgener, David Brian
Burghart, Daniel Laurence
Burke, Daniel Martin
*Burke, Dennis Edward
*Burke, Thomas Leo
Burleson, Robert Ralph
Burns, Robert Brian, Jr.
Burritt, Scott Allan
Burrows, Robert L.

*Burson, Craig Niman
Burson, Gary Herbert
Burson, John Stephen
Buschbach, Thomas Richard
Buss, Stephen Alan
*Butler, Gerald Joseph
Buttinger, Paul Richard
Button, James Edward
Butts, Larry John
Cabay, Terrence Allen
Calcagno, Robert Samuel
Caldwell, Michael Ward
Caldwell, William Patrick
Calvert, David Michael
*Calvetti, Pamela Jean
*Campbell, Clive Douglas
Cardwell, Robert Thomas
Carico, John William
Carkin, James Warren
Carlson, Steve Carl
Carrick, Jonathan Robert
Carrison, Craig Louis
Carroll, Kenneth James
Carstens, Richard Stover
Carter, Joel Steven
Caruana, Roger James
Cascio, Anthony Thomas
Case, Jack Nelson
Caulfield, Edward Michael
Cech, Thomas Joseph
*Chan, Jimmy Siu-Leung
Chan, Mike Hiusing
Chan, Richard A.
*Chan, Wai Kung
*Chapin, William Pond, III
*Chapman, Edward Allen
Chapman, George Emil
Chapman, Wayne Allen
Check, Geoffrey David
Chen, Herbert
*Chesley, Patrick John
Childress, Neil Baker
*Choi, Tatyin Boniface
Chrisman, Bruce Charl
Christ, Alan Richard
Christensen, Glenn Michael
Christoff, Douglas Nick
Chu, Michael Paul
Clapman, Myrim
Clark, George Leslie, Jr.
*Clark, Linda Jean
Clary, Michael Dean
*Clemens, Michael John
*Clements, Ernest Vinton, II
Coberly, Glen Carter
Cochran, John David
Coleman, James Joseph
Collins, Jeffrey Craig
Collins, Michael David
Collord, Ross Brian
Comerford, Nicholas Brian
Condreva, Kenneth James
Connolly, James Michael
Conour, John Franklin
Conrad, Gary Richard

*Conway, George Edward
Cooling, Thomas Lee
*Cooper, George Kyle
*Cooper, Larry Philip
Correale, Michael Gene
Costa, John Louis
Costello, Dan Dominic
*Coultas, Dewey Howard
Coulter, George Albert
Cousineau, Thomas Joseph
Coutant, Alan Robert
Cox, James Edward, Jr.
*Cox, Steven Charles
*Cralley, William Edward
Crawford, John Roger
Crawford, Timothy Lee
Crome, Victor Paul, Jr.
*Cromley, John Timothy
Crozier, Terry Ernest
Crump, John George
Crylen, Edward Anthony
Csanda, David Lee
Culver, Steven Randall
*Cunningham, John Tracy
*Cuplin, Richard Paul
Cusick, Robert William
Daily, Wayne Emerson, Jr.
Dale, Donald Allen, Jr.
Dama, Keith Allen
Daniels, Mark Francis
Danner, Gregory James
Darzinskis, Kazimir Reynold
Daugherty, James Lee
Daum, Patrick Lynn
Davenport, Fred Thomas, Jr.
Davenport, Lynn Anderson, Jr.
*Davis, Harry Glenn
*Davis, Kathryn Ann
*Davis, Randall Douglas
Davis, Robert Wayne
Davis, Stephen Duane
*Davison, Dwight Oran
Dawson, Bernarr Everett, Jr.
*Debates, Anthony Louis
Debolt, Robert Dale
Debouck, Michael Jules
Degraaf, Douglas Warren
Deisinger, Robert David
Denardis, Michael William
Dennhardt, Walter H. J.
Denny, Steven Kay
Denslow, David Allen
de Para, Domingo Enrigue
Detwiler, Timothy Lee
Devine, James Thomas
*Deweese, Joseph Edward
Dierckman, Thomas Edward
Dietzler, Daniel Patrick
Dilley, Larry Dale
Divito, Anthony Stanley
Dobratz, Glenn Eric
Dobrovolny, James Lawrence
*Dodgson, David Scott
*Dolegowski, John Richard
*Dominik, Daniel Frank

Donahue, Daniel Michael
Donaldson, George Easton, III
*Dorgan, Timothy Moody
Doty, Richard Allen
Doud, Gary Ray
*Dowden, Douglas Calhoun
Dowell, David Harry
Downing, Todd Ralph
Drake, Allen Carl
*Drake, Bradley Kent
*Dresch, Henry Joseph
Driemeyer, Daniel Edward
Duback, David William
Dunlap, Thomas Donald
Dunn, Thomas McDonald
Dunning, Michael Francis
Durrenberger, Robert Scott
Durtschi, William George
Durward, Bruce Stuart
Dyck, Rodney I. J.
Dykstra, Larry Robert
Dykstra, Roger Everett
Easler, Dean Edward
Ebersole, Gary Lee
Ecke, Gary James
Eckert, Anthony DeWitt
Edelbrock, John Frances, Jr.
*Edstrom, Robert Charles
Edwards, John Francis
Edwards, Jon Jeffrey
*Eggerding, Carl Louis
Ehrgott, John Francis
Ehrlich, Edward Stanley
Ekblad, James Alan
Ekstrand, Daniel Ross
Elbl, Michael William
Elliott, James Edward
*Elliott, Ronald Lee
*Ellis, William Thomas
Else, Daniel Henry, III
Elsesser, Michael Ray
Emery, Warren Lee
Engel, Steven Edward
*Englund, Charles Jeffrey
Enstrom, Kenneth Dean
Ephraim, Gary David
Epstein, Lloyd Mark
Erickson, Keith Randall
Erickson, Paul Milton
*Erickson, Stephen Lee
*Erin, Rod
Ernst, Gregory John
Evans, Donald Clark
Evans, William Theodore
Ewing, Donald Lee
Ewoldt, Robert George
Eyfells, Ingolfur Helgi
Faber, John Pierre
Fabin, Paul
*Fajfar, Dennis John
Falk, Jerry Lynn
Faust, William Wayne
*Fawcett, Bradly Kevin
Fay, Joseph William
*Feinberg, Stephen Jay

*FELDMAN, MARK IRWIN
FELDMANN, MARK RUSSELL
FELLMAN, CHARLES WALTER
FERETICH, ROBERT ANTHONY
FESL, JAMES JOSEPH
FEYEN, GORDON
*FIDUK, KENNETH WALTER, JR.
*FIELD, DONALD MARTIN
FIELD, SCOTT ROBERT
FILEWICZ, MARK VINCENT
FIMOFF, MARK JAY
FINKE, ROBERT LAWRENCE
FISHER, DAVE HENRY
FISHER, PAUL ADRIAN
FISHER, TODD ALAN
*FITZHENRY, PATRICK
*FJERSTAD, ERIK ALLEN
FLACH, MICHAEL GENE
FLANAGAN, PATRICK BRENTON
*FLASCH, FRANK LEONARD
*FLOROS, MICHAEL ANTHONY
FOAT, GALEN DELBERT
FOLKERTS, CHARLES HENRY
FOLLIS, WILLIAM JOSEPH
FOLTZ, NORMA LOUIS
*FONTANA, THOMAS PAUL
FORBES, RICHARD ALLEN
FORDHAM, MARK EVERETT
*FORSBERG, THOMAS WAYNE
*FORSE, ROGER JAMES
FORTSCHNEIDER, DAVID
FOSTER, STEPHAN LYLE
FOUTCH, DOUGLAS ALLEN
FRAILEY, MAX LEE
FRANCKOWAIK, RICHARD
FRANK, DOUGLAS NEAL
FRANKLIN, MICHAEL STEVEN
FRANKLIN, SHELDON NORMAN
*FRANTSI, PHILIP CHARLES
*FRAZIER, RODNEY LYNN
FRAZIER, TERRY LEE
*FREDERICKSON, DAVID LYNN
FREESE, JOHN DAVID
*FRETT, MICHAEL CHARLES
FREUND, THOMAS JAMES
FREY, PAUL DIXON
FRICKE, RICHARD THOMAS
FRILING, PAUL MICHAEL
FRITCH, HARVEY LEO
FRITZ, FREDERICK JOSEPH
FRITZ, RONALD EUGENE
*FRONCZAK, FRANK JOHN, JR.
FROST, JAMES LEROY
FRUS, JOHN ROBERT
*FRYKMAN, DANIEL PAUL
FTACEK, ANDREW PHILIP, JR.
*FULLER, KIM FRANCIS
*FUOSS, DENNIS EDWARD
FUQUA, DIRK BRIAN
FURLAN, JAMES EDWARD
FURMAN, RICHARD LOUIS
*GABRIEL, KEITH ROBERT
GAC, FRANK DAVID
*GALLAGHER, DANIEL THOMAS
GALLAGHER, ROBERT WILLIAM

GARD, GAYLORD LYNN
GARDNER, BENJAMIN, JR.
GARDZE, ERIC PAUL, JR.
GARNER, JAMES MICHAEL
GARRISON, GARY DEAN
GARROTT, FREDRICK CLINTON
GATES, MARKLAND THAYER
GATS, JAMES PAUL
GAULT, WAYNE B.
GAVENDA, ROBERT ANTHONY
GAZDA, PHILIP ALLEN
GEDDES, BRUCE DAVID
*GEHRIG, DOUGLAS BRUCE
*GEHRING, DURWARD JAMES
*GEHRING, ROBERT ELLIOTT
*GEHRT, CARL LEE
GENCZO, STEVEN GEORGE
GENTRY, DANIEL HESLER
GEORGE, DONALD JOHN
GERLACH, KARL ROBERT
GERSHON, MICHAEL RICHARD
GIBALA, ROCCO
GIBBONS, JAMES JOSEPH
GIBBS, RONALD THOMAS
GIBES, JOSEPH GERALD
GIBSON, ERNEST LEE
GIBSON, TERRENCE LYNN
GIES, JOHN VICTOR
GIGER, DONALD WAYNE
GILBERT, GREGORY STEVEN
GILLEN, MICHAEL PATRICK
GILLHOUSE, DAVID ROBERT
GILLIS, JAMES ANDREW
GILMORE, DOUG JOHN
GILMORE, MERLE LEE
GISINGER, JACK LORIN
GIURATO, ROBERT SANTO
GJETNES, IVAR
*GLADHILL, THEODORE WILLIAM, JR.
*GLAZER, MARVIN ALAN
*GLEASON, JAMES N.
GLETTY, BRUCE EDWARD
*GLICK, JEFFREY SINCLAIR
*GLICKER, JOSEPH LAWRENCE
GMITEREK, HENRY STANLEY
GMITRO, ARTHUR FRANK, JR.
GOETZMANN, JOHN PAUL
GOLDBERG, WILLIAM JAY
GOODAPPLE, PAUL THOMAS
GOODING, MICHAEL JOHN
*GOODMAN, ALLAN LEE
GORDON, RICHARD BENJAMIN
GORENS, EDWARD HARRISON, JR.
GORSUCH, JEFFERY SCOT
GOTSCHALL, STANLEY GEORGE
GOTTEMOLLER, PAUL JOSEPH
GOUDIE, JAMES EDWARD
GRAFF, RICHARD FRANCIS
*GRAHAM, GEORGE WADE
GRAUL, CHARLES HERBERT
GRAY, DAVID PAUL
GREEN, GEORGE EDWARD
GREEN, HAROLD KENNETH
GREEN, KENNETH J.
GREENE, HOWARD CARY

38

GREENE, TERRY GENE
GREENING, LANCE ROBERT
GREENLEE, WILLIAM JOHN
*GREENWALD, CARL JOSEPH
GREER, WILBUR CHARLES
GREGOR, JOHN DAVID
GRESH, JOHN DALLAS
GRGAS, JOHN MICHAEL
GRIEB, DONALD LEON
GRIMMELBEIN, MARK WILLARD
GRISOLANO, JAMES MARTIN, JR.
*GRMAN, MICHAEL EDWARD
GROENE, CHARLES STANLEY
GROENE, LAWRENCE ROBERT
GRONLI, MICHAEL EDWARD
GROTH, STEVEN LOUIS
GROVES, HAROLD JAMES
GUINN, RICHARD ALAN
GULLEDGE, JOHN HOWARD
GUNDLACH, GREGORY JOHN
GUNN, DONALD BRUCE
GUNNARSSON, THOR
GUNTHER, ROBERT WILLIAM
GUSTAFSON, ROBERT JOHN
*HAAR, THOMAS BERNARD
HAAS, DANIEL LOUIS
HAAS, RUDOLPH RALPH
HACK, RANDOLPH LEONARD
HAEGER, ALLAN ROBERT
*HAGAN, WILLIAM KELLY, III
HAGEMEYER, LAWRENCE P.
HAGEN, DAVID LOUIS
HAGENSICK, JOHN LOUIS
HAHN, ROBERT WILLIAM
HAHN, THOMAS FREDRICK
*HAINAUT, JOHN JOSEPH
HALL, DOUGLAS RALPH
HALL, JAMES LOWELL
HALL, RANDOLPH LEE
HALLENE, ALAN M.
HALLEY, DAVID ROSS
HALLOWELL, RICHARD A.
HAMMAN, JOHN MILROY
HAMMERICH, THOMAS ALAN
HAMMES, ROBERT MATTHEW, JR.
HAMMOND, JEFFREY KEITH
HAMMOND, JOHN B.
*HANCOCK, JOHN DAVID
HANLON, JAMES ALAN
HANNA, BRUCE FRANCIS
HANSEN, KENNETH ADOLPH
*HANSON, HOWARD PAUL
HANSON, MELBA MCCALLISTER
HANSON, RICHARD CRAIG
HAPP, JAMES LEO
HAPPEL, FREDERICK JOSEPH
*HARLAN, JERRY WILLIAM, JR.
HARMESON, TERRY ALAN
HARRINGTON, THOMAS ARTHUR
*HARRINGTON, TIMOTHY ALAN
HARRIS, RICHARD DANIEL
*HARRIS, RICHARD SHUTT
HARRISON, MICHAEL WATT
HARSHA, DARYL EUGENE
HART, BURTON LEE

*HARTWIG, JOHN LEWIN
HARTY, DANIEL PATRICK
HARZ, HAROLD DAVID
HASEGAWA, WAYNE KAZUMI
*HASKIN, ROGER LEE
*HASSELBACHER, KEVIN
HATFIELD, DONALD EUGENE
HATTENDORF, DONALD WILLIAM
HAUB, WILLIAM CLIFFORD
HAUCK, REED KEITH
HAUGHNEY, GARY VINCENT
HAWES, ROBERT TURLEY
*HAWORTH, ROBERT HUGH
HEATH, DAVID LEE
HEBDON, DAVID E.
*HEDRICK, JAMES ALLEN
HEFNER, ROBERT EDWARD
HEIDEMANN, STANLEY FRANCIS
HEIMANN, WILLIAM CHARLES
HEINKING, GARY
HEISS, DIRK FREDERICK
HEITSCHMIDT, WILLIAM ROBERT
HELD, THOMAS ANTHONY
HELFRICH, DONALD LEE
HELM, RANDALL PAUL
HELSTROM, DENNIS DEAN
*HEMPHILL, STUART RANDOLPH
HEMSTREET, EDWARD ALAN
HENDERSON, GORDON WILLIAM
HENDERSON, JAMES ALAN, JR.
HENDRICKS, JERRY DEAN
HENDRICKSON, PHILIP DALE
HENNEGAN, NEAL MICHAEL
HENRICHS, MARK ALAN
HENRY, DAVID GERARD
HENSLER, WILLIAM JOHN
*HERBERGER, GARY RICHARD
*HERLIEN, ROBERT ALLEN
HERMAN, RAY MICHAEL
*HERNES, ERIK
HERREWEYERS, JEROME KAREL
HERRON, LESTER WYNN
HERSEE, STEPHEN ALLEN
HICKS, KENNETH BENJAMIN
*HIGGINS, BRYON MARK
*HIGHLAND, WILLIAM ROBERT
*HILBERT, STEVEN RAY
HILL, THOMAS ANDREW
*HINCH, DAVID LEROY
HINE, MARK LANE
HINKLE, RUSSELL DALE
*HINRICHS, RICHARD LEROY
HINZ, PAUL ROBERT
HITT, GLENN DAVID
HITZEROTH, ROBERT WESLEY
HO, BILL PANG
*HO, DAVID SUMING
*HOCHSCHILD, RICHARD NEIL
HODGE, WILLIAM ANDREW
HOEFLINGER, JAY PHILIP
HOENE, KENNETH FRANCIS
HOFFMAN, ROBERT PAUL
HOFFMAN, STEVEN CRAIG
HOGANSON, GEORGE EDWARD
HOLDEN, JOHN WILLIAM

39

Holecek, Bruce Robert
*Holland, Gregory
Hollatz, Lawrence Carl
Holliday, Paul Kenneth
*Hollingshead, Mark Alan
Holmen, Ralph Warren
Holtz, Thomas Marcus
Holz, Paul David
Hood, James Louis
Hoover, Keith Martin
*Hopkins, Harland Glenn
*Hopp, Randolph Lee
Horak, William Charles
*Hoskins, Andrew Charles
Houck, John David
Houkom, John Arnold
*Howe, James Richard
*Howland, Dennis Ray
Hoy, Michael Lee
*Hoyt, Roger Franklin
Hryncewicz, Casimir Vincent
Hubble, Steven George
*Huber, Bruce Alan
*Huber, Bruce Alan
Huber, Phillip Stanley
Hudzik, Robert Joseph
Hughes, John Sefton
Hughes, Scott Edward
Hughes, Victor Wallace, Jr.
Hui, Andy Man-Chan
Huizenga, John Raymond
Huling, Keith Robin
Hull, John Robert
Humphrey, Michael Owen
Hunsinger, Charles Ray, Jr.
*Hunt, Roger Allan
Hunter, Anthony William
Hurvitz, Bruce Leslie
Husser, Dewayne Leroy
Hussey, Frank Spencer, III
Hutter, Gary Michael
Hyzer, Peter Christopher
Ignatowicz, Steven Allan
*Ingold, Henry Willard
*Ingram, Larry Stephen
*Ingram, Richard George
Irvin, Mark Alan
Isaacson, Robert Edward
Ivsin, Michal
*Jacobus, Charles J.
Jacques, John Donald
Jaeger, David Thomas
Jakse, Nancy Ellen
Jakupcak, Kenneth Andrew
*James, David Christopher
Janczak, Richard Thomas
*Janke, Mark Charles
Jankowski, Chester Francis
Jansen, Leonard Herman
Jansen, Virgil William
Jarnholm, Arne Richard
Jarvis, Larry Michael
*Javid, Shabon Harold
*Jecmen, Robert Milton
Jenkins, Lewis

Jenkins, Michael Owen
*Jenkins, Thomas Edward
Jensen, Stephen Myron
Jett, Bryan Thomas
Jirkovsky, Alan George
*Johnson, Bruce Allen
Johnson, Donald Ray
Johnson, Duane Henry
*Johnson, Gary Burton
Johnson, Glenn Robert
Johnson, John Delmer
*Johnson, John Henry
Johnson, Keith Robert
Johnson, Kenneth Arthur
*Johnson, Leonard Kurt
*Johnson, Martin Jerome
Johnson, Peter Robert
*Johnson, Richard Harold
*Jones, Brent Rodney
Jones, Charles Allen
Jorgensen, Kenneth Arthur
Juhl, Gary Alan
Jule, Robert William
Jupin, David Wayne
*Jurich, Dale Rade
*Jurkin, Gary James
*Kaar, David Richard
*Kahn, Robert Charles
Kaiser, Fred Chris
*Kaiser, Joseph Matthew
Kaiser, Sidney Vaughn
*Kaminski, Stephen Joseph
Kane, Patrick Timothy
Kania, Bruce John
Kannall, Gregory Alan
Kannenberg, Richard Edwin
Kant, Steven Douglas
Kao, William Hsia
*Kappes, Joseph Mark
Kapral, Dennis Henry
Kaspar, Gary Charles
Kassel, James William
Kaufman, James Matthew
Kazenske, Edward Robert
Keal, Dean Harry
*Keasler, Robert Neil
Keasler, William Edward, Jr.
Keeley, Patrick Christopher
Keene, Donald Willfred
*Keiler, James Calvin
Kempf, John Joseph
Kennedy, Edward Jerome
*Kerans, Karen Sue
Kerchenfaut, Michael Roy
Kerr, Michael Edward
Kerstein, Paul Alan
Kersten, Frederick Poole
*Kesaris, Jim Tom
Kessler, James Joseph, Jr.
Kessler, John Warren
Kettman, David Lee
Kidd, David Michael
Kidd, Ronald Wayne
Kilar, Joseph Henry
Kilty, Roger Steven

40

KINNEY, CAROLYN MARGARET
*KIPP, ROBERT MARION
KIRK, ROBERT MICHAEL
KIRK, STEPHEN ALAN
KIRKENDOLL, ROBERT PATRICK
KITCHEN, JERRY NORMAN
*KLAMM, RICHARD DALE
*KLAZURA, PAUL JOSEPH
KLECKER, JOHN LAWRENCE
KLECKNER, KENNETH BERL
*KLEIN, CHARLES ALLEN
KLENKE, JAMES ROBERT
KLINE, GEOFFREY CAMPBELL
KLINE, THOMAS FRATER
KLING, THOMAS JOSEPH
*KLOCKE, NORMAN LEE
KLOSS, DENNIS JOHN
KLOSTERMANN, NORBERT
KNAPP, DAVID JOSEPH
KNAPP, KIRK OWEN
*KNAPP, RICHARD LEE
*KNEISEL, THOMAS FREDRIC
KNELL, CHARLES PINCOFFS
KNEPP, GARY LYNN
KNIGHT, CHARLES WILLIAM
*KNOWLTON, GORDON RAY
KOCH, LARRY WARREN
KOCH, ROGER DALE
KOCIAN, GENE JAMES
*KOEHLER, THOMAS LEE
KOELLING, MARK ALAN
KOHLMEIER, JAMES ALLEN
KOLAZ, DAVID JAMES
KOMER, ALBERT GEORGE
KONEN, BRUCE PAUL
KONRAD, WILLIAM KURTIS
*KORKOWSKI, JAMES ANTON
KOSCIK, RICHARD ALLEN
KOSKI, GERALD WILLIAM
KOSTER, FREDERICK JULIUS
KOTLARIK, JOHN JOSEPH, JR.
*KOWALL, RICHARD JOSEPH
KOWALL, ROBERT THOMAS
KRAKER, ROBERT GILBERT
KRAUS, GEORGE ALBERT
*KRAUSE, KENNETH EDWARD
*KRAVITZ, KENNETH MICHAEL
KRAWITZ, JEFFREY SIMS
KRAYBILL, DANIEL DUNSMORE
*KRAZINSKI, JOHN LEO
KREHBIEL, COURTNEY EVANS
KREMPELY, DENNIS THOMAS
*KRIZ, DAVID G. C.
KRIZ, KENNETH JOSEPH
KROMPHARDT, JAMES FREDERICK, II
KRUSH, ROBERT JOHN
KRUTA, JOE NICK
KRUZIC, RONALD WALTER
KUHFUSS, ALVIN LEE, JR.
KUHN, ROBERT HENRY
KUJOVICH, LAWRENCE ROBERT
KULL, JOHN DAVID
KUNZ, GARY LOUIS
KURAS, JOHN CHARLES
KUROWSKI, JAMES ANTHONY

KURTH, DALE ROBERT
KUSEK, THOMAS H.
KWITKOWSKI, PETER ALLEN
LABEDZ, GERALD PAUL
LACERENZA, MARK DOMINIC
*LACEY, WILLIAM ANDREW
LA FRANK, SAMUEL EARL
LAMB, JEFFRY EARL
LAMONICA, MICHAEL ANTHONY
LAMSZUS, JANE MARIE
LAMSZUS, JOHN GEORGE
LANAHAN, MICHAEL JAMES
*LANCASTER, DAVID RUSSELL
LANE, DENNIS DEL
*LANE, PHILIP JAMES
LANG, DAVID JAMES
*LANGMAN, CHARLES HENRY
LANZEN, BRIAN ARTHUR
LARSON, DEAN WESLEY
LARSON, DOUGLAS ERIK
LARSON, DUANE PAUL
LARSON, STEVEN ARTHUR
*LASH, RALPH MORGAN
LASSWELL, DAVID CHARLES
LATHROPE, MICHAEL FRANKLIN
LATREILLE, RENEE F.
LATTAL, JOSEPH MATTHEW
LAUF, ROBERT JOHN
*LAWS, JOHN WILLIAM
*LAWSON, MARK RICHARD
LAWSON, STEPHEN CRAIG
LAY, MARK ALLEN
LEAMON, JOHN ARTHUR
LEANG, WILLIAM NIM
LEBENSORGER, WILLIAM
LEDEN, WILLIAM EARL
LEDUC, ROGER PAUL
LEE, ALFRED MING-HUNG
LEE, ROGER EDWARD
LEEBRICK, JOHN RANDOLPH
LEFFINGWELL, DEAN ALLAN
*LEGARE, OWEN LEONARD
LEHMAN, PAUL JOSEPH
*LEHMANN, RANDALL EARL
*LEHNEN, DAVID CHARLES
LELLMAN, JAMES JOHN
LEMAN, MARCUS LEE
*LEMAN, MARVIN GENE
LEMAR, JAMES KENNEDY
*LEMCOE, ROBERT LEWIS
*LEMEIN, GREGG DOUGLAS
LENAHAN, RICHARD MICHAEL
*LENTINE, FRANK GEORGE
LEO, RICHARD JOSEPH
LEONARD, MICHAEL LYNN
LEONG, JOHNNY MAY
LEUNG, CASEY KA CHAI
LEVEK, RAYMOND JOSEPH
LEVIE, JAMES HOWARD
LEVINE, HAROLD JAY
LICINA, GEORGE JOSEPH
LIND, ALLEN EDWARD
LINDEN, DAVID WARNER
LINDGREN, TIMOTHY FREDERICK
LINDSEY, DONALD ROY

41

LIONBERGER, EDWARD EARL
LIPPY, DAVID PAUL
LITTLE, CHARLES CHRISTOPHER
LITTLE, JAMES DANIEL
LITTLE, MICHAEL RAY
LITZ, EMIL JOE
*LIU, WING KI
*LOB, CLIFFORD GODFREY
LOEDING, WILLIAM LAURENCE
LOEHR, ROBERT JOHN
LOEW, FREDERICK ALLEN
*LOHMANN, WALTER EDWARD
LORENTZ, CARL WINFRED
LORENTZ, EDWARD CHARLES
LOVEKAMP, JAMES MICHAEL
*LOWE, JOHN CHEUNG
LOWER, JOHN GREGORY
LOWSTUTER, BRUCE RICHARD
LOWSTUTER, WILLIAM ROBERT, JR.
*LUCIER, TERRENCE ARTHUR
*LUDOWISE, MICHAEL JOSEPH
LUDWIG, STEVE
LUEBS, CRAIG JOHN
LUFKIN, JOHN KIMBALL
LUHR, ROBERT JOSEPH
LULEWICZ, PHILIP FRANCIS
*LUXION, DENNIS WAYNE
MACKIN, EDMUND FRANCIS, JR.
MACRIS, THOMAS DEAN
MADONIA, JOHN JOSEPH
MAHACHEK, DAVID LEE
*MAJCHROWICZ, DENNIS MICHAEL
*MAK, ALAN SUNG-CHI
MAK, KUI NANG
MAKAR, JOHN ANTON
MALAISE, MAURICE GLENN
MALE, RUTH ANN
MALEKSETIAN, AZAD
MALLEN, RICHARD FELIX
*MALLIN, THOMAS WAYNE
*MANCINI, LOUIS JOSEPH
MANCZAK, JOHN EDWARD
MANN, STANLEY LINDEN
MANNING, PATRICK FRANCIS
MAPLE, ROBERT EDGAR
MARCHI, STEPHEN ALBERT
MARCONETT, BRUCE LYNN
MARCYK, GERALD T.
MARENTIC, MICHAEL JAMES
MARIETTA, GARY LEE
*MARION, BRAD ALAN
*MARION, RAYMOND HOMER
MARLIN, MICHAEL PAUL
*MARSHALL, RICHARD ALAN
*MARSHALLA, ROBERT ALVIN
MARTIN, BRUCE ALAN
MARTIN, JAMES ARTHUR
*MARTINEAU, WALTER STILLGER
*MARTINEK, STEPHEN JOHN
MASON, GREGORY A.
MASON, JERRY LEE
*MASON, WILLIAM ERNEST
*MAST, PETER KARL
MATESKI, JAMES EDWARD
*MATHEWSON, THEODORE DAVID

MATIS, LOUIS PAUL
MATONE, PHILIP JEAN
MATTHEWS, WILLIAM RICHARD
MAUGHMER, MARK DAVID
MAY, DAVID VINCENT
MAYER, WILLIAM JOHN
MAZAWA, ROBERT JIRO
McCABE, CHARLES KEVIN
McCARREN, DANIEL STEPHEN
*McCLARY, ELMER R.
*McCLEISH, MICHAEL LAWRENCE
*McCOY, MICHAEL DENT
McCOY, RICHARD WAYNE
McGINNIS, JAMES
McGOWAN, PHILIP JAMES
McGUIRE, EDWARD VINCENT
McKIBBEN, CLAUDE FRANK
McKINNEY, BILL DEAN
*McKOWN, RUSSELL CARL
*McLEVIGE, WILLIAM VICTOR
McNAMARA, JAMES ARTHUR
McNAUGHTON, JAMES LLOYD
*McNEESE, DENNIS THOMAS
MEADOWS, BYRON DAVID
*MEARA, JAMES LEWIS
MEDINE, ALLEN JOSEPH
MEEKER, JIM ROBERT
*MEIER, DANA GLENN
MEIER, PAUL FERD
MEISNER, DAVID BRUCE
MEISNER, MICHAEL JAMES
MEISTER, GEORGE PHILLIP
*MEIXNER, ROBERT HAY, JR.
MELICHER, STEPHEN ALAN
MELLER, DAVID VICTOR
MELVIN, RICHARD OWEN
MENCHHOFF, JERRY ALLAN
MENNENGA, LOWELL ERNEST
MENTKOWSKI, TIMOTHY FRANCIS
MENTZER, RAY ALLEN
MESBAH, BEDI
*MEVERT, DAVID WAYNE
MEYER, DAVID FREDERICK
MEYER, LEONARD CLEMENS
MICHELS, THOMAS JOSEPH
MIELE, MICHAEL ANTHONY
MIELEC, ROGER WLADIMAR
MIFFLIN, JOHN STEPHEN
MIKKELSEN, MICHAEL JAMES
MIKOLAITIS, JAMES CRAIG
MILBRAND, JOHN FRANCIS
*MILLER, BRIAN THOMAS
MILLER, GLENN HENRY
MILLER, JOSEPH LAWRENCE
MILLER, MELVIN
MILNER, BRIAN ROSS
MILSTEIN, SIDNEY MARK
MINDOCK, KEVIN LEE
MINER, WILLIAM HOWARD
*MITCHELL, BRADLEY WILLIAM
MITCHELL, ROBERT DAVID
*MITCHELL, STANLEY EUGENE
MIX, KEVIN JAY
MIZE, JOHN MELVIN
MOBURG, RICHARD HOWARD

42

MOELLER, DARYL DWAYNE
MOHAUPT, RICHARD BRUCE
MOLITOR, MICHAEL JAMES
MONCELLE, MICHAEL EUGENE
MONSON, TYRUS KENT
MOOGK, GARY WILLIAM
MOORE, JAMES CLARE, III
MOORE, JEFFREY ARTHUR
MOORE, MCKINLEY
MOORE, WILLIAM ALBERT
MORACHE, MICHAEL ALBERT
MORAVEC, ROBERT JOHN
MORBY, ALLAN ROGER
*MOREY, ROBERT EDWARD
MORRIS, CHARLES DONALD
MORRIS, JOHN ANTHONY
MORRISON, STEVEN LEON
MORTENSEN, HAROLD HENRY
MOTTL, GLEN JEROME
MOULTON, STEPHEN WAYNE
MUCCI, DAVID MICHAEL
MUELLER, CRAIG ROBERT
*MUELLER, JAMES JOSEPH
MUELLER, RAYMOND CHARLES
*MUELLER, STEVE ROGER
*MUELLER, THOMAS JAMES
MUHONEN, GARY MARK
MUNSON, JOHN MICHAEL
MUNTNER, MICHAEL STEVEN
MUNTON, DARRELL EDWARD
MURAMOTO, SIDNEY WARREN
*MURIN, CAROL JEAN
MURPHY, WILLIAM THOMAS
MURRAY, RICHARD CHARLES, II
*MUSE, JOHN EDWARD
MUSIAL, MICHAEL EDWARD
MUSIAL, MICHAEL EDWARD
MUSUR, ROBERT JOSEPH
*MYERS, HERBERT ALLEN
NAGEL, RICHARD ARMIN
NAHLIK, FRANK JOSEPH
NALYWAJKO, MICHAEL IHOR
*NAZIMEK, LARRY EDWARD
NEFF, ANDREW NELSON
NEGELE, JAMES ROBERT
NEITZKE, THOMAS GEORGE
*NELSON, DANNY LEE
NELSON, JOHN FRANKLIN, JR.
NELSON, MARK WILLIAM
NELSON, PAUL KENNETH
*NELSON, THOMAS EVERETT
*NELSON, WILLIAM EDWARD
NESPECHAL, ROBERT JOHN, JR.
NEUMAN, GLEN A.
NEVINGER, RONALD DALE
NEWELL, DONALD MARK
NEWHAGEN, PAUL
NICHOLS, WILLIAM EDWARD
*NICKOLLS, JOHN RICHARD
NICOL, THOMAS HOWARD
NIEHAUS, JEFFREY ALAN
*NIEHOFF, DENNIS DEAN
NIEMANN, DAVID ALOYS
NIEMI, TRACEY JON
NIESTRADT, JAMES EUGENE

NOGGLE, THOMAS LYNN
*NORDSTROM, ERIC WALTER
NORDSTROM, PETER JOHN
NORTH, MARK HUNTINGTON
NORTON, HERBIE RAY
NOSAKA, FRED GARY
*NOVAK, GREGORY CLEMENT
*NOVARIA, ROBERT JOHN
NOVEY, WILLIAM EDWARD
*NOWAK, EDWARD DANIEL
*NYSTROM, GUSTAV ADOLPH
*NYSTROM, HALVARD EDWARD
O'BRIEN, LARRY SCOTT
OCHS, DAVID NICHOLAS
O'CONNELL, RICHARD HARRIS
O'CONNOR, DONALD STEPHEN
*O'DONNELL, JOHN PATRICK
OEDEWALDT, WAYNE ROY
OERTLEY, THOMAS EARL
OFNER, CLYDE MANNE
*OGLE, JAMES ADELBERT
OKEREN, IZIM
OLAND, C. BARRY
OLDHAM, JAMES ROBERT
OLIVER, BRUCE ALAN
OLKIEWICZ, EDWARD DENNIS
OLMSTEAD, ALVIN DALE
*OLSEN, CRAIG ALAN
OMHOLT-JENSEN, JAN
ONISCHUK, STEVEN JAMES
OPREA, DAVID MITCHELL
*ORAVIS, LARRY THOMAS
O'REILLY, MARGARET MARY
ORR, PHILIP BRIAN
ORTSCHEID, ROBERT ALLEN
OSBURN, KEITH DUANE
OSTENDORF, DAVID ERNEST
*OSTERTAG, EDWARD LOUIS
OSWALD, KEITH JOSEPH
*OVERMYER, PHILLIP IRVIN
OVERTON, TREVOR CHARLES
OZOR, JOSEPH EVARIS
PAGE, ROBERT ALLEN
PAGEL, SHERWOOD HARRY
PAINE, ARTHUR RAY
PALMORE, LARRY MITCHELL
*PARK, STEPHEN MICHAEL
PARKER, DENNIS WINSLOW
PARKER, JOHN WAYNE
*PARKER, KENNETH PAUL
PARKES, JOHN JOSEPH
PARKINSON, RICHARD GILL
*PARKS, DAVID MOORE
PARKS, RODNEY THOMAS
PATANELLA, JAMES ERNEST
PATRICK, FREDRICK ALLEN
PATRICK, HAROLD EUGENE
PATTERSON, JAMES EDWARD
*PEARSON, JAMES PETER
PEARSON, KENNETH WAYNE
PECK, DON E.
PECK, KEN E.
PEDERSEN, RAYMOND F.
PEO, GEORGE EDWIN, JR.
PEPPING, RICHARD EDWIN

43

PERISHO, RONALD JAY
*PERKO, LAWRENCE NEAL
*PERRY, THOMAS JAY
*PERSCHNICK, GENE ALLEN
*PERSIANI, GUIDO F.
PERZ, JOAN C.
PERZ, MICHAEL MARTIN
PESSIN, STUART IVAN
*PETERS, JOHN MATTHEW
PETERSEN, GARY RICHARD
PETERSON, GARY ALLEN
PETERSON, HARRY WILLIAM
PETERSON, LEON CURTIS
PETERSON, LEONARD SIMON
PETERSON, ROBERT KEITH
PETRILLI, JOSEPH FABIAN
PETTERSEN, MICHAEL SCOTT
*PETTITT, KENNETH DALE
PETTY, THOMAS DAVID
*PFAENDER, THOMAS GEORGE
PFAU, LARRY JOSEPH
PHELAN, TERRENCE ROBERT
PHILLIPS, GREGORY SCOT
*PHILLIPS, JOHN VINCENT
PICKARD, SCOTT STREET
PIENKOS, JAMES MICHAEL
*PIEPER, RICHARD WAYNE
PIERRE, WAYNE FORREST
PILLOTE, DELPHINE MARIE
PINTO, CLIFFORD WALTER
PIOTROWSKI, THOMAS CARL
*PISCHKE, KEITH MARTIN
PLAGGE, GLENN DONALD
PLENCNER, ROBERT MICHAEL
*PLENIEWICZ, RICHARD
*PLEWA, JAMES WILFRED
POHLMAN, JEFFREY THOMAS
POHLMANN, KENNETH CRAIG
POLESKY, RICHARD WILLIAM
POLLOCK, RANDALL JAMES
POLSON, DUANE ROBERT
PONSONBY, RALPH EDWARD
*POPE, PAUL WILLIAM
PORT, ROBERT DAVID
*PORTER, ROBERT LEE
POSKA, FREDERICK JAMES
POTT, EDWARD JAMES
POTTER, DON HOLLIS, JR.
POULAKOS, EMMANUEL MIKE
*POVILUS, DAVID STEPHEN
POVSE, FRANK LEO
POWELL, TERRY NORMAN
POWERS, ROBERT THOMAS
PRATTEN, DON H.
PREDICK, PAUL ROBERT
PRETNAR, MICHAEL WILLIAM
PREY, JEROME WILLIAM
PRICE, KENNETH DAVID
PRICE, RICHARD KENTON
PRIEGNITZ, ROBERT ARTHUR
PROSECKY, MICHAEL ANTHONY
PROSISE, JAMES ROBERT
PRUSKI, BOHDAN THOMAS
PUNCHES, DENNIS ORRIS
PURDY, DAVID JOHN

PURTLE, GEORGE ALAN
PUZEY, HAROLD WILLIAM
QUAKA, THOMAS EDWARD
QUILLINAN, QUINN WILLIAM
RADOCHONSKI, PIERRE ANDRE
RAINES, RICHARD DEAN
RAKERS, JAMES BERNARD
RAMQUIST, FREDERICK CARL, JR.
RANDALL, MARK JOHN
RANDELL, LARRY PAUL
RANDOLPH, WILLIAM WOOD
RANGE, BONNIE RUTH
RANSOME, FREDERICK DAVID
RASBID, LAWRENCE WILLIAM
*RATH, GALEN DONALD
RAUH, MICHAEL MERLYN
RAUSCH, JACOB HENRY
*RAUSCH, PATRICK GLENN
RAUSER, LARRY WAYNE
*RAY, ALAN BENJAMIN
RAYMER, JERRY NORMAN
*READ, STEVEN EWING
REAVILL, SCOTT LOVITT
REDING, ROBERT ALLEN
REDLICH, JAMES WILLIAM
REED, LARRY DEAN
*REED, RICHARD CHARLES
REEDY, JOSEPH BARRETT
*REETZ, KEITH ERNEST
REICHLE, JOSEPH ARTHUR
*REISINGER, LEE WALTER
REISSIG, WALTER CHARLES
REMESCH, ANTHONY JOSEPH
RENFRO, CLIFFORD WAYNE
RENO, JEFFREY MICHAEL
RENWICK, BRIAN LEE
RETTBERG, WILLIAM ARTHUR
RICCA, DAVID ERNEST
RICCA, LESLIE AARON
RICE, JAMES COLLINS
RICE, JEROME
RICHARDS, STEPHEN JOHN
*RICKER, RANDALL EDWARD
RIEGER, GEORGE ERNEST
*RIEGER, RODNEY WALTER
RIEKE, BRENT EDWARD
RIGGINS, ROBERT ELDON
RITCHEY, BRUCE NEAL
ROBERTS, LARRY KEITH
*ROBERTSON, ALAN SPENCE
ROBINS, DAVID STANLEY
*ROCKENBACH, PHILIP CATLOW
ROEDIGER, GARY ARTHUR
*ROEPKE, ROBERT WAYNE
ROESCHLEY, STEPHEN RAYMOND
*ROGERS, BARRY WILLIAM
ROGERS, DAVID MARTIN
*ROLEY, DANIEL GAY
*ROLEY, DAVID RAY
ROLEY, ROBERT DOYLE
ROLL, JOHN LINDEN
RONEY, JAMES PHILIP
*ROOSE, THOMAS ROBERT
ROSBOROUGH, GEORGE WILLIAM
ROSCETTI, THOMAS LEE

44

Rose, James Edward
Rose, Richard A.
Rosen, Joseph Nathan
Rosenbarger, Robert
Rosenberg, Earl Wayne
Rosenberg, Irving Charles
Rosenow, Darold K.
Rosner, Raymond James
Roth, Francis Dallier
*Roth, Steven Douglas
*Roth, William Henry
Rouse, Wesley David
Rubenacker, Larry Joseph
*Ruby, Robert Allen
Ruehrwein, Donald Neil
Ruge, George Norman
Rupp, Stephen Francis
Rush, James Harvey
Rybel, Vincent Walter
Rybel, William John
Ryden, Steven William
*Ryder, David Allen
Rydzewski, Lawrence Emil
Rymas, Chrysilis Marie
*Safford, James Harvey
*Saller, Richard Paul
Salm, Robert Jay
Salnick, Richard Eugene
Samata, Sam Nick·
*Sammann, Ernest Albert
*Sances, James John
Santangelo, James Angelo
Santic, Martin George
Sarmiento, Joseph Joachim
Satterthwaite, Mark Cameron
Satterwhite, David Glenn
Sbertoli, Robert Louis, Jr·
Scales, Robert Prado
Scattergood, Stephen John
Schaal, Kevin Dean
Schaefer, Mark Alan
Schaffner, Roger Rollins
*Schaidle, Charles Lee
Schaller, Richard Frank
Scherffius, James Hurley
*Schermerhorn, Roy De Wain
*Schiavoni, Roger Michael
*Schlembach, James Jay
Schlembach, John Michael
Schlesinger, Morton Lee ·
*Schmidt, John William
Schmitt, James Crispin
Schmudde, James Frederick
Schnake, Mark Arthur
Schnayer, Jerold Bruce
*Schneider, David Ray
Schneider, Gilbert Lee
*Schneider, Ronald Wilbert
*Schoenberg, Kurt Francis
*Schottman, Frederick Joseph
*Schranz, Norbert Johannes
Schreiber, Brian Edward
Schriver, Robert Edward Patrick
Schroeder, Paul Robert
Schroeder, Stephen Martin

Schrof, Larry Don
Schuch, Paul Michael
Schutte, John David
*Schwartz, William Henry
Schwartzberg, Allen Paul
Schwarz, Frank Gregory
Schweigert, Alan Lee
*Schweitzer, Eric Allin
Schwerin, Leroy Frank, Jr·
Seaton, Paul Ellwood
Seeber, Kim Everett
Seid, William
*Seitz, Ernest Frederick
*Selander, John Michael
*Selbrede, Steven Charles
Selby, John Hunter
Senft, Werner Heinz
Seng, Michael Orris
Senneff, Michael Dale
Sensenbrenner, Kenneth
*Severin, Warren Donald
Shaff, Frederick Wayne
Shaffer, Ronald Allan
*Sharkey, John Thomas
Shaver, Cecil Bruce
Shaw, Dennis John
Shaw, Frank
Sheaff, Charles Milton
Shearer, Terrance Lee
Sheldon, Gene Pierce
Shelton, Larry Wayne
Sherman, Lawrence Elliot
*Shewmaker, Ronald Dean
Shimomura, Gary Takeo
Shinn, Richard Allan
Shockey, Daniel Phillip
Shook, Kenneth Robert
Shook, Roger Lynn
Shoop, John Clarence
Shulman, Mark Michael
Shultz, Richard Dean
Sickinger, Daniel Louis
Sieracki, Raymond Joseph
Sieracki, Richard Joseph
Sieu, Benny Lou
*Silva-Tulla, Francisco
Simkus, Mindaugas Anthony
Simmons, Gary Gene
Sinder, Dale Robert·
Sitrick, David Howard
*Skager, Paul Steven
Sliva, Oscar Joseph
Slown, David John
Slusher, Carroll Wayne
Smaga, John Andrew
*Smith, Brian Lester
Smith, Daniel Burton
Smith, Daniel Jay
Smith, Gary George
Smith, James Blain, Jr·
Smith, James Edward
Smith, James William
*Smith, Keith Lon
Smith, Michael Frederick
Smith, Robert Arthur

45

*Smith, Susan Diane
*Snodgrass, Kirk Allen
Snoke, Thomas Edwin
Snyder, Steven Daniel
Snyder, Terry N.
Snyder, William George
*Sommer, Henry Joseph, III
*Sommers, David Arthur
Sonneville, Stephen Thomas
Soper, Michael Butler
Soppet, William Kevin
Spacinsky, John Joseph
Spencer, Glenn Richard
*Spetz, Gary Wayne
*Spicer, David Alan
Spielman, Stephen Christie
Spier, Edward Michael
*Spilker, Robert Leonard
*Spinhirne, James Dale
Spoor, Robert Louis
Squillo, Paul Stephen
Stahl, Charles Sumner
*Stahlhut, Randall Kent
Staley, Bruce Mitchell
Stamerjohn, Ralph Warren
Stamp, Stephen Lloyd
Standerwick, Bruce Bertrand
Stanford, Raymond Alden
*Stangel, Gregory Lee
Stanish, Michael Albert
*Stanley, Galen Ward
Stanley, Tobin Alexander
Stanowski, David Richard
Staton, Joseph Michael
Steffen, David Eugene
Steffen, Ronald Wayne
Stejskal, Frank Paul
Stella, Mario Anthony
Stenzel, William John
Sternstein, Allan Joe
Stewart, Kathleen Anne
*Stinson, Kenneth Richard
Stirniman, Robert Paul
Stock, Darrell Allen
Stockner, Alan Ray
Stoller, George Edward
*Stoltz, Terry Lee
Stone, Maureen Celinda
Storm, Stewart Lee
Stotmeister, Kevin Stockel
Stout, Alan Cavitt
Strahl, Gerald Alan
Strain, George Michael
Strand, Robert Raymond
Streitmatter, Cleon Carl
Streitmatter, Michael Jay
Strohacker, Fred Martin
Subject, David Paul
Such, Mark Robert
*Sudlow, William Joseph
*Sue, Harry
Suhre, Dennis Ray
Sullivan, James Allen
Sullivan, Randall L.

Sulo, Robert Michael
Summers, Ralph William
Sunleaf, David Reed, Jr.
Suter, Ronald Eugene
Sutherland, Robert, Jr.
Sutter, Craig Bernard
*Sutton, Kenneth Charles
Sutton, Ronald Lee
*Sutton, Stephen Arthur
Swartwout, Mark Wesley
Swearingen, Steven Lee
Swiatowiec, Frank John
Swinderman, Robert Todd
Szymanski, Alan Richard
Takagishi, Stephen Kurt
Talbert, David Floyd
*Talmadge, Richard Neal
Tangalos, Dennis Anthony
Tanner, Joseph Richard
*Tarabori, James Allen
*Taylor, Bradley Alan
Taylor, Gary Steve
Taylor, Larry Eugene
Taylor, Tim Edward
Taylor, William Michael
Taylor, William Randall
Tedrahn, David Charles
Tehan, Michael James
*Terlizzi, Eric Lewis
Terry, Dennis William
Terry, Robert Edward
Testin, Robert A.
Theis, Randall Lee
Thelan, John Dero
Theobald, Michael Ray
Thies, Gregory Thomas
Thiessen, Jonathon Wayne
Tholl, Donald Eugene
*Thoman, Gary Edward
Thompson, David Anthony
Thompson, Dean Robert
Thompson, James Jay
Thompson, Mark H.
*Thompson, Robert Ray
Thompson, Steven Ross
Tice, Lee Don
Tiffany, Harry Wayne
Timmermann, Thomas William
Tolliver, Mark Evan
*Tomlinson, Carole Ann
Topel, Frank William
Toporek, Morris
Touchberry, Robert Walton, Jr.
*Toy, Albert Victor
Traber, Thomas Alan
Trachtenbarg, David Edward
Trapp, Cheryl Ann
*Trautman, Jack Paul
Trebelhorn, Richard James
Tremblay, Michael Anthony
*Trent, Ernest Lee, Jr.
Trinh, Le Gia
Tripp, David Herbert
*Trojan, William Thomas

TRONC, MARK ALAN
TROPPITO, ANTHONY JOSEPH
TRIUMPINSKI, THOMAS ELLIS
*TRYTTEN, STEVEN EARL
TSE, KUM-SUEN
TUCKER, PAUL THOMAS
TULEJA, THOMAS FELIX
*TUREK, MARK EDWARD
*TURNER, BRYCE ELLIS
TURNER, JOHN ALGER
TYGRET, REGINALD LEE
*UBELL, FRANKLIN DAVID
*UDWARI, JOSEF JOHN
*UFKES, TED GENE
*ULVILA, JACOB WALTER
UNGER, DAVID EARL
UNZICKER, DENNIS LYNN
URBANI, ROGER LAWRENCE
UREK, JAMES FRANK
VALENTA, JOSEPH FRANK
VANAKEN, HARRY WILSON
VAN ARSDALL, PAUL JON
VAN AUWELAER, JAMES MICHAEL
VAN BLADEREN, JOHN ALBERT
*VAN BLARICUM, MICHAEL
VANCE, GARY MILES
VANDERSPOOL, JAN PETER, II
VANDERWERFF, JOSEPH ALAN
VAN HOOZEN, ALLEN LEE
VAN SCHYNDEL, ROBERT LYNN
VARSHNEY, PRAMOD KUHAR
VAUGHN, CLIFFORD LISLE
VAUGHN, JERRY WAYNE
VEDDER, HELLMUTH
*VENEZIA, KENNETH RAY
VERBIN, JEFFREY HAROLD
VERCELLINO, DAVID LEE
VERSHAW, JAMES THOMAS
VIITA, JOHN WAYNE
VISSER, JOHN RICHARD
VOEGELE, JAMES WALDEN
VOELZ, JEFFREY FREDERICK
VOLK, MICHAEL WAYNE
VOLTAGGIO, FRANK THOMAS
*VONBEHREN, AUGUST ALAN
VOSS, GEORGE DENNIS
*VYDUNA, JAMES BRENT
WAGNER, EUGENE JOSEPH
*WAGNER, JERRY ALLEN
WAGNER, RALPH JAMES
*WAGNER, WILLIAM CHARLES, JR.
WAGONER, JOSEPH LARRY
*WAHLERT, STEVEN LEE
*WAIT, JAY JENNER
WALDEN, GARY DEAN
*WALDROP, PARK DAVON
WALGRAVE, STEVEN CHARLES
WALKER, MICHAEL EUGENE
WALL, RICHARD FRANCIS, JR.
WALLACE, RICHARD READE
WALLEN, MICHAEL GLENN
WALTER, PAUL FRANCIS
*WALTERS, DONALD SCOTT
WALTERS, GARY BRIAN

*WALTERS, ROBERT STEVEN
WALTERS, TIMOTHY LAWTON
WANZEK, STEPHEN JOHN
WARD, JAMES
WARD, ROBERT DEE
WARNER, TERRY WAYNE
WARREN, JOHN MICHAEL
WASHBURN, MARK FISHER
WATKINS, ALBERT LEO
WATSON, JAMES STUART
WATSON, ROBERT JOHN
*WEATHERHEAD, PAUL DAVID
WEAVER, MARK DENNIS
WEAVER, VAUN CLAYTON
WEBBER, MICHAEL ANDREW
WEBBER, ROBERT CHAPMAN
WEBER, TIMOTHY JOHN
WEEKS, ROBERT JOHN
WEGLARZ, DENNIS MICHAEL
WEIBEL, ROBERT JOHN
*WEIK, RICHARD DALE
*WEIKART, GEORGE SCOTT
WEINBERG, JOHN STEVEN
*WEINZIERL, THOMAS ALLEN
*WEISHAR, MICHAEL CHARLES
WELSCH, CLETUS JAMES
WELSH, RIKKI LYNN
WEMLINGER, JOHN CHARLES
*WEN, KUO YEN
WENDEL, JAMES PAUL
WENNER, THOMAS JOHN
WENTHE, GARY DALE
WERESZCZYNSKI, JOHN STEPHEN
WERNER, JOHN RAMON
WERNER, WILLIAM DENNIS
WESSEL, RICHARD LEE
WETENKAMP, SCOTT FRANKLIN
*WEYGANDT, STEVEN LEE
*WEYRAUCH, JOHN ROBERT
WHEELER, JONATHAN SPARKS
WHISTON, BRIAN RICHARD
*WHITE, ANDREW BURTON
WHITE, JOHN CLINTON
WHITE, WILLIAM RAYMOND
WHITTAKER, PAUL ALLEN
WICKLEIN, ROBERT HENRY
*WIELAND, DONALD LEE
WIKHOLM, ROYCE JOHN
WILBER, CLYDE ALLEN
WILDEMUTH, JAMES HAROLD
*WILKEN, GARY ALLEN
*WILKENS, TERRY LELAND
WILLENBORG, DAVID LEE
WILLIAMS, ALLAN RICHARD
*WILLIAMS, BRUCE JOHN
WILLIAMS, DAVID WALTER
*WILLIAMS, EARL HARMON
WILLIAMS, H. EVAN, IV
*WILLIAMS, JOHN JAY
WILLIAMS, RHON LINN
*WILLIS, JEFFREY OWEN
WILLMER, DORIS INGLESE
WILLMER, JAMES LESTER
WILLSON, LAWRENCE WENDELL, JR.

WILNER, DOUGLASS OWEN
*WILSON, DONALD EUGENE
WILSON, DONALD JAY
WILSON, GARY ALAN
*WINCEK, THOMAS JAMES
*WINTER, STEPHEN MICHAL
WINTERS, PATRICIA ANN
*WISNIEWSKI, CHARMAINE
WISSEHR, JAMES HAROLD
WITHROW, DANIEL CHARLES
*WITTE, BENJAMIN MICHAEL
WITTMER, DALE EDWARD
WOEHR, WILLIAM AINLEY, II
*WOLF, GARY LEO
WONG, BERT KWOCK WAI
WONG, KAI SIN
WONG, TSZE YUE
WOO, RICHARD MOY
*WOODARD, SCOTT EUGENE
WOODWORTH, LARRY ARNOLD
WOODYARD, JOHN PHILIP
WRAIGHT, ROBERT CLAY
WROBLEWSKI, KENNETH ANDREW
WRONKIEWICZ, JAMES ANDREW
WRONKIEWICZ, ROBERT DANIAL
WUBBEN, JULIAN EDWARD
*WUBBEN, ROBERT CLEMENT
*WUEBBLES, DONALD JAMES
WUELLNER, JOSEPH WILLIAM
*WUELLNER, WILLIAM WALTER
WUNDERLICH, MITCHELL
*WUTTKE, STEPHEN ANTHONY
WYNES, KENNETH DALE
*YAGUCHI, KOJI

YANG, CHARLES Y.
*YARRINGTON, PAUL
YAU, JOHN C.
YEDINAK, JAMES EDWARD
YELVERTON, ROBERT GLENN
*YERGES, JOHN RICHARD
YIM, KALVIN WAI-KIN
YOCKEY, LYLE DUANE
YORK, BRUCE ALLAN
YORK, GARY MARTIN
YORK, JOHN ROBERT
YOSHIMURA, OWEN KEHAULANA SHINZO
*YOUNG, BENEDICT LOUIS
*YOUNG, GREGORY
YOUNG, HARRY CHIN
YOUNG, WILLIAM FREDERIC
*YOUNKER, WILLIS FRED
*YUEN, SIK KEE
ZACHERT, DAVID LEE
*ZACK, GREGORY WILLIAM
*ZACK, JAMES JEFFREY
*ZANCHO, WILLIAM FRANK
ZANONI, JOSEPH EUGENE
ZAVERL, FRANK
ZBOROWSKI, DAVID GEORGE
ZDANOWICZ, RICHARD JOSEPH
ZDARSKY, MICHAEL GEORGE
ZEWDE, ELIAS
ZICK, GREGORY LEONARD
*ZIELINSKI, EDWARD LEE
ZINN, CHARLES MADISON
ZOLINE, KENNETH OLIN
ZORN, JOE ALLEN

## COLLEGE OF FINE AND APPLIED ARTS

ABBOTT, SUSAN JEAN
ABELS, DAWN ADRIAN
ABLEMAN, ANDREA ELLEN
ABRAHAM, MAVIS ANN
ABRAMS, FRED JAY
*ABRAMSON, DAVID VICTOR
ACKERMAN, JOAN MARIE
ADAMS, JUDE BURKE
ADAMS, LARRY LANE
ADAMS, ROBERT DARYL
*ADAMS, VICKI LYNN
ALBERTSON, BARBARA JILL
ALBERTSON, THOMAS JEFFREY
ALEXANDER, CHARLES REID
ALLEN, KATHERINE GRACE
*ALLEN, MARIBETH
ALTHEIDE, JERILYN SUE
*ALTSCHUL, MARLA KOLS
*AMDAL, JAMES RUSSELL
ANCHOR, CHARLENE KAREN
ANDERSON, ALICE VICTORIA
ANDERSON, DIANE LYNN
ANDERSON, JAMES WALLACE
ANDERSON, MARILYN EVA
ANDERSON, MORRY RAY
ANDERSON, TIMOTHY LEE
ANDERSON, WILLIAM LIPPINCOTT, JR.
ANDRE, JEFFREY ALLEN

ANGERAME, WAYNE MICHAEL
ARKISS, GENISE JOY
ARMON, ROBERT ANDREW
ARONSON, CAROLYN JANE
ASHER, JON F.
ATCHISON, LINDA JO
ATWOOD, CHARLES LEROY
AUFMUTH, MARY ANN
AUMILLER, BILL JOHN
AUSTIN, HOWARD BROOKS
*BABBITT, JEAN HANCOCK
*BACCHI, DIANE MARIE
BACH, ROBERT O'BANNON
BAHR, RANDOLPH CHARLES
BAIRD, JAMES ADAM
BAJARS, RITA NORA
BAKER, BARBARA ANN
BAKER, DANIEL LEE, JR.
BAKER, DAVID GLEN
*BARBER, KATHLEEN MARIE
BARFORD, DAVID CHRISTOPHER
BARNES, CRAIG MARTIN
BARNES, MARCIA DUNDORE
BARNES, STEVEN RESSOR
BARNEY, CAROL ROSS
BARRY, EDWARD JOHN
BARTLETT, EVAN ALAN
*BARTLING, CHRISTINE ELAINE

48

BARTOS, MARK FRANCIS
BARWICK, CYNTHIA FULGHUM
BASH, PATRICIA JO
BATH, THOMAS JAMES
BATTISTONI, ORCHARD LYNN
BAUER, KNUT T.
BAUMGARTEN, DEAN JOSEPH
*BAUSER, JOHN EDWARD
BEAN, CHARLES EDWARD
BECK, BARBARA LOUISE
BECKER, RICHARD ALAN
BEGICH, MICHAEL THOMAS
BEGLEY, DOUGLAS GILBERT
BEHLES, KENNETH LAMBERT
BEHMER, CARL FRANK
BEIRIGER, SUSAN CHRISTINE
BEKENSTEIN, SUSAN
BENDEL, SUSAN GALE
BENNER, BETH ELLEN
BENNETT, CHRISTINE
*BENOLKEN, SARAH LESLIE
BENSON, FRANK TIPTON, JR.
BENTE, ROSS JOSEPH
BERENSON, SHARON MAE
*BERG, MARY CAROLE
BERGER, MICHAEL STEVEN
BERLE, JAMES ANDREW
BERMAN, MONA RITA
BERNBAUM, ADRIEN SUE
BERNSTEIN, FRANK J.
BERSHAD, BLAINE D.
BESCHORNER, RANDALL LEE
*BISHOP, STEVEN E.
BISHOP, THOMAS BURKE, JR.
BISHOP, WILLIAM RANDOLPH
BITTNER, SAMUEL PHILLIP
*BJORSETH, KATHLEEN MARIE
BLACK, JAMES HENRY
BLACKMORE, TIMOTHY WILLIAMS
BLANE, BARBARA ALLYN
BLANK, WILLIAM CHARLES
BLOCK, MARY RENEE
BLOECKS, RENATE SIEGRID
BLUCKER, JAMES DWIGHT
BLUMENTHAL, DIANE H.
BLUMENTHAL, MARC JEFFREY
BOAN, JAMES SCOTT
BOB, SUSAN LINDA
*BODLE, MARGERY ANN
*BODNAR, PETER DAVID
*BOEHNERT, JUDY MARTHA
BOGDAN, LINDA ESTHER
BOGUE, TAMARA CLAIRE
BOHAN, KIMBERLY LINNEA
BOLSHERT, JOHN PAUL
BOLOZKY, NETA
*BOND, DIANE CHRISTINE
BONO, STEVEN BUCKLEY
*BOONE, CHERYL RUTH
BORAK, ANDREA JUDITH
BORGESON, JEFFREY RICHARD
BORGSMILLER, SANDRA KAY
BOROWSKI, MICHAEL CARL
BOSTIAN, SANDRA LEE
BOWLIN, HOWARD BRUCE

BOYDSTUN, JAY BRYAN
BOYER, WILLIAM DAVID
BOZARTH, JOHN LUTHER
BRACE, SHARON MARGARET
*BRASHIER, REBECCA JANE
BREEZE, CYNTHIA MASSANARI
BRENGLE, JOHN MATHIAS
BREWBAKER, DANIEL MARTIN
BRIDGHAM, STEVEN WAYNE
BRIGGS, SARA GAIL
*BRIGHT, PEGGY RENEE
BRILL, LINDA ALLISON
*BRIN, ALICE FRANCES
BRINZA, SHELLEY ANN
*BRITTAIN, RICHARD GRAY
*BRODSKY, DANIEL PAUL
BROOCKS, GAY GEORGIA
BROOKS, JANICE
BROOKS, NANCY SUE
BROWN, CAROLYN GARFIELD
*BROWN, CHRISTOPHER GROVE
BROWN, GERALD WILLIAM
BROWN, JERRY JOHN
BROWN, RICHARD EDWARD, JR.
*BROWN, ROGER MARK
BROWN, THOMAS ROBERT
BROWNER, WILLIAM JOHN
BRUBAKER, THOMAS COSTELLO
BRUCE, DIANE LESLIE
BUCHA, JUDITH KAE
BUGBEE, CHRIS ALLEN
BUILTA, MARTHEA RAY
BULLOCK, PAMELA LOUISE
*BURD, MARY L.
BURGHART, JEAN NANCY
BURGIN, MARTHA DELL
BURKHART, ELLEN KATHRINE
BURLEY, BARBARA OCHS
BURNHAM, SHIRLEY SEMINGSON
BURNS, DONNA MARY
BURNS, GARY CURTIS
*BURNS, LAURENCE CORMICK, JR.
BURTON, JEFFREY WADE
BUTERA, SUSAN DIANE
BYERLY, STEPHEN LAVERNE
BYRNE, CHRISTOPHER MARBURY
BYRNE, GRACE ELEANOR
CABELL, ELISABETHANN
CAFOUROS, SUZANNE ANDRE
CAHN, FREDERICK HANKE
*CAIN, JOHN DAVID
CAIN, JOHN HOWARD
CALVO, MARY ELIZABETH
*CAMPBELL, BILLIE LOUISE
*CAMPBELL, JEANNETTE MAY
CAMPHOUSE, WILLIAM MARK
CANADAY, HOLLIS BETH
CARDENAS, RUDOLPH PALOMO
CARON, BARBARA JOAN
CARPENTER, CAROL MARGARET
CARPENTER, JOHN FREDERICK
CARREN, HOWARD LEWIS
CARY, PHILIP STEPHEN
CASSINELLI, PETER JOSEPH
CASSIOPPI, MARIE PAULETTE

49

CAWLEY, GEORGIA LEE
CAWN, GARY MARC
CECH, MARVIN KEITH
CHANG, MICHAEL LOH TIEN
CHAPIN, NELL MARIE
*CHARNEY, WAYNE MICHAEL
CHASTAIN, SUSAN ELIZABETH
CHAUDOIR, LEONARD HOLLIS
CHEE, WILBERT CHUNGFUN
CHELSETH, ROBERT STEPHEN
CHEN, ANDREW CHIA-CHING
CHENAIL, MARK STEPHEN
CHENEY, LARRY ALLEN
CHENEY, MICHAEL ROBERT
CHICHESTER, KATHY-LEE
CHICKE, KATHLEEN
CHILCOTE, PHILIP KEITH
CHIPMAN, JOHN ALBERT
*CHOISSER, SHARON MARSHAK
*CHRISTIANSEN, LIZA GENE
*CIEMIEGA, DAVID JEFFREY
CIONI, RAYMOND PETER
CIOPER, ANTHONY PAUL
CIRANGLE, ERNEST FRANK
CLARK, BRUCE ARNOTT
CLARK, MARY JANET
CLARK, PATRICIA HELEN
CLARY, PHILLIP STANLEY
CLAY, ROBERT RAYMOND
*CLAYTON, CHRISTINE FRANCESCA
CLOE, JOHN MICHAEL
CLOTFELTER, JAY KENT
COE, KATHY JEAN
COHN, LINDA SUE
*COLE, CLAYTON CAMMETT
COLEMAN, JACQUELINE ANN
COLLINS, DAVID ALLEN
*COLLINS, MARY MARGARET
COLLMAN, SALLY SUE
CONLEY, COLLEEN ELIZABETH
CONNELL, MICHAEL IRRMANN
CONNER, NANCY RIEDELL
CONNOLLY, MARY CAREN
COOPER, VICTORIA ANNE
COOPERMAN, JANE SARA
CORADINI, TERRENCE DOMENIC
*CORBETT, PATRICIA LEE
*CORIELL, DIANE MAXINE
CORMAN, ILENE ESTHER
*CORONA, DAVID ANTHONY
CORUSH, JERROLD STEVEN
COSTELLO, DENNIS ROBERT
COURVOISIER, NANCY DOROTHY
COYLE, LAURA MARY
CRANE, CATHERINE LOUISE
CRENSHAW, SARAH LOUISE
CRNKOVICH, CHARLES MIRKO
*CROHAN, ROBERT EDWARD
CRONE, JAMES LEE
CROW, RANDALL KENYON
CUNNINGHAM, HELENA SCHADD
CUNNINGHAM, JOHN FRANCIS
CURTIN, MARK ROBERT
CURTIS, JONATHAN ULREY
CYGOTTE, STEVEN RICHARD

CYROG, JAYNE ANN
DAHL, ROBERT JOHN
*DAMICO, DONALD PATRICK
DANCA, ALEXANDER EMANUEL
*DANENBERG, GAIL DIANE
DANGERFIELD, PHILIP LEWIS
DAVIDOFF, SUSAN HARRIET
DAVIDSON, LINDSAY ALAN
*DAVIS, BARBARA ANN
*DAVIS, DENISE MARIE
*DAVIS, RHEA ELLEN
DAWE, REBECCA SEIGLAR
DE COSTER, STEPHEN MICHAEL
DEFOREST, THOMAS RICHARD
DEFOTIS, CONSTANCE
DEKKER, DIANE JUNE
DELHEIMER, DENNIS MARSH
DEMENT, HENRY ROBERT
DEMOS, STANLEY GEORGE
DENNY, STEVEN ROY
DENSLOW, MARTHA FRANCES
DE PIETRO, RUSSELL JOSEPH
DE VACHT, GLORIA LOUISE
*DEVIN, LONNIE KEITH
DE VOSS, JOSEPH SHERRILL
DEWES, LESLIE JAMES
*DICKEY, KATHARINE SUE
DICKINSON, WILLIAM KENT
*DICKMAN, BETTY JANE
*DICKMAN, THETA ANN
DIETRICH, SUSAN ERDELYAN
DIFFERDING, JAMES CHARLES
DILLER, MARILYN ANN
DILLINGHAM, LARRY MAX
DILLOW, CONNIE JEAN
DIMIT, JOHN HILL, JR.
DINGER, KARL EDWARD
DI NOVO, BARBARA SCHROEDER
DIPPEL, KATHRYN SUSAN
DITCHKUS, DAVID WILLIAM
DIXON, MICHAEL ALBERT
DIXON, RANDALL GORDON
*DODDS, JOANNE ELIZABETH
DOLE, KEVIN DAVID
DONAHUE, JANE MARIE
DONALDSON, LESLIE SUE
DORNAUS, SARA JEANNE
DOWNING, REBECCA ANN
DRAP, ALBERT JOSEPH, JR.
DRAYTON, CAROL JEAN GOWLER
DRAYTON, JOHN ROBERT
DRIGGERS, MICHAEL KEITH
DROPKO, DANIEL GLENN
DUBBS, JUDITH CANDICE
DUBOIS, JEANNE MARIE
DUCHON, MARTHA WITKOWSKI
DUGINGER, MARILYN MARGARET
*DUNKER, AMALIE PAULINE
DUNLAP, RAYMOND NELSON
DURKEE, DEONNA REE
DURKIN, PAUL BARTELL, JR.
*DYAR, JANICE MARIE
DYMIT, JOSEPH MICHAEL
EARP, LAWRENCE MARSHBURN
EASLEY, SYRAL WAYNE

ECKARD, BONNIE JEAN
*ECKSTEIN, BEVERLY JO
EDWARDS, MICHAEL GEORGE
EDWARDS, WILLIAM HENRY
EGAN, WILLIAM KEITH
EGLOFF, WILLIAM MERRILL
EHLBECK, MICHAEL WILLIAM
EIKE, STEVEN EUGENE
*EIKENBERRY, JAMES OWEN
EIMER, RONALD WILLIAM
EISENSTEIN, SUSAN GAIL
EKSTRAND, RICHARD LEE
ELIAS, JOHN CHARLES
ELKUSS, BRONWYN CAROL
ELLISTON, RONALD JAMES
ELMORE, MARK ALAN
ELMORE, VIRGINIA KATHLEEN
ELSTNER, MARK LEONARD
EMRICH, MARY J.
ENG, OCK DOON
ENGELHARDT, JOHN PAUL
ENGSTRAND, THOMAS BERNARD
EPPSTEIN, SAMUEL DAVID, JR.
*EPSTEIN, BEVERLY ANN
ERBACH, EDWARD ALAN
ERICKSON, CAREY VEDICK
ERICKSON, LINDA ELLEN
ERICKSON, LYNNE SCROGGS
ESSERMAN, DALE LYNN
ETZEL, LINDA MARIE
ETZKORN, SHEILA MARIE
EVANS, PAMELA ANN
EYLES, RANDALL ARTHUR
FABER, CELESTE BAUER
FAIKUS, SUZANNE
FARNSWORTH, GEOFFREY
FAYFAR, STANLEY CASPER, JR.
FECHTER, ANITA SOPHIE
*FEDER, MARC SHELLY
*FEELEY, JEANNE EDITH
FELDMAN, IRA FREDERICK
*FELDMAN, JAY HOWARD
FELDPAUSCH, JOAN TROWBRIDGE
FELDT, DANIEL DONALD
FENCL, RICHARD ERVIN
FENN, MARSHA LOUISE
FIALA, THOMAS JOSEPH
FIELD, ANN ELIZABETH
FIFIELD, WILLIAM LEWIS, JR.
FILIPPI, LAWRENCE PAUL
FIN, TERESA MARIE
FINBLOOM, NEIL MARK
FINGER, MARK JAMES
FIPPEN, CHERYL LYNN
FIRSZT, STEVEN ANTHONY
FISCHER, BRIAN TOM
*FISCHER, HAROLD ALAN
FISHER, ANNE MARIE
FITZHUGH, JAMES RICHARD
FITZPATRICK, DIANNE TECKENBROCK
FLACK, STEVEN L.
FLEIG, WILBUR JOHN, JR.
FLETCHER, DEBORAH MAY
FLETCHER, MICHAEL STEVEN
FLINT, VIVIAN WILLINGHAM

FOGELBERG, DANIEL GRAYLING
FOOTE, SUSAN MESKILL
FORD, MARY GARDNER
FORD, ROBERT WALTER
FOREMAN, GARY DEAN
FORSELL, JACK MARK
FORSNER, CORINNE VIRGINIA
FORTNER, DAVID WILLIAM
FORTUNA, WILLIAM FRANK, II
FOSTER, ORLAND TERRELL
*FOX, CAROL ILENE
FOX, JOANNE KAY
FRANCH, KENNETH DAVID
FRANKE, MICHAEL ALLEN
FREDRIKSON, JEAN MARIE
FREEDMAN, LAUREN RAE
FREEDMAN, NANCY CAROL
FREESE, CHRISSIE EUGENE
FREMIN, HERBERT JOSEPH
FREUND, ADRIAN PAUL
FREY, JOAN HORN
FRINK, RONALD WAYNE
*FRISBIE, ANNE CELESTE
FRITH, EUGENIA CAROL
FROEHLIG, JOHN ARTHUR
FRONCZAK, MARY MARGARET
FROST, PATRICIA ANNE
FROST, THOMAS J.
*FUCHS, NANCY MELINDA
*FUCHS, RICHARD CHARLES
FUGMAN, ROBERT EDWARD
FULGENZI, JAMES LAWRENCE
FULTON, JOHN ROBERT
FUNG, LANCE DOUGLAS
FUNG, MATTHEW KEN
GABRIELSE, THERESA KLEIN
*GABRIELSON, EDWARD WILLIAM
GAETANO, CAROL SUSAN
GAGOSIAN, STEPHEN DOUGLAS
GAHR, THOMAS AUSTIN
*GALLAGHER, DONNA LEE
GALLIVAN, MARILYN SUE
GALLOWAY, DAVID ARTHUR
*GARBE, KIRK DOUGLAS
GARBER, JOSEPH LEROY
GARDEI, BRIAN ROBERT
GARR, GINGER MARIE
GARRET, ESTHER LEE
GASS, VIRGIL J.
*GAWLIK, STEVEN JOHN
*GELLAR, JAMES KENT
GERMAN, SANDRA LYNN
GERSICH, ANDREW JAMES
GERSON, JANET CLASTER
GIBBAR, PERCY JAMES, JR.
GIBBONS, DONNA JEAN
GIBBS, WESLEY FAYETTE, JR.
GIBSON, MICHAEL ALLEN
*GILES, JOHN EDWIN
GILGENBACH, JAMES EDWARD
*GILLESPIE, MONTE CRAIG
GILLHOUSE, LAWRENCE MICHAEL
GILMORE, FREDERICK EDWIN
GIUNTOLI, PHILIP ALFRED
GIZYNSKI, SHARON LOUISE

51

GLADSTONE, BRYAN WILLIAM
GLADSTONE, RITA ELLEN
GLASER, HEIDI ELIZABETH
GLASS, LINDA MAE
GLEASON, WILLIAM ALFRED
GLEAVE, FREDERICK WILHELMS
GLICK, PAMELA LYNN
*GLOVER, JOHN FRANKLIN
GODAR, MARY KATHRYN
GOETTING, MARK LOUIS
GOGLIA, FREDERICK JOSEPH
GOLAS, DONALD DENNIS
GOLDBERG, STEVEN WILLIAM
*GOLDENBERG, LEON
GOLDENBERG, THOMAS EDWARD
GOLDIS, NORMAN Z.
GOLDNER, ARTHUR ABRAHAM
GOLDSTEAD, ROBERT WARREN
GOLDSTEIN, HARVEY JAY
GOLDSTEIN, MARNA PAT
GOLDSTEIN, PERRY
GOLDSTEIN, ROBYN ELYSE
GOLKOWSKI, GREGORY EDWARD
GONIA, LAURENCE STEPHEN
GOOD, NICHOLAS EUGENE
*GOODFRIEND, ARTHUR ALLEN
GOODKIN, IRA
GOODMAN, SUE ELAINE
GOOUD, GEORGE STEPHEN
GORDON, MICHAEL DAVID
*GORMAN, LAWRENCE JOHN
GOZDZIALSKI, JAMES STANLEY
GRACEFFA, THOMAS GREGORY
GRANT, AUBREY URIEL
GRATTEAU, PHILLIP ROY
*GRAY, GEORGENE ELLEN
GREEN, LINDA MARIE
GREGG, KAREN CHRISTINE
GREGORY, ADRIANNE DANILE
*GREIVE, ANNETTE LOUISE
*GREMBOWICZ, MONICA JEAN
GRENNAN, DEBRA JOAN
*GRESEY, JENNIFER JANE
GRIEBENOW, ROBERT RICHARD
GRIFFARD, THOMAS JAMES
GRIFFITH, JEFFREY ALAN
GRIGUS, CAROL ANN
GRIMES, JAMES JOSEPH
GRODY, ANNETTE MARY
GROEBE, KIMBERLY ANN
*GRONEWOLD, MARCIA DEE
GROSS, JAN MELODY
GROSS, ROBERT MITCHELL
GROSS, WALTER STEVEN
*GROSSBERG, STEPHEN JAY
GROSSMAN, LARRY HERBERT
GROVE, GREGORY RONALD
GROVE, SHARON KAY
GRUBE, SUSAN PALMER
GUITHER, GEOFFREY PAUL
GUREWITZ, PAULA SUE
GUSSE, GARETH RENE
GUSTIE, KARLA KAY
GUTNIK, SUSAN ILENE

GUY, THEODORE KING
GYLLSTROM, THOMAS HAROLD
HAAKE, MICHAEL LEE
HABERKORN, MICHAEL HARRY
HABLEY, TERRY PHILLIPS
HAEGER, LINDA PAULEY
HAEGER, RICHARD SCOTT
HAEGSTROM, JOHN ARTHUR
HAHN, RUSSELL SCOTT
*HAHN, STEPHEN RAY
HAKES, BETH LIVINGSTON
HALBACH, ROBERT WILLIAM
HALFVARSON, ERIC FOY
HALIK, GEORGE RAYMOND
HALL, CATHERINE JOANNE
HALL, JANICE
HALL, LOUIS OLLMAN
*HALLMARK, ROGER ALAN
*HAMBY, MARK
HAMILTON, SARAH GARLAND
HANAMOTO, CLAIRE MASA
HANDELMAN, SUSAN
*HANNULA, THOMAS LEO
*HANSEN, EDMUND JOSEPH
HANSON, CRAIG ANTHONY
HANSON, ERICA JEAN
HAPAG, DONNA MARIE
HARDTKE, MIMI LISABETH
*HARMS, DIANE SUE
HARRIS, BONNIE JEAN
HARRIS, STEVEN RAY
HART, ERNEST CARROLL
HARTMANN, CARL LEE
HARTMANN, MARK CHARLES
HASENBERG, JOHN MELVIN
HASON, NINO
HATCH, DEBORAH McCOWN
HAUPTFUEHRER, DAWNA LYNNE
*HAWKINS, THOMAS WAYNE
HAWKINSON, WILLIAM WALTON
HAYES, ROLAND LEE
*HAYMAN, SARAH
HAYS, JONATHAN VINCENT
HEALY, DAVID ARTHUR
HEATH, JOHN ROBERT
HEHN, JACK WILLIAM
HEIDELMEIER, BONNIE JEAN
HEIDIG, ROSEMARY FRANCES
HEILE, BARBARA ANNE
HEIMANN, CONSTANCE ELLA
HEITZMAN, FRANK EDWARD
HELANDER, DANIEL JAMES
HENDERSON, SONDRA CAROLE
*HENDRICKS, MICHAEL GEORGE
HENRICKS, MADELINE CLAIRE
HENRY, ROBERT JOSEPH
HERBST, BRUCE RAYMOND
HEREN, LAWRENCE PHILIP
HERM, LAURIE DAVIES
HERM, LORRAINE RUETER
HESELOV, CAROLE BONNIE
HESSE, WENDY ANN
HESSELSCHWERDT, STEVE PAUL
*HEUERTZ, CHARLES MATHIAS

52

HICKLE, GREGORY ALAN
*HICKS, JEFFREY LYNN
HIGHTOWER, JANE E.
HILL, RICHARD SCOTT
HILLS, SALLY LUCILE
HILTENBRAND, WILLIAM
*HIMEL, RAYMOND LARRY
HINES, WALTER EARL
*HINTON, JAMES EUGENE
*HIPSKY, BARBARA GAIL
HIRSCHHORN, SUSAN FAY
HODAK, LAWRENCE JOHN
HODEL, RONNIE LEE
HOERR, WILLIAM ALAN
HOFELDT, WILLIAM ALAN
HOFFMAN, THOMAS CRAIG
HOFMAIER, THOMAS GEORGE
HOGAN, STEPHEN MICHAEL
HOHN, CHRISTOPHER CARL
HOIT, MICHAEL IAN
HOLECHEK, PAUL EUGENE
HOLLOWAY, SHARRON DENISE
HOLT, RITA ANNE
HOMUTH, LARRY JOHN
*HONN, STANLEY LOREN
HOOD, JANE ANN
HOOK, WILLIAM GARY
HOPPER, PAULA ROSE
HORBINSKI, DENNIS JEROME
HORVATH, STEVEN JOHN
HOUDEN, PATRICIA ANN
HOULIHAN, EDWARD MICHAEL
HOWELL, WILLIAM LEIGHTON, JR.
HOWIE, MARY JUDITH
*HRUBY, PATRICIA ANNE
HRVOL, ROSALIE KOTWAS
HUBLER, STUART ALDEN
HUDSON, CHRIS ALLEN
HUEHLS, LLOYD BRIAN
HULTING, NANCY KRUMM
HUMMEL, JOHN STEPHAN
HUMPHRIES, DENNIS RICHARD
HUTCHENS, GORDON BRUCE
JUNGST, MARILYN LEE
HUTCHINS, NANCY ANN
HUTCHISON, JANET ALDEN
HWA, NANCEE
HYTOFF, BRIAN MICHAEL
IPPOLITO, CHERYL DIANE
IRELAN, UNA MANETTA
IVERSON, THOMAS ELDEN
JACK, BRIAN MALCOLM
JACKSON, ISABELLE CELESTE
JACKSON, MICHAEL BURNELL
JACOBSON, BRUCE JOHN
JACOBSON, SUSAN ALICE
JAFFE, STEVEN HARVEY
*JAKES, DOLORES RITA
JAMROK, ROSE ANNE
JANKOUSKY, EVELYN ANN
*JANSEN, JAMES HOWARD
JANSEN, KATE CARUS
JANZEN, SHARON BETTY
JASTROW, WILLIAM TENNANT

JEAKINS, DANIEL LEE
*JENNINGS, TERESE LESLIE
JOHANSEN, STENFORD KIM
JOHNSON, ALAN GORDON
JOHNSON, DIANE RUTH
*JOHNSON, GARY KEITH
JOHNSON, HENRY ERIC
JOHNSON, JANE CECILIA
JOHNSON, JEAN ANN
JOHNSON, JOHN WILLIAM
JOHNSON, MARTIN HARRY
*JOHNSON, MICHAEL CRAFT
JOHNSON, RALPH EVERETT
JOHNSON, RANDOLPH
JOHNSON, ROBERT WAYNE
*JOHNSON, RONALD BERT
JOHNSON, SHEILA CRUMP
*JOHNSON, SUSAN MARY
JOHNSON, SUZANNE
JOHNSON, WILLIAM LEE
JOHNSTON, THOMAS BENJAMIN
JONES, ERIC LEE
JONES, JAKE ANDERSON, III
*JONES, KAREN LYNN
JONES, NANCY LYN
JONESON, DALE ALAN
*JOSWICK, RICHARD BERNARD, JR.
JUNGER, DAVID JOHN
*JUNGK, RICHARD ANDREW
*KAISER, CHARLES LEE
KAISER, DENNIS LEE
KALVELAGE, GERALD C.
KALVER, GAIL ELLEN
*KAPCHE, JAMES ALBERT
KAPLAN, ILENE SHERYL
KAPUSTKA, LAWRENCE JEROME
KARANUSIC, MAYA TATIANA
KARLQUIST, DAVID WILLIAM
KASTHOLM, JOHN, III
KEATING, EDWARD JOSEPH
*KECK, WILLIAM FOLEY
KEFFER, KATHRYN GRACE
KELLOGG, JAMES EDWIN
KELLY, KEVIN WILLIAM
KELLY, MARGOT CELESTE
*KELLY, MILTON DOW
KELLY, SUZANNE ELIZABETH
KELTON, CHRISTOPHER TWISS
KENNEDY, MARY KATHLEEN
KERESTES, TIMOTHY PATRICK
KERRICK, MARY ELIZABETH
KERSCHNER, MORLEY I.
*KILBANE, ROBBYN LESLIE
KIMME, DENNIS ALAN
KIMMICH, JOHN EDWARD
KIMPTON, JEFFREY SCOTT
KINCAID, KAROL LYNNE
KINDRED, BARBARA SUE
KING, DAVID MERRILL
KING, MICHAEL PATRICK
KING, NANCY JO
KINGERY, NANCY KATHLEEN
KIVLAND, BONNIE JEAN
KIZEVIC, JOSEPH GREG

KLEMM, MARGARET ANNE
KLICKNA, KIM
KLIMA, ARTHUR JAMES, JR.
KLOOCK, JANET ELIZABETH
*KLOSTERMAN, JAMES CARL
KNAAK, LINDA RUTH
KNIGHT, DOUGLAS JAMES
*KNOX, DAVID EARL
KOBOS, REBECCA MARIE
KOBUS, RICHARD LAWRENCE
KOCH, LAURIE ANN
KOEBBEMAN, KATHLEEN LENSKE
KOEHLER, GALE JOSEPH
KOEHLER, THOMAS COCHRAN
KOENTOPP, KURT KREAHLER
KOLLINS, APHRODITE FRANCES
KONSLER, CAROLE LYNN
KOPAN, NICHOLAS
KOPCHELL, MARK CRAIG
KORSGARD, WILLIAM WEBSTER
*KOSMACH, GEORGE STEPHEN
KOSOVSKI, MAURA SUE
KOST, STEPHENIE ROSE
KOSTELECKY, JAN
*KOSTELNICK, CHARLES JOHN
KOVELL, RICHARD LEE
KOWALL, KENNETH ROBERT
KRAJEWSKI, DANIEL JOSEPH
KREJCI, RONALD FRED
KRESS, CHARLES WILLIAM, JR.
*KRIDER, ALAN JAMES
*KRISTEN, CHRISTINE ELAINE
KROMM, LEROY G.
KRUEGER, JOYCE LYN
KRUSE, SUSAN LAURA
KSANDER, MOLLY ROWE
KUBALA, THOMAS ALLEN
KUBY, ANDREW EWING, III
KUCHLER, VICTOR RAYMOND
KUFFNER, DAVID JOHN
KUHN, JANINE ARDELL
KUJAWSKI, MARY THERESE
KULA, JOHN JOSEPH
KUMNICK, RICHARD ALLEN
*KUNTZ, JANE ELIZABETH
KUROWSKI, MARY LEE
KUSZ, JOHN PAUL
KUTSCHE, JEFFREY PAUL
LACH, NORMAN LESTER
LAESCH, ELLEN MARIE
LAFLEUR, ALBERT LEROY
LAMB, KENNETH STUART
LAMBERT, DIANA
LAMBERT, MICHAEL TERRANCE
LANDAHL, GREGORY WILLIAM
LANDIS, DEBORAH WALKER
*LANDIS, EDITH LOUISE
LANGE, BARBARA ANN
LANGERMAN, DEBORAH JO
LANGLEY, DENNIS WARREN
*LAREN, TIMOTHY DANIEL
LAROCK, RALPH CORLISS
LARSEN, MARCIA KAY
LARSON, DAVID WILLARD
LARSON, LAURA-LEE

LARSON, ROBERT STEVEN
*LARSON, TIM PHILIP
LARUE, JACQUELINE
LARVENZ, KENNETH MICHAEL
LASALLE, DANA LOUISE
LASKOWSKI, RUDOLPH JOSEPH
LASSER, BRIAN ALAN
*LASZEWSKI, MARILYN BRDA
LAUDERDALE, MONICA LEE
LAURIDSEN, CYNTHIA ANN
LAUTERSTEIN, DAVID JOSEPH
LAVINE, GLENN
LAZAR, WALTER PAUL
LE, CHI-SANH
LEATHERWOOD, MARYA LEONA
LEBARRON, LINDA BANKS
LEE, CHOW JUNG
LEE, GAIL LENA
LEFF, DEAN BURL
LEFORT, JO CHRISTINE
LEHMANN, CARLA MARIE
LEIS, JANE KATHERINE
LEONARD, GARRY STEPHEN
*LERITZ, JAMES PETER
LESTER, GREGG HARVEY
LESTER, KATHRYN EDNA
LEUCHS, EDWARD CHARLES
LEV, JAMES ROY
LEVAN, STEVE DONALD
LEVIN, RICHARD LESLIE
*LEVIN, SANDRA ALENE
LVORA, CHRISTINE FRANCES
LEVY, SANFORD SCOTT
LIDRAL, KAREL ARTHUR
LIEBER, THOMAS ALAN
LIEBLING, JEFFREY SCOTT
LILJA, NANCY KAY
*LINARD, RITA ANN
LINCICOME, RICK ALLEN
LINCOLN, LINDA LEE
LINDABERRY, DOUGLAS
LINDBLAD, JOHN EMIL
LINDSEY, JOHN RUSSELL
LINGEMAN, ALISON ADAIR
LINGRELL, KAREN NANI
LINN, DANIEL SAMUEL
LINN, GRETCHEN MARTHA
*LINTZENICH, ROBERT WILLIAM
LISHKA, GERALD R.
LLARENA, PELAYO
LODAL, BETH ANN
LODUHA, PAUL PAT
LOMPERIS, JUDITH ANN
LONG, EDNA LEE
LONG, JUDY KAYE
LOOK, DAVID WALTER
LOOMER, LEANNA DAWN
LOTHROP, JAMES DENNY
LOUGH, VIRGINIA
LOUGHMAN, PHILIP GREGORY
LOVE, CYNTHIA ANNE
LOVELESS, GEANNE MARIE
LOY, DEAN STANTON
LOZAR, ROBERT CARL
LUBBEN, SUZANNE MARIE

54

*LUDWIG, ELIZABETH CAROL
*LUEBKE, CHARLES MARTIN
LUEBKEMAN, DAVID JOHN
*LUM, GERALD HOONG WUN
LUNT, DANIEL LEE
MABRAY, SUSAN K.
MACDONALD, JAMES MARVIN
*MACGREGOR, STEVEN WILLIAM
MACHACEK, ROBERT WILLIAM
MACK, GARY MICHAEL
MACRAE, MARK LAWRENCE
MACRIS, NICHOLAS STEPHEN
MAEGLIN, KRISANNE
MAINES, PENELOPE DEBORAH
MALLORY, STEPHEN WESLEY
*MAMMINGA, JAMES ROBERT
MANGO, ROBERT JOSEPH
MANLEY, LYNN W.
MANLEY, SUSAN K.
MANN, FRED RAY
MANN, JAMES NEWTON, JR.
MANNIK, MART RAYMOND
MANNING, JENNIFER L.
MANSFIELD, RICHARD STEVEN
MARCOWITZ, JEFFREY LEE
*MARGOLIS, KAREN JUNE
MARGOLIS, TOBY HELENE
*MARK, JEFFREY SCOTT
MARKS, JOYCE SILBERSTEIN
MARLOWE, FAYE SUSAN
MARLOWE, LINDA SUE
MARRONE, DAVID ALLEN
MARSHALL, WILLIAM GEORGE
*MARTERSTECK, CHRISTOPHER PAUL
MARTIN, JAMES P.
MARTIN, JANE ANNE
MARTIN, JOHN RAYMOND, JR.
MARTIN, NANCY LOU
*MARTIN, SUSAN LYNN
MARTINEK, LAUREL ELOISE
MARTING, JOHN CHARLES
MARVELLI, PATRICIA MARIE
MARX, CHRISTY LYNN
MARZAL, VINCENT ANDREW
MARZEN, RENA MILLER
MASLOVITZ, ROCHELLE CELIA
MASNY, MICHAEL GARY
MASSIE, KENT LIND
MATHESON, VANCE LEE
MATIS, CRAIG
MATTHEIS, BETTY SUE
MATTHEWS, SUSAN ALLENE
MAXWELL, MARILYN JO
MAXWELL, MARTHA FRITTS
MAY, JUDY PATRICIA
MAY, THEODORE A.
MAY, WILLIAM ALAN
MAYER, WILLIAM CLIFFORD
MAYLAND, RUTH ANN
MAYORAS, DOUGLAS ALLAN
MAZZERI, PETER JOSEPH
McBRIDE, MARY ANN
McCAFFERY, MARGARET GAGE
McCARTHY, LAURIE ANN
McCARTY, JOHN CHRISTOPHER

McCAULEY, JOSEPH EDWIN, III
McCLURE, MARSHA JANE
*McCLUSKEY, NANCY LEA
McCUE, THOMAS EDWARD
McCULLAGH, GRANT GIBSON
McCULLEY, MICHAEL TODD
*McDERMOTT, TERRI JEAN
McDONALD, BETH MARIE
McDONNELL, BARBARA ANN
McDONOUGH, MARLAINE JOYCE
*McELWAIN, JANICE MARIE
McFADDEN, ANDREA PISTORIUS
McGARRY, PATRICIA JOSEPHINE
McGINNIS, MICHAEL THOMAS
McGINNIS, MIKE JOHN
McGLORY, ANDREW VERNIN
McGOWN, DOUGLAS HICKOK
McHENRY, SALLIE ANN
McINTYRE, JANET KATHLEEN
*McKAY, SHERRY MAE
McMAKIN, DEAN ELLERSLIE
McMURTRIE, BRUCE ELLIOTT
McNAMARA, JOHN BAILEY
McNEELY, JAMES HARRY
McPHEE, RICHARD JEFFREY
McPHERSON, LINDA CAROL
McQUEEN, RUTH ANN
McSORLEY, THOMAS LEE, JR.
*McWILLIAMS, RONALD DUANE
McWILLIAMS, STEPHEN JAMES
MEACHAM, HOWARD DENNIS
MEACHUM, CAROL JO
MEATTE, MARK CASEY
MEDLEY, MALINDA JANE
MEHLER, LEE NORMAN
MEID, PATRICIA ANN
MELAHN, LEROY CARL
MELDGIN, LINDA ANN
MELLER, LEE RAYMOND
MELOTTE, RALLS CALLAWAY
MENDENHALL, JOHN PAUL
MENN, MICHAEL ALAN
MENZEL, DAVID LEE
MERRICK, JILL SUZANNE
*MERTZ, LINDA MARY
MESSENGER, SHARON MARIE
MESSMAN, GERALD PAUL
METZGER, HAROLD FRANK
MEYER, ALLEN EARL
MEYER, DENNIS PAUL
MEYER, MICHAEL LAWRENCE
MICHALEK, MARILYN JEAN
MICHELAU, SANDRA LEE
MIENER, ROBERT GLENN
*MIKULA, BARBARA JEAN
MILES, DONNA LENORE
MILLER, CURTIS ANTON
MILLER, DOUGLAS HOWARD
MILLER, JANET MOCHEL
MILLER, KENNETH EDWARD
MILLER, KERRY JEAN
MILLER, LINDA KAY
MILLER, MARGUERITE ANNE
MILLER, VICKI LYNN
MILLETT, MARK LEWIS

MILLS, BARBARA KAY
MINK, CHARLES PAUL
MINTZ, PATRICIA FAYE
*MITCHELL, JAMES WHITNEY
MITCHELL, JANE ALLISON
MITTELSTAEDT, LINDA PAULINE
MODRIC, RUTH KAREN
MOHLER, ROBERTA JANE
MOK, LEWIS STEPHEN
*MOLDENHAUER, JUDITH ANN
MOLINARO, MICHAEL JEROME
MONKKONEN, GAYLE ARDELLE
MONSON, ANNE
MOORE, ALFRED LEON
MOORE, ANDREW JAY
MOORE, SUSAN ELAINE
MORFORD, LYNN ELLEN
MORGAN, MARGARET ELIZABETH
MORITZ, FREDRIC ALAN
*MORRISON, BARRY ANTHIS
MOSES, BARBARA SUSAN
MOYER, ELAINE SUZANNE
MRAZ, COLLEEN JOY
MUEHLEMANN, JAMES ROY
MUEHLENBEIN, DAN EDWARD
MUELLER, MICHAEL D.
MUFF, JOHN CHRISTOPHER
MULA, THOMAS PAUL
MULKEY, HEATHER LYNN
*MULLIN, LINDA KAY
MULVIHILL, COLLEEN YVONNE
MURPHY, CHARLES JOSEPH
MURPHY, THERESE ANN
MYERS, STEVEN RAY
NACHTMANN, RITA CLAIRE
NAFZIGER, TIMOTHY ALAN
NAPIER, THOMAS ROY
NATIELLO, BARBARA GAY
NAUERT, DOLORES ANN
NEAL, WILLIAM ROBERT
NELSON, DEBRA JUNE
NELSON, JOANN GRECORICH
NELSON, KENNETH RUSSELL
NEPON, JANICE LAURY
NEWTON, DALE EDWIN
NEWTON, SARAH JONES
NICOL, JEANNE MARIE
NIEMIEC, MARILYNN LOUISE
NISBET, WALKER ALLEN
NISBETT, JANET ELAINE
NOLTE, THEODORE C., JR.
NORRIS, KENT ALAN
NOTHEISEN, LAURIN DIANE
NOTTOLI, JANICE ANN
O'BOYLE, SUSAN ELLEN
O'BRIEN, DANIEL STEVEN
O'BRIEN, MARYBETH KATHLINE
OECHSEL, JEANNE ANN
O'HARA, RICHARD EDWARD
OLMSTEAD, SARAH LOUISE
OLSON, BENJAMIN HARRY
OLSON, KATHRYN LAMAN
OLTMANNS, LARRY KARL
ORBAN, CONNIE DIANE
O'ROURKE, BERNARD JOSEPH

ORR, RICHARD KENNETH
ORTBAL, JOHN DAVID
OSWALD, GAYLE LOUISE
OVERMAN, GUY JENNINGS, JR.
*OVITSKY, DENNIS J.
OWEN, HOWARD HENRY
OWENS, MARCIA JANE
PAAPE, JOHN CONRAD
PACE, JOEL MILLER
PACHOLKE, JAMES BENHART
*PACKARD, HILARY ANN
PAGE, PATRICIA LYNN
PAHN, JOEL ALAN
PAINE, CECELIA ROSE
PALLAS, BRENT JACK
PALMER, LARRY ALAN
PALMERI, MARCIA KATHERINE
PANIKIS, KIRK GEORGE
PANN, HAROLD DAVID
PARKIN, JUDD LOVETT
PARKS, BARRY JAMES
PARKS, MARCIA MARIE
PARSHALL, STEVEN ANTHONY
PASTORE, JOHN JOSEPH
PATTEN, CRAIG MICHAEL
PATTERSON, THOMAS MARC
PAUKSTIS, STEVEN JUDE
PAULSEN, ARNE JAMES
*PEARCE, MARTHA MORRIS
PEARSON, DEBORAH JANE
PEARSON, HEATHER JEAN
PECENY, MARY CHRISTINE
PECK, LINDA GAIL
PEDERSEN, AUDREY MARSHA
PERLMAN, HOWARD ALAN
PERRY, RICHARD EUGENE
PESCHE, NICOLETTE ANN
PETERS, AMY ELIZABETH
PETERS, NANCY ANN
PETERSEN, EDWARD ALLEN, III
PETERSON, DAVID GEORGE
PETERSON, JANET RUTH
PETERSON, NEAL WRIGHT
PETTIJOHN, TERRY LEE
PETTIT, JAMES CURTIS
PEYLA, PATRICIA ANN
PFEIFER, BONNIE FREDIN
PIASKOWY, ANDREW JAMES
PIATT, JAMES HOBART
PIAZZA, JAN
PICKER, RONALD STEVEN
PICKREL, SHEILA SUE
PIERCE, KENNETH REID
PIERCE, MICHAEL EDWARD
PIERDILUCA, MICHAEL VINCENT
PIERSON, STEVEN JAMES
PIET, JANE MARIE
PIETRZAK, LAWRENCE RICHARD
PILTZ, GLENDA SUE
*PINZARRONE, PAUL FRANK
PIPKIN, CYNTHIA ELIZABETH
PISTORIUS, NANCY JEAN
PLESKOW, DEBORAH GAIL
*PLONDKE, JAMES CHARLES
POCIASK, THOMAS JOHN

56

*POESCHL, ROBERT HENRY
POHLMAN, JUDITH KAY
POLENSKY, PEGGY ANN
POORMON, JANICE LEE
POPE, ROY EDWARD
POPELKA, JASON PAUL
POPKO, SUSAN ELLEN
*PORTER, STEVEN MICHAEL
PORTO, MARY JO
POWELL, JAMES MAHLON
POWELL, SUSAN MARIE
POWER, ROBERT JAMES
*PRENTICE, KIM DONALD
PRICE, CAROL SUSAN
PRICE, MARK STEVEN
PRIMMER, ANITA DIANNE
PRITIKIN, ARLENE MYRA
*PRIZER, STEPHEN E.
PROBST, DAVID GLEN
PROPER, ROBERTA SUSAN
PROPES, PATRICIA MASURAT
PRUET, MELISSA SUE
PUSICH, MICHAEL MORRIS
QUAST, JAMES JEFFREY
RABBERS, JILL KORGIE
RABCHUK, MARY KATHRYN
*RADES, NANCY LEE
RADOSTA, ELIZABETH ANN
*RADWINE, SAMUEL BENJAMIN
RAGONA, JOHN EDWARD
RAIFF, JANET
RAIMAN, RANDALL GRANT
RAMP, PAMELA OSBURN
RANDALL, DEBORAH SUE
RANGE, GARY JOSEPH
RANKAITIS, SUSAN ANNE
*RAPACZ, RONALD RICHARD
RASCOE, CHERYL ROACH
READ, PHILLIP N.
REAGAN, ROSS STANTON
REBECHINI, ALICE IRENE
REDDY, THOMAS MARTIN
REEDER, DENNIS CLYDE
*REEM, DENISE ELAINE
REIMER, FRANCIE JOAN
REINWAND, STEPHAN FRANCIS
RENKEN, SCOTT KARDELL
REPLINGER, ROBERT LOUIS
REQUA, SUSAN IRENE
RETZSCH, BRUCE WARD
REUL, JAMES GAYLAND
*REVAK, MARY LOUISE
REYNOLDS, DALLAS KENT
REYNOLDS, MARY KAY
RHEA, LORA LEE
RICH, LARRY LAVERNE
RICHARDSON, VERLIN DEAN
RICHTER, ELVER STUART
RICK, JAMES S.
RICKER, SUSAN LOUISE
RICKETTS, JOHN ARMON
*RIEDELL, CAROLYN BETH
RIES, TERRY ALLEN
RILEY, ANN ROGERS
RITCHER, GARY KIPP

RIVES, KATHRYN WINIFRED
ROAKS, LINDA LAMBERT
*ROBERTSON, BARBARA ANNE
ROBINSON, RANDALL SCOTT
ROCK, ROY BRADLEY
RODIN, JOANNE DALE
ROECKER, FREDERICK JOHN
ROECKER, JAMES ALLEN
ROESCH, DEIDRE ANN
ROESKE, MARILYN HATLEY
ROGAL, BRIAN JAY
ROGERS, LORLYS
*ROLLAND, JOHN PAUL
ROMEIN, STEPHEN DOYLE
ROMINE, DEBORAH KAY
RONAYNE, DIANA GLENN
ROPER, TYRONE DELANO
ROSE, RICHARD HERSCHEL
*ROSEN, ALAN MARC
*ROSEN, ELLEN
ROSEN, ROBERT MANDEL
ROSENBLUM, MARTIN JAY
ROSENZWEIG, ALAN DAVID
ROSS, ALLEN MOREY, JR.
*ROSS, SUSAN ELIZABETH
ROTH, DEBORAH
*ROTTMAN, DAVID BRUCE
ROUSH, RICHARD WALTER
ROZICH, ROBERT LEE
RUBIN, FRED A.
RUDDELL, DEBORAH GLEZEN
RUETER, ELAINE HELEN
RULE, HOWARD KEITH
*RUNDELL, KATHRYN LUTZ
RUSHING, PAUL DANA
RUSSELL, ALAN HUGH
*RUTGARD, MARLA BETH
RUZICH, STEPHEN GEORGE
RYBAR, LINDA JOYCE
RYERSON, WAYNE THOMAS
SABIN, NETTIE FAYE
SAFFIR, JANICE TERRY
*SAGE, VICTOR THOMAS
SAKS, ARNOLD HENRY
SALEMI, PETER JOSEPH
SALIS, NANCY
SALM, KURT LEE
SALMAN, RANDY KEITH
SALMO, VIRGINIA ANN
*SALZMAN, MELINDA CANDACE
*SAMARAS, KATHRYN THEODORA
SAMBORSKI, ROBERT
SANDA, DONALD JOSEPH
SANOSKI, PAMELA JEANNE
*SARFATTY, GEORGE MAY
SARTORE, STEPHAN JOHN
SASSE, WENDY JO
SAUERBRUNN, DEANNA DOWNING
SAUNDERS, JOHN TIMOTHY
SAUSSER, MARTHA CLAIRE
SAXLER, ROBERT JOSEPH
SAXNER, JANET RAE
SCALISE, RONALD ALAN
SCALZITTI, LUANNE MARIE
SCHAFER, KATHRYN CHARLOTTE

SCHEAFNOCKER, GLENN SCOTT
SCHEFFLER, NANCY LYNN
SCHEIN, FREDERICK LESTER
SCHEMSKE, SANDRA GAIL
SCHERMERHORN, MARILYN SHEA
SCHICKEDANZ, JOHN CHARLES
SCHLEMBACH, DAVID LENHART
SCHLIPF, JANET SUE
SCHMIDT, MARK STEPHAN
SCHMIDT, SHARON ANN
SCHMIDT, THOMAS WILLIAM
SCHMITT, MARY KATHERINE
SCHNEIDER, GEORGE EDWARD
SCHNEIDER, MARC DAVID
SCHNEIDER, RICHARD LOUIS
SCHOENEMAN, LARRY
SCHOFIELD, DONALD WAYNE
SCHOLTENS, EUGENE EDWARD
SCHOTT, LAWRENCE HENRY
*SCHRAM, RICHARD MICHAEL
SCHRAUF, LINDA MAE
*SCHROEDER, WILLIAM JOHN
SCHUETTE, KARLYN ANN
SCHUETTE, LYNN VIRGINIA
SCHULTZ, JEAN ELLEN
SCHULTZ, KATHY ANN
SCIBONA, GUY THOMAS
SCOPP, PHILIP BRUCE
*SCOTT, ROBERT WILLIAM
SCOUFFAS, JOHN RICHARD
SEELIG, JEROME MARC
SEGAL, NATHANIEL JAY
SEGEL, MARC KALMAN
SELLERS, EARLANE L.
SELLKE, DAVE WILLIAM
SELON, MICHAEL DAVID
SERFASS, ROSALIND ELAINE
SEXTON, JOHN PAUL
SEXTON, TIMOTHY JOSEPH
*SHAFER, JAMES BRADLEY
*SHAFER, WILLIAM LEE
SHAFFER, DUANE LESLIE
SHAPIRO, ROBYN G.
SHARPE, BEN GRIDLEY
SHAW, DAVID JOHN
SHERFEY, WILLIAM JOSEPH
SHERWIN, NANCY JEAN
SHIELS, LINDA HARRIS
SHODA, GARRY TAKASHI
SHOEMAKER, DENNIS DUANE
SHOGREN, SANDRA JEANNE
SHRIBER, PAUL EUGENE
SHULMAN, SALO LEE
SIBLEY, JACKIE RUTH
SIBLEY, RICKI DEAN
SIEGEL, KEITH HERBERT
SIEGLER, RICHARD DENNIS
SILVERN, PAUL JEFFREY
SIMERL, LAUREL ANN
SIMON, JAMES LEO
SINGLETON, DEBORAH ANN
SIREN, RAUL ALVAR ROGER
SISTER MARY FRANCELLA WARD
SKELTON, BRIAN LAUFER
SKELTON, JAMES DWIGHT

SKIBBE, JANET RUTH
SKIDMORE, RONALD HARTSON
SKOKOWSKI, HENRY
SKOLNIK, CAROL SUE
*SKWERES, MARY ANN
SLACK, JAMES LEE
SLATTERY, JOAN MARY
SLAVIN, JANET SUE
*SLEZAK, CHARLENE MARIE
SLIVKA, VINCENT, III
*SLOAN, EUGENE DENNIS
SLOAN, PAMELA MARIE
SLUTSKY, RAEL DON
*SMAARDYK, JANE ELLEN
SMALLER, DANA LYNN
SMARON, RONALD JOSEPH
SMITH, BRADLEY THOMAS
SMITH, CRAIG MALCOLM
*SMITH, DAVID MOCK
SMITH, HEATHER CHRISTINE
SMITH, JAMES MERLYN, JR.
SMITH, KAREN ELIZABETH
SMITH, LARRY L.
SMITH, NANCY LOUISE
*SMITH, TRACY
SMITH, WAYNE EVAN
SNIDER, LARRY ALAN
*SNODGRASS, JOYCE LYNN
*SNOEYENBOS, SUE
*SOMENZI, CANDACE JOYCE
SOMMER, KATHRYN LEIGH
SONDEJ, DENISE
SOO, SHIRLEY ANN
*SORENSEN, GARY LEE
SORENSON, LARRY RICHARD
SOROKIN, BEVERLY ROSE
*SOROSKY, LAURA JEAN
SOSIN, LYNNE CAROL
SPANGLER, PSYCHE MARTINA
SPERSRUD, NORMAN CARL
*SPINDLER, JEAN MARY
SPRINGFIELD, EZELL
SPRINGMAN, JOHN MARSHALL
STALTER, DANIEL JOSEPH
STANIS, MARIANNE CAROL
*STANLEY, DAVID WARREN
STARK, MARGARET MARY
STARR, DOROTHY ANN
STARR, WILLIAM ERNEST
STASIEK, ROBERT JOSEPH
STAUFFENBERG, STEPHEN FRANZ
STEICHEN, MARY KATHERINE
STEIN, NORMA JEAN
*STEINKE, TERRY MICHAEL
STERBA, STEVEN CHARLES
STERN, CAROL
STERN, PAULA JOAN
STERN, RICHARD BENNETT
STICHA, MARK WITTWER
STICKLER, SARA LYNN
STIEGEMEIER, TAMRA LYNN
STOCK, KENNETH RICHARD
STONE, REBECCA ANN
*STONE, TERRY MICHAEL
STONEHAM, SANDRA LEE

58

STOOPS, WALTER ROBERT
STORM, KRISTINE
STOVALL, THOMAS STUART
STOVER, MERRY BETH
*STRANDBERG, PAMELA RAYMONDE
STRANDELL, DONALD ROBERT
STRANG, TIMOTHY HUGH
STRAUB, BEVERLY CHRISTINE
STRONG, BARBARA JEAN
STRONG, MARGARET LYNN
STRUM, JERRY SCOTT
SUE, IVAN PETER
SULLIVAN, JORETTA BARNETT
SUMMERS, JAMES DOUGLAS
SUTTLES, KERRY LYNN
SWAIM, SHERYL ANN
SWANSON, JANE ELIZABETH
SWANSON, PHILIP ALFRED
SWANSON, SHIRLEY IRENE
SWEENEY, DAVID RAY
*SWIFT, SUSAN LEE
SWISHER, GAYLORD HULETT
SYVERSON, ELIZABETH ANNE
SZARY, SANDRA ANNE
SZERSZEN, CAROL ANN
TALAMO, JOHN JERRY, II
TANNER, THEODORE LEA, JR.
TASA, DAVID WAYNE
TERAMOTO, BRUCE TAKAO
TERDICH, JOHN GEORGE
TETON, GAIL RENNY
THAYER, NANCY DARLE
THEWIS, ALBERT GERBEN, JR.
*THIEL, ERIC GEORGE
THOMAS, BARBARA
*THOMAS, DEBRA LOUISE
THOMAS, JUNE E.
THOMAS, PATRICIA RICH
THOMAS, ROBERT GREGORY
THOMAS, ROBERT RAY
THORNBERRY, MARTHA LYNN
*THUN, NANCY LEE
THURMAN, BRUCE RANDOLPH
TIMRECK, THEODORE WILLIAM, JR.
TITONE, DREW
*TOMISEK, JANE ELIZABETH
TONELLI, GAIL LYNN
TOPPING, HARRY FRANKLYN
TOWER, RICHARD WILLIAM
TOWNER, ROBERT LEMUEL
TRAINOR, DENNIS RICHARD
*TRIPLETT, KEVIN TIMOTHY
TRITT, TERRY LEE
TROGDON, DARYL ANN
*TROMPETER, WILLIAM EDWARD
TROSKY, GEORGE ALBERT
TRUE, GREGORY THOMAS
TRUITT, HENRY
*TRYBA, HOLLY ANNE
TSIOURIS, ARTHUR CHRIS
TURNBAUGH, ANNE
TURNBULL, GUY ANTHONY
TURNER, GEORGE EDWIN
TURNER, KATHY ALTA
TURNER, LEE CHESTER

TUTTLE, ANN
TUTTLE, GARY JOSEPH
UDOW, MICHAEL WILLIAM
USELDING, LINDA JEAN
UTLEY, BEVERLY JANE
*VALENTINE, CATHY LOUISE
*VANDRESER, PATRICIA LOU
VANHORNE, JOHN TAYLOR
*VANLANDINGHAM, JOHN THOMAS
VANTELLINGEN, FREDRIC GOUDY
VAVRA, GREGG ARNOLD
VEAL, LARRY JONATHAN
VEHLOW, PAUL EDWARD
VENTURA, PATRICK JOSEPH
VETTER, LINDA SCHEU
VICK, LYNN MARGARET
VINCENT, SHARRON LEE
VLADIKA, KATHLENE VIRGINIA
*WACK, RICHARD GEORGE
WAFLER, TERRY ALAN
*WAGNER, NANCY LEE
WAGNER, RICHARD MARK
WAGNER, TERRY LEE
WAKELAND, LEZLIE CHRISTINE
WALDMANN, KAREN RAE
WALDORF, WILLIAM JOHN
WALKER, EDITH SHARON
*WALKER, STEVEN CHARLES
*WALL, PAMELA ANN
WARGO, CHRISTINE ANN
WARHOL, CINDY ANNETTE
WARING, SARAH ELIZABETH
WARNECKE, DENNIS RAY
WARREN, MICHAEL THOMAS
*WASSERMAN, LOUIS
WATKINS, RICHARD KENT
*WATSON, GEORGE CHAPMAN
WATSON, RESA MARGARET
WEBER, CHRISTINA ANN
WEDEKING, EDWINA COONS
WEEKS, ARTHUR BRUCE
WEEKS, DAVID GEORGE
WEIGOLD, CALVIN CLARENCE
WEINBERG, MARIAN J.
WEINSTEIN, ELLEN
WEINTROB, DEBORAH LYNN
WEINZERL, THOMAS HERBERT
WEISBERG, ANNETTE RUTH
WEISHAUPT, LAUREL ANN
*WEISKOPF, JOAN
WEISS, CARLA MURBACH
WEISS, ROBERT LOUIS, JR.
WELKER, JON WHITNEY
WELKER, RITA ROGOWSKI
WELLMAN, DAVID HARVEY
WELLS, KERMIT JACK
WENDELL, STEVEN JOHN
WENDT, GARY FREDERICK
WENNER, GERALD PAUL
WERCH, SHIFRA ELKA
WERHAN, LEE WESTBY
WERMCRANTZ, JOHN DENNIS
WEST, MICHAEL ARTHUR
WEST, MICHAEL GORDON
WEST, TIMOTHY EDWARD

*Westcott, William Warren
Westlake, Walton Harvey
*Weyrauch, John Benjamin
Wheeler, Jill Glenene
White, Christine Gayle
White, Christine Susanne
White, Diane Katherine
White, Eileen Foote
White, John Abiathar
White, Larry James
White, Roger Gail
Wicks, James William
Wideburg, Charles Allen
Wiesenmeyer, Hilda R.
Wiggins, Jerome Grier
*Wilbrandt, Laurence Arthur
Wild, Arthur Monroe
*Wildman, Linda
Wilks, Andrew Carleton
Willard, Lee Ella
Williams, Russell Kenneth
Williams, Terry Lee
Williamson, Janet Lee
Wills, Scott Gordon
Wilson, Carol Haddon
Wilson, Michael Wayne
Wilson, Scott Curtis
Windmiller, Anne Christina
Wittkamp, Jonathan Herbert
*Woertz, Glenn Russell
Wolfer, Tina
Wolinsky, Robert Joel
Wollam, Pamela Jean

Wolske, Donna Lee
*Wong, Betty Pendleton
Wood, Patricia Anne
Woodhouse, David Conley
Wozniak, Pamela Ann
Wray, Christine Johanna
Wray, Gregory George
Wright, James William
*Wrigley, Carole Jean
Wuellner, Christopher John
Wurth, Michael Elbert
Yang, Vivian E. Ping
Yanney, Joan Elizabeth
Yassky, Charles Lewis
Yoshizumi, Curtis
Young, Janis Ann
Yousling, Sara Jane
Zachman, Mark T.
Zadora, Walter Lawrence
*Zajonc, Margaret Elizabeth
Zakaras, Robert Ernest
Zebrauskas, Kristine Jane
*Zeck, William John
Zeigler, Barbara Ann
Zeitlin, Oreen Inez
Zelent, Joan Lori
Zimmerman, Ann Margaret
Zimmerman, Frank William
Zimmerman, Susan Babette
Zobac, Gregory Scott
*Zorns, Susan Wagner
Zukerman, Ilene

## COLLEGE OF LIBERAL ARTS AND SCIENCES

Aaron, Philip Stewart
Aaron, Robert Lloyd
*Abel, Jacqueline J.
Abell, Mary Ann
Abelson, Richard William
Abraham, Thomas Henry
Abrajano, Barbara Jean
Abramat, Hans-Dieter
Abrams, Elyse Joy
Abrams, Jeffrey Ray
*Abrams, Marilyn Adrian
Abramson, Janice Myra
Ackerman, Cinda Jean
Adajian, Michael Bird
Adams, Bobbie Lynne
Adams, Carolyn Jean
Adams, Jay William
Adams, John Merlin
Adams, Kathleen McBride
*Adams, Martha Jean
Adams, Richard Leigh
Adams, Vera Ann
Adelman, Nancy Susan
*Ader, Richard Alan
Aderhold, Deborah Lee
Adkins, Mia K.
Adkins, Wilma Carol
*Adkisson, Stanley White
*Adler, Joan Marie

Ager, Bonita Mary
*Agins, Ann Sherry
Agnello, Ninfa
Agran, Rhonda Marlene
Agre, Norman Eugene
Agron, Shelia Hope
Ahern, Arthur Francis
*Ahern, Thomas Jeffrey
*Ahlf, Ann Junetta
Aiken, John Drake
*Aiken, Richard Chalon
*Aikus, Dorothy Ann
Akerhaugen, Ellen Ann
Akers, Marcelle Jeanine
*Akulow, Oksana Antoinette
Alban, Laurie Sue
Albano, Deborah Linn
Albrecht, Carol Jean
*Albrecht, David Walter
*Albun, Carl Jerome
Alden, John Freeman
Alderman, Brenda E.
*Alderson, Susan Kay
Aldrich, Eric Lynn
Aldrich, Phyllis Jeanne
Aldridge, Margaret Bryan
Alexander, Michael Myron
Alexander, Stephen D.
Aliabadi, Youssef Samadi

60

ALLEN, BARBARA LYNN
*ALLEN, CAROL ANN
ALLEN, CATHERINE LUCILE
ALLEN, CYNTHIA JEANNE
*ALLEN, DAVID MICHAEL
ALLEN, ERIC LYNN
ALLEN, GARY BRUCE
ALLEN, HEIDI THRESE
ALLEN, JOHN STEPHEN
ALLEN, KENNETH BRADFORD
*ALLEN, RICHARD BLAIR
ALLEN, ROBIN HARRYETTE
ALLEN, SARAH CATHERINE
ALLEN, TRACEY LEE
ALLENDER, JULIE ANN
ALLENSWORTH, THOMAS ELMER, JR.
ALLETAG, NANCY SUE
ALLIN, MARY MARGARET
ALLISON, BONNIE JUNE
*ALLSWANG, BARRY STEVEN
ALMBERG, MARK JOHN
*ALMGREN, NANCY ANNE
ALMY, KATHLEEN MARY
*ALONZO, AIDA MARGUERITE
ALPER, MARLA KAY
ALPERN, RONALD STUART
*ALTER, BARBARA PHYLLIS
ALTER, JAN HELEN
ALTGILBERS, MARGARET ANN
ALTSCHUL, BETTY JEAN
ALTSTIEL, LARRY D.
ALVEY, LARRY RUSSELL
AMADOR, LAURA KATHERINE
*AMBERG, ELIZABETH ANNE
AMBERG, SUSAN JEAN
AMBRE, JOSEPH PAUL
AMENT, SUSIE
AMES, MELINDA LEET
AMIDON, RUTH ELLEN
*AMLING, JENNIFER LOUISE
AMONI, LARRY MICHAEL
AMORUSO, WILLIAM BRUCE
AMRAM, JACK CHRISTOPHER
AMUNDSEN, DORIS JEAN
ANDELMAN, LYNN JUEL
ANDERMANN, RONALD EDWARD
ANDERS, MARJORIE JEAN
ANDERSEN, BARBARA LEE
ANDERSEN, DENNIS L.
*ANDERSEN, HENRY THOMAS
ANDERSEN, MARY K.
ANDERSON, BARBARA JAN
ANDERSON, BERNADETTE
*ANDERSON, CAROL LINNEA
ANDERSON, CHERYL LYNN
ANDERSON, CHRISTINE MARRA
ANDERSON, CRIS JANA
ANDERSON, DOROTHY
*ANDERSON, JUDITH LEE
*ANDERSON, KATHLEEN ANN
ANDERSON, KIMBALL RICHARD
*ANDERSON, KIRK PAUL
ANDERSON, MARLA JEAN
*ANDERSON, NEAL FREDERICK
*ANDERSON, NEAL GEORGE

ANDERSON, PAMELA KAY
ANDERSON, PATRICIA CHABOT
ANDERSON, PAULA CATT
ANDERSON, RICHARD WARREN
ANDERSON, ROBERT ALTON
ANDERSON, RONALD STANLEY
ANDERSON, SHARON ROSE
ANDERSON, SHERYL ANN
ANDERSON, STEPHEN CRAIG
*ANDERSON, STEPHEN KEITH
*ANDERSON, STEVEN GEORGE
ANDERSON, SUSAN MARY
*ANDERSON, THOMAS ERNEST
*ANDERSON, THOMAS ROY
ANDERTON, STEPHEN SCOTT
*ANDREAS, NANCY ELAINE
ANDREWS, CONNIE SUE
ANDREWS, DEBORAH ELIZABETH
ANDREWS, GEORGE JAMES
ANDRYSIAK, DAVID MICHAEL
ANGELINI, ROXANNE SUE
ANGLESANO, ANNETTE MARIE
*ANKIN, MICHAEL GARY
*ANSEL, LESLIE FERN
*ANSEL, MARC JOEL
*ANSPACH, KENNETH GORDON
ANTONIU, KATHLEEN RAE
ANTRIM, GAIL LYNN
ANTRIM, PAMELA JEAN
*APCEL, MELISSA ANN
APPEL, CURTIS H.
*APPLE, NEAL LOUIS
ARCHAMBAULT, CAROL RENEE
ARDIZZONE, ANTHONY VITO
ARENSON, PETER TODD
*ARENSON, SUSAN LESLIE
ARIENT, PATRICIA ANN
ARIEW, SUSAN ANDRIETTE
*ARMETTA, NANCY ANNE
ARNETT, KATHLEEN ANN
ARNOLD, DOUGLAS STRACHAN
ARNOLD, JEAN MARIAN
ARNOLD, JOSEPH AYLSWORTH
ARNOLD, LOUANNE K.
*ARNOLD, SANDRA KAY
ARNOTE, JAN GAYLE
ARNTZEN, DAVID MATTHEW
ASCHAUER, MARTIN NICHOLAS
*ASCHAUER, RUTH ELLEN
*ASCHOFF, JOHN GEORGE
ASH, JANE ELIZABETH
*ASHAMY, CORINNE MARIE
ASHBROOK, JOHN MARK
ASHBURN, NANCY FARRAR
*ASHER, IRA MANUEL
ASHER, KAREN DIANE
*ASHER, SHARON KAY
*ASHKINAZ, MARK DENNIS
*ASHLEY, DANIEL JOSEPH
*ASHLEY, LANE JOHN
*ASPER, CHERYL DEONNE
*ASPER, GLORIA ELLEN
ASSINK, ANNE HOEKSTRA
ASTROTH, JEFFREY DALE
ATCHISON, LINDA JO

61

\*ATE, LYNN MARIE
ATHERTON, KIRBY KATHRYN
ATKIN, SUSAN JEAN
ATKINS, BEVERLY ANN
ATKINS, JEFFREY ALAN
\*ATKINSON, DAVID EDWIN
ATLAS, ALVIN CHARLES
\*ATLAS, BARRY FOSTER
\*ATLAS, MARILYN JUDITH
ATON, RUTH CHRISTINE
\*ATTIG, LINDA MARIE
\*AUBRECHT, KATHRYN ANNE
AUDIA, LINDA MARIE
AUERBACH, MYRON BAYARD
\*AUERBACH, VIVIAN SUE
\*AUFDERHEIDE, ANN BELLE
AULT, DONALD FRED
AURIEMMO, LANA PATRICIA
AUSTIN, BOBBY WAYNE
AXEN, KAREL JEAN
AXT, RANDOLPH WILLIAM
AYRES, ROBERT ANDREW
AZZARELLO, ELLEN JAYNE
BABB, JAMES LOWELL
BABCOCK, PHYLLIS ANN
\*BACE, LYNN ALEXANDRIA
BACH, CATHERINE MAE
\*BACH, MARY LOIS
BACHELDER, LYNN ANN
BACHHUBER, ROBERT WILLIAM
\*BACHHUBER, WENDY LOVELLA
BACKE, CAROL LYNNE
BACKER, SUSAN KAY
\*BACKS, WILLIAM MARTIN
BACZYNSKI, JAMES MICHAEL
BADESCH, ROBERT THEODORE
\*BAECHLE, DANIEL ARTHUR
\*BAEDER, ALICE JOYCE
BAER, DAVID ANTHONY
BAER, LAURIE JEAN
BAER, ROBERT SCOTT
\*BAGLEY, KATHY ANNE
BAILEN, JOHN RICHARD
BAILEY, BONNIE ISABEL
BAILEY, MARSHA LYNN
BAILEY, PAMELA MARY
BAILEY, SUSAN JANET
BAIRD, MICHAEL DANE
BAITS, ROBERT HAROLD
BAKER, ALAN GREGORY
BAKER, AMELIA SMITH
BAKER, BARBARA CAROL
\*BAKER, BARBARA ELLEN
BAKER, DAVID BRUCE
\*BAKER, ELIZABETH RUTH
BAKER, FRANK MATTOON
BAKER, JAMES ALLEN
\*BAKER, JO ANN
BAKER, JOHN ALAN
BAKER, KATHY LOUISE
BAKER, MARGARET LYNNE
BAKER, MARILYN BONNIE
BAKER, MARVIN JOEL
BAKER, NANCY KRISTINE

BAKER, ROBERT CHARLES
BALASI, MARK GEOFFREY
\*BALBACH, EDITH DE WITT
BALDO, ELIZABETH
BALDUS, DAWN MARIE
BALDWIN, GARY EUGENE
BALDWIN, GERALD ERWIN
BALGLEY, KATHLEEN ANNE
BALINSKI, KENNETH ANDREW
BALL, THERESE ANN
BALMES, JOHN RANDOLPH
BALMES, SHARON NIMER
\*BAMBERGER, JUDY ANN
BANDSTRA, BARRY LOUIS
BANDY, JOHN ROBERTS
BANGHAM, MARY RAFTERY
BANICH, WILLIAM RUDY
BAQUERO, INES OLGA
BARAGLIA, JAMES PASQUAL
BARANCHIK, MARC
BARBER, MARSHA ANN
BARCH, PAULA BATES
BARD, HELENE MELODY
BARDWICK, PETER ALAN
BAREITHER, DANIEL JOSEPH
BAREN, BEVERLY ELLEN
BAREN, TERRY ALLEN
\*BARFIELD, HENRY HARVEY
BARGER, ROBERT KNIGHT
\*BARGREN, PAUL EUGENE
\*BARK, MARLA EILEEN
BARKEI, CAROLYNE JOY
\*BARNARD, MARY KAY
BARNARD, CHRISTIE KAY
BARNARD, STEVEN CHARLES
BARNAS, DANIEL RAYMOND
BARNES, GARY
BARNES, GEORGIA ANN
BARNES, HENRY MARSHALL
\*BARNES, MALCOLM DUNCAN
BARNES, PAUL FREDERICK
BARNES, WILLIAM HUBBARD
\*BARNETT, BENITA KAYE
BARNETT, GEORGE AARON
BARNETT, J. BRIAN
BARNETT, JANE ELLEN
BARNETT, JO ANN
BARNETT, PAUL ALAN
BARNOW, MARLA SUE
\*BARON, DENNIS JOSEPH
BARR, MARTIN PHILLIP
BARRATT, STEPHEN JOHN
BARRETT, ARTHUR KENNETH
BARRETT, MARY SUE
BARRETT, MICHAEL P.
BARRETT, WILLIAM JOSEPH, JR.
BARRON, MARGARET MARY
BARRON, PAUL WILLIAM
\*BARRY, CATHERINE MARY
BARSANTI, CARL MICHAEL
BARSKY, GARY JAY
\*BARTASH, JOANNE MARGARET
BARTEL, LANCE BRIAN
\*BARTEL, RICHARD JOSEPH

*Bartenstein, Julie
Bartfield, Steven
Barth, Elizabeth Shirley
Bartlett, Judith Jean
Bartlett, Judy Eileen
Bartlett, Richard Stephen
Bartlotti, Leonard Napoleon
Bartoli, Constance Irene
Bartoloni, Mary Kathleen
*Barton, Christine Ann
Barton, James Derek
*Barton, James Michael
Barylske, Theodore Edward
Basile, Evelyn Louise
*Baskin, Craig Paul
*Basofin, Peter
*Bass, Deborah Sue
*Bass, Murry Alan
Bass, Steven Allen
*Bassett, John Kaericher
*Bastian, John Frederic
Batchelder, Sue Ellen
Bateman, Kristine Marie
Bates, Robert Joseph, Jr.
Batista, David Eugene
*Batko, Kenneth Alan
Batricevich, Dale Roberta
Battershell, Larry Joe
Battle, Porter Leon
Baucom, Donna Gansman
Baudino, Lowanda Fay
*Bauer, David Carl
Bauer, Joanne Linda
*Bauer, Nancy Ann
*Bauer, Nancy Kathleen
*Bauer, Stephen Mark
Baugh, Gary Norman
Baum, Michael Lin
Bayer, Robert Gene
Bazzetta, James Joseph
Beach, David Kent
Beach, Mary Elizabeth
*Beal, Richard Lee
Bean, Theodore William, Jr.
Beard, Paula Gwen
Beard, Rhonda Kaye
Bearden, Frances Palmatier
Beare, Janis Gay
Beasley, Patricia Gay
Beatty, Randolph Paul
Beaudway, Janet Ann
Beberman, John Russell
Beck, Barbara Jo
Beck, Janet Janeen
Beck, John Leonard
Beck, Paul John
Beck, Penny Jo
Beck, Sue Ellen
Beck, William Austin
Becker, Cathie Ann
Becker, Harold Glenn
Becker, Jan Allen
*Becker, Kenneth Michael
Becker, Linda Hope

Becker, Tessia Ruth
*Becker, William Bradley
Beckerman, Grace Elisabeth
Beckett, John Steven
*Beckfeld, Mary Catharine
Bedford, Shelley Renee
Bednar, Susan Gail
Bedows, Elliott David
*Been, Steven Allan
Beer, Joan Louise
Begley, James Baker
*Begoun, Avis Joy
Behensky, James Frank, Jr.
Behensky, Patricia Marie
Bein, Richard Paul
Bekermeier, Linda Anne
Belden, Jeffery Lewis
Beldin, Joan Evelyn
Belgrad, Barbara Ilene
Bell, Cynthia Susan
*Bell, Debra Susan
*Bell, Laird Arthur
Bell, Patricia Marie
*Bellairs, Jerald Michael
Bellen, Janice Marie
Beeler, Stephen Mark
Bellis, Marilyn Lee
Belmont, Fredrick Alan
Belokon, Elaine A.
Belsley, Kathryn Gene
Bemi, Michael Joseph
Benchik, Barbara Ann
*Benedict, William Waite
Benes, Marygrace
Benewich, Kathleen Susan
Benn, Howard Phillip
Bennett, Alice Bernice
*Bennett, Barbara Ann
Bennett, Evan David
*Bennett, Frederick Peter
Bennett, Sari Johanna
Bennett, Steven Bradley
Bennison, Marcia Kay
*Benson, Cheryl Yvonne
Benson, J. Daniel
Benson, Leland Nathan
*Bentcover, Teri Lynn
Benthaus, Julie Lynn
Benton, Anthony Stuart
*Benton, Ronald Lilyard
Berauer, Linda Maria
*Berbaum, Michael Lawrence
Berfield, Margo
Berg, Kathleen Pierce
Berg, Steven Wayne
Berger, Arlene Rosalyn
*Berger, Brian Bernard
Berger, Cathy Michele
*Berger, Daniel Benjamin
*Berger, Debra Eve
Berger, Gary Lee
Berger, Joel Emanuel
Berger, Lorelle Hilary
Bergling, Frederick Robert

63

*Bergman, Gary Lee
Bergstrom, Robin Phillip
Berk, Mitchell Lewis
Berke, Samuel David
*Berkel, Edgar Leonard
Berklacich, Frank Martin
Berkman, Peter Michael
*Berkowicz, Howard Hyman
Berkowitz, Judith
*Berkowitz, Richard Alan
*Berkson, Andrea Joy
Berkson, Candice Jill
*Berliant, Marc Norman
Berman, Barbara Helene
*Berman, Bonnie Sue
Berman, Carol Lynn .
Berman, Cheryl Rae
*Berman, Marna Ann
Berman, Richard Alan
*Berman, Scott Zane
*Berman, Stephen Alan
Berman, Wendy Carol
Bermingham, Charles Edward
Bernacki, Marylou
Bernardi, John Vincent
*Bernardy, Johanna Mary
Berner, Gregory Peter
Bernhard, Donna J.
Bernickas, John Victor
*Bernsee, Robert William
*Bernstein, Alan David
*Bernstein, Avis Mell
Bernstein, Gail Sandra
Berstein, Helane Iris
Bernstein, Karen Susan
Bernstein, Robin Marlene
*Bernthal, David Gary
Bero, Carol Ann
Berry, Catherine Ann
Berry, David Philip
Berry, Linda Rachel
Berry, Susan Lynn
Bersche, Gerald Lotz
*Bersin, Alex Geoffrey
*Berson, Bruce Alan
*Bertelsen, Julia Sue
Berthold, Robert Craig
Bertolet, James Cecil
*Bertram, Carolyn Margaret
*Bertschy, Timothy Louis
Besore, Mary Ann
Bethune, Christine Louise
Betka, Lois Emele
Betz, Karen Margaret
Bewersdorf, James William
Beyda, Marcia Lynn
*Bial, Raymond Steven
*Biancalana, Flora Ermenia
*Bible, Claudia Enzinna
Bible, Dana King
*Bibly, Kathrine
*Bicek, Margaret Jane
Bickus, Julie Jean
Bidenkap, Jay Lance
Biderman, Robert James

Bidwell, Vanda Irene
Bieber, Susan
Bielema, Brian Jay
Bieschke, Colleen Ellyn
Biesemeier, Donald, Jr.
Biliack, Stuart Andrew
*Bill, Linda Marie
*Biller, Carol Naomi
Billig, Linda Lee
Billman, Barbara Jeanne
*Bilyeu, Thomas Michael
Bindenagel, James Dale
Binder, Patti Joan
*Binenfeld, Jan Susan
*Binkin, Geri Suzanne
*Bird, Donald Merle
Bird, Ronald Frank
Birkenkamp, Ray Thomas
Birkey, Jacqueline Ekstam
*Birstein, Karen Sue
Bisberg, Kathleen Florilla
Bishir, Joan Kathleen
*Bitzer, John Le Roy
Bivins, Walter Perry
Bjorseth, Richard Edward
Black, Ellen Jean
Black, Jennifer Jane
Black, Kathleen Wynne
Black, Marcia Lea
Black, Mark Morris
Blackwelder, Peggy Jean
Blackwell, Donald Kimble
Blahnik, Theresa May
Blair, Melvin Robert
Blake, David Robert
Blakeman, Clyde Thomas
*Blanc, Peter Leon
Blanchard, Ann Elizabeth
Blanchet, Nancy Ann
Blanco, Jose Manuel
Blanco, Sandra Kay
Bland, Dianna Sue
Blanding, Bonnie June
Blank, Richard Gerald
Blank, Virginia Ross
*Blazek, Judith Jean
*Blessman, Barbara Kay
*Blitstein, Mark David
*Bloch, Elizabeth Mara
Bloch, Rosanne Louise
*Block, James Irwin
Blodgett, Dennis Jay
Bloemendaal, Ralph Edwin
*Bloemer, Robert William
Bloese, Rodney Thomas
*Blom, Bernhard Emile
*Blonn, Rebecca Ann
Bloom, Barbara Lea
Bloom, Irving Aaron
Bloom, Mark Lawrence
*Bluestone, Robin Joy
*Bluhm, Karen Esworthy
Bluhm, Ronald Ray
Blum, Arthur Lee
Blum, Eugene Jay

*Blum, Rosanne Dea
Blum, Steven Terry
Blum, Susan Andrea
Blumenfield, Shelley
Blumenthal, Howard Michael
Blunier, Doris Elaine
Blustein, Judy Roberta
Boas, Linda Ann
Boborci, Joseph Frank
Bock, Karen Leah
*Bodem, Charles Rene
Bodnar, Susan Maria
*Bodznick, David Alan
Boehm, Frederick Joseph, II
Boelter, Virginia Marie
Boesen, Thomas Peter
Bogaerts, Stephen Craig
*Bohan, Daniel James
*Bohl, Betty Jean
Bohlen, Christopher Wayne
Bohn, Anna Elizabeth
Bohrer, Bruce Frederick
*Boime, Susan Ilene
Boin, James Joseph
*Boksa, Karen Ann
*Bokuniewicz, Henry Joseph
Boland, Kathleen Ursula
Bolin, Gloria Arlene
Bollweg, Doris Elaine
Bolmey, Carlos Alberto
Bolton, James Roberts, Jr.
Bombach, Barbara Ann
*Bonansinga, Michael Joseph
Bonas, Julie Eileen
Bone, Sharon Kay
Bonetti, William Carl
*Bonnell, Linda Marie
*Bonnom, Randall Curry
*Bond, Bette Lynne
Bookman, Alan Sherman
Books, Donald Kent
Bookshester, Joyce
*Boone, Luann Tucker
Booth, Douglas Allen
*Boraz, Royce Ellen
*Bordeaux, David Henry
Borden, Adrianne Naoma
Borek, Sam
Borgstede, James Paul
Boria, Philip Joseph
*Borok, Robert I.
Borovec, Jacquelyn Messmore
Borre, Kristen Sue
*Borrenpohl, Lavonne
*Borrenpohl, Nancy Lee
*Bortz, Sheri Lee
Borys, Cynthia Anne
Borzoni, Christine Eileen
Bosanac, Stevan Nicholas
Boss, Margaret Allison
Bost, Barbara Ann
Bostic, Victoria Elizabeth
Bostrom, Mary Beth
*Botteron, Mary Alice
*Boucek, Carol Lyne

*Boudart, Mary Gene
Bouillon, Michael Ray
Bouwkamp, Thomas Gerald
Bowen, Kevin Francis
Bowen, Pamela Susan
*Bowen, Robert Evans
Bowers, James Lamar, Jr.
Bowles, Jeanette Mosher
Bowman, Jeanne Marie
Bowman, Linda Marie
Bows, Ronna Lynn
Bowton, Constance Gail
Bowton, David Lowell
Boxerman, Naomi Lee
Boxley, Mark Lane
Boyd, Brian Edward
Boyd, Mary Lena
Boyd, Patricia Anne
*Boyington, Barbara Ann
*Boyle, Martha Ann
Brach, Donna Jean
Brackett, John Alan
Bradford, Jacqueline Ann
Bradle, William Ramesey
Bradley, Cynthia Roberta
*Bradley, Katie Rachel
Bradna, Marylou Ann
*Brady, Richard Allen
*Brainerd, Susan Ellen
Bralley, Patricia
Brandon, Lawonda Quintella
Brands, Rosanne Miller
Brandstrader, Janet Roberta
Branman, Larry Allan
Branz, Jeanne Louise
*Brash, Richard Alan
Bratrude, Pamela Susan
*Bratton, Jay Philip
Bratu, Randall Peter
*Brauer, Mary Alice
Braugher, Cheryl Anita
Braun, Bonnie Sue
Braun, Donald Peter
Braun, Jerome Sheldon
Braun, Nancy Elizabeth
Braun, William David
Braun, William Joseph
Braverman, Blair Iran
*Braverman, Marla Dee
*Bredberg, Daniel Jon
Bredberg, Karl August
Breen, Joseph Richard
Breeze, Clark Alan
Breitenstein, Francis
Breitowich, Alan David
Bremer, Charles Dale
Brenner, Barbara Jean
*Brenner, Karen Lynn
Brenner, Scott Douglas
Brese, Denis James
Bresnahan, Kerry Ann
Bresnan, Regina Frances
Bress, Larry Kenneth
Bressman, Robert Allen
*Brethauer, Todd Steven

65

BRETT, RANDALL PHILIP
BREWER, JOANNA MAE
*BREWER, MICHAEL LYNN
BRICHTA, RAND E.
BRICKER, KATHY E.
BRICKETT, PAUL ALAN
*BRICKMAN, JEFFREY MARTIN
*BRIDGES, SHARON LEA
*BRIDGWATER, GARY ROBERT
BRIDWELL, ELIZABETH ANN
BRIELER, ANTHONY WAYNE
BRIESKE, TINA MARIE
BRIGGS, LAURA E.
BRIGGS, MICHAEL JOE
BRIGHT, BEVERLY ANN
BRIGHT, JUNE ADELE
BRIGHTON, WILLIAM DAVID
*BRIGHTWELL, MARTHA VIRGINIA
*BRILL, BETTE SUE
BRINKMAN, DANIEL JOHN
BRINKMAN, JAMES EDWARD
BRINKMAN, SUSAN JEAN
BRINKMANN, KATHLEEN ANN
BRISCOE, MARCIA JANE
BRISKMAN, ETHEL
BRITSKY, MARINA ANNE
BRITTIN, WILLIAM ALAN
BROADUS, JOHN ROBERT
BROCK, JUDITH DAVIS
BROCKER, KENNETH ROBERT
BROCKMAN, LAURA CAROL
BROCKMANN, FREDERICK RUSSELL, JR.
BROCKMEYER, CHERYL ANN
BRODE, ELVIN LELAND, JR.
BRODEMUS, JOHN STANLEY
BRODEMUS, ROBERT MARK
BRODER, JEFFREY KENT
BRODERICK, THOMAS F.
BRODHEAD, JANE DOROTHY
*BRODIN, MARY ELLEN
BRODSKY, GEORGE DANNY
*BRODSKY, MICHAEL AARON
BRODY, ADRIAN LYNN
BROEKER, DEBORAH ANN
BROEKER, JOAN CELESTE
BROHMAN, SUSAN ROSE
BROKAW, SUSAN LOCKWOOD
BRONSTEIN, LINDA GUSTAFSON
BROOKMAN, BARBARA JEAN
*BROOKS, EILEEN DEBORAH
*BROOKS, RICHARD LYNN
BROSIOUS, MARY ANNE
BROSIOUS, RITA ANNE
BROUDO, MARC
*BROUWER, JOEKIE
BROWN, BARRY WAYNE
BROWN, BRUCE TODD
BROWN, CYNTHIA JOY
BROWN, DANIEL HARRY
BROWN, DEBORAH SUE
BROWN, ELIZABETH ANNE
BROWN, JAMES MICHAEL
BROWN, KATHLEEN MARY
BROWN, LAUREN ANN
BROWN, LAWRENCE P.

BROWN, MARK LESLIE
BROWN, MICHAEL ELLIOT
BROWN, PAMELA RUTH
BROWN, PATRICE CATHERINE
BROWN, PRISCILLA JANE
*BROWN, ROBILEE
BROWN, STEWART JAY
BROWN, TIMOTHY W.
BROWNE, YVONNE A.
BROWNSTEIN, CAROL SUE
BRUBAKER, CRAIG
BRUBAKER, POLLY BRISTOL
*BRUCAT, CYNTHIA ANN
*BRUCE, ROBERT JAMES
BRUGENHEMKE, MARY JANE
*BRUHN, JOANNE ELIZABETH
BRUIN, CHRISTINE MARIE
BRUMIS, MELODY
*BRUMLEVE, CHARLES EVAN
*BRUMLEVE, TIMOTHY ROBERT
BRUMM, NANCY JOHANSEN
BRUNE, MARTHA
BRUNET, ROBERT WALTER
BRUNKER, DAVID LAWRENCE
*BRUNO, ELIZABETH ALEXANDRA
BRUNO, MARY ANN
BRUNOEHLER, WANDA LYNN
*BRUSH, JAMES RICHARD
BRUSKI, SANDRA LYNN
BRYAN, GARY EARL
BRYAN, KATHLEEN LYNNE
BRYANT, TERRY LYNNE
BRYER, ANDREA SUE
BRYNER, JAMES MARTIN
BUBERT, JOHN ROLLIN
BUCHER, CRYSTAL DAWN
BUCHOLTZ, KATHLEEN L.
*BUCHSBAUM, YAEL
BUCKHIESTER, BONNIE ELIZABETH
BUCKHOLDT, CHRISTINE
BUCKINGHAM, BARBARA FRANCES
BUCKLES, NEIL EUGENE
BUCZYNA, LINDA ANN
*BUDDE, JANE MARGARET
BUDNIK, JUDITH ANN
BUDZ, JACK THEODORE
*BUDZ, JEROME THOMAS
*BUDZIK, PHILIP MARTIN
*BUERCKHOLTZ, MARY PATRICIA
*BUHAI, BETSY EILEEN
BUHSE, JILL ANN
BINAUSKAS, ALDONA IRENE
BUIS, REBECCA JANE
BUJALSKI, JANICE MARIE
BULAWA, DENNIS EDWARD
BULL, REX WARREN
BULMASH, ANN LYNN
*BULTAS, JANICE FITZGERALD
*BUNCH, DEBRA JEANNE
BUNGER, BONNIE BELCHIK
BURBICK, JOSEPH MICHAEL
BURCH, ROBERT JOSEPH
*BURCH, WILLIAM ALLEN
BURD, WILLIAM EDWARD
BURDEN, JOSEPH RICHARD

BURGESON, LINDA ELLEN
BURGESS, SHARON LYNN
BURGHARD, HENRIETTE KRISTIN
BURGUM, CELESTE AMELIA
BURKE, CHRISTOPHER RAYMOND
BURKE, MARGARET MARY
BURKE, RICHARD EDMUND
BURKE, WILLIAM CARL, JR.
BURKHALTER, JOHN FRED
BURKHARDT, TERRY JOHN
*BURKHOLDER, KATHLEEN
*BURNETT, JOHN CARLOS, JR.
BURNETTE, DOROTHY ANN
BURNS, EDWARD J.
BURNS, JULIE ELLEN
BURNS, LESLIE LEE
BURNS, THOMAS MICHAEL
BURROUGHS, EILEEN FRANCES
BURSON, LOREN SCOTT
BURSON, MICHAEL ALLEN
BURSTEIN, TOBY
BURTON, CHARLES A.
BURTON, CHARLES MARVIN
BURY, SHARON LEE
BUS, KENNETH PAUL
BUSCH, CAROL NOEL
BUSH, DEBORAH SUE
*BUSHEE, DEBRA GRACE
BUSHING, LYNN RIPPEL
*BUSHMAN, MARY ANN
BUSHNICK, PHILIP NEIL
BUSS, DONALD CLAYTON
BUSSE, JOAN HEATHER
*BUSSELL, DIANA BOLZ
BUSTER, KAREN JACQUELINE
BUTE, DANIEL JOHN
BUTH, DONALD GEORGE
BUTITTA, JOHN MICHAEL
*BUTLER, AUDREY KAY
BUTLER, JOHN ALAN
*BUTLER, JOHN CHRISTIAN
BUTLER, MARIE
*BUTTERFIELD, CAROLE DIANE
BUY, KAREN ALICE
BYERLY, FLOYD CHARLES
*BYERS, DAVID JOHN
BYRNE, BARBARA LAMBERT
*BYRNE, DAVID UDELL
BYRNE, ROBERT JOHN
*BYTHELL, CAROL ANN
*CABAY, BARBARA LYNNE
CABRERA, LOUISE MARIE
*CACCIATO, DARLENE
CACHEVKI, KAREN
*CADY, RALPH LOWELL
*CAFARELLA, JEAN MARIE
*CAHILL, ANNE LOUISE
CAHILL, JOHN ANDREW
*CAINE, JANET ANN
CALCESE, WILLIAM GERALD
CALDERO, CARMEN
CALEBAUGH, DONALD LAWRENCE
CALHOUN, ISAAC FRANK
CALLANAN, MARTHA ANN
CALLION, ETHELYN MILDRED

CAMERON, LINDA LOUISE
CAMERON, WILLIAM ALLEN
*CAMILLO, SUSAN MILDRED
CAMMON, DALE LEE
*CAMODECA, SILVIO JOSEPH
CAMPANELLA, CARL JOSEPH
*CAMPBELL, DAVID BATES
CAMPBELL, DEBORAH JOAN
CAMPBELL, JAMES EARL
CAMPBELL, JOSEPH MASON
CAMPBELL, MARY CATHERINE
CAMPBELL, MARY ELIZABETH
CAMPBELL, NANCY JANE
CAMPBELL, RICHARD DENNIS
CAMPBELL, TED SCOTT
*CAMPBELL, WILLIAM DWIGHT
CANADY, BLANTON THANDREUS
CANEL, ROBERT LOUIS
CANNAN, JUDITH ANN
CANNELIN, MARGARET RUTH
CANNELL, CAROL ANNETTE
CANNON, JAMES CLINTON
CANTRALL, DENISE GILOMEN
*CANTRELL, MICHAEL ALAN
*CAPUTO, TONI JO
*CARAVELLI, JAMES FERDINAND
CARAWAY, MYRA SUE
CARBARY, JAMES FRANKLIN
CARDELLA, RICHARD GEORGE
*CARDELLI, JAMES ALLEN
CAREY, DOUGLAS LEE
CAREY, RICHARD PETER
CARIUS, JEFFREY RAPP
CARIUS, JULIE KRAUT
*CARKEEK, THOMAS GERALD
CARLBERG, KRISTINA LOUISE
CARLEY, STEPHEN EDWARD
*CARLINO, NANCY ANNE
*CARLSON, ALLEN MARK
*CARLSON, BRUCE ELBERT
*CARLSON, EVELYN LOUISE
CARLSON, JANET RISTOW
CARLSON, JOAN DIANE
*CARLSON, JUNE EILEEN
CARLSON, KAREN SUE
CARLSON, KRISTINE MAE
CARLSON, RICHARD ALLEN
CARLSON, SHARLENE HELEN
CARLSON, STEVEN CRAIG
CARLTON, REBECCA ANN
CARLTON, SARAH LEE
CARLYLE, SANDRA RAE
*CARPENTER, HENRY ALAN
*CARPENTER, ROBERT BRUCE
*CARR, FRANKLIN DEAN
CARR, JOSEPH CONRAD, II
CARR, MICHAEL JOSEPH
CARRIE, LYNN MARIE
CARRIGLIO, JACK JOSEPH
CARROLL, ANN CHARNETZKI
CARROLL, MONICA
CARROLL, SUSAN LEE
*CARTER, CAROLYN ELIZABETH
CARTER, CATHERINE CAULFIELD
CARTER, CLAUDIA SUE

67

*Carter, David A.
Carter, Stephen Rich
Cartwright, Max David
Carver, Margaret Mary
*Casagrande, James Bert
Cascia, Mark Andrew
*Case, Jimmie Arden
*Casella, Gail Jane
*Caselton, Marilyn Sue
Casey, John Shephard
Casey, Nancy McDaniel
Cash, Richard Joel
Cashman, James Francis
*Casperson, Paul Gordon
Cassidy, Rosanne
Casson, Richard Thomas
Castagno, Barbara Ann
Castan, Ronald Francis
Castleman, Linda Marie
Catalano, Anthony Francis
Catania, Frank Joseph
Catlin, Marilyn Janette
Catron, David Owen
Catto, Loretta
Cavanaugh, Raymond Joseph
Cave, Mary Kuzera
Cavender, Teresa Elizabeth
*Cederholm, Fred William
Celesk, Roger Allan
Cella, Paul Arthur
Center, David Steven
Center, Robert Allen
Cepicky, Jacquelyn Lee
Cercone, David Joseph
Cerda, Jane Elizabeth
*Cerrone, Kimberlie Louise
*Cesarone, Bernard Joseph
Chaben, Susan Phyllis
Chace, Gordon Kenneth
Chace, Shella Odom
Chakoian, Martin Henry
Chalcraft, Joyce Kay
Chalfen, Marc James
Chalupnicek, Alan Jerome
Chamberlain, Ellen Marie
Chamberlin, John Gilchrist
Chambers, Patrick Thaddeus
Chambers, Ronald Michael
*Chamot, Ernest Walter
Chan, Daisy Shun-Lan
Chan, Eva Yulan
*Chandler, Elaine Eleanor
Chandler, Gloria Snowden
Chang, Chin-Chin
*Chao, Nancy Shan
*Chapman, Lee James
Chapman, Marcia Ruth
*Charness, Neal Marc
Chase, Richard Dana
Chase, Robert S.
*Chauncey, Joan Margaret
*Chausow, Alan Martin
Chavarry, Roberto George
*Cheek, Becky Joanne
*Cheek, Charles Edward

Cheever, Sheryl Lynn
Chelcun, Greg William
*Chen, Peter Yale
*Chen, Tsun-Huei
Cheng, Linda
Cheng, Peter James
Cheng, Steven
Chergoski, Pamela Jean
Cherney, David Todd
Cherry, Thornton Eugene
Cherveny, Ronald George
Chesna, Laura Anne
*Chesrow, George W.
Chess, Susan Therese
*Chevalier, Mary Margaret
Cheverud, Thomas Robert
Chew, Deborah La Vaugn
*Chewning, Diane Sue
Chicoine, Stephen Duane
Chicoine, Susan Elizabeth
Chidster, Marjorie Sue
Chilberg, Peggy Jo
Chiligiris, Mary Evan Thea
*Chipman, Jeffrey Thomas
*Chisek, Michael Andrew
Chisholm, Mary Catherine
Chodera, Susan Mary
Chong, Dianne
*Chorba, Carol Ann
Chrisman, Richard Angus
Christen, Barbara Ann
*Christen, Darryl Keith
*Christensen, Alice Faye
Christensen, Gary Marvin
*Christensen, Rose Ann
*Christiansen, David Karl
*Christiansen, John Hadley
Christiansen, Nancy Ann
*Christman, Kathy Lynn
Christofanelli, Robin Lynn
*Christoff, Richard Wayne
Christoffersen, Alan Bruce
*Christofferson, April
Christon, Stephen Paul
Chrusciel, Sophia Elizabeth
Chu, Grace Tena
Chvosta, Ruth Anne
Chwistek, Lois Jean
*Cicero, Joan Grace
Cieply, Brian Andrew
Cihlar, Dorothy Jeanne
Cihlar, Ronald Lee
Cima, Lawrence Malcolm
Cinotto, James Hale
Cifra, Dale Leonard
Ciskowski, Robert Dennis
*Cizmar, Dawn Kathleen
Claggett, James Rogers
Clamage, Arthur Earl
*Clancy, Michael John
Claricoates, Gregory James
Clark, Carol Ann
Clark, Carolyn
Clark, Cheryl Jean
*Clark, Craig Robert

68

CLARK, CYNTHIA LOUISE
CLARK, HORACE POMEROY
CLARK, LINDA ANNE
CLARK, LINDA SUE
CLARK, LYNN MILLER
CLARK, PETER PICQUET
CLARK, RAMONA THERESE
CLARK, ROBERT JORDAN
CLARK, SHARON LINDA
CLARKE, STEPHEN FERGUSON
CLARKSON, MARY PRUDENCE
CLAUSEN, WALTER SCOTT
CLAY, GLORIA J. DUNHAM
CLAYPOOL, CONSTANCE JANE
CLAYTON, ALBERT TRACY
CLAYTON, JAMES DENNIS
CLAYTON, JANE CHRISTINE
CLEMENS, KAREN RUTH
CLENNON, SUZANNE FRANCES
CLIFTON, MITCHELL HOWARD
CLIFTON, PAMELA P.
CLINE, LYNN STUCK
CLINTON, DAVID WILLIAM
CLODFELTER, LINDSAY D.
CLUM, MARY ANN
CLYNE, DAVID WILLIAM
COADY, JOHN PATRICK
COATES, RENATA GOELLNER
COATS, DONALD WAYNE
*COBB, MICHAEL ALLAN
*COBBLE, JAMES FORREST, JR.
COFONE, FRANK, JR.
COGGESHALL, ALICE JEAN
COGHLAN, MARGARET MARY
COHEN, ALBERT SAMUEL
COHEN, BETTE JO
COHEN, BONNIE KAY
COHEN, DAVID ALAN
*COHEN, GERALD ALAN
COHEN, HOWARD J.
COHEN, JEFFREY DAVID
COHEN, JUDITH ANNE
COHEN, JUDY MAE
COHEN, JULIE HARRIET
COHEN, LAWRENCE ALAN
COHEN, MARSHALL DAVID
COHEN, MITCHELL ROBERT
*COHEN, MYRON SCOTT
COHN, ARNOLD KEITH
COHN, DORITH RAFAELA
COHN, JOANNE
COHN, LAURIE ELLEN
*COHN, MARJORIE LYNN
COHN, RALPH MICHAEL
COKER, VIRGIL MORRIS
COLBERG, ANNE IONE
COLBERT, JANET LYNN
*COLBERT, MARC HALL
COLBERT, SUSAN ELYSE
*COLBURN, THERESE JEAN
*COLBY, VIRGINIA GAYE
COLE, HELENE MARTHA
COLE, JULIE BETH
*COLE, NANCY SUE
COLE, VALERIE Y.

COLEAN, GLORIA MARIE
COLET, JIM GLENN
COLLIER, GLENN HAVEN
*COLLIER, SARA ELLEN
COLLINS, CATHERINE MARY
*COLLINS, CHARLES PATRICK
COLLINS, ELIZABETH LYNN
COLLINS, JAMES LINTON
COLLINS, JEAN
COLLINS, LINDA SUSAN
COLLINS, ROBERT JEFFREY
*COLLINS, SUSAN LEE
COLLONS, CINDY JOY
COLLYER, CATHLEEN ANN
COLTHURST, NANINE CARTIER
COMBS, CATHLEEN MARIA
*COMFORT, NANCY LYNN
*COMPTON, CHARLES CARSON
COMPTON, MARILYN MARTHA
CONDON, JANE CHANTAL
CONE, RAYMOND BARRY
CONFORTI, PAUL MICHAEL
CONLON, EDWARD JOSEPH
CONLON, GEORGIA SUE
CONLON, MARY ALICE
CONLON, PATRICIA ANN
CONNELLY, STEPHEN DUANE
CONNOR, SHARON ANN
CONOVER, PATRICIA ANN
CONRADI, ROBERT ALLEN
*CONROY, KATHLEEN RANDALL
CONSTAN, ATHANASEA NANCY
CONSTAN, EVANGELO THEODORE
CONSTANTINE, CAROL ANN
CONVERSE, PHILIP MEAD
CONWAY, PETER NOEL
COOK, DAVID MICHAEL
*COOK, JEFFREY STEVEN
*COOK, KARA LINDA
COOK, MARILYN
*COOK, MARTIN LEO
COOK, RONNA JOY
COOK, THOMAS RUSH
COOK, WILLIAM ROBERT, JR.
COOKE, DAVID HARLAN
COOPER, ANN THOMAS
COOPER, DAVID MARTIN
COOPER, ELIOT DAVID
COOPER, JAMES EVERETT, JR.
COOPER, KATHRYN DENISE
COOPER, PHILIP ASA
COOPER, ROBERT BERNARD
COOPER, ROBERT CHARLES
COPPER, KEVIN BRUCE
CORBAN, GAYLE L.
CORCORAN, MARY PAT
CORDULACK, SHELLEY WOOD
CORK, TIMOTHY RYAN
CORLEY, JOHN WILLIAM
*CORN, LILA SARAH
CORNER, BRADLEY ROBERTS
CORTESI, ROBERT RAYNOLD
CORWIN, DEBORAH WELLS
COSER, RICHARD JOSEPH
COSGROVE, DAN THOMAS

69

*COSGROVE, DONNA MARIA
COSGROVE, MARY FRANCES
COSTELLO, JAMES JOSEPH, JR.
COSTELLO, SUSAN ELIZABETH
COSTLEY, LINDA SUE
COTNER, CHARLES LELAND
*COTTINGHAM, JOHN THEODORE
COUGHLAN, LORETTA RAHAS
*COUGHLIN, COLLEEN DENISE
COUGHLIN, PATRICIA ANN
COUGHLIN, WENDY RITA
COULIAS, DALE CHRISTINE
COULTAS, NANCY CHARLENE
*COURNOYER, ANN KATHRYN
COURT, CHARLES MICHAEL
*COURTNAGE, SUSAN LOUISE
COURVOISIER, JOAN MARIE
COVINGTON, RICHARD WARREN, JR.
COWAN, JOAN LOUISE
COWAN, LETA CAROL
COWAN, STEPHEN DAVIS
COX, ELLEN MARY
*COX, GRACE ELIZABETH
*COX, RICHARD NORMAN
COY, BARBARA LEE
COYNE, JOHN ANDERSON
*CRABILL, MARY ATONINA
CRABTREE, CAROLYN LOUISE
*CRAIN, DEBRA NAN
*CRAIN, MARTIN ROSS
CRAMER, CONSTANCE BETH
CRAMER, MARK JAY
CRANDALL, CLAUDIA ANGELA
CRANE, CHARLES FREDERICK
CRANE, CONSTANCE CAROLYN
CRANE, JAMES KENNETH
CRANE, JILL
CRANE, ROBERT GARY
CRANK, JERRY MICHAEL
CRATER, BARBARA ANN
CRAWFORD, CATHERINE SUE
CRAWFORD, JUDY
CRAWFORD, LORNA CLAIRE
CRAWFORD, ROBERT DALE
CRAWLEY, GAYLE DOROTHY
CREDICOTT, DAVID EDWARD
CREEK, MARDENA BRIDGES
CREEL, DAVID RUSSELL
CRIPE, JEAN ELIZABETH
*CRISEL, JERRY EARL
CRISP, BARBARA JEAN
CRITES, ELLEN CARROLL
CRITTENDEN, ANITA DELOIS
CROFT, MICHAEL ZALMAN
*CROFT, STEVEN MARTIN
CROISANT, WILLIAM, JR.
CROKER, REBECCA ANN
CROMBIE, PETER BLYTH
CRONAU, CHRISTINE
*CRONE, CHARLES LYNN
CRONE, RICHARD LAWRENCE
CROOKS, KENNETH RICHARD
CROSS, ALICE JEAN
CROSS, ANITA LYNN
*CROSS, JANET ANN

*CROSSAN, BRUCE GREGORY
CROUSE, SHIRLEY LOUISE
CROWE, MICHAEL JAMES
CROWLEY, CANDICE ANN
CROWLEY, CATHERINE CLAIRE
CROWLEY, MICHAEL JOSEPH
CULBERT, BRUCE PARKER
CULLEN, PATRICE JOAN
*CUMBY, CHARLES CARLYLE, JR.
CUMBY, MICHAEL CHARLES
CUMMER, CONSTANCE LAURENCE
CUMMINS, DENISE LOUISE
CUNNINGHAM, ANNE M.
CUNNINGHAM, LEE RUSSELL
CUNNINGHAM, MARY PAULA
*CUPEC, JAMES CHRISTOPHER
*CURATOLA, SANDRA ANNE
*CURRAN, KRISTINE MARIE
CURRIE, CHARLES PETER
CURRIE, ROBERT EDWARD
CURTIS, CAROLYN SUE
CURTIS, JAMES-WYLIE ALLISON, II
CURTIS, NANCY ELIZABETH
CURTRIGHT, JANE ANN
CURTTRIGHT, JOHN MALCOLM, III
CUTLER, CAROLE ANN
CUTLER, DEBORAH SUSAN
CUTLER, ROBERT BRIAN
CUTTONE, DONNA MARIE
CYBUL, CYNTHIA LOUISE
*CYGAN, EDWARD ANTHONY
CYGNAR, BRUCE ARN
*CYPHERS, ANN MARIE
CZAPAR, CAROL ANN
CZERNEDA, ROSEMARY ANNE
CZESTOCHOWSKI, JOSEPH, JR.
*DACHMAN, CAREY BENNETT
*DAGEN, NANCY ELAINE
DAGGITT, MARGARET SUE
*DAGUE, MARTHA JO
DAHLGREN, LEONARD ROY
DAHLKE, CHARLES KENRICK
DAHLSTRAND, AVA CHRISTINE
*DAILEY, CHRISTINE LOUISE
DALE, BARBARA LOUISE
DALEY, ANN MAUREEN
DALEY, PATRICIA JANE
*D'AMBROGIO, MARGARET MARY
DAMER, MARY KAY
D'AMICO, ANGELINA CHRISTINE
DAMLER, JAMES MICHAEL
DAMON, DAVID ANTHONY
DAMOS, JAMES ROBERT
DANCASTER, LINDA SUE
DANDELLES, RICHARD LEE
DANGLES, GEORGE JOHN
DANHAUS, PAUL EDWARD
*DANIELS, LESLEY DIANE
DANIELSON, LINDA SUE
DANIELSON, STEVEN LOUIS
DANLEY, ROBERT BRUCE
*DANNENFELDT, DIANE SUE
DAPRON, HARRY LEE
DARMSTADTER, LYNN ELLEN
DARNELL, CAROL LYNN

70

DARNELL, DEBRA MAY
DARNER, ROBERT GRAHAM
DAU, KATHLEEN ELIZABETH
DAUBS, JANIE JO
*DAUGHERITY, KERRY LEE
DAUM, THOMAS DILLON
DAVENPORT, JACK BASTIN
DAVID, DONALD CARY
*DAVID, JACQUELINE DEBORAH
*DAVID, MYRNA ANN
DAVIDSON, DENISE GOLDIE
*DAVIDSON, JAMES BENJAMIN
DAVIDSON, ROBERT GEORGE, JR.
*DAVIDSON, VICTOR LESTER
*DAVIS, BRIDGET IONA
*DAVIS, CAROL BETH
DAVIS, CATHLEEN ANNE
DAVIS, CYNTHIA SUE
DAVIS, DIANA PEARL
DAVIS, DOLORES JEAN
DAVIS, DONNA SUZANNE
DAVIS, ELLEN NESSA
DAVIS, ERNEST EDMUND
*DAVIS, JAMES FREDERICK
DAVIS, JANET LYNN
DAVIS, JARY EILEEN
DAVIS, JOEL JAY
DAVIS, JUDY ELLEN
DAVIS, JUDY ROLENE
*DAVIS, LAURA REBECCA
DAVIS, LLOYD STEPHEN
DAVIS, NANCY MARIE
DAVIS, PAMELA KAY
*DAVIS, PAULA WINSOR
DAVIS, PHILLIP VINCENT
*DAVIS, ROBERT WENDELL
DAVIS, STUART ALLEN
DAVIS, SYLVIA BETH
DAVIS, THOMAS PATRICK
DAVIS, WAYNE ALAN
DAWN, JULIA ANNE
*DAWSON, CLYDE WILLIAM
DAY, DALE RICHARD
*DAY, GREGORY LLOYD
*DAY, RICHARD JOSEPH
DAYTON, ELIZABETH ANN
DAYTON, KAY ELLEN
DEAN, CAROL ANN
DEAN, JAMES WILLIAM
*DEAN, KAREN ANNE
DEAN, PAULA MARIE
*DEAN, STACY LILLIAN
DEARDORFF, THOMAS CLARE
DEBATES, MARYJO
DEBRUYCKERE, DIANE MARIE
DECHO, JANET ANN
DECKER, DONITA INEZ
DECKER, MARC CONWAY
DECOSTER, LOREN REED
*DECYK, ROXANNE JEAN
DEDECKER, KATHLEEN ANN
DEFRANK, MICHAEL NICHOLAS
DEFRONZO, MICHAEL
DEGRANDE, GARY GASTON
DEGUIRE, DENISE MARIE

DEGUIRE, PETER JAMES
DEHN, JEFFREY LEE
DELABAR, PAMELA ANN
*DELANEY, CAROL JEAN
DELAP, TIMOTHY KEITH
DELAURA, RONALD EDWARD
DELFIACCO, LINDA MARIE
*DELHEIMER, STEVEN CRAIG
DELIN, BARRY STEVEN
DELL, LINDA LOUISE
DELLAS, HERCULES ALEXANDER
*DELVENTO, CONNIE ANN
DEMARCO, MARGARET SUE
DEMARS, ROBIN A.
DEMMERT, JAMES JOSEPH
DEMPSEY, PAUL NICHOLAS
DENARDO, KAREN MARIE
DENAULT, JOHN MELVIN
DENIS, CLYDE LOUIS
DENIS, SUSAN MARIE
DENNARD, RONNIE MIKE
*DENNIS, JON EDWARD
DENNIS, PATRICK LEE
DENNIS, WILLIAM MICHAEL
DENNISTON, ANN CAROL
*DENNY, JACK WARREN
*DENOV, ANGELA MARIE
DENOVO, ROBERT CHARLES
DENTON, DENNIS WILLIAM
*DENTON, DIANE LYNN
DEPINTO, JACQUELINE MARIE
*DEPKE, JANET MARIE
DEPLONTY, JANICE RUTH
DEREX, MICHAEL S.
DERUNTZ, MICHAEL LEO
*DESCHENE, STEVEN RICHARD
DESROSIERS, DORIS RITA
DESSOUKY, IBTESAM ABDEL
DESTEFANO, JAMES NICHOLAS
DETAR, MARVIN BRADFORD
DETELLA, KATHERINE MARIE
DETERS, ROBERT LOUIS
DETTNER, ROBERT CLYDE
DEUTSCHER, JANICE LOUISE
DEVENS, CHARLES J.
DEVERELL, DAVID ANTONIE
DEVINE, DANIEL JAMES
DEVINEY, MADELINE JOSEPHINE
DEVON, MARILYN C.
*DEVORE, CYNTHIA LYNNE
*DEVUONO, MARY
DEVUONO, PATRICK MICHAEL
DEWALT, STEPHEN RALPH
DEWITT, DIANE MARIE
DIAMENT, FAYE HELEN
DIBIASE, DENISE MARGERITE
DICKEY, ADELINE ELINOR
DICKEY, LYNN ESTELLE
*DICKEY, MICHAEL DENE
DICKEY, SARAJANE
*DICKLER, LINDA GAIL
*DIDECH, DEAN MICHAEL
DIDOMENICO, JANET MAY
DIEHL, KAREN ANN
DIEHL, MARY ELIZABETH

71

ENGELHARDT, LUDWIG ENGELBERT
ENGELHARDT, WILLIAM FOSTER
ENGLAND, STEPHEN JAMES
ENGLER, SHERI JARVA
ENGSTROM, JAMES CARL
*ENGSTROM, KATHY SUSAN
ENLOW, WILLIAM RICHARD
ENNIS, MAUREEN ANN
ENTMAN, BRUCE ROGER
EOVALDI, PAULA KAY
*EPHRON, MARK STEVEN
*EPPING, MYRA LYNN
EPPINK, BETTY ANN
*EPPLIN, EUGENE HERMAN
*EPPLIN, JEROME JOSEPH
EPPLIN, MARGARET ANN
*EPSKY, MARILYN RUTH
EPSTEIN, BOB ERIC
EPSTEIN, EDWARD LAWRENCE
EPSTEIN, JANE ANN
*EPSTEIN, MARC ALAN
ERCIUS, MARK STEVEN
*ERDE, MARY ANNE
*ERHARDT, PENNY JANE
ERICKSON, JAMES EDWARD
ERICKSON, JONATHAN ROBERT
ERICKSON, MARSHA LYNN
*ERICKSON, PAMELA IRENE
ERICKSON, TERYL LYNN
ERKERT, ALLEN CHRISTIAN
ERKERT, ROSEMARY LEE
ERLANDSON, MARY ELLEN
ERNEST, PAMELA JANE
ERNST, DAVID EARL
ERNSTEIN, BARBARA JEAN
ERVIN, LESLIE DUKE
ERWIN, MICHELE ANN
ESBROOK, DAVID GEORGE
ESCHENFELDER, MARY LOUISE
ESKER, KATHRYN JANE
ESKER, STEPHEN CHARLES
*ESSENFELD, IDYTH
*ESSENPREIS, PATRICIA SUE
ESSER, DALE LESLIE
ESSERMAN, BONNIE ROSE
ETCHASON, CHERLYN SUE
*EUSTICE, DEBORAH CLARE
*EVANS, MARGARET ANN
EVANS, SCOTT WADE
EVANS, SUSAN LOUISE
EVERHART, BARBARA EILEEN
EVERS, LARRY WILLIAM
EVRARD, STEPHEN KENT
*EWAN, JANE MARIE
*EWAN, JUDITH ANN
EWANIC, DEBRA EVON
*EWERS, THOMAS BEARD
EWING, GENE EDWARD
EWING, VANESSA GARCIA-SERRA
EWTON, JOHN HOUSTON
*EYCHANER, BARBARA ANN
EZRING, MURRAY
FABER, EMILY CHRISTINE
FABIAN, DIANE CHARLOTTE
FABRIZIO, JAMES ROCCO

FABRIZIO, JUDITH EILEEN
FADER, RONALD ALAN
FAGAN, KATHLEEN THERESA
*FAIR, C. JAMES
FAIRBANK, WILLIAM ALLEN
FAKLIS, NICHOLAS JOHN
FALCONIO, LINDA SUE
FALK, SUSAN
FALK, ZENA MARLYN
*FALKENTHAL, SCOTT VON
*FALTUS, VICKI LYNN
FANCHER, DOROTHY FRANCES
*FARBER, DANIEL ALAN
FARBER, NEIL HOWARD
FARBER, SUSAN DONNA
FARBY, BARBARA SUSAN
FARKAS, JACQUES NATHAN
FARKAS, REGINA ESTELLE
FARLEY, LAURA LYNN
*FARMER, ROGER ALAN
*FARNER, SUSAN MARIE
FARNHAM, LINDA JANE
*FARNHAM, NANCY ELLEN
FARRELL, JANICE LOUISE
FARRINGTON, THOMAS ARTHUR
*FARRUGGIA, ROBERT VANCE
FASSETT, NANCY JEAN
FASULES, JAMES WALTER
*FAULSTICH, GRETCHEN ANN
*FAULSTICH, LEO JOSEPH
FAUST, MARSHA ANNE
*FAVERO, KEVIN THOMAS
FAY, TIM JAMES
FAYMONVILLE, LORETTA ANN
*FEDROWITZ, JOSEPH HENRY
FEHST, GERALDINE RAE
FEIGER, KATHERINE JOANNE
FEINBERG, JOYCE MARILYN
FEINBERG, STEVEN BRUCE
FEINGOLD, JEFFREY M.
FEINSTEIN, RENEE ILENE
*FEIST, ELLEN SUE
FEIST, LINDA LEE
*FELDMAN, ANITA SUSAN
*FELDMAN, JAMES EDWARD
FELDMAN, JEROME IRA
*FELDMAN, ROBERT JOEL
*FELDMAN, STEVEN
*FELL, DAVID ALAN
FELLMAN, JANICE LYNN
FELLNER, KAREN JEAN
*FELLOWS, LELAND GARY
*FELSENTHAL, CAROL GREENBERG
FELSENTHAL, RANDY I.
*FELSENTHAL, STEVEN ALTUS
*FENBERG, SUSAN LYNN
FENCL, GLENN FRED
FENDER, SUSAN
FENNESSEY, KIMBERLY SUE
FENSKE, GREGG RICHARD
FERENCE, GEORGIA ANN
FERENCZ, GLENN EDWARD
FERGUSON, REBECCA KETTELKAMP
FERNALD, STEPHEN CRAIG
*FERRIS, ROGER ALAN

74

Ferry, Carole Lynn
Ferry, John Lyman
Fett, Day Ann
*Fett, William Frederick
Feuer, Debora Hope
Fey, Justine Louise
*Fiarman, Lawrence Morris
Ficek, Judith Ann
*Fiedler, Ellen Victoria
Fiegenbaum, Steven James
*Field, Daniel Playfair
*Field, Jean Ann
*Field, Steven David
Field, Susan Frances
Fieldhouse, James McKay
Fields, Gary Lynn
*Fields, Jacqueline Elaine
Fields, Scott Ira
Fieleke, Curtis Stuart
*Fierstein, Ira
*Fifield, Barbara Jean
Figatner, Joel Garrett
Filion, Mary Agnes
Finch, Angeline
Finch, Anna Lee
*Fincke, Debra Marie
Fine, Steven Michael
Fink, Esther
Fink, Ilene Gwen
*Fink, Marsha Ann
*Finkbeiner, Drucilla
*Finke, Jeffrey Wayne
*Finkel, Barry Sholem
*Finkelstein, Michael
Finks, Nancy Jean
Finks, Sara Ann
*Finley, Robert Coe III
Finn, Thomas William
*Finnerman, Doris Susan
Finnerty, Donna Jean
Finno, Joan Clare
Fiorenza, John Peter
Firestone, Diane Sharon
Firfer, Barbara Jan
Fischer, Karen Inger
*Fischer, Laurence Eliot
Fischer, Willard John
Fish, Gail
Fisher, Andrea Regina
*Fisher, Anna Marie
*Fisher, Joy Deborah
Fisher, Kenneth Howard
Fisher, Merle Beth
*Fisher, Raymond Lee
*Fisher, Richard Stuart
Fisher, Scott Harley
Fisher, Scott Irwin
Fisher, Sherry Kay
*Fisher, Stephen Craig
*Fishman, Adrianne May
*Fishman, Regina Mary
Fishman, Steven Allan
Fitch, Cherlynne Sue
*Fitzer, Susan Louise
*Fitzgerald, Catherine

*Fitzgerald, Joan Marie
Fitzgerald, Laurel Anne
Fitzpatrick, Linda Marie
Fitzpatrick, Rita Denise
Flach, Philip Leo
Flahaven, Judith Ann
Flake, John Joel
Flanagan, Stephen Mark
Flanegin, Joan
Flanegin, Sharon
Flannell, Danny Leon
Flannigan, Timothy Richard
Flatner, Cindy Thea
Flaxman, Cheryll Dawn
*Fleagle, John Thomas
Fleener, Christine Diane
Fleetwood, Robert Sparks
Fleischer, Kenneth Jeffrey
*Fleming, Elizabeth Charlene
Fleming, Linda Sue
Fleming, Yvonne Jeannai
*Flessner, Stephen Mark
Flettre, Margaret Ann
Flicht, Myra Lynne
Flint, Patricia Ann
Flom, Karen Ann
Flood, Susan Jane
*Flora, Janice Elaine
Flora, Steven Kent
Floyd, Bruce Martin
Fluck, Deanna Mae
Fluegge, Marylou Catherine
*Flynn, James Edward
Flysche, Bruce Lee
*Fogel, Maureen Gail
*Fohrman, Linda Leslie
*Fohrman, Monica Marcia
Folk, Daniel Hall
Fondrie, Barbara Kay
*Foote, Robert Allan
Foran, Linda Lee
*Foran, Paul Gordon
*Forbes, Stephen Harding
Forcade, Michael Charles
Ford, Avalon Lora
*Ford, Jeffrey Barry
Foreman, Hannah Sutherland
Foreman, Janice Gail
Foreman, Syd Alan
Fornelli, Rita Marie
Forry, Sally Jane
Forse, Barbara Janette
Forsythe, Gary E.
Fortman, Christine Marie
Fortmeyer, Ruth Ann
Fortner, Phyllis Hasbrouck
*Foster, Craig Stephen
Foster, James Campbell
Foster, Judith Ann
Foster, Lynn Caroline
*Foster, Mary Alice
Foulds, Leslie Jean
Fournie, Raymond Richard
Foutris, Christine Sophia
Fox, Cynthia Jean

75

Fox, Janet Elaine
Fox, Joel Birk
Fox, Karen Wendy
Fox, Sheryl Diane
*Fox, Susan Nancy
Frakes, Audrey Mae
Fralick, Janet Lee
Franchi, Filis Sarae
Francis, Mary Ann
*Frank, Charles Roy
*Frank, Geri
Frank, Jeron Michael
Frank, John Peter
Frank, Richard David
Frank, Sharon Louise
Frank, Steven Lee
*Franks, William Dale
Franson, James Carl
Frantz, Dennis Andrew
*Frantz, Larry Thomas
Fraser, Susan Elizabeth
Fratello, Daniel Armond
Freddy, Colleen Irene
Frederick, Pamela Kay
Frederick, Richard Claeys
Freding, Cheryl Hill
Fredman, Mark Steven
Fredericks, Jeffrey Reed
Fredrikson, Jo Anne
Freedman, Laura Beth
*Freedman, Shelley Beth
*Freedman, Susan Russelle
Freeman, Donna Jean
Freeman, Laurie Lynn
Freeman, Lisa Edith
*Freeman, Maynard Lloyd
Freeman, Steven Dale
Freibaum, Barnard
Freiboth, William Henry
Freidin, Jay David
*Freidinger, Joy Lynn
*Freireich, Valerie Jane
Freisinger, Sheldon David
French, Edward Harry
Frey, Barry A.
Frey, Deborah Ann
Frey, Mark Charles
Frey, Robert William
Freyman, William Charles
Fricke, Mary Jane
*Friedland, Mary Kathryn
*Friedland, Nancy Ellen
Friedlander, Arnold Marvin
Friedlander, Kenneth
*Friedman, Andrea Joan
Friedman, Caryn Beth
*Friedman, Darlene Donna
Friedman, Debbie Marsha
*Friedman, Deborah Jane
Friedman, Debra Fran
Friedman, Jamie Rose
*Friedman, Joel
*Friedman, Judith Cherie
Friedman, Lee
Friedman, Leslie Arlen

Friedman, Marcia Toni
*Friedman, Paul Jay
*Friedman, Sandra Lee
*Friedman, Stephen Joel
Friedstat, Robert Alan
Friend, Kathleen D.
Frisbie, Thomas Richard
Frishman, Richard Allen
Fritsch, April Marie
*Fritsch, Jane Frances
*Fritsch, Kathleen Christine
Fritz, Joanne
Fritz, Stephen Glenn
Fritzen, Jorja Carol
Frjelich, Kenneth
From, Bernice Louise
Froom, Joan Elizabeth
Fruin, Stephen Francis
Frydman, Sharon
Frye, Karen Ruth
Frykman, Duane Victor
*Fuchs, Elaine Viola
Fuchs, Linda Ann
Fugami, Carol Jane
*Fujii, Midori
Fujimoto, Gordon Takeo
Fuller, Faye Irwin
*Fuller, Theodore Darrel
Fulton, Gwendolyn Carol
Funk, Connie Sue
*Funk, David Bruce
Funk, James Eugene
Furar, Carol Ann
*Furlong, Joanne Catherine
Furmanek, Andrea Estelle
Gabbert, Janis Ann
Gac, Martha Harriet
Gaebler, Deborah Jean
Gaffron, Robert Arthur, Jr.
*Gagerman, Janice Raye
Gahwiler, Barbara Lynn
*Gaines, Carol Anne
*Gaines, Kay Barrett
Gaines, Robert Alan
Gaines, Sam
Gainey, Barbara Lynn
Galbraith, Sue Zane
Gale, Virginia Anne
Galecke, Gary Allen
Galen, Nancy Doyle
*Galford, Terese Linda
Gallagher, Daniel Harry
Galle, Joyce Marie
Gallisath, Barbara Lynn
Galt, Enone Sue
Ganakos, Barbara Elaine
Gannon, David Lee
Ganske, Kenneth Ralph
Ganski, Linda Susan
*Garb, Jeffrey Louis
Garbe, Paul Le Roy
Garbutt, James Cameron
*Gardner, Jane Ellen
*Gardner, Phyllis Irene
Gardner, Robert Edward

76

GARESCHE, GAIL MARIE
GARFIELD, ALAN H.
GARFIELD, LAREN H.
*GARFINKEL, DONNA JEAN
GARFINKEL, ELAINE KEOWN
GARGO, STEVEN FRANKLYN
GARMAGER, KRISTOFER
*GARRETSON, SARAH MELINDA
GARRETT, DANE WILLIAM
GARRY, DONNA MARIE
GARRY, MARK THOMAS
GARTON, BARBARA ANDERSON
GARTON, INA MALINDA
GARVEY, MICHAEL STEPHEN
*GARVEY, NANCY ANN
GARWIN, ARTHUR HARRIS
GARWOOD, JANE LOUISE
GASKE, MARGARET AGNES
GASS, CECELIA CATHERINE
GASS, ZACHARY IRVING
GAST, JAMES ALAN
*GAST, MICHAEL J.
GAST, SUSAN SMITH
GASTON, STANLEY JAMES
GATES, JOELEN JERI
GATEWOOD, JOHN BROOKING
*GATSIS, KAREN
*GATSIS, RENEE
GATZIOLIS, SOPHIA
*GAUDIOSO, LYNN MARIE
GAUEN, KEITH ALAN
GAUEN, MARY ABBOTT
*GAULT, LONNE KATHRYN
GAULT, LUCINDA LEE
*GAVARES, NICKI JO
GAVLIN, NANCY LYNN
*GALVIN, SUZANNE
*GAVZER, LAURA NAN
GAYDEN, LOU WILLIE
*GAYER, ROBERT JOSEPH
GEARY, MARY CAROL
GECAN, GARY JOHN
GECAN, PAMELA SUE
GEDEN, WILLIAM FRANCIS
GEE, CAROLYN ELLEN
GEHRKE, SHERRY LYNN
GEIDERMAN, GAIL LINDA
*GEIDERMAN, JOEL MARTIN
GEIGER, DEBORAH ANN
GEIGER, VIVIENNE LEE
GEISSAL, DRUSILLA BURNHAM
GELDER, BRADLEY STUART
GELFELD, ADRIENNE RUTH
GELLER, LYNDA GRAFINGER
GENI, LAWRENCE RYAN
GENOVESE, THOMAS MICHAEL
GENT, NANCY CATHERINE
GENTEMAN, CAROL JEAN
GENTRY, URANIA ELISABETH
*GEORGE, JOHN MARTIN, JR.
GEORGE, KERRY EARL
*GEORGE, PAUL MICHAEL
GEPHART, MARY FRANCES
GERALD, MARILYN LEE
GERALD, NEIL DOUGLAS

GERBER, ANITA SUE
GERBER, BRUCE STEVEN
GERBER, GARY EUGENE
GERBER, LOWELL IAN
GERBER, RICHARD LARRY
*GERBER, ROBIN MARLA
GERDES, ROGER ALLEN
GERDY, LINDA MAUREEN
GEREMIA, NATALIE ANN
GERL, JAMES DANIEL
GERNAND, CHRISTOPHER JON
*GERRITY, ANNE THERESE
GERSBAUGH, CHRISTINE HELEN
GERSHON, SHARON KAY
GERSICK, SHELLEY ANN
GERSON, DAVID ROSS
*GERSTEIN, ROESIA HILDY
GERSTEN, JEFFREY LAWRENCE
*GERSTNER, WILLIAM CARL
*GERTEN, LAWRENCE JOSEPH
GERTSCH, RUSSELL HAYWARD
GESCHKE, WAYNE BERNARD
GETSON, PAMELA ROSE
GIACOMINI, KATHLEEN COONS
GIAMPOLI, FRANK JOSEPH
GIANNESCHI, CYNTHIA VICTORIA
GIANNESCHI, DANISE MARY
GIANNETTI, LINDA KATHLEEN
*GIBBONS, KATHLEEN KAY
GIBLICHMAN, MERLE BETH
GIBRICH, CRAIG ELLIS
GIBSON, GAIL ELAINE
GIBSON, KATHLEEN ROSE
*GIBSON, STEPHEN ALBERT
GIBSON, SUE ANN
GIERING, ROBERT RICHARD
GIERMAN, MARY KAY
*GIERMAN, SHARON FAY
GIERSCH, EILEEN FRANCES
GIGLIO, LORA FRANCES
*GIGLOTTO, JOSEPH MORGAN
GILBERT, CHARLES FRANK
*GILBERT, JOHN LAURENCE
GILBERT, JOHN PHIL
GILDIG, THOMAS JOHN
GILES, GEOFFREY LYNN
GILES, JANICE FISHER
GILL, DAVID BRADLEY
GILL, STANLEY DALE
GILLENWATER, STEVEN ROBERT
*GILLESPIE, DANIEL LESTER
GILLESPIE, JOAN MARY
GILLESPIE, MARTIN PETER
GILLETTE, RICHARD HARRY
GILLIAM, JAMES KARL
GILLIAND, DONNA JEAN
GILLIARD, DONALD WILLIAM
GILLINGHAM, JOHN CHARLES
GILLMAN, MARGARET MARY
*GILMAN, ALAN DAVID
GILMORE, THOMAS GENE
GILSTRAP, NANCY JEANNE
GINDER, GORDON DEAN
GINGERICH, DOROTHY CAROL
*GINN, DARYL

77

GINSBERG, LESLIE JAN
GINSBERG, RICHARD LESLIE
*GINSBURG, ELLIOT KIBA
GINSBURG, MARVIN LESLIE
*GINTZLER, JANICE MAE
GIORDANO, JOSEPH ANTHONY
GIORDANO, KAREN SIMPSON
*GIROUD, JORGE MANUEL
GITELIS, MICHAEL
GITELIS, STEVEN
GITLIS, KARYN RAE
GITMAN, DAVID
GIULIETTI, ROSALIND VIRGINIA
GIUNTOLI, AVA BRODY
GIVEN, GAY PATRICIA
GIVEN, THOMAS WILLIAM
*GIVENS, SALLY LOUISE
GLAS, CORINNE LORRAINE
GLASGOW, JAMES WILLIAM
*GLASSMAN, ROBERT M.
GLASSNER, BARRY LAWRENCE
GLATT, BARBARA SUE
GLATTMAN, ROSLYN LEE
GLAZE, KURT TOBEY
GLEASON, PATRICIA A.
*GLEASON, VICKI LEE
GLEESPEN, DONNA MARIE
GLENNON, KATHLEEN
*GLESNE, CORRINE ELAINE
*GLICK, DONALD LEE
GLICK, ROBERTA P.
*GLICKSON, SCOTT LESTER
GLIDDON, SCOTT WENTZ
*GLIEBERMAN, BRUCE ALLEN
GLINBERG, ROBERT HENRY
*GLISKER, JANICE LYNN
GLOBERSON, TERRY LEE
*GLOSS, DIANNE MARIE
GLOWACZ, SUSAN GAIL
GLOWINSKI, ANNE MARIE
GLUSKIN, LAWRENCE ELLIOTT
GLUT, PAULETTE ARLAYNE
*GNAVI, WALTER MICHAEL, JR.
GNIEWEK, DARLA RAE
*GOBEN, BETTY ANN
GOBLE, BONNIE JOANN
GOBLE, JANICE ELAINE
GOCH, MARTIN GENE
GODDARD, MARY SUZANNE
GODFREY, JENNIFER MICHELE
GODLEWSKI, PAUL STANLEY
GODOWSKI, THERESA LOUISE
GODWIN, MILTON CHARLES, JR.
*GOECKNER, DANIEL JOSEPH
GOETZKE, MARK ALAN
GOGGINS, MAUREEN IRENE
*GOGOLA, PAULINE KAY
GOLAB, JAN EDWARD
GOLAS, RUTH MARIE
GOLD, DAVID LAWRENCE
GOLD, DEBORAH TOBY
GOLD, DIANE MARIE
*GOLD, HARRIET LYNN
*GOLD, JAMES HAGLER
GOLD, JEFFREY ALLEN

GOLD, MARK ALAN
GOLD, RUSSELL STUART
GOLD, THERESA
GOLDBERG, HERBERT LOUIS
*GOLDBERG, JANIS KAY
*GOLDBERG, MARLENE SUE
GOLDBERG, MARTIN HAROLD
GOLDBERG, MAXINE JOY
*GOLDBERG, MICHAEL JEROME
GOLDBERG, ROBERT C.
GOLDBERG, STEVEN ELLIOT
GOLDBERG, SUSAN CAROL
*GOLDBERGER, GAIL E.
*GOLDENBERG, LARRY STEVEN
GOLDFEIN, LARRY KENNETH
GOLDFLIES, MITCHELL LEE
*GOLDHOR, ELIZABETH PAYNE
*GOLDMAN, ALAN LEE
GOLDMAN, ALAN NEAL
*GOLDMAN, BARBARA MAXINE
*GOLDMAN, DAVID ECKSTEIN
GOLDMAN, DAVID MARC
GOLDMAN, JAMES NORMAN
*GOLDMAN, JEFFREY HOWARD
GOLDMAN, JOSHUA WILLIAMS
GOLDMAN, MAVIS GERALD
*GOLDMAN, MYRNA
GOLDMAN, PAULA LAURETTE
GOLDMAN, RUTH SUSAN
GOLDMAN, TOBY MARCIA
GOLDRICH, HOWARD MICHAEL
*GOLDSCHMIDT, MICHAEL ARNOLD
GOLDSMITH, STEWART PETER
*GOLDSTEIN, JAMES ALAN
GOLDSTEIN, JAY LAWRENCE
GOLDSTEIN, JUDY ANN
GOLDSTEIN, LAURENCE JAYE
GOLDSTEIN, WAYNE MARTIN
GOLDWASSER, KATHERINE
GOLIO, JAMES PETER
GOLLUB, ALLEN BENJAMIN
GOLMAN, GAIL SUSAN
GOMBERG, BETH MELISSA
GONTERMAN, KARA JEAN
GONZALEZ, REBECCA
GOODE, JOANNE LESLI
*GOODELL, JOHN ROBERT
*GOODIN, FRANK LEE
GOODMAN, BETH FRANCINE
GOODMAN, BRUCE DAVID
GOODMAN, CAROLYN JEAN
GOODMAN, KAREN RUTH
GOODMAN, RICHARD LAWRENCE
*GOODMAN, ROBERT ALLEN
*GOODWIN, SARAH ANN
GOOLEY, JANET SUE
GOOT, ARNOLD LARRY
GOOTZEIT, DEBRA SARA
GORDEN, SUSAN ANNETTE
*GORDON, GLENDA GAY
*GORDON, JANICE S.
GORDON, RUSSELL HUNTER
GORDON, YALE MICHAEL
GORE, CAROL LEE
GORE, CHARLES PHILIP

78

GORENZ, RICHARD JOSEPH
GORINI, HELEN MARY
GORMAN, DONALD JAMES
*GORSHE, RANDAL LOUIS
GOSPODARCZYK, MARGARET FRANCIS
GOSS, MARIANN ELIZABETH
GOTTEINER, ROBIN DALE
*GOTTFRIED, JOAN MAE
GOULD, ARTHUR EDWIN
GOULD, MARCIA ELAINE
*GOULKA, JOANNE LYNN
*GOUNDAS, CHRISTINE
GOWDY, LIZA
*GOWLER, VICKI S.
*GRABLE, PAULA
GRABNER, PATRICIA CHENOWETH
GRABOW, KAREN MINDA
GRACHAN, ALLAN FRANCIS
GRACZYK, PAULETTE MARIE
GRADY, DANIEL CLAY
GRAESSER, ROBERT JULIUS
GRAHAM, KATHLEEN ANNE
*GRAMAN, THOMAS LOWELL
GRAMM, PATRICIA MARLEEN
GRANAT, ALAN LESLIE
*GRANATH, JAMES WILTON
GRANS, SUSAN ELLEN
GRANT, CELIA MARY
*GRANT, DEBRA SUE
GRANT, WILLIAM MICHAEL
*GRASSEL, KEITH ALAN
*GRAUEL, NED WILLIAM
GRAVES, DOUGLAS BRUCE
GRAVES, KAYE MARIE
GRAWEY, LYNETTE KAY
GRAY, BECKY JEAN
GRAY, DEBORAH SUSAN
*GRAY, JULIE ANN
GRAY, THELMA SHARON
*GRAZIAN, JAN ELLEN
GRAZIAN, LAURIE JEAN
GREAGER, JOHN ALLISON, II
GREAVES, ELIZABETH JANE
*GREAVES, WILLIAM WALTER
GREBENAR, SANDRA LEE
*GREDE, MARY ALICE
GREEN, DEBRA SACKS
GREEN, ELIZABETH IRENE
GREEN, FRANCINE NICOLE
GREEN, KAREN JOY
GREEN, LAWRENCE ARTHUR
GREEN, MARGARET JORDAN
GREEN, MARGARETTE BERTHA
GREEN, RICHARD JORDAN
GREEN, RONALD GRANT
GREEN, SHARRI ESTHER
GREEN, SUSAN MARGARET
GREENBERG, BARRY SCOTT
GREENBERG, LYNN
GREENE, BRENDAN DAVID
GREENE, KEVIN PETER
GREENE, WILLIAM MICHAEL
GREENFELDT, BARBARA LEE
GREENFIELD, DEBORAH NAN
*GREENFIELD, HAZEL GRETA

GREENFIELD, PAUL STEVEN
GREENLEE, ANNE
GREENOUGH, KIMBALL EVANS
GREENSPAHN, BARBARA HOLLIS
*GREENSPAHN, BRUCE ROBERT
GREENSPAN, BENNETT STEVEN
GREENSTEIN, LARRY PHILLIP
GREFFE, ANNETTA JEAN
*GREGER, NANCY GAY
GREGORCY, GLENN MARCEL
GREGORY, CAROLINE GRACE
GREINER, STEVEN PAUL
*GREISDORF, ANNA
GREISMAN, ROBERT STEWART
GRESCHEK, KATHLEEN ANNE
GRESS, DIRK WILHELM
GRETSCHMANN, KENNETH
*GRIDER, JOHN BURNHAM
*GRIEME, LINDA JO
GRIERSON, ANDY RAY
GRIESEMER, CHARLES TOWNSEND
GRIFFIN, DEBORAH LEE
GRIFFIN, LORRAINE ELLEN
GRIFFIN, TERESA MARIE
GRIFFITH, HARRY DURLAND
*GRIFFITH, LAWRENCE BRADLEY
GRIGG, ANN ELLIS
GRIGGS, J. RICHARD
GRIMM, EVELYN ELIZABETH
*GRISLIS, AIVAR ROLAND
GRISOLANO, KATHY
*GRITCHEN, LYLE STEVEN
GRITTON, ROSANNE
GROCHOCINSKI, DAVID EDWARD
GROESCH, GARY L.
GROFF, SUSAN ELLEN
*GROH, ANNETTE MARIE
*GROM, PATRICIA ANNE
GRONER, JEFFREY PHILLIP
GROOME, JUDITH KAY
GROSS, ALAN MARK
GROSS, ANDREA FRANCES
*GROSS, GARY EVAN
GROSSE, MICHAEL WILLIAM
GROSSE, ROBERT CHARLES
GROSSMAN, DENNIS LE ROY
*GROSSMAN, NEIL MARC
GROSSMARK, MARLENE LYNN
GROT, SANDRA KAY
GROTRIAN, TIMOTHY MARK
GRUBE, LINDA KAY
GRUZALSKI, PHIL ARTHUR
GRYGA, MARGARET MARY
GSCHWEND, JOHN ARTHUR
GUALANO, RICHARD LOUIS
GUCCIONE, JOHN MORGAN
GUBELER, ANN
*GUGLIELMI, THOMAS
GUICE, VIOLA MURIEL
GUIDO, DIANE CHRISTINE
GUINN, LINDA LILLETTE
*GULLANG, DEBORAH JEAN
GULLBERG, JAMES ROBERT
GULLICKSON, JAMES ALLAN
GUM, MARY ELAINE

79

GUNDERSON, MARK ROBERT
GUNN, STEVEN CARL
GUNNER, SANDRA HILL
GUNTERMAN, CAROL ANNE
GUNTHNER, ROBERT JAMES
GURGA, LEROY STEVEN
GURION, HENRY BARUCH
GURWITZ, DEBORAH SUZETTE
GUSE, MICHAEL PAUL
GUSTAFSON, CATHERINE MARIE
GUSTAFSON, CHARLES BERNARD
*GUSTAFSON, ERIC SCOTT
*GUSTAFSON, WILLIAM BENEDETTI
GUTENKAUF, LINDA ANN
GUTHMANN, JOEL EDWARD
GUTHRIE, GALE JO
*GUTHRIE, JANET ELAINE
GUTMAN, JOEL HOWARD
GUTNIK, RANDI BETH
*GUTTU, SHARA LEE
GUYTON, THOMAS LEE
GVILLO, KATHERINE KACENA
GWIZDALSKI, BONITA
*HAAS, DANIEL DILLON
HAAS, DEBORAH RUTH
*HAAS, JOHN CHARLES
*HAAS, MARY CATHERINE
HABECK, CARMEN CHRISTA
HABECOST, CHRISTY CAROL
*HACK, GREGORY PAUL
HACKETT, KATHLEEN THERESE
HACKMANN, WILLIAM STERLING
HADLEY, LYNN
HAFNER, THOMAS BENNETT
HAGAN, SUSAN RUTH
HAGEN, JAMES EDWIN
HAGG, CHRISTINE IONE
HAHN, FREDRICK W., JR.
HAHN, JESSICA MARGRIT
HAHN, JONATHAN HERMAN
*HAHN, NANCY ELLEN
HAHN, SANDRA LEE
*HAHN, STEPHEN ROBERT
HAHN, TERRI SUZANNE
*HALBACH, JOSEPH L.
*HALBUR, JOHN DAVID
HALE, LINDA W.
HALEY, DELORES ANN
HALFAR, STEPHEN ARTHUR
HALFFIELD, DONALD RICHARD, JR.
HALL, BARBARA LEE
HALL, BENJAMIN JOSEPH
HALL, BRENDA ROSSON
HALL, DIANA SUE
HALL, JAMES ROBERT
HALL, JEFFREY SCOTT
HALL, JESSIE MAE
HALL, JUNE PENELOPE
HALL, MELVIN EDDIE
HALL, MICHAEL JAMES
HALL, MICHAEL ROBERT
HALL, RALPH MICHAEL
HALL, RAYNARD VILLA
HALL, RUTH ANN
HALL, SHARON DOWERS

HALL, TERRI ROXANNE
HALL, THOMAS WILLIAM
*HALLER, SUSAN KATHERINE
HALLERUD, DAVID MICHAEL
HALLINAN, JOAN MARJORIE
*HALLSTROM, ARONA HORVITZ
HALPER, JOEL DAVID
*HALPERN, BARBARA KAY
HALPERN, SHARYL ANN
HALVERSON, JULIE ANN
*HALVORSON, SCOTT ALAN
HAM, THERESA MARIE
HAMAND, MARTHA CAROL
*HAMILOS, DANIEL LEE
HAMILTON, JOHN WILLIAM
HAMILTON, LYNN BETZ
HAMILTON, MARY JANE
HAMILTON, REED ALAN
HAMILTON, WANDA JEAN
HAMMEL, JAMES EDWIN
HAMMER, CHRISTINE ANNE
HAMMOND, DOUGLAS EDWARD
HANCOCK, JOHN MICHAEL
HANCOCK, LIZA BETH
HANCOCK, MARTHA ANN
HANDLER, ALICE ELAINE
*HANDLER, JOEL FRANCIS
HANDLEY, BONNIE LOUISE
HANDLEY, PATRICIA ANN
HANDWERGER, CAROL JUDITH
*HANEY, CYNTHIA KAY
HANING, RICHARD DALE
*HANKIN, ARONA
*HANKINS, GAIL JACQUELINE
HANKINSON, ANITA JANE
*HANLYN, CAREN M.
HANN, ELIZABETH KATHLEEN
HANN, RANDY RAYMOND
HANNA, JEANNE TINSLEY
*HANNASCH, JAMES DONALD
*HANNO, MILDRED SARA
HANRAHAN, PATRICK RALPH
HANSEN, BARBARA EILEEN
HANSEN, DEBORAH ANN
HANSEN, DON WILLIAM
HANSEN, ERIC JOHN
*HANSEN, JONATHAN CURTIS
HANSEN, LAWRENCE JEFFREY
HANSEN, LINDA SUE
HANSEN, MICHAEL JOHN
HANSEN, SUSAN MARIE
HANSON, GWEN
HANSON, HOLLY DIANE
HANSON, JANIS ANN
*HANSON, JOHN HOLDEN, JR.
HARDERS, ROBERT TERRENCE
HARDIN, MICHAEL WILLIAM
HARDT, PEGGY ANN
HARDY, BETSY LEWIS
*HARDY, H. STEPHEN
*HARPST, WILLIAM FREDERICK
HARJU, MARK RALPH
HARKINS, SUSAN KAY
*HARM, THOMAS ANDREW
HARMON, JANET MARIE

80

HARMON, JOSEPH EMMETT
HARMON, MARGARET SUE
HARMS, ALFRED GLEN, JR.
HARMS, CAROL ANN
*HARMS, CHARLOTTE ESTELLE
HARMS, DANIEL CARL
*HARMS, MARCIA JANE
HARMS, MARY LAZZARI
*HARPER, DENVER
HARPER, GREGORY LEE
*HARPER, SCOTT THOMAS
*HARPESTAD, ALICIA ANN
*HARR, RHONDA JOY
HARRE, CHARLENE MICHELE
HARRELL, HARLAN LEE
HARRING, MICHAEL ADRIAN
HARRINGTON, MARY CATHERINE
HARRINGTON, WARREN JOSEPH
HARRIS, DAVID MICHAEL
HARRIS, DAVID MICHAEL
HARRIS, DONNA JEANNE
HARRIS, GARY BURTON
HARRIS, GEORGETTE NINA
HARRIS, HARLENE DEBRA
*HARRIS, HAROLD LANE
HARRIS, ILA
*HARRIS, MAX LAWRENCE
HARRIS, PHILIP SHERIDAN
HARRIS, RICHARD JOSEPH
HARRIS, RICHARD JOSEPH
HARRIS, ROBIN GAY
HARRIS, STEVE
HARRIS, TIMOTHY MICHAEL
HARRIS, TONY RAY
HARRIS, YOLANDA
HARRISON, CONNIE JEAN
HARRISON, DANIEL JEROME
HARRISON, EDWARD ALLEN
*HARRISON, HAROLD HENRY
*HARRISON, KRISTINE ORCUTT
HARRISON, TODD FREDERICK
HARSHFIELD, JANETTE DENE
HARSHMAN, HELEN HEY
HART, LINDA LABUDA
HART, ROBERT MCDOWELL
HARTER, SCOTT ALLISON
HARTFORD, KATHLEEN MARY
HARTH, DONALD EDWARD
HARTLEY, PAMELA JEAN
HARTMAN, ALAN FRANK
HARTMAN, ANN ELIZABETH
*HARTMAN, DEBORAH LYNN
HARTMAN, HAROLD BEERS, II
HARTMAN, MICHAEL J.
*HARTMANN, KENNETH ORVEL
*HARTMANN, PAULA KAREN
HARTSHORN, MARTHA ANNE
*HARVEY, LYNN
HARVEY, MARIAN MOORE
*HARVEY, SCOTT MINER
*HASBACH, KATHLEEN ELLEN
HASENYAGER, JAMES RICHARD
HASKINS, CHARLES GREGORY, JR.
HASTINGS, CHARLES NICHOLAS
HATFIELD, MARY LESLIE

HATHAWAY, CHARLA BERYL
HATHAWAY, MARGARET VANDERVEER
*HATHAWAY, WILLIAM LUTHER
HAUFF, DOROTHY MAE
HAUG, DEBORAH MARIE
HAUGHEY, IRENE KATHRYN
HAUPTLE, MARY ELIZABETH
*HAUSMAN, BARBARA JO
*HAVILL, JUANITA RUTH
HAVRANEK, ROSEMARY
HAWKER, GREGORY ALAN
HAWKINS, WILLIAM ROBERT
*HAWN, JEANINE HAMACHER
HAWTREE, JAMES STEVEN
HAYASHI, NANCY MASUMI
HAYASHI, TOSHIO
HAYES, DAVID MICHAEL
HAYES, GWENDOLYN ANN
HAYES, JOHN CHARLES, JR.
HAYES, KATHLEEN ELIZABETH
HAYES, LYDIA BELLE
HAYN, DON PORTOR
*HAYNES, ROBERT PAUL
*HAYS, PHILIP GRANVILLE
HAYSE, KAREN MARIE
HAYWARD, LESLIE BARBARA
HEADY, GEORGE BRISCOE
HEALY, RICHARD WILLIAM
HEALY, THOMAS EUGENE
HEARD, BARBARA JO
HEBEISEN, CHERYL DAWN
HEBERER, DWIGHT HERBERT
HEBRANK, WILLIAM ROBERT
HEBRON, WILLIAM STEPHEN
HECKER, JAMES MILLARD
HECTOR, RICHARD EDWARD
HEDBERG, BARBARA LYNN
HEDBERG, SUSAN JEAN
*HEDGES, JOAN C.
HEDRICH, NORMAN
HEDSTROM, MARY LOU
HEFFLEY, EARLE FRANKLIN, III
HEGG, ARLENE PATRICIA
HEHNER, JANICE JEAN
HEIDECKER, JOAN MARIE
HEIDELBERG, JAMES EDWIN
HEIDEMAN, JACQUELYN SUE
*HEIL, NANCY JO
HEIM, SANDRA LEA
HEIMBACH, CYNTHIA JOAN
HEIMBURGER, RUTH ELAINE
*HEIMLICH, ESTHER
HEINRICH, THOMAS H.
*HEINSEN, LINDSAY WITT
HEINZ, BARBARA KATHRYN
*HEINZ, KENNETH JOHN
HEISE, RAYMOND LEE
*HEISS, HOWARD EDWARD
*HEISTERMAN, JANE MARIE
HEITSCH, BARBARA ANN
*HEITSCH, JANET MARIE
HEITZ, HENRY KEVIN
HEITZMAN, MARY KATHERINE
HELLER, DAVID M.
*HELLER, HARLAN KENT

81

\*HELLMAN, ALAN LEE
HELLMAN, HOWARD MARVIN
HELM, STEVEN PAUL
HELMS, DEBORAH LYNN
\*HELMS, MARILYN HRUSKA
HELSPER, NORMA JANE
HEMPEN, CAROLYN JOAN
\*HENDEE, RANDAL JAMES
HENDERSON, BURRELL EUGENE
HENDERSON, GARY STARK
\*HENDERSON, HARRY GEORGE
HENDERSON, MARK NELSON
HENDERSON, MERRILL DOUGLASS
\*HENDERSON, RICHARD CLARK
HENDERSON, WILLIAM RICHARD
HENDRICKS, WENDY CARLETTE
HENDRICKSEN, CAROL ELIZABETH
HENDRIX, MERLE GENE
\*HENDRIX, PATRICIA ANN
HENINGER, STEPHEN DON
HENKIN, AVIS ILENE
HENNEGAN, MARGARET ANN
HENNENFENT, DONNA JEAN
HENRICKS, JOHN DAVID
HENSCHEN, SHARON MARIE
HENSLEY, DANNY GENE
HENSLEY, JOHN BROOKS
\*HENSLEY, MARILYN JOANNE
HENSOLD, JACK OLIVER
\*HERBERT, PATRICIA IRENE
\*HERBSTER, BARBARA ANN
\*HERBSTMAN, BRYNA GAIL
HERBSTMAN, BURTON LEE
HERDRICH, KATHRYN ANN
\*HERGET, ROBERT THOMAS
\*HERM, JOHN WHITTON
\*HERMAN, HOLLY LYNN
HERMAN, MICHAEL JOHN
\*HERMAN, PAUL RODNEY
HERMAN, ROBERT DONALD
\*HERNANDEZ, DONALD JAMES
HERRICK, ELIZABETH ANN
HERRSTROM, GAIL ADELE
HERRSTROM, SYLVIA JEAN
HERSCHBACH, MARY PITTAS
\*HERSH, ADRIENNE JOY
\*HERSON, ALBERT IRWIN
HERTEL, PAMELA ANNE
HERZOG, MARTHA LYNN
HERZOG, WENDY ANN
\*HESLER, SUSAN DIANA
HESS, EDWARD FREDERICK, III
HESS, PAMELA ANN
HESSELL, CHARLES BARRY
HETT, DAVID SCOTT
HEWITT, ELIZABETH ANN
HEWITT, JAYE PATRICIA
HEWITT, WILLIAM GENE, JR.
HEWKIN, GREGORY CHARLES
HEYER, CONSTANCE JOAN
HEYMAN, PATRICIA ANN
HICKEN, MARY SCHMIDT
HICKMAN, ANDREW DISNEY
HICKMAN, PAUL ADDISON
HICKMAN, SUSAN KAY

HICKOK, JUDY ANN
HICKS, DEBORAH LOUISE
HIERONYMUS, CATHERINE
HIGDON, MATTHEW L.
HIGGINS, SUZANNE
HIGHSMITH, CHERYL EILEEN
HIGHT, DOUGLAS SCOTT
HIGHTMAN, PHILIP CARL
\*HILDEBRAND, ANNE MARION
\*HILDEBRAND, BARBARA JEAN
\*HILEMAN, KATHLEEN ANN
HILL, CLOYDIA FAYE
HILL, JOHN CHARLES
HILL, MARCIA SUE
HILL, MARTIN ELLSWORTH
\*HILL, NANCY JEAN
HILL, RONALD STEWART
HILL, YOSHIKO
HILLAN, JUDITH LYNN
\*HILLMAN, CAROL LYNN
HILLS, LARRY JAMES
HILTON, RICHARD STENCE
HIMEL, LORRAYNE VICTORIA
HIMLEY, MARGARET HUENGMANN
HIMSTEDT, SHARON ALBERTA
HINDMAN, JOHN ROBERT
HINDS, NANCY LEE
HINKLE, RONALD LELAND
HINMAN, MARCIA ANN
HINO, ELSBETH
HINRICHSEN, JAMES JOEL
HINSHAW, PAUL ONEIL
\*HINSON, VICKI LYNN
HINTHORN, JAMES LESLIE
HINUEBER, JEFFREY GEORGE
\*HIRCHERT, KURT WALTER
\*HIRSCH, KAREN IRENE
HIRSCH, RONNIE JAY
HIRSCHTICK, ROBERT EDWARD
HIRYAK, PEGGY LOUISE
\*HISER, MARK WARREN
HISER, MARTHA LOUISE
HITCHCOCK, MARY ELLEN
HITCHENS, SHARON RAE
HITCHINS, RANDA SUE
HITTLE, RICHARD MERLE
HIXSON, JENNIFER QUEDNAU
\*HIXSON, MARY ALICE
\*HLADY, GARY WALTER
\*HLAVACEK, MARGARET HELEN
\*HO, ELLEN YUAN-CHU
\*HOAG, MARGARET MARY
\*HOBFOLL, STEVAN EARL
HOCENIC, DENISE JOANNE
HOCK, DIANE LUCILLE
HODES, GAIL DARA
HODGETT, CANDACE MARIE
\*HOEFLER, KATHLEEN THERESE
HOEGL, EUNICE ADRIAN
HOELTZNER, LINDA MARY
\*HOESTEREY, BARBARA LOUISE
HOFFING, ANN JUDITH
HOFFMAN, ALAN DALE
\*HOFFMAN, ALAN WAYNE
HOFFMAN, ALLEN EDWARD

82

HOFFMAN, ARLENE JOYCE
HOFFMAN, CHARLES WILLIAM
HOFFMAN, DENNIS
HOFFMAN, DONALD LEE
HOFFMAN, JAMES EDWARD
*HOFFMAN, PATRICIA ANN
*HOFFMAN, PATRICIA ELEANOR
HOFFMAN, ROBERT JAY
HOFFMAN, ROBERT STEVEN
HOFFMANN, CANDACE KAY
*HOFMANN, ROBERT THOMAS
HOFSTRA, ROBERT J.
*HOGAN, LINDA EVELYN
HOGREWE, BONNIE SUE
*HOHENSTEIN, JAMES HOWARD
HOHULIN, CONNIE TESSIER
*HOHULIN, KEITH RICHARD
HOKE, DALE WILLIAM
*HOKE, FRANCIS ELLET
HOLADAY, BRUCE LEES
HOLCOMB, RUTH ALICE
*HOLEMAN, TIMOTHY ALAN
HOLLE, LOIS MILDRED
HOLLE, PAMELA DALE
HOLLENBERG, CHERI LYNNE
*HOLLEYMAN, KIRK BRADFORD
HOLLINGER, LINDA ANN
HOLM, LINDA MARIE
*HOLM, MICHAEL JAMES
HOLMAN, WILLIAM KARL
*HOLMBERG, CHARLES VICTOR
*HOLMEN, PHYLLIS JANE
HOLMGREN, MARY LYNN
HOLMQUIST, ANTONE GAYLORD
HOLMSTROM, CAROL JEAN
HOLMSTROM, JOHN THEODORE
HOLT, JEAN ALICE
*HOLT, ROBERT WALLACE
*HOLT, WILLIAM MARTIN
*HOLTZBLATT, LESTER JOSEPH
HOLTZMAN, ROBERTA SUE
HOLUB, GEORGE LEE
HOLUB, LOUIS ALLEN
HOLUM, IVAN WILLY
HOLZMAN, NANCY SUE
HOMAN, DAN CHARLES
HOMER, JEFFREY B.
HOMICZ, DIANE MARIE
HOMMEL, CHARLES THOMAS
HONIGBERG, MICHELE CARYN
HOOKER, JOSEPH EDWARD
HOOPER, MARGARET ANN
HOOVER, ELLAN JEAN
HOPKINS, WILLIAM PAUL
HOPPE, MARK WILLIAM
*HORBERG, LAWRENCE KENNETH
HORLER, NORMAN VICTOR
HORN, LORRAINE KAY
HORNBUCKLE, SHARON LEE
HORNE, DOYLE JACKSON
*HORNER, RICHARD ALLEN
*HORNKOHL, RHODA GWEN
*HOROWITZ, JORDAN JAY
*HORTON, JENNIFER KAY
HORVATH, CARY ALEXANDER

HORVATH, JAMES LEE
*HORWITZ, MARSHA
HORWITZ, SHELLEY MARLA
HOSKIN, JOHN HIRAM
HOSKINS, TERESA LEIGH
HOSTERT, JOHN DAVID
HOSTETTER, BETH ANN
HOTT, MARTHA JANE
HOUFEK, CAROLYN FAYE
*HOUGEN, CARLENE DORAN
HOUGHTON, JO ANN MCKOWN
HOULDSWORTH, PATRICIA LYNN
HOUSE, DEBORAH MARY
*HOUSTON, DENNIS MICHAEL
*HOUSTON, ELISABETH GALLEY
HOUSTON, GREGORY KEVIN
HOUSTON, ROGER LEE
HOUTZEL, RAYMOND WILLIAM
*HOVEY, MICHAEL CURTISS
*HOWARD, CRAIG PHILLIP
HOWARD, JEANNE ANN
HOWARD, JOSEPH OMAR
HOWARD, STACEY ANN
HOWE, PEGGY ANN
HOWE, RICHARD HERBERT
HOWELL, WILLIAM CHARLES
HOWSER, RICHARD GLEN
HOYERMAN, JANICE SUE
HOYNE, CAROLYN MARIE
HREHA, KATHLEEN MARY
*HUBBARD, JENNIFER VALENCIA
HUBER, ANNA CHRISTINE
HUBER, NANCY BRIGGS
HUCK, ROBERT LEO
*HUCKO, JOSEPHINE THERESA
*HUDDLESTON, RODNEY KURT
HUDSON, CAROLINE
HUDSON, ELIZABETH FARR
*HUDSON, TIGHE FRANCIS
*HUDSON, VALORIE ANN
HUEBNER, DENNIS LAVERNE
*HUENEMANN, KAREN ELIZABETH
*HUFF, MARTHA ELIZABETH
HUFF, STEPHEN MEEKINS
*HUFFMAN, PATRICIA JAN
*HUGHES, CAROL ANN
*HUGHES, CAROL JANE
HUGHES, PATRICIA ANNE
HUGHEY, SUSAN ELIZABETH
HUGUELET, JEFFREY CHARLES
HUIZENGA, LINDA RUTH
HULL, CAMILLA SUE
*HULSEBERG, JUDITH LYNN
HULSEY, LESLIE LYNN
HULT, KEITH CARLTON
HUME, RHONDA GAYLE
*HUMPHREVILLE, ANNE ELIZABETH
HUMPHREVILLE, MARILYN
HUNGER, LIANE JEAN
HUNSINGER, PENNY PARKER
HUNT, GREGORY PAUL
HUNT, IVA JEAN
HUNT, KENNETH FRANKLIN
HUNT, STEPHEN RICHARD
HUNTER, JAMES EUGENE

83

HUNTER, JOY DEE
HUNTER, MARK RAYMOND
HUNTER, SUZANN FAYE
HURSCH, JULIE ANNA
HURSEY, RALPH MICHAEL
HURST, JIMMY RAY
HURST, KAREN LYNETTE
HURT, CONSTANCE MARIE
HUSMANN, CHRISTIE ELIZABETH
HUSS, JULIE ADAIR
HUTCHINSON, LELAND WILLIAM, JR.
HUTCHISON, SHELDON BUTT
*HUTSON, MILES AUSTIN
HUTTON, CATHY LEE
HUTTON, DONALD WAYNE, II
HYDE, WILLIAM PARSON
*HYKAN, ROBERT ALAN
*HYMAN, DAVID BRUCE
*HYMEL, SHELLEY CLAIRE
HYMEN, ROGER JOHN
*IANNI, MARY ELAINE
ICHEN, LILA
IGNASIAK, KATHLEEN ALICE
IHRIG, LLOYD ROBERT
IKLER, JEFFREY MELVIN
ILLING, SUSAN MARY
IMBERT, EARL ARTHUR
*INCAPRERO, JOSEPH FRANK
INGALLS, CAROLYN
*INGRASSIA, LAWRENCE ANDREW
INGRASSIA, SUSAN MAKULEC
INGWER, MARSHA JUDITH
INLANDER, DAVID WILLIAM
INMAN, MARGARET ANN
*INMAN, STEPHEN JOHN
INSKEEP, SUSAN LOOMIS
*IRION, SUSAN ELIZABETH
IRWIN, DEBORAH ANN
ISAACS, SUSAN CAROLE
ISAACSON, IRA JAY
ISAAK, EUGENE DENNIS
*ISBELL, SUSAN MARY
ISENBURG, LARRY DALE
ISENHART, ROSEMARY SWARTZ
ISHAM, MARK FREDERIC
ISSAK, BARBARA ELLEN
ITKIN, NANCY ANNETTE
IVERSON, DENNIS WAYNE
IWAMOTO, KRISTINE H.
IZENMAN, MICKEY
JABLONSKY, LINDA SUSAN
JABLONSKY, MARY LOUISE
JACHIMEK, LINDA JULIA
JACK, MARILEE PATRICIA
JACKANICZ, DONALD WAYNE
JACKLIN, JUDITH VICTORIA
*JACKSON, ANN LOUISE
JACKSON, ARETHA
*JACKSON, BARBARA ELLEN
JACKSON, DOUGLAS ARTHUR
*JACKSON, GREGORY WAYNE
JACKSON, JUANITA MARLENE
JACKSON, MARY PATRICIA
*JACKSON, RICHARD ADRIAN
JACKSON, SALLY ANN

JACKSON, THOMAS VICTOR
JACOB, HELENE BONNIE
*JACOBI, NEAL HENRY
JACOBS, ALISON
JACOBS, DONALD MOOR
*JACOBS, ELLEN
*JACOBS, FRED LAWRENCE
JACOBS, JEAN BRELOS
*JACOBSEN, CARL LAWRENCE
JACOBSEN, JOHN KURT
*JACOBSON, JOANNE
JACOBSON, LORETTA JEAN
*JACOBSON, MARION DANIELA
*JACOBSON, SHELLEY ANNE
JACOBSON, WAYNE STEVEN
JACOT, DONALD RICHARD
JACQUES, VIRGUS DENNIS
JAFFE, AUSTIN JAY
JAMES, HARDIN THOMAS, JR.
JAMES, JENNIFER ALMA
*JAMIESON, MICHAEL WARREN
JAMRISKO, STEVEN FRANCIS
JANES, DAVID DEAN
*JANES, ELIZABETH ANN
JANES, JOHN RAYMOND, JR.
JANICKI, ANTHONY JAMES
JANKAUSKIS, LINDA JEAN
*JANNOTTA, DANIEL JOSEPH
*JANOSIK, RICHARD BARRY
JANOTA, ROBERT RAYMOND
JANOWSKI, JEAN MARIE
JANSSEN, SHARON ELAINE
JANUZIK, GALE ANN
JARBOE, JACQUELYN CLARE
JARCHOW, KATHLEEN ANN
*JARMAN, PRISCILLA SUE
JAROSCH, LYNELL PLAS
JAROSZ, SHARON HELEN
*JARRELL, RONALD GENE
JARVIS, THOMAS LEE
JASINSKI, CAROL ANNE
JASINSKI, CLEMENTINE HELENE
JASMICK, ADAM WILBUR
JASPER, JERRY GEORGE
*JAUHOLA, CHRISTINE ANN
JAVUREK, CLAYTON GEORGE
JAVUREK, JEFFREY JAY
*JAWOREK, MICHAEL ANDREW
JAYNE, LINDA LEE
JECKEL, LAWRENCE LEE
JEFFERSON, MARK ALAN
JEFFREY, JEANNE MILDRED
JEFFREY, TERRY DAVID
*JENIK, ROBERT A.
*JENKINS, RHONDA SUE
*JENNE, ROBERT CHARLES
JENNER, CAROL BETH
*JENNINGS, ELIZABETH ANNE
JENO, MARYELLEN
JENSEN, CLARK DAVID
JENSEN, JULIE ANNE
*JENSEN, KIRK BRADLEY
JENSEN, ROBERT ALAN
JEPSEN, PHILLIP RICHMOND
JERRELL, THOMAS AHRENS, JR.

84

Jeske, Kenneth Lloyd
Jeske, Richard Thomas
*Jeske, Susan Ellen
*Jespersen, Carol Anne
Jetton, Merlin Ford
*Jezek, Kenneth Charles
*Jezik, Marie Lilette
Jezik, Vera Sairlette
Jilek, Anita Gail
*Joergens, Renee Sue
Johns, Stephanie Ann
Johnson, Adele Marie
*Johnson, Allan Hale
Johnson, Belinda Anne
Johnson, Bruce Roy
Johnson, Candice Anne
*Johnson, Christine Ann
*Johnson, Christine Mary
*Johnson, Cynthia Kay
Johnson, David Bert
Johnson, David Ray
Johnson, Diane Holly
Johnson, Donald Ray
Johnson, Donn Edward
*Johnson, Donna Lee
Johnson, Douglas Haynes
Johnson, Ellen Carol .
*Johnson, Ellen Linnea
*Johnson, Gloria Jean
Johnson, Gregory Richard
Johnson, Izona
Johnson, James Allen
*Johnson, Janet Catherine
Johnson, Janis Aileen
Johnson, Jay Dean
Johnson, Jeffrey Kendall
Johnson, Jerolene Jeffrey
Johnson, John David
Johnson, Karen Diane
Johnson, Karen Ellen
Johnson, Kathleen Jean
Johnson, Kathleen Nell
Johnson, Kenneth Alvin
*Johnson, Lawrence Lynn
*Johnson, Leslie Susan
Johnson, Louise Marie
Johnson, Lucinda Nelson
*Johnson, Lynn Ann
Johnson, Marilyn Lea
Johnson, Marjean Kay
Johnson, Mary Kirby
Johnson, Pamela Clarice
Johnson, Patricia Ann
Johnson, Patricia Ann
Johnson, Rebecca Lynn
Johnson, Robert Clarence
Johnson, Stephen Craig
Johnson, Steven Ralph
*Johnson, Susan A.
Johnson, Terry Duane
Johnson, Vicki A.
Johnson, Warren Dale
Johnston, David Alexander
Johnston, Richard Kyle
*Johnston, Sarah Louise

Johnston, Steven Craig
*Jollie, Malcolm Richard
Jonas, Joanne
Jones, Barbara Ann
Jones, Barbara Gaye
Jones, Brian John
Jones, Dean Paul
*Jones, Debora Sue
Jones, Lee Allen
Jones, Lela Claire
Jones, Marilyn Edith
Jones, Marion Herrietta
Jones, Mary Susan
Jones, McKinley Alfred
*Jones, Patricia Ann
Jones, Paula Jean
Jones, Portia Rita
*Jones, Richard Michael
Jones, Ronald Scott
Jones, Wendy D.
Joos, Maralee Anne
Jordan, Ann Downen
Jordan, Eugene Noel
Jordan, Judith Ann
Jordan, Sharon Ann
Jordan, Vida
*Jorgensen, Sharon Susan
Joseph, Gary Mark
Joseph, Raymond Alphonso
*Josephson, Donna Lynn
Jost, Robert Charles
Joyce, Christopher Patrick
Judd, John Howard
Judd, Laurie Maureen
Judson, Douglas Austin
*Judy, Conna Elizabeth
*Juell, Merry Kendricks
*Junck, Larry Richard
*Junkus, Joan Cleopha
Juola, John Phillip
*Juraska, Kathleen M.
Jurgens, Carl Edward
Jurgens, Larry Charles
Jursinic, Susan Berger
Jury, Carolyn
*Just, Lawrence Edward
Kaegi, Charles Edward, Jr.
Kaelin, Thomas Mark
Kahn, Adrianne Bette
Kahn, Deborah Jean
Kahn, Helen Sue
Kahn, Marcy Helene
Kahn, Marla Rae
Kahn, Susan Marcia
*Kahn, Wendy H.
*Kahr, Helga
Kaim, Alan Michael
Kaiser, Jeffery Dean
Kaiser, Madeleine Marie
Kakita, Harriet Eiko
Kalachnik, Mark Joseph
*Kalin, Daniel Howard
Kalin, Gene Stuart
Kalinak, Kathryn Marie
Kalish, David Ray

85

*Kalish, Mark A.
Kalish, Steve Brian
Kalivoda, Kathryn Ann
Kalivoda, Paula Jean
Kalnitz, Joanne Harriet
Kamenear, Charleyne
Kamenear, Linda Robyn
Kaminen, Carol Jean
*Kaminski, James Stanley
*Kaminski, Thomas Michael
Kamm, Cheryl Lee
Kamm, Marlene Sue
*Kammenzind, Richard Henry
Kammlade, Marilyn Elizabeth
Kamowski, Richard Michael
*Kampf, Elizabeth
*Kamrava, Masoud
Kane, Dennis Joseph
*Kant, Carol Rochelle
*Kant, Renee Judith
*Kanter, Charlene Ruth
Kanter, Janice
Kanter, Joanne
Kanter, Richard Joel
Kantor, Merry Blake
Kantor, Susan Marie
Kaplan, Blair Hale
Kaplan, Bruce Lewis
*Kaplan, Daryl
Kaplan, Debra Helene
Kaplan, Henrietta Reva
Kaplan, Maeta
Kaplan, Philip Alan
Kaplan, Sharon Faye
*Kapp, Jeffrey Allen
Kappes, Jorja Neupert
Kapros, Laura Elizabeth
*Karabin, Marybeth
Karczewski, Leonard Peter
Kareken, John Alexander
Karel, John Allen
*Karela, James Francis
*Karesh, John Winkler
Karkos, Jerie Beth
*Karl, Linda Ann
Karl, Pamela Sue
*Karlen, Douglas Melvin
*Karlinsky, Lana Rebecca
Karnes, Diane Susan
Karnett, Vinetta Jean
Karon, Minda Sue
*Karps, Paul David
Karras, Maureen Georgia
Kartun, Allan David
*Kasab, Farida
Kasak, Mary Ellen
Kasanov, Joel Steven
Kash, Gary G.
Kason, Bonnie Ann
Kasper, Ellen Jane
Kasper, Lloyd Howard
Kasprzycki, Elizabeth M.
Kassanits, Frank James
Kassly, Carol Susan

Kastigar, Linda Jean
*Katerndahl, David Arthur
Kato, Joanne Masaye
Katz, Irene Tobe
Katz, Ivy Rae
*Katz, Lee David
Katz, Robert Sanford
Katz, Susan Ava
Kauffman, Sandra Ellen
*Kaufman, Alan Scott
Kaufman, Bruce David
*Kaufman, Dale M.
*Kaufman, David Joseph
Kaufman, James Allen
Kautz, Susan Jane
Kavanaugh, Margaret Mary
Kavitt, Barbara Joy
*Kawamura, Charlene Katsuko
Kay, Michael Richard
Kay, Robert Knox
Kazama, Rodney Mitsuo
Kazmercak, Susan Margaret
Kazuk, Kathleen
Kazuk, Susan
*Kearley, Timothy George
*Kearney, James Allen
*Kearns, Lisa Therese
Keating, Genevieve Warble
Keca, Daniel Joseph, Jr.
Keehn, Susan Jane
Keevil, Charles Henry
*Kefer, John Arthur
Kehoe, Danea M.
Kehr, Debera Juanita
Kehrberg, Christine Lynn
*Keil, Edward Byron
Keisler, Gail Mae
*Kelikian, Alice Arshalooys
Kelikian, Armen Sirigan
*Keller, Gema Ellen
Keller, James Ray
Keller, Patricia Ann
*Keller, Susan Louise
*Kelley, Karen Raye
Kelley, Lynda Lorraine
Kelley, Michael Stephen
Kellner, Barbara Elise
Kelly, Brighid Anne
Kelly, Mary Ellen
Kelly, Michael Burch
Kelly, Patricia Lynn
Kelly, Richard Edward
Kelly, Sally Beaurling
Kelly, Susan Margaret
Kelly, William Dunham, Jr.
Kelm, Beverly Ann
Kelm, Stephen Edward
Kelsey, Christine Gioia
*Kemp, Allen Phillip
Kemp, Nancy Marie
Kendall, Donna Jean
Kendall, Wendy Loy
*Kendrick, Laura Jean
Kenis, Linda Joy

86

KENNARD, DONALD RAY
KENNARD, RUTH IRENE
KENNEDY, BRENDA TOOLEY
*KENNEDY, LORA MAUREEN
KENNEDY, LUKE J.
KENNEDY, PATRICIA ANN
*KENNEDY, THOMAS JOHN
KENNEL, BRIAN CHARLES
KENNER, LARRY ALAN
*KENNY, DIANE MARIE
*KEOGH, RITA LAPPIN
KEOGH, ROBERT ALLEN
*KEPES, KATHRYN LUCILE
*KEPFORD, KIRBY BERNARD
KEPLEY, VANCE IVAN, JR.
KERASOTES, DEAN LOUIS
KERBER, JOAN THOMPSON
KERCHNER, GEORGE JOHN
KERKOVE, BARBARA ANN
KERNER, DORA
KERO, MARIANNE
KEROFF, FREDERICK MICHAEL
*KERR, STANLEY PAUL
KERRICK, SANDRA SUE
KERSHNER, ADENA CLAIRE
*KESLER, JAMES LESTER
*KESLER, LINDA SUE
KESLER, PHILIP ROY
KESSLER, ALAN TODD
*KESSLER, HAROLD ALLAN
KETTWICH, DONALD LEE
*KEWLEY, WAYNE KENNETH
KEYES, CHARLES DAYTON
KEYSOR, RIC EDGAR
KHESHGI, ZAREENA B.
KIBERT, RONALD EDWARD
*KIBIKAS, WILLIAM ALAN
*KIBURZ, ARNOLD JOHN, III
KIDD, JEANNE MARGARET
KIEBACK, LOIS E.
KIELHORN, JANET SUE
KIELIAN, GERALD GEORGE
KIELTYKA, DAVID EUGENE
KIERIG, PAUL NICHOLAS
KIERNAN, SUSAN GAEL
KIES, KARLA KLARE
KILEY, JAN
*KIMBERLEY, WANDA JEAN
KIME, DONNA LOUISE
*KIMMEL, THOMAS ALLEN
KINCAID, MAUREEN ANN
*KINCZEWSKI, KATHY ANN
*KING, ARTHUR RAYMOND
KING, BARBARA ELLEN
KING, BARBARA LYNNE
KING, LINDA LOUISE
KING, MARGARET FRANCES
*KING, MARK REID
KING, MICHAEL RICHARD
*KING, ROBIN GAYLE
*KING, WILLIAM ARTHUR
KING, WILLIAM PATRICK, JR.
KINGSLEY, RONALD LEON
KINSINGER, DAVID WAYNE

KINZER, LAURA JOAN
KIPNIS, EDITH
KIPNIS, ELLEN HOLLIS
KIPPER, MARY ANN
KIRBY, JOHN RODNEY
KIRBY, KATHLEEN MARIE
KIRCHHERR, JAMES KENNETH
*KIRCHHOFER, MARK LYNN
KIRCHHOFF, CYNTHIA JOYCE
KIRILUK, HAROLD JAMES
KIRK, PAMELA ANN
KIRK, SUSAN PAMELA
KIRKCONNELL, KRISTIN JANET
KIRKENDALL, CHRISTOPHER INGLE
KIRKPATRICK, BRUCE LEONARD
*KIRKPATRICK, KEN FLOYD
KIRKPATRICK, PATRICIA LEE
KIRKWOOD, JUDITH ANN
*KIRSCHTEN, BARBARA LOUISE
KIRSTEIN, JULIA ELLEN
KISILL, CAROL JEANNETTE
*KISTLER, JOAN LOEL
*KITE, STEVEN B.
KJELL, BRADLEY PRYOR
KLAGES, PETER HENRY
*KLAUKE, SALLY ANN
KLEIDON, CAROL ANN
KLEIN, BEVERLEY JANIS
KLEIN, BONNIE GALE
KLEIN, LARRY BEN
KLEIN, LYNN ELLEN
KLEIN, MARGARET ANN
KLEIN, MARTIN EDWARD
*KLEIN, NEAL ALAN
KLEIN, PAULA ANN
*KLEIN, ROSEMARY
KLEKAMP, DAVID HARLEN
KLEMPNER, MARTIN JAY
*KLEMT, LAURA LIEBERMAN
*KLESH, JOHN ROBERT
KLETT, JEFFREY HARRY
*KLETT, KRISTI LYNN
KLICK, JUDY ANN
KLIER, GENE ANN FRANCES
KLIMO, PAMELA LOUISE
KLINE, JAMES WILLIAM
KLINGER, GARY DEAN
KLINGLER, ROBERT JOHN
KLIPOWICZ, STEVEN WAYNE
KLIPPERT, LINDA SUSAN
KLITCHMAN, RICHARD GREGORY
*KLOBUCHAR, RICHARD LOUIS
*KLOTTER, KEVIN ALBERT
KLOWDEN, JOYCE ANN
KLYNSTRA, MELINDA LOU
KMETZ, ANNE MARIE
KMIEC, DENNIS CHARLES
KNAAK, BEVERLY JEAN
*KNAPP, THOMAS JOSEPH
KNAUER, CHARLINDA
*KNECHT, ROBERT NEAL
KNECHT, RONALD LEE
*KNELL, CHARLES DENNE
KNETSCH, TANA SUE

KNIEPKAMP, MARY MARGARET
KNIERING, JOHN HOVELL
*KNIGHT, CHARLES DANIEL
KNIGHT, MARK VENARD
KNIGHT, PAMELA JAMES
KNIRSCH, JAMES ROBERT
KNISKERN, DAVID PAUL
KNISS, RONALD EUGENE
KNODLE, BEVERLY ANN
KNOKE, GARY ALAN
KNOPF, REBEKAH CAROLINE
KNUDSON, DENNIS LEROY
KNUE, GEORGE MICHAEL
*KNUTSON, DIANA MARLESE
KOBLER, MARY ALICE
KOBOSKY, JUDY KAY
KOBRITZ, LAUREN SUSAN
KOBUSSEN, ANTHONY JOHN
KOBYLECKY, JOHN GEORGE
KOBYLECKY, JUDITH KATERINE
*KOGAL, LOUISE MARIE
KOCH, LEON WILLIAM
KOCH, MICHAEL SILAS
KOE, FRANK, JR.
KOE, KWOCK KOONG
KOEHL, JACQUELINE SUE
KOENIG, MARILYN GAIL
KOEPKE, LINDA CHWIERUT
*KOEPPEN, BRUCE MICHAEL
KOERMENDY, ADRIENNE
KOERNER, JOHN EDNAR
*KOERNER, KAREN SUE
*KOESTER, CONNIE KAY
*KOESTERER, MARY PATRICIA
*KOHL, KATHLEEN HARRIET
*KOIDIN, ELLEN SUE
*KOLB, GEOFFREY KEITH
KOLBUK, MICHAEL TED
KOLENS, SUSAN MARY
KOLESAR, MARCY ANN
*KOLL, STEVEN ALLAN
KOLMAN, MARGARET MARY
KOLTER, MARSHA LYNNE
KOLTSE, GEORGE
*KOLTUN, PHILIP LOUIS
KOMORN, MARGO
KONDA, JEAN MARY
*KONOPKA, ALLAN EUGENE
KONRAD, PATRICIA FRANCES
KONRATH, DONALD JOSEPH
KOOB, DENISE
KOOLISH, MEGAN IRENE
*KOONCE, WAYNE ALLAN
KOPEC, ANDREW MICHAEL
KOPERA, ANNE THERESE
KOPISCH, JAMES ARTHUR
KOPP, JANICE ANN
KOPP, JEAN CAROL
*KOPP, MARLENE ELAINE
*KOPPLIN, JUDITH ANN
KORB, ANNE DOUGLAS
KORBA, ROSEMARY
KORDICK, JEAN LOUISE
*KOREN, NANCY MARIE
KORENBLIT, ALLEN DAVID

*KORENGOLD, HELEN LEAH
*KOREY, MICHAEL STEVEN
KORKOWSKI, SARAH HANEY
KORN, CHERI MERLE
*KORNBLATT, IRA BENNETT
*KORNBLITH, SANDER JAY
KORNBLUM, BARBARA LEE
KORS, BRIAN ALAN
*KORSHAK, SHELLEY JOYCE
KORTE, NIC EUGENE
KORZEC, KATHLEEN FRANCINE
KOSOVSKI, ROBIN
*KOSS, LOIS GEORGIA
KOSTAL, JERI LEE
KOSTEL, PAUL JOHN
*KOSTER, ELAINE MASSOCK
KOSTER, JUDY
*KOTEK, JOSEPH JOHN
*KOTIN, ANTHONY M.
KOTTEMANN, BRUCE CHARLES
*KOVAL, JOAN BEVERLY
KOVAR, PETER SCOTT
KOWALCZYK, JAMES JOSEPH
KOWALKE, PAULA L.
KOWALSKI, BRIAN
KOWALSKI, ELAINE MARIE
KOZELKA, ROBERT STEPHEN
KOZIK, THOMAS JOSEPH
*KOZIKOWSKI, CONSTANCE ANN
KOZLOFF, JOANNE GAIL
KOZLOW, KAREN H.
*KOZLOWSKI, BARBARA LUKJANOW
*KOZLOWSKI, BEATRICE A.
KRAFT, CLAIRE IRENE
*KRAFT, DIANA MARIE
*KRAKAUER, NEIL JORDAN
*KRAMER, BARBARA LYNN
*KRAMER, JEFFREY
*KRAMER, LESLIE ANN
KRAMER, ROBERT WALTER
KRAMER, RONALD JAMES
KRAMPER, BRUCE JOHN
KRASINSKI, KEITH MICHAEL
*KRASNOW, RENEE CAROL
KRAUSE, MARTIN FRANZ, JR.
KRAUSS, JOHN PAUL
KRAUSS, MARGARET L.
*KRAUSZ, NIKY LYNN
KRAUT, JEROME RICHARD
KRAVISH, JUDITH MAE
KRAVITZ, HOWARD MICHAEL
*KRAVITZ, MARILYN AVIS
KRAWCZYK, LYNN ANN
KREBS, KURT HENRY, JR.
KREITER, MARC STEVEN
KREPS, NANCY JO
*KRESCA, LINDA JEAN
*KRESL, JOANNE AMALIA
KRETT, KAREN MARY
KREUSCH, KAROLYN JEAN
KRICHEVSKY, LAURA ELLEN
KRIEBLE, KRISTINE SUZANNE
*KRIECHBAUM, JEANNE LYNN
KRIEGER, DIANE WILDERMUTH
KRIESHOK, THOMAS STEPHEN

KRIISA, THOMAS ENN
KRILE, CHARLES ADAM
*KRISCHER, JOEL ERNEST
KRIZ, DAVID G. C.
KROGSRUD, L. STEPHEN
KROHE, MARY CHARLENE
KROL, EDWARD MICHAEL
KROL, KATHLEEN ANN
KRON, NICHOLAS GERARD
*KRON, PRISCILLA LOUISE
KRUEGER, KEITH WILLIAM
KRUEGER, KURT ALLEN
KRUG, KAREN LEE
*KRUGER, CHRISTINE ANN
*KRUGER, KATHRYN DIANE
*KRUGER, SARAH LYNN
*KRUGGEL, KIM ELIZABETH
KRUGMAN, ARLENE IRIS
*KRUIDENIER, JAMES FRANCIS
KRUIDENIER, JOHN ROBERT
*KRULE, ELAINE ROCHELLE
KRULEWITCH, HARRY SCOTT
*KRUPKA, MILES ALBERT
KRUPP, KATHERINE JEAN
KUBCZAK, JAMES THOMAS
KUBECZKO, PATRICIA ANN
KUBIAK, RONALD RICHARD
KUCESKI, CHRISTINA
KUCHARCZYK, BARBARA ANN
KUCHEN, CATHERINE ANN
KUCHINSKY, MARCIA ANN
KUCZERPA, CAROLE ANN
KUDIRKA, A. GEORGE
KUEHLING, ROSE ELLEN
KUEHN, CLYDE LOUIS
KUEHN, JANET WHITE
KUEHN, LYNN
KUEPER, ELIZABETH JANE
KUHL, PHYLLIS JEAN
KUHLI, SARA EDITH
KUHLMAN, KAY ROEDER
KUHN, DONNA LYNN
KUHN, MARGARET ALISON
KUHN, MARSHA ANN
KUHN, MAUREEN ROSE
KUJAWINSKI, THOMAS AGUINAS
*KULCZEWSKI, ALAN JOSE
KULIKOWSKI, LINDA MARIE
KULTON, BARBARA ANN
KULWIN, MAURY HAROLD
KUMAKI, MARGARET ANN
KUMOREK, RAYMOND THOMAS
KUNDE, BRADFORD JAMES
KUNNEMANN, RHONDA LYNN
KUNTZ, PAULA MARIE
KUNTZ, RAYMOND CARL
*KUPEC, LYNN MARIE
KUPSKY, DOLORES HELEN
*KURLINKUS, DAVID JOSEPH
*KURTOCK, SARAH BETH
KURTZ, BRENDA HOPE
*KURTZ, DONALD LESTER
KURTZ, SHEILA LORRAINE
KURYLO, CATHERINE ANN
KURZ, DAVID WAYNE

KURZ, THERESE MARIE
KURZEJA, PAUL LOUIS
KUSHMUK, JAMES WALTER
KUSHNER, MARK STEPHEN
KUSHNER, SHARON JOYCE
KUTSCH, BONNIE MARIE
KUTZ, KATHRYN JEANICE
KUZIAN, SANDRA ADEN
KUZMINSKI, DAVID JOSE
KWASMAN, MARC GARY
*KWINN, PATRICIA ANNE
KWOH, JUO-WEI ROSIE
*LABOTKA, RICHARD JOHN
*LABOTKA, THEODORE CHARLES
LACHKY, JOSEPH NOEL
LACK, CHERYL SIMMONS
*LACKMAN, SARAH
*LADEVICH, LAUREL ANNE
*LADOLCE, DEBORAH LEE
LADOLCE, DENISE ANN
*LADOUCEUR, LYNN ELLEN
LADWIG, GAIL JEAN
LAFF, NED SCOTT
LAFFEY, CHARLOTTE MELBY
LAFLEUR, MARY SUE
*LAFORCE, NORMAN CHARLES
*LAFRANCO, ROSALIE ANN
LAGERQUIST, LINDA CAROL
*LAGNADO, DAGMAR MARIA
LAHEY, LINDA MARIE
LAIRD, SANDRA DEE
*LAJACK, LEXINE MAGDALENE
LAKE, RHONDA KAY
LALLA, DOUGLAS JOHN
*LAMARRE, ARTHUR GERALD
LAMB, CONSTANCE SUE
LAMB, EUGENIA ELIZABETH
LAMB, MICHELLE EVA
*LAMBERT, ERNESTINE LEA
LAMBERT, LINDA MARIE
LAMBOOY, MARY ANNE
LAMM, MARC STUART
LAMMERS, MARK RONALD
*LAMORTE, JOSEPHINE
LAMPO, JOSEPH
*LANCE, SANDRA EILEEN
LAND, PETER WILLIAM
LANDESMAN, TOBY ANN
LANDGRAF, MARSHA JEAN
*LANDWEHR, BARBARA DE WOLF
LANDY, CRAIG ALAN
LANE, CHARLES RAY
*LANE, PHILIP EDWARD
*LANG, JANET MARY
LANG, LOUIS ISADORE
LANGER, BARBARA ELLEN
LANGLOIS, DON PAUL
LANGMEAD, LAUREN LOUISE
LANNIN, SUSAN DENISE
LANSFORD, JAMES EDWARD
LANSING, SUEANNE
LANSPERY, GLORIA JEAN
LANTZ, DAVID ALAN
LANTZ, PATRICK EUGENE
LANUCHA, MARY LOU

89

LAPAT, MICHAEL JAMES
LAPIDOS, RALPH CARY
LAPOLLA, JAMES PETER
LAPP, KATHLEEN SUE
LAPP, SUSAN KAY
LARABEE, JUDITH MARIE
*LARCOMBE, ELSA M.
LAREY, BETH ANN
*LARIMER, MARK WILLIAM
LARISON, BRENDA IRENE
LARMORE, GERRY KENT
LAROCCO, JAMES ROY
LAROCQUE, BARBARA JEAN
LAROSE, ROGER WALTER
*LARSEN, TERESA ANNETTE
LARSON, CYNTHIA SUE
*LARSON, DEBORAH LYNN
LARSON, ELLEN
LARSON, JOHN LEONARD
LARSON, LINDA ANN
LARSON, MICHAEL JOSEPH
LARSON, PHYLLIS CHARLENE
LARSON, ROBERT MILTON
*LARSON, ROGER WILLIAM
LASKY, JOSEPH LOUIS
*LASSNER, MICHAEL WALTER
LATCH, MARK HARRINGTON
LATHROPE, ALICE ELIZABETH
*LATOS, LINDA ANN
LAUBE, CATHERINE SUE
LAUBSTED, PENELOPE
LAUCK, RITA JEANNINE
*LAUDE, JOHN WILLIAM
LAUDER, DAVID CHARLES
LAUFFENBURGER, SANDRA
LAUGHLIN, JAMES EVERETT
*LAUNSPACH, JEAN ANNE
LAVANDER, JEANNETTE MARIE
*LAVELLE, CHRISTINE
LAVELLE, JAMES ROBERT
LAVIGUEUR, MAITA GOLDSTEIN
LAVIOLETTE, MARY JOSEPHINE
*LAWICKI, JOY MARIE
LAWLER, CONNIE GOKEN
*LAWLER, DEL EDGAR
LAWLER, KEITH BRIAN
LAWLOR, LAWRENCE MARK
LAWLOR, MARY LEE
LAWRENCE, PATRICIA LOUISE
*LAWRENCE, PETER KENNETH
LAWS, MARVIN NEAL
LAWSON, JOAN
LAWTON, NANCY JANE
*LAWTON, ROBERT LAWRENCE
LAZ, BARBARA JEAN
LAZAR, PAMELA BETH
LAZARUS, JAY LAWRENCE
*LEAHY, CYNTHIA KAY
LEAHY, WILLIAM EDWARD
LEAVER, JANET KAY
*LEAVITT, ILONA SUE
LEAVITT, STEVEN WARREN
LEBLOND, DAVID JOSEPH
LECHOWICZ, PATRICIA ANN
LECOMTE, JOHN ROBERT

*LEDBETTER, ALAN RICHARD
LEDUC, JUDITH ANN
LEE, ALVINA EWING
LEE, BETTY
LEE, BONNIE JEAN
LEE, EDWIN KING
LEE, FLORA M.
LEE, KAREN JANET
LEE, RICHARD ALAN
LEE, STEPHANIE LORRAINE
LEE, STEPHEN CRAIG
LEE, TRACY ALAN
LEEBRICK, KAREN GRAY
LEEDS, MICHAEL SETH
LEEFERS, LARRY ALAN
LEEN, CAROL LOUISE
LEESMAN, KAREN SUE
LEFCOURT, RONALD LEWIS
LEFFKOWITZ, LAUREEN
LEFORGE, JUDITH
LEGEL, DENNIS RAE
LEGGS, TONI ELIZABETH
LEHARES, WILLIAM PAUL
LEHER, PAUL SHERIDAN
*LEHMANN, JAY ALAN
LEHR, JUDITH
*LEHR, LESLIE IAN
LEHR, NOLA RUTH
LEHTO, MARGARET ANN
*LEIBACH, STEVEN JAY
*LEIBSON, DAVID ALAN
*LEIBSON, PAUL JOSEPH
LEIBY, JACK LE ROY
LEIDING, REBA MELINDA
LEININGER, DAVID ALFRED
LEITNER, GREGORY LESTER
LEMNA, CAROL BODOH
LEMON, DAVID EDWARD
LENAHAN, JAMES JOSEPH
LENAHAN, JOHN THOMAS
LENGFELDER, JULIE ROSE
LENKAITIS, LYNDA ANN
LENNY, DAVID MAURICE
LEO, JANICE MARIE
LEONARD, JAMES RUSSELL
LEONARD, MARGARET MARY
LEONG, DENNIS WEE.
*LEOPOLD, WILBUR RICHARD, III
*LEPINSKY, SUSAN IRIS
*LEPPERD, THOMAS EDWIN, III
LEPSCIER, JOHN OLIVER, JR.
LERFELT, REBECCA B.
*LERITZ, JAYNE MARIE
*LERNER, EDWARD MARK
LERNER, JANE L.
LERNER, PEARL EVE
LERNER, WAYNE MICHAEL
LESHT, ROBERTA ANN
*LESK, HELENE
*LESLIE, CYNTHIA GAIL
LESLIE, RICHARD MICHAEL
LESNER, LYNN MICHAEL
LESNIAK, GREGORY JOSEPH
LESS, LARRY PAUL
*LESS, YVONNE VIRGINIA

90

*LESSARIS, CONSTANCE ANDREA
LESSER, FERN MYRA
LESTER, LINDA SUE
LESTER, REBECCA
LESZKIEWICZ, JOANNE MARGARET
LEUBRIE, WILLIAM ROBERT
LEUTLOFF, CYNTHIA ANNE
LEVANDER, LARK DAWN
LEVENS, JEFFREY B.
LEVENSTEIN, GARY IRWIN
LEVERICH, RICHARD B.
*LEVIE, MARK ROBERT
LEVIN, ARNOLD LAWRENCE
LEVIN, BARBARA MARILYN
LEVIN, BARRY CHARLES
LEVIN, BARRY SCOTT
LEVIN, IRA M.
LEVIN, JOEL C.
*LEVIN, MARK HOWARD
LEVIN, ROBERT MICHAEL
*LEVIN, SHELLEY
LEVIN, TEDD
*LEVINE, BARBARA ANNE
LEVINE, DARRYL ADAM
LEVINE, JOSEPH DOUGLAS
LEVINE, RICHARD JAMES
LEVINE, ROBERT MILES
LEVINE, SUSAN CAROL
*LEVINSON, GARY ELDEN
LEVINSON, LOUIS HENRY
*LEVINSON, ROBERTA ANN
*LEVINSON, STEPHEN GREG
*LEVIT, SHARON IDALIE
LEVITT, MARTIN JAY
LEVY, JOHN ISAAC
LEVY, LAURA
LEVY, MICHAEL MARC
LEVY, NANCY JEANNE
*LEVY, PETER ALEXANDER
*LEWANDOWSKI, SUSAN CAROLE
*LEWIS, EDWARD RUSSELL
LEWIS, EVELYN BETH
LEWIS, GERALD HOWARD
LEWIS, JAMES CHARLES
LEWIS, KATHRYN ANN
LEWIS, LAURA
LEWIS, MOLLY ANNE
LEWIS, RHONDA MARIA
LEWIS, ROBERT WAYNE
LEWIS, RONDA KAY
LIBERG, GAIL ANNE
LICARI, SAMUEL JOHN
LICHON, FRANCIS STANLEY
LICHTENSTEIN, ALAN LOUIS
LICKISS, KAREN PATRICIA
*LIDINSKY, PAMELA ANN
*LIEBER, DEBORAH LEE
LIEBERMAN, DAVID ROBERT
LIEBERMAN, MARCIA JOAN
LIEBOVICH, LOUIS WILLIAM
*LIEBOVITZ, SUSAN GAIL
LIEBRECHT, JANE MARIE
*LIECHTY, RICHARD DAVID
LIEFER, BETTY L.
*LIENESCH, MICHAEL FREDERICK

LIETZ, STEPHEN THEODORE
*LIFTON, LLOYD BERNARD
LIGON, ELIZABETH ADELE
LILLIENFELD, ROCHELLE
*LILLIG, KIMBERLY KAY
LIMA, SAMUEL S., JR.
LINABURY, ELIZABETH ANNE
LINAS, CHRISTINE
LIND, JANICE MARIE
*LIND, RICHARD ELLIS
LINDBLAD, LANA MARIE
*LINDEMANN, GARY EDWARD
LINDER, BARBARA HOLST
*LINDER, DAVID CHARLES
*LINDER, SHARON MARIE
LINDGREN, NANCY EILEEN
LINDLEY, CRAIG CHARLES
LINDQUIST, JUDITH ANN
*LINDQUIST, KENNETH WILLIAM
*LINDQUIST, SANDRA JEAN
LINDQUIST, SUSAN LEE
LINDQUIST, WILLIAM CARL
LINDSAY, JOHN ARTHUR
LINDSAY, LAWRENCE EDWARD
*LINK, KATHLEEN MARY
*LINN, EDWARD SHELDON
LINSKY, MILES ALAN
LINSTER, CHARLES ANDREW
*LIPKIN, DAVID MICHAEL
*LIPPI, BARBARA JEAN
LIPPOLD, KAREN MARIE
LIPPOLD, KATHRYN GAE
*LIPSCHULTZ, CLAIRE MARCIA
LIPSHULTZ, RONALD JAY
LIPSKY, EDWARD S.
*LIPSON, SELMA JANE
*LIPTRAP, JAMES MATTHEWS
*LISS, PAUL LLOYD
LISS, SHEILA RUTH
*LISSAK, DEBRA JO
LISTON, JEANETTE KAY
*LITCHFIELD, WILLIAM JOHN
LITOBORSKI, LAWRENCE CARL
*LITTLE, DANIEL EASTMAN
*LITTLE, ROBERTA DOROTHY
LITTLE, WILLIAM LAVERNE, JR.
*LIVELY, PAUL TURNER
LIVERGOOD, LINDA KATHLEEN
LIVERTON, CATHLEEN ANNE
LIVEY, JAY ALBERT
LLOYD, DAVID HANCOCK
LOBELL, DAVID PRICE
LOBERG, SUZANNE SCOTT
LOBOSCO, ANTOINETTE
LOGIN, MITCHELL ROY
LOCKE, FRANCES RITA
*LOCKMILLER, RICHARD GORDON
LOEB, DIANE SUE
LOEB, EDWARD NORMAL
LOEBACH, BARBARA KAY
LOEBACH, RUTH ANN
LOECHELL, KIRSTEN ANN
*LOEHMAN, WILLIAM CHARLES
LOESSEL, MARGO SUE
LOEWEN, DAVID BARRETT

LOEWENSTEINER, DANIEL
LOFTUS, MARY LOUISE
LOGIUDICE, JOSEPH FRANCIS
*LOHRMANN, JANET ALICE
LOHSE, PATRICIA MARIE
LOIACONO, MADELINE CATHERINE
LOISELLE, LINDA ANN
*LOMBARDI, MICHELLE JEAN
LOMBARDI, SUSAN ANNE
*LOMPERIS, LINDA SUSAN
LONCKA, SHIRLEY MARIE
LONG, ALLAN KEITH
*LONG, DIANE MARY
*LONG, JOHN PERRY
LONG, KATHLEEN CLARE
LONG, MARTIN PETER
*LONG, REBECCA LOUISE
LOOCHTAN, RICHARD MARC
*LOOKER, PATRICIA ANN
LOOKINGBILL, DARRELL
LOPATIN, MICHAEL ALAN
*LOPEZ, TONY STEVEN
*LORBER, MARC IRWIN
*LORD, ROBERT JOHN
LORE, SHARON DIANE
LORGE, MICHAEL MAURICE
*LOSASSO, LEA ANN
LOTEMPIO, SUSAN MERRILL
LOTKA, KENNETH ALAN
*LOTTES, STEVEN ARTHUR
LOVE, MADELAINE MARIE
*LOVELACE, DAVID BRYAN
LOVENTHAL, ANN MARJORY
*LOVINGER, NAOMI ANN
*LOW, TOM WILLIAM
LOWE, RICHARD WILLIAM
LOWERY, ELIZABETH ELLEN
LOWREY, BRADLEY JOHN
LOWRY, MARY LYNN
*LOWRY, MICHAEL MURDOCK
LOWRY, WILLIAM EDWARD
LOXAS, GEORGENE
LUBER, JOAN MICHELLE
*LUBIEN, RAYMOND BERNARD
*LUBIN, STUART FREDRIC
*LUCAS, ANDREW DANIEL
LUCAS, LINDA MARY
LUCK, SUSAN TROTTER
LUCZAJ, PATRICIA ORGAN
LUCZKIW, WALTER JOHN
*LUDEWIG, DONNA JOYCE
LUDWIG, MARY JO
*LUECKING, JAMES GEORGE
LUEDERS, SCOTT WILLIAM
*LUETKEMEYER, JOHN LAWRENCE
LUKAS, JAMES CHRISTOPHER
*LUKEN, BONNIE LOUISE
LUM, KENNETH LANG
LUMPKIN, PAUL DAVID
LUNDAHL, JANICE KATHLEEN
*LUNDBERG, JEAN MARIE
LUNDBERG, MARY DIANE
LUNDE, PAULA ANN
*LUNDFELT, JEAN KATHLEEN
LUNDFELT, STEPHEN JAMES

LUNDGREN, CHERYL ANN
LUNDGREN, DIANE RUTH
LUNDQUIST, ROY ARTHUR
LUNT, JANA ROTZ
LUPINEK, JAN ALAN
LUSTER, GORDON RAY
LUTHY, LISA ANN
LUTZ, JOLEEN MARGARET
LUTZ, KATHY ALESANDRINI
LYLE, CHARLA HOPE
LYLE, KAREN KAY
LYMAN, MARTHA ANN
*LYNCH, DENNIS EUGENE
*LYNCH, FRANCIS LUKE
LYNCH, ROBERT JOSEPH
LYNGAAS, MICHAEL EDWARD
LYNK, JUDITH ANN
LYNN, MARY ELIZABETH
LYON, FRANCES IRENE
LYTLE, NANCY MARGARET
*MAACK, RODNEY ALAN
MAAS, JOSEPH THOMAS
MABRY, THOMAS WILLIAM
MACARTHUR, MARY
MACHALA, JOYCE CATHERINE
MACIEJEWSKI, RICHARD PETER
*MACK, JEFFREY TAYLOR
*MACKE, DAVID LYNN
*MACKEY, SHEILA KAY
MACKOWIAK, MARILYN IRENE
MACLEOD, BARBARA JEAN
MACMARTIN, ELIZABETH ANN
*MACRANDER, ALBERT TIEMEN
MACZEK, EUGENE ROBERT
MADDEN, DAVID MARVIN
MADDOX, PAMELA KAY
MADDUX, HOWARD RAYMOND, JR.
MADEJ, BARBARA ANN
MADENBERG, DAVID RICHARD
MADISON, ROGER DALE
*MADSEN, ELIZABETH CHRISTINE
MADSEN, JANET LYNN
MADSEN, MARK CARL
MADSEN, SANDRA KAREN
*MAEDA, FRANCES SUSAN
MAFFIA, CHRISTINE
MAGELLI, NANCY LICKSTON
MAGILL, JAMES LOUIS
MAGILL, REBECCA NORRIS
MAGLOTT, LARRY FRANKLIN
*MAGNER, JAMES ARTHUR
MAGSAMEN, KATHRYN ANN
MAHER, HARRY ELLSWORTH
MAHER, RICHARD JEFFREY
MAHONEY, ROSLYN MARY
MAHOOD, MELISSA
MAIER, JOSEPH PETER
MAIERHOFER, ROBERT LEE
*MAIERHOFER, WILLIAM JAMES
MAISIAK, RICHARD STANLEY
MAISTO, KEITH DOUGLAS
*MAJKO, RICHARD MICHAEL
MAKI, LINDA JOY
MAKURA, TENDAI
MALAGA, JOSEPH FRANK, JR.

*MALEK, MARTHA MARY
MALEN, JUDITH LOUISE
*MALEY, DALE MURRAY
MALINA, JO ANN
MALINSKY, STEVEN PAUL
MALKI, ALAN ELLA
MALL, RONALD MARTIN
*MALLOY, ROBERT GERALD
*MALMROSE, JOHN HERBERT
MALONE, MARY KIM
MALONE, MICHAEL PATRICK
MALOVANY, HOWARD
MALTEN, KATHLEEN SUE
MAMMINGA, MARGARET OATMAN
*MAN, DIANE GAIL
MAN, JACQUELINE ANNETTE
MAN, NORMAN LEE
MANCUSO, CYNTHIA CAROL
MANDEL, DOUGLAS JOSEPH
MANDELL, MARIANNE
*MANDELL, MICHAEL STEVEN
MANGAN, BONNIE FAY
MANGAS, MARY ELLEN
*MANGEL, MARC STEVEN
MANGIERI, CHRISTINE RAE
*MANGURTEN, MICHAEL LEONARD
MANIFOLD, PATRICIA ANN
MANIS, LYNN DORSEY
MANKEY, JENNIFER SUSAN
MANLEY, MARGARET ANN
MANLEY, REBECCA
MANN, JAY MAY
MANN, JUDITH KAY
MANN, KEITH BRUCE
MANN, KENT ROBERT
MANN, MARK STEPHEN
*MANN, SHELDON H.
*MANN, STEWART RALPH
MANN, THOMAS WILLIAM
MANNA, LYNNE SUSAN
MANNINEN, CHARLES OLIVER
MANNS, WILLIAM JOSEPH, JR.
MANUS, SUSAN
MARANTZ, MARLA JANE
MARBACH, WALTER JOHN
MARCADO, SUSAN JILL
MARCANO, GLADYS ESTHER
MARCEAU, JANICE CONSTANCE
MARCHEN, GAYLE ELIZABETH
MARCHESE, FRANK JOSEPH
MARCHI, CATHERINE A.
*MARCHIANDO, ALBERT WILLIAM
MARCINEK, MARIANNE
MARCUS, HAL IRVING
MARCUS, JAN RICKA
*MARCUS, LAURA NAN
MARCUS, MARC RICHARD
*MARCUS, RICHARD HARVEY
MARCUS, RICHARD JAY
*MARDER, ROBERT JOEL
MARGOLIN, ANDREA FAY
MARGOLIN, DAVID IRA
MARGOLIS, MARLA JAN
MARIK, WARREN JOSEPH
MARIN, CAROL ANN

*MARINO, JOANNE GAYLE
MARINO, PAMELA JEAN
MARKEY, JANICE S.
*MARKMAN, BARBARA ELLEN
MARKOVITZ, DENNIS IRVIN
MARKOWSKI, MICHAEL ROBERT
MARKS, LESLEE ANN
*MARKS, PEGGY DIANE
MARKS, WILLIAM E.
MARLATT, SHAWN RENEE
MARLIN, JOHN CARL
*MARLIN, JON MICHAEL
MARMILLION, PAUL EVAN
MARPLE, WENDELL DEAN
MARQUESS, CYNTHIA HARRIET
MARQUEZ, IRENE
MARQUIS, PAULETTE R.
MARQUIS, ROBERT JOHN
MARRON, JAMIE PATRICIA
MARSH, EMILY JEAN
*MARSHAK, LAURA ELLEN
MARSHALL, ROGER GARTH
MARSHALL, STEVEN ARTHUR
MARSHALL, VICKI JO
*MARSHALLA, LINDA ROSE
MARTAN, JOSEPH RUDOLF
MARTENS, CARL WILLIAM
MARTENS, CAROL LYNN
*MARTENS, CHRISTINE LEE
*MARTENS, KATHRYN IRENE
*MARTIN, DAVID STUART
*MARTIN, DIANE MARIE
*MARTIN, ELLEN MYRTLE
MARTIN, JAMES ALBERT
MARTIN, KATHIE
MARTIN, MARILOU
MARTIN, ROBERT ALAN
MARTINA, JOSEPH PHILIP
MARTINDALE, DIANE SHERRY
*MARTINEAU, PAUL ROBERT
MARTINO, CLAUDIA
MARTINUCCI, GABRIELLA
MARTZ, DEBRA ANN
MARUKO, KEIKO
MARUNA, JACQUELINE
*MARX, DONNA JEAN
*MARZEC, MARIANNE MARGARET
*MASHKES, SUSAN
MASON, DAVID JOHN
MASON, EDWARD VINCENT
MASON, JAMES RICHARD
MASON, RICHARD JOSEPH
MASON, VERA ERNESTINE
MASSEY, LANNY EDWARD
*MASSEY, NATHAN ANDERSON
*MASSEY, SANDRA GOSSEN
*MASSINGILL, MARSHA ELAINE
MAST, CATHERINE SUE
*MAST, PHILIP EDWARD
*MASULIS, CHRISTINE MARY
*MATAYOSHI, EDMUND DENNIS
MATEER, JACQUELYN HENKIN
MATEJCAK, RAYMOND JOSEPH
MATEJKO, JANICE ESTELLE
MATEK, BETH SAMUEL

MATEVICH, PETER MICHAEL
MATHENY, PATRICIA
MATHEWS, AVA JOY
MATHIS, JEANINE CAROL
MATORY, JO ANN
MATRANGA, MATTHEW FRANCIS
MATSON, HARRISON EUGENE
MATTCHEN, PATRICIA KANT
MATTHEIS, JAMES RALPH
*MATTHEWS, SHELDON HAROLD
*MATTHIAS, LINDA KAY
*MATTIS, HENRY EDWARD
MATTIX, DANA MONTELLE
MATTSON, JAMES WILLIAM
MATTSON, RICHARD LEONARD
MATUGA, JOSEPH PAUL
MATUSZEWSKI, ANNE ELEANOR
MATZKO, PAUL, JR.
*MAURER, CHRISTOPHER ARMAND
MAURER, DAVID L.
MAURER, REGINA ANN
MAURIDES, ELLANI JO
MAWHINEY, BONNIE JEAN
MAXHEIMER, JEAN ELLEN
*MAXON, LINDA SUE
MAXWELL, GAIL
*MAXWELL, MARGO JEAN
*MAXWELL, MICHAEL BRUCE
MAXWELL, RICHARD WILLIAM
MAY, JOY ROSAMOND
MAY, MARCIA MAGGIORE
MAY, NANCY K.
MAY, SUSAN
MAYER, ALICE EVELYN
*MAYER, CYNTHIA ANN
MAYER, ELEANOR
*MAYER, JEAN MARY
MAYER, JEANNE DOOLITTLE
MAYER, PATRICIA ANN
MAYER, ROBERT K.
MAYER, SCOTT ALAN
MAYEROFF, JERRY MICHAEL
MAYFIELD, JOHN MORGAN
MAYLAND, POLLY NAN
MAYO, CHARLES FRANKLIN
MAYSE, MARK ALAN
MAZE, JUDITH ANN
*MAZZONE, THEODORE
MCALPINE, GEORGE JAMES
MCAULIFFE, JOAN PATRICIA
MCCABE, KATHLEEN ANN
MCCALL, LINDSAY LARUE
*MCCANE, CECILIA GAY
*MCCANN, PHYLLIS RUTH
MCCANN, WILLIAM HAROLD
MCCARTHY, GAIL KATHLEEN
MCCARTHY, PATRICIA ANN
· MCCARTHY, PATRICIA ANN
MCCARTHY, WILLIAM ROBERT
MCCARTY, MARY MARGARET
MCCAULEY, JOHN PATRICK
MCCAULEY, MARLIN DON
*MCCLELLAN, GAIL JEAN
MCCLELLAN, LEONARD
*MCCLELLAND, GARY MILES

McCLENNY, RUTH LORRAINE
McCLINTOCK, GREGORY KENT
McCLUSKEY, ROBERT A.
*McCOLLUM, TOQUALEE
*McCORMICK, JANICE
McCOY, REBECCA SUSAN
*McCOY, ROBERT GEORGE
McCOY, STEVEN GEORGE
McCRAW, THOMAS ERWIN
*McCULLOCH, ELLEN ANN
McCUMBER, THOMAS LOGAN
McCURDY, DAVID SCOTT
McCURDY, PATRICIA LYNN
McCURDY, VICKY LYNN
McDADE, LINNA SPRINGER
McDANIEL, DAVID JAMES
McDANIEL, LINDA KAY
McDANIEL, WILLIAM CHERRY
McDERMOTT, KATHLEEN ANN
McDONALD, CATHERINE MARION
McDONALD, DAVID LEE
*McDONALD, KEVIN JAMES
McDONALD, LEE FOSTER
McDONALD, MAUREEN ROSE
McDONALD, PAUL ANDERS
McDONNELL, MARY FRANCES
McDOWELL, LAURIE ANN
McELLIGOTT, MARY ELLEN
McELLIGOTT, ROBERT MICHAEL
*McELROY, BRENDA JOYCE
McELVAIN, L. PATRICK
*McELVAINE, MICHAEL D.
McELWAIN, ROBERT DOUGLAS
*McENROE, JOHN THOMAS
*McEWAN, BETTE EVELYN
McFADDEN, JAMES EARL
McGARY, SUSAN JANE
McGEE, CECELIA YVETTE
McGEOUGH, PAMELA ANN
*McGETRICK, JOHN JOSEPH
McGILL, JEFFREY CHARLES
McGINTY, MICHAEL
McGIVNEY, NANCY MARIE
McGONNAGLE, JAMES DAVID
McGOUGH, TIMOTHY PATRICK
*McGOVNEY, JAMES EUGENE
McGRADY, DOUGLAS JAMES
*McGRATH, ANN TERESA
McGRATH, KATHERINE MARY
McGRATH, NEAL FRANCIS
*McGREAL, DONNA LYNN
McGUIRE, JAMES THOMAS
*McGUIRE, JOHN WILSON
*McGUIRE, MARGARET J.
McGUIRE, MAUREEN ANN
McGUIRE, THOMAS PATRICK
McGURK, JAMES ARTHUR
*McHENRY, SUSAN ALICE
McINTOSH, HUGH EUGENE
McINTOSH, L. K.
McKAHAN, KATHLEEN HELEN
*McKECHNIE, JAMES KEITH
*McKECHNIE, THELMA LOUISE
McKELVIE, MARK RICHARD
McKENZIE, KATHLEEN MARIE

McKENZIE, MARK WILLIAM
McKIBBIN, JOHN GATES
McKINLEY, MARGARET ELIZABETH
McKINNEY, KARYL LYNN
McKIRGAN, NANCY ANN
*McKNIGHT, RICHARD SAMUEL, JR.
*McLEAN, CHRISTINE ROSE
*McLEES, MARILYN MAY
McLOUGHLIN, SUSAN ADELL
*McMAHON, KATHLEEN AGNES
McMAHON, MARY EDNA
*McMAHON, MARY JEANNETTE
McMILLAN, CHARLES ANSON
*McMILLIN, KIM IRVING
McMURRAY, LAURA ELIZABETH
McNABB, LOUIS JOSEPH
McNALLY, DEBORAH JOAN
*McNAMARA, PHYLLIS ANNE
McNAMARA, SUSAN MARIE
McNAMEE, BARBARA ANNE
McNEILL, MYRNA RAE
*McNETT, MICHAEL EDWARD
McNICHOLS, DANIEL LAWRENCE, JR.
McQUEEN, CHARLES EDWARD
*McQUEEN, CHARLES RAY
McREYNOLDS, DANA ROY
McROBERTS, KAREN MARIE
McWILLIAMS, JULIE
MEACHUM, BRUCE JAY
*MEDENIS, ISMENE
MEERS, SHARON SUE
MEESSMANN, DANIEL GEORGE
MEGGINSON, SANDRA KAY
MEHL, DAVID ARTHUR
*MEIER DUANE, EDWARD
MEILINGER, JOHN HUGH
MEINERT, JOHN CHRISTIAN
*MEINHEIT, CATHERINE JOANNE
MEINHEIT, SUZANNE MARIE
*MEINHOLD, JANE MAY
*MEINKE, LINDA MARION
MEISELS, HENRY ISAAC
MEISENBACH, JOSEPH ANTHONY
*MEISNER, KEITH GEORGE
MEISNER, MARY JOAN
*MEISS, HARRIETTE LEONA
MEISTAS, LINDA SUSAN
*MEISTER, SUSAN JOY
*MELCHER, RICHARD EARL
MELCHERT, CARLA JEAN
MELCHING, MOLLY JANE
*MELDI, DOMINIC MATTHEW
MELER, REBECCA ANN
MELIA, MARY JEAN
MELLICK, EDWARD RONALD
*MELLOW, JULIE ANNE
MELMAN, JANET EILEEN
MELNICK, NINA
MELNIK, JOYCE CAROL
*MELNYK, JOHN G.
*MELTZER, MICHAEL HOWARD
MELVIN, ANNE MURIEL
MELVIN, MARIANNE RUE
*MELVIN, TYRONE RAY
*MENASCE, JULIE

MENCHOFF, JERRY ALLAN
*MENDELOWITZ, DAVID SAMUEL
MENDIUS, BARBARA JANE
MENDOZA, MYRIAM DE JESUS
*MENEGHINI, ROBERT
*MENG, RONALD LESLIE
*MENGES, CHRISTOPHER MARTIN
*MENNENGA, ARLENE KAY
*MENNIE, SCOTT DONALD
MENZEL, SUSAN JEANNE
MERCER, BARBARA CROWLEY
MEREL, RONALD HOWARD
MERHLEY, LINDA MAY
*MERKEL, LINDA CATHERINE
*MERKEL, ROBERT RAYMOND
*MERKER, ROBERT IRVING
MERLIE, MELISSA ANN
MERLIE, MICHAEL JOHN
*MERNIN, CATHERINE SUE
MERRICK, ROBERT ERVIN
MERRION, MICHAEL THOMAS
MERRITT, LORENCE H.
MERRITT, SEARS WILLIAM
MERTES, PATRICE SUSAN
MERTES, SUSAN
MESETZ, PENNY LEE
MESEWICZ, NORMAN
MESICH, JAMES JOHN
MESKAUSKAS, NORA DENICE
MESSENGER, DAVID LAWRENCE
MESSINA, JAN CARYLE
MESSMAN, JOHN HENRY
MESSMAN, RONALD ALBERT
MESSMER, JANET CHRISTINE
*METCALF, ROBERT ALAN
*METRICK, SCOTT ALAN
METSKAS, NANETTE MARY
METTLING, STEPHEN R.
METZ, PETER ROBERT
METZ, RAYMOND JOSEPH
METZ, RICHARD CHARLES
METZ, RUSSELL ALLEN
*MEYER, DAVID WARREN
MEYER, DIANE M.
MEYER, ELKE
MEYER, JANE ANN
*MEYER, JOAN ELLEN
MEYER, JUDITH MARY
MEYERS, GLENNA RUTH
MEYERS, PAMELA ANN
MICHAEL, MARYJANE SHAND
MICHAEL, PHILLIP EUGENE
MICHAELS, CHERYL MARY
*MICHAELS, DEBBIE LYNN
MICHELSEN, LINDA JEAN
MICHELSON, BELINDA GAIL
MICHIELSEN, PEGGY ANNE
MICKELBERRY, ORVILLE DEAN
*MICKENBECKER, KATHLEEN
MICKENBECKGER, THERESE MARIE
*MIDDLETON, KEVIN EUGENE
*MIELING, TERENCE MICHAEL
*MIERNICKI, MARYANN CATHERINE
*MIGALSKI, MICHAEL EUGENE
*MIGDOW, JEFFREY ARTHUR

*MIGIELICZ, FRANCES ANNE
*MIGLIN, BRUCE PAUL
MIKES, JOY FRANCES
MIKLES, FREDIKA ARLENE
MIKOLS, THAD E.
MIKULIC, CAROLYN
*MILES, DONALD EUGENE
MILES, JANE VICIC
*MILES, KATHY TUNNICLIFF
*MILES, LINDA MARIE
MILES, WILLIAM CHARLES
MILESKI, JUDITH ELLEN
MILKE, JUDITH MARIE
MILKOWSKI, ANDREW LESTER
MILLARD, ANTHONY JAY
MILLARD, PATRICIA ANN
MILLER, ALAN EARL
MILLER, ARLENE CLAIRE
MILLER, BRENDA ANN
MILLER, BRIAN NORMAN
MILLER, BRUCE DAVID
*MILLER, BRUCE NATHAN
*MILLER, CARLA SUZANNE
MILLER, CHERYL ALLYN
MILLER, CHRISTINE KAREN
MILLER, CYNTHIA LOUISE
MILLER, DAVID GEORGE
MILLER, DAVID JOHN
MILLER, DEBRA SUE
MILLER, DIANA LYNN
MILLER, DONNA G.
*MILLER, GARY J.
MILLER, GERALD JAMES
*MILLER, JANE ANN
*MILLER, JANENE CHRISTINE
MILLER, JANET BOSLEY
MILLER, JANICE MARIE
MILLER, JEREMY NORMAN
*MILLER, JOHN E.
MILLER, JOHN ENGEL
*MILLER, JUDITH MERLE
MILLER, JUDY KAY
*MILLER, KAREN ANNE
*MILLER, KAREN LEAH
MILLER, KRISTINE MARIE
*MILLER, LARRY EVAN
*MILLER, LINDA ANN
MILLER, LINDA REUBEN
*MILLER, LINDA SUSAN
MILLER, LINDA TAYLOR
MILLER, LOIS ROCHELLE
MILLER, MARY JUSTINE
MILLER, MARYBETH GEANIOUS
*MILLER, MELISSA GAY
MILLER, NORMAN LOUIS
MILLER, PAMELA CLAIRE
MILLER, PATRICIA ANN
MILLER, RICHARD WILLIAM
MILLER, ROBERT ALAN
MILLER, RODNEY KERMAN
*MILLER, RONALD DWIGHT
*MILLER, SANDRA
MILLER, SANDRA FAIRBANKS
MILLER, SCOTT MARTIN

MILLER, SHAYLE
MILLER, SIDNEY ROBERT
MILLER, SUE RAU
*MILLER, SUZANNE VIRGINIA
*MILLER, VINCENT THOMAS
MILLER, WARREN GLENN
MILLER, WENDY DEE
MILLER, WENDY MARA
MILLHOUSER, ROBERT JOHN
MILLIGAN, KEVIN RUPERT
MILLMAN, GWENN
MILNER, PATRICIA KAY
MILOCH, KAREN ELLEN
MILSK, NORMAN VICTOR
MILTON, JUDITH ELLEN
MINDRUM, ROBERT LYNN
*MINER, DONALD LEE
MINICK, RICHARD DALE
MINIKEL, JEFFREY LEE
MINIKEL, SUSAN CAROL
MINISCALCO, JUDITH ANN
*MINNICK, CRAIG ALAN
MINOR, PENELOPE ANN
*MINTON, MARK ALLEN
MINUS, BRUCE ALLEN
MIRANDA, ROSE NAOMI
*MIS, BARBARA BERNICE
MISIORA, BERNADINE MARY
MITA, NORA KATHLEEN
MITCHARD, JACQUELYN GAYE
MITCHELL, BARBARA LEE
MITCHELL, DENNIS FLOYD
MITCHELL, JANE TERESA
MITCHELL, JEAN MARIE
MITCHELL, JERRY VICTOR
*MITCHELL, KAY ANN
MITCHELL, NATALIE CHARLOTTE
MITCHELL, RUSINE
MITCHELL, SALLY JO
MITCHELL, THOMAS EVANS, JR.
MITCHUM, KENNETH LYNN
MITRICK, MICHAEL FRANIS
MITRICK, VERONICA JEAN
MITSIS, CHRISOULA
MITTELMAN, SHARON ILENE
MIZE, STANLEY ALLEN
MLODINOFF, RHONDA LYNN
MOATE, NANCY KAY
MOBURG, CHARLES EVERETT
*MOELLER, RAYMOND JOSEPH, JR.
MOEN, CRAIG ALAN
MOEWS, CYNTHIA MARIE
*MOEWS, LAWRENCE PAUL
*MOGILL, MICHAEL ALAN
MOHR, DEBORAH L.
MOLINAR, JOHN LOUIS
*MOLINARI, JANET ELLEN
*MOLL, DANIEL WILLARD
MOLODOW, LYNDA
MONGEAU, DENISE MARIE
MONIER, JAY RUSSELL
MONKS, BARBARA EVE
MONROE, JAMES DAVID
MONROE, WILLIAM KIMBRO

Monteith, Phyllis Ann
Montemayor, David
Monts, David Lee
*Monypenny, Alice
Monypenny, Laura
Moody, Garry Lane
*Moody, Mary Ann
Moody, Susan Elizabeth
Moon, Michael Mark
Moore, Barbara Bunker
Moore, Catherine Anne
Moore, Debra Lee
*Moore, Diane Elaine
Moore, Elizabeth Ann
Moore, Kevin Anthony
*Moore, Lee Eugene
Moore, Melvin Maurice
*Moore, Patricia Ruth
*Moore, Patrick James
Moore, Robert Charles
Moore, Stephen James
Morales, Lydia Esther
*Moran, Donald Will
Morava, Carol Susan
Moreland, Bernice Roberts
Moreno, Samuel Praxed
Morford, Raymond Scott, Jr.
Morgan, Edward Alan
Morgan, John Grant
Morgan, Marian Louise
Morgan, Michelle Loretta
Moriarty, David John
Morin, Catherine Louise
Moritz, Sandra Ruth
Morris, Bertram Charles, Jr.
Morris, Billy Joe
*Morris, Clifford Theadore
Morris, Gregory Edward
Morris, John Albert
Morris, Kathleen Ann
Morris, Margaret Norman
Morris, Richard Dale
Morris, Veronica A. J.
Morrison, David Lloyd
Morrison, Matthew Greenwood
Morrison, Wildey David, Jr.
Morrow, Rebecca Anne
Mortimore, Robert Harry
Morton, Carolyn Ann
Morton, Kathleen Marie
Morton, Sally Jean
Moschel, Bruce Cary
Mosely, Jeannine
*Moser, Elizabeth Ann
Mosher, Ralph Paul
*Mosher, Sharon
Mosny, Emil Kenneth
Moss, Kalene Elizabeth
Moss, Mark Thomas
Moss, Merilyn Sue
Moss, Robert J.
Mossberger, Gregg Lee
Motel, Joel Lurie
Motel, Robert Alan

Motenko, Gail Lynn
Mott, Dennis Delbert
Motycka, Susan Lynn
Movesian, Stephen Joseph
Mowers, Leila Sue
Moy, Mark Munk
Moy, Mary Mee
Moy, May May
Moye, Christine Elizabeth
Moyer, Mark Albert
Moyer, Thomas William
Mudron, Maureen Dolores
Mueller, James Irwin
Mueller, Linda Sarah
Muench, Jacqelyn Rae
Muhs, Laurie Jo
Mui, Ruth
*Muirhead, Martha Pocklington
Mularz, Thomas Edward
*Mulcahney, Robert William
*Mulch, Robert F., Jr.
Mulder, Gail Marie
Mulhall, Martin Francis
Mullarkey, Thomasina Maeve
Mullen, Maureen Anne
*Mulligan, Patricia Ann
Mulrooney, Raymond James
Mulroy, Maureen Bridges
*Mulroy, Patrick Francis
Mumm, Rosemary Sue
Mumm, Russell Craig
Munaretto, Raymond Frank
Munch, Nancy Jeanne
*Munch, Paul Thomas
*Mundt, Gordon Kenneth
Munson, Arnold Isaac
Muraski, Mary Jean
Murdock, Joseph Patrick
*Murowchick, Linda Sue
Murphy, Angela Regina
Murphy, Cathleen Colette
*Murphy, Janis Irene
Murphy, Linda Ann
Murphy, Lynne Alison
Murphy, Marianna
Murphy, Mary Cathleen
*Murphy, Robert Joseph
Murphy, Shirley Ann
Murphy, William Scott
Murray, Barbara Cathryn
*Murray, Christopher Cameron
Musikantow, Robert Allen
Muslin, Steven Barry
Muszynski, David Donald
Muszynski, Irvin Lawrence, Jr.
Mutaw, Kathleen Eleanor
Myer, Sally Kay
*Myers, John Riley
Myers, Terry Lee
Myles, Barbara Clancy
Myles, Raymond
Myrent, Debra Karen
*Naab, Elisabeth Maria
Nachtmann, Christine Marie

NADARSKI, JUDITH ANN
*NAFSHUN, MAXINE LOU
NAGLE, CHRISTINE ANN
NAGLE, JANIE BETH
NAGLE, MARY BETH
NAHLIK, RICHARD LAWRENCE
*NAKASHIMA, CATHY YURI
NANUS, SUSAN LEIGH
NARTKER, CYNTHIA CASS
NASLUND, HOWARD RICHARD
NASLUND, LINDA RUTH
NASRALLAH, JOANNE
NAST, JUDITH ANN
NATHAN, JOHN EDWARD
NAUGHTON, PATRICIA ANN
NAUYOK, GEORGE FREDERICK, JR.
NAVIN, PETER BERNARD
*NEAL, PHILLIP GRANT
NEBOSKA, ELIZABETH GUNTY
*NEEDELMAN, HOWARD WILLIAM
NEER, MICHAEL R.
NEGRETE, LOLA JEAN
NEIWEEM, BERNARD MICHAEL
NELLE, MARIANNE
NELSON, CYNTHIA CATHLEEN
NELSON, FLORENCE MACNEIL
NELSON, FRED ALLAN
NELSON, GEOFFREY BYRON
NELSON, KATHLEEN LOIS
NELSON, PEGGY LEE
*NELSON, RICHARD HERBERT
NELSON, ROBERT CURTIS
NELSON, RONALD DAVID
*NELSON, RUSSELL WILLIAM
NELSON, STEPHEN TORREY
NELSON, TERRY LEE
NELSON, WILLIAM DELBERT
NEMANICH, EUGENE JOHN
NEMECEK, MARTIN ANTHONY
NEMETH, LUDWIG WOLFGANG
NEPOTE, JOSEPH JOHN, II
NESBIT, JOHN ARTHUR
*NESBIT, ROGER WILLIAM
NESBITT, STEPHEN LEE
*NESHEIM, SANDRA LYNN
NESVIG, JACKLYN ANNE
NESVIG, KRISTIN LOUISE
*NETEMEYER, PATRICK RALPH
*NETHERTON, MARTHA JANE
NETTELHORST, SUSAN
NETTLES, STEVEN SCOTT
NEUBERGER, ANDREA ROSE
NEUBERGER, GAY CLAIRE
NEUMANN, BETH ANN
NEUMANN, NANCY LOUISE
NEUMARK, JONATHAN JAY
NEUMEYER, FREDERICK SCOTT
NEUNABER, DEBORAH DEE
NEUREUTHER, JANET EILEEN
NEUSTADT, DONALD HOWARD
NEWBERRY, RALPH JEFFREY
*NEWELL, LARRY MICHAEL
NEWLAND, THERYL ELAINE
NEWLIN, JAMES ROBERT, JR.
NEWMAN, LYNNE MARCIA

NEWMAN, ROBERT HARRY
NEWMAN, ROBERT N.
NEWTON, DAVID R.
NEWTON, GRANT LEWIS
NEWTON, MICHAEL ALLEN
*NIBECK, BARBARA JEANNE
NICHOLAS, MARGARET JO
*NICHOLS, RONDA ANNETTE
*NICHOLSON, DEBRA JEAN
NICHOLSON, GARRY CORNELL
*NICHOLSON, PETER ALLEN
*NICHELSON, LEE ERNST
NICKSARLIAN, MARY HELEN
NICKSARLIAN, SONYA
NICKUM, GARY JOHN
*NICOL, ARTHUR DUEY
*NIEBRUGGE, DANIEL JOSEPH
NIEBUHR, BRUCE RICHARD
NIED, JANICE JUDITH
NIEDER, JULIE DEBORAH
NIEDER, MARILYN ANNE
NIEDERMAYER, LYNN MARIE
NIELSEN, EILEEN ANN
NIELSEN, LINDA LOUISE
NIELSEN, PAUL HOWARD
NIEMAN, JOYCE ANN
NIEMANN, GAIL ANN
NIEMANN, JANET KAYE
NIEMI, V. BRIAN
NIMZ, CHERYL KEISTER
*NIPPA, DOUGLAS LAWRENCE
NISBET, PATRICIA FLORENCE
*NISBET, ROBIN WEBB
NISHIMOTO, WARREN SEIJI
NISSAN, KATHLEEN BECKER
NITEKMAN, DEBORAH ANN
NITKA, BENJAMIN SOLOMON
NITZKIN, JEFFREY LEE
NIX, KENNETH RICHARD
NIXON, LINDA JOY
*NOBLE, SCOTT WILLIAM
NOBLE, SHANNON MARIE
*NOBLE, WILLIAM WYGLE
NOFFKE, MATTHEW WALTER
NOHL, DANIEL EUGENE
NOLAN, CAROL ANNE
NOLAN, JOHN MICHAEL
NOLAN, MARGARET MARY
NOLAN, MARY ELLEN
NOLAN, DAVID FREEMAN
NOLLER, THOMAS WAYNE
NOONAN, DEBORAH GAIL
NOONAN, MARGARET ANN
*NORDBERG, DONALD EDWARD
*NORDGREN, CAROL ANN
*NORDHEDEN, ANGELENE CARLA
NORDQUIST, RONALD DALE
*NOREM, JOLENE FERN
NORMAN, ROSANNE
NORMAND, CLARENCE WILLIAM
NORRIS, JOHN WILLIAM
NORRIS, JULIE ANN
NORRIS, LYNDA LOUISE
NORTH, ALICE MARIE
NORTH, ROBERT ARTHUR

NORTHROP, ROGER JOHN
*NORTON, PATRICIA KERR
*NOSEK, RICHARD DOUGLAS
NOSKO, JUDITH ELLEN
NOTHDURFT, GRACE LOUISE
NOTHNAGEL, MARGARET ELIZABETH
NOTTOLI, MARGARET MARY
NOVAK, DEBORAH GAIL
NOVAK, ELAINE SUSAN
NOVAK, JANET ANN
NOVAK, LINDA JEANNE
NOVICK, ALAN JEFFREY
NOVICK, WILLIAM PAUL
NOVY, DAVID RICHARD
NOVY, STEVEN BRADLEY
NOWARD, CHRISTI LEA
NUDO, ALAN FRANK
NUGER, PAULA JOYCE
*NUMRICH, PAUL DAVID
NUSTRA, CHERYL SUE
NUTE, CHARLES ROBERT
NUTTALL, CHRISTINE ANNE
*NUTTALL, JOHN LAWRENCE, III
*NUTTING, DEBORAH LANDIS
NYHOLT, DEBORAH LYNN
*NYHOLT, PAMELA ANN
NYLUND, MARY KAY
NYMAN, ALICE JEAN
NYMAN, EMILY ADELE
*OAKES, DAVID WAYNE
OAKES, HOWARD LEE
OAKS, JOHN DARREN
*OBENAUF, CARL DEAN
OBERLIN, LORRIE ANN
O'BRIEN, KATHLEEN MARY
O'BRIEN, LISA MARY
O'BRIEN, THOMAS PATRICK
*O'BYRNE, STEPHEN MICHAEL
OCKERT, JILL ANN
O'CONNELL, KATHLEEN MARY
*O'CONNELL, SHIRLEY GRAY
O'CONNOR, GARY LEN
O'CONNOR, MARIAN ELIZABETH
*O'CONNOR, MARY ELIZABETH
O'CONNOR, MATTHEW RICHARD
O'CONNOR, SUSAN JANE
*ODDO, SANDRA MARIE
ODELL, ALICE ELAINE
*ODELL, STEVEN JAMES
O'DONNELL, JAMES FRANCIS
*O'DONNELL, KATHLEEN MARIE
O'DONOGHUE, MICHAEL JAMES
O'DWYER, PAMELA GREEN
OEHMKE, RONALD TAYLOR
*OERTEL, NANCY MARIE
*OGDEN, JOAN MARY
OGDEN, JOANN MASSA
*OGLE, KAREN ANN
OGLESBY, WANDA JEAN
OGOLIN, WILLIAM JOSEPH, JR.
O'GRADY, ALICE PATRICIA
*OGRON, JANET SUE
O'HARA, MICHAEL WILLIAM
O'HARA, PATRICK JOSEPH
*OHLEMILLER, GARY WAYNE

OHLENDORF, RICHARD JAMES
OHMAN, KATHLEEN MARIE
*OHMAN, SANDRA MAE
OHR, DEBORAH COVENY
OI, LILLY
OKEN, STUART MICHAEL
OKERSTROM, MARK WILLIAM
OLDHAM, RUTH LILLIAN
OLEARY, KATHLEEN ANNE
OLEARY, SHEILA
*OLECK, PATRICIA LYNN
OLESKER, KATHY JEAN
OLIC, RUTH LORRAINE
OLSEN, BRET GEORGE
OLSEN, CAROL ANN
OLSEN, CHRISTINE LOUISE
OLSEN, JANELLEN
OLSEN, MARGARET SUSAN
OLSON, ALLEN WADE
*OLSON, BETTY SCHMIDT
OLSON, DEBORAH RUTH
OLSON, ELIZABETH ANN
OLSON, KAREN HELEN
*OLSON, LINDA JEAN
OLSON, MARCIA JO
OLSON, ROBERT LOUIS
OLSON, VICKI MAY
OMAHEN, SUSAN CLAIR
OMALLEY, BERNARD MICHAEL
OMALLEY, KATHLEEN ANN
OMELL, STACEY KYLE
ONEAL, LARRY DWAYNE
ONERHEIM, CAROL OLSON
OPOLION, JACK LOUIS
OPPENHEIM, MARK GORDON
OPPENHEIMER, WILLIAM JOSEPH
OPPERMAN, LINDA JANE
*ORAM, RICHARD WHITE
ORCUTT, DANIEL WITHERBEE
ORDAL, CAROLYN ANN
ORELOVE, FRED PAUL
*ORNSTEIN, BARBARA ELLEN
ORR, BRUCE WAYNE
ORR, HAROLD DOUGLAS
ORRIS, HOLLY ANITA
ORSAY, CHARLES PRESTON
*ORTHWEIN, KARLA FRANCES
ORTO, FRANKLIN SAMUEL
OSBERG, ANNE ELIZABETH
OSBORNE, CERETTA ARLENE
OSGOOD, JUDY KAY
OSHEL, MICHAEL VAL
OSTENDORF, JOELLEN
OSTERBERGER, LARRY DALE
OSTERBUR, CAROL LYNN
*OSTERBUR, CYNTHIA ANN
*OSTLER, RAYMOND JOHN
*OSTREICHER, JEFFREY IAN
OSTREM, DAWN EMITA
OSTRENGA, BERNADINE ANN
OSTROF, ADRIANE B.
OSTROWSKI, IRENE MARIE
OSTROWSKI, PATRICIA LEE
OTEY, NANCY ANN
OTMASKIN, DENNIS JOHN

O'TOOLE, FRANCIS MICHAEL
OTRÈMBIAK, MICHAEL MARTIN
OTTO, CRAIG WARREN
OURADA, ROBYN RUTH
OUTLAW, JESSE
OUTTEN, TERESA ANN
OVERMAN, GREGORY SCOTT
OVERMAN, WILLIAM HENRY
OWEN, CAROL DORIS
OWEN, JOANNE STARK
OWEN, MARTHA MCLEAN
OWEN, THOMAS EDWARD
OWENS, LINDA JEANNEAN
OWINGS, NICK STAFFORD
*OZYURT, YILDIZ GULER
PACANOWSKI, RONALD FRANCES
PACENTA, WENDY LEE
PACEY, STEPHEN ROBBINS
PACHTER, FREDERICK JO
*PACIN, MARILYN SUE
*PACINI, CHARLES MICHAEL
PADEN, ROGER KENNETH
PAGE, PATRICIA ANN
PAGONE, VINCENT CHARLES
PAGORIA, SHARON MARIE
PAHUCHY, ANNA
*PAINE, THEODORE EDWARD
PAINTER, STEVEN ANDREW
PAISLEY, DEEANN
PALBY, SUSAN CYRILLA
PALIJ, SUSAN ANDERSON
PALKO, JUDITH ANNE
PALLY, EVA CAROLINE
PALM, CATHERINE ANN
PALMATIER, NANCY ANN
PALMER, FRED JAY
PALMER, LOIS MARIE
PALMER, PATRICIA JEANNE
*PALMER, RICHARD ALLEN
*PAMPE, MARCIA LEE
*PAMPEL, FRED CARROLL, JR.
PAN, LINDA YING-ZE
PANCOTTO, LINDA RAE
PANFIL, LEROY FELIX, JR.
PAPKE, MARY ELIZABETH
PAPPAS, MARCUS ANDREWS
PARDYS, MICHAEL ALAN
PARISH, JAMES MICHAEL
*PARISH, SYLVIA NELLE
PARK, JOHN MORROW
PARKER, BRIAN DAVID
*PARKER, MARLA JAN
PARKHURST, CHRISTINA LOUISE
PARKINSON, ANN NORTH
PARKS, JULIA LYNN
PARKS, PAMELA ANN
*PARKS, PAUL BROWNLEE
PARKS, STEVE ALAN
PARR, BILLIE JO
PARRISH, JANICE BETH
PARRISH, MARY DIANE
PARRO, CRAIG DENNIS
PARSONS, ANNA CHRISTINA
PARSONS, GERALDINE STOCKHAM
PARSONS, JON RICHARD

PARSONS, LYNN ELLEN
*PARTH, DONALD JAMES
PARYS, MARY LOUISE
*PASSAFIUME, DIANNE MARIE
*PATCH, ROBERT WARNER
PATEJUNAS, CONSTANCE
*PATEK, KATHERINE JANE
PATEY, JEREMY WILDER
*PATINKIN, LYNN DIANE
*PATINKIN, TERRY ALLAN
*PATIS, KENNETH HAROLD
PATRICK, SHAWN STEPHEN
PATTERSON, CAROL ANN
*PATTERSON, CHARLES STEWART
PATTERSON, CHRISTOPHER HOLDEN
*PATTERSON, MARK ALLEN
PATTERSON, POLA NOAH
*PATTERSON, SUSAN CAROL
PATTERSON, SUSAN HANNA
PATTERSON, SUSAN L.
PATTERSON, TARA MARIE
PATTERSON, TRUDI ALICE
PAUL, DENISE MARIA
PAUL, MARLA HELENE
PAULASKAS, ANNETTE MARIE
PAULL, MATTHEW HOWARD
*PAVISH, DANNY LEE
PAVLETIC, MARY ANN
PAWELAK, JAMES EUGENE
PAWELAK, JEROME EDWIN
*PAYNE, JAMES GREGORY
*PAZERO, JOSEPH EDWARD, JR.
PEALE, THOMAS RAY
PEARCE, DAVID ALAN
PEARD, BEVERLY ADELE
*PEARLMAN, BARBARA RUTH
PEARLMAN, ELLEN LINDA
PEARLMAN, ROBERT STUART
PEARSE, MARY KATHRYN
*PEARSON, JOHN CLAUDE
PEARSON, LAUREL WEBSTER
*PEARSON, RICHARD WARREN
*PEARSON, WILLIAM RAYMOND
PEASE, SARAH GORTNER
*PEAVOY, SUSAN JOAN
PECH, WILLIAM CARY
*PECHTER, EDWARD ALLEN
PECHTER, GARY EDWARD
*PECK, MICHAEL ROBERT
PECK, PATRICIA ANN
PECK, RAYMOND KEITH
PEDERSEN, ROBERT GLEN
PEEK, KAREN LYNN
PEER, SANDRA FAYE
PEKALA, RAE SUSAN
PEKAR, RUSSELL GEORGE
PELANT, EDWARD DANIEL
*PELC, PAULETTE AYN
PELLIKAN, CHRISTOPHER
PELTZ, FREDERICK DOUGLAS
PEMBERTON, SCOTT BENDER
PEMBERTON, STEPHEN CARLYSLE
*PEMPER, MARY JANET
PENCE, PAMELA JEAN
*PENCE, ROBERT JOHN

100

PENKAVA, ROBERTA
PENN, CANDACE MARIE
PENNELL, DANNY JOE
PENNER, RAYMOND GEORGE, JR.
*PEO, MARGARET LOUISE
*PEPPER, DANIEL
PEPPING, JENNIFER JEAN
PERBOHNER, JOHN JAY
*PERCEFULL, AARON WILLIAM
PERELMAN, ROBERT DAVID
PERKERS, KENT JORDAN
PERKINS, CAROL ANN
PERKINS, KEVIN PATRICK
PERKINS, THOMAS WILLIAM
PERKINSON, DAVID PAUL
PERKOFF, DAVID ALAN
PERLEN, MARK ROY
*PERLMAN, BRUCE STEPHEN
PERLMAN, REID MICHAEL
*PERLOW, DAVID LEE
PERLOW, MADELINE
PERMUT, STEVEN LARRY
PERRIER, JANICE PERKINS
PERRINO, LUCRETIA ALINE
PERRY, RALPH WAYNE
PERTILE, ELLEN LYNN
PESKIN, BARBARA LYNNE
PESTELL, BRUCE EDWARD
*PESTIEN, RICHARD ARTHUR
PETER, MARY HEBRON
PETERS, FARLEY MILLS
PETERS, NANCY
*PETERS, NIKI KAY
PETERS, RENEE KATHALEEN
PETERSEN, JANET F.
PETERSEN, JUNE ELLEN
PETERSEN, LINDA RAE
PETERSEN, MARSHA GAY
PETERSON, CARLA
*PETERSON, CHRISTOPHER MERLE
PETERSON, DAVID EDWARD
PETERSON, GAIL FERNE
*PETERSON, GEORGE ALLEN
*PETERSON, GORDON EDMOND, II
PETERSON, JAMES DOUGLAS
PETERSON, JOHN ANDREW
PETERSON, KEITH ALAN
*PETERSON, LARRY DEAN
PETERSON, LINDA ELLIS
*PETERSON, LORETTA MARIE
PETERSON, LYNETTE ANNE
PETERSON, MERRITT RAMSEY
PETERSON, PAUL LEONARD
PETITJEAN, DAWN YVONNE
*PETITT, KATHY ALENE
PETKUS, LAWRENCE LEE
PETREK, FRANCIS RAYMOND
PETRIGALA, BARRY EDWARD
PETROSKEY, DOROTHY CAROLYN
PETRY, JANET KAY
PETRY, JOSEPHINE ANNE
PETTAY, ROBERT HENRY
PETTI, ROBERT CHARLES
*PETTIBONE, JILL ELIZABETH
PETTIS, ROXANN

*PETTIT, MARTHA ANN
PETTIT, REID ALLEN
PETTY, DENNIS GUY
PETZING, ROBERT DALE
PFEFFERLE, NORMAN WALTER
*PFLAUM, SUSAN MARIE
PHALEN, JOHN WILLIAM
*PHELAN, JAMES HARRY
PHELAN, PATRICIA MAUREEN
PHILIPAITIS, GREGORY RAYMOND
*PHILIPPE, KATHERINE ELSA
PHILIPPI, THOMAS RICHARD
*PHILLIPS, BEVERLY RUTH
PHILLIPS, CAROL ANN
PHILLIPS, DONALD MARK
PHILLIPS, ELLIOTT RICHARD
PHILLIPS, GWEN E.
PHILLIPS, LAWRENCE RICHARD
*PHILLIPS, ROBERT EDWIN
PHILLIPS, ROBERT JOSEPH
PHIPPS, KELSEY JANE
PIACENTI, MERLE ANGELD
PIACENTINI, RITA ELIZA
PIATT, THOMAS JOHN
PICK, MICHAEL ARTHUR
PICKARD, DAWN
*PICKERING, BETH ANNE
PICKERING, JOHN
PICKERING, SALLY VICTORIA
*PICL, FRANK MATTHEW
PIEKARZ, JUDY IRENE
*PIENKOS, PHILIP THOMAS
*PIEPER, CAROL ELAINE
PIETRZAK, MICHAEL JOSEPH
PIETSEK, DAVID JEAN JACQUES
PIFKE, ROBERT CHARLES, JR.
PIKE, GERALD ADOLPH
PILE, LARRY WILLIAM
PILGRIM, LAURA JEAN
PILIBOSIAN, DIANE JEAN
PILLING, SUE ANN
PILZ, DAVID PAUL
PIME, LESLIE IRA
PINES, BONNIE JOY
PINES, JAN PHYLLIS
PINTO, ILZA MARIA FERREIRA
PINZUR, MICHAEL STEVEN
PIPER, PATRICIA KATE
PIPER, RONALD ROBERT
PISTORIUS, ROSEMARY
*PITTROFF, KATHRYN EVELYN
PITTS, ALBERT LEWIS
PITTS, ALICE ANN
PITTS, EMILY LARUE
PLACEK, BRUCE PHILLIP
PLACKE, JOAN WOOD
*PLASS, JANE PAULA
PLATT, CYNTHIA ANN
*PLATTNER, PAUL FREDRICK
PLAYER, J. SCOT
PLECKI, GERARD DAVID
PLESKO, JEFFREY MICHAEL
PLESKO, JOHN TODD
*PLESKO, TIMOTHY JOHN
*PLETCHER, WILLIAM RANDALL

101

PLEVIAK, JOHN ARTHUR
PLIKAITIS, PATRICIA ROZYCKI
PLINSKE, LUCIA SUE
*PLOETZ, CATHERINE SUE
PLOTKIN, STEVEN JOEL
PLOTKIN, WENDY
PLUMLEY, CHRISTINE MYRA
PNAZEK, KARL STEVEN
POCHOS, STEPHEN P.
*PODLIPNIK, CAROL JOY
*POEHLER, DAVID WAYNE
POEPSEL, JAMES EDWARD
POFFENBERGER, CRAIG ALAN
POGOFSKY, TERRY JAY
*POHLOD, PATRICIA ANN
POHNAN, WILLIAM GEORGE
*POKER, DAVID BRIAN
*POKORNY, JACQUELINE ANN
POLACEK, DENISE CATHERINE
POLACH, RAYMOND FRANK
POLAN, DAVID JAY
*POLIN, GLENN MICHAEL
POLITO, MARIAN
POLJACK, DIANE MARY
POLK, CARLA RAE
POLK, JANINE LYN
POLLACK, SHARON LEE
POLLANS, LANNIE AARON
POLLOCK, AUDREY MARGO
POLLOCK, TERI SUSAN
*POLLYEA, EDWARD JAY
POLON, JEFFREY MICHAEL
*POMRENKE, BONNIE JOYCE
*POOLE, DORIS J. G.
POPE, JAMES WILLIAM
POPE, RICHARD STINSON
*POPE, RICHARD TRAVIS
POPE, WHITNEY SUZANNE
POPHAM, TERESA VALERIE
POPMA, CHRISTOPHER MARLOTH
POPOVICH, DONNA
PORDY, MICHAEL GREGORY
POREBSKI, JAMES MATTHEW
PORTER, BELINDA JOYCE
*PORTER, DARCY ANN
PORTER, JOHN WENDELL
PORTER, LAWRENCE NATHANIEL, JR.
PORTER, MARY ANN
PORTER, MARY JOSEPHINE
PORTER, ROBERT DONALD
*POST, WARREN MICHAEL
POSTULA, KATHLEEN MAUER
POSTULA, MICHAEL JOSEPH
POTEMPA, GREGORY LOUIS
POTISH, HERBERT AARON
POTTEBAUM, JAMES ANTHONY
POTTS, CAROLYN JEAN
*POTTS, KENNETH CHARLES
*POTTS, MARY JOAN
*POULTON, MARY SUZANNE
*POVILUS, ROGER PETER
*POWELL, MARITA ANN
POWELL, PAULA LOU
POWER, DIANE ELIZABETH
POWERS, CHARLES HENRY, JR.

POWERS, JANIS ELIZABETH
POWERS, THOMAS ANTHONY
POWLEY, DOUGLAS JACK
POY, PAUL CHRISTOPHER
*POY, PAULA
POYSER, JOAN R.
POZULP, KEITH RAYMOND
PRAG, LAUREL ELLEN
*PRANAITIS, ALPHONSE JOAN
*PRANGE, CLARICE DIANE
PRATT, HAROLD THORNTON
*PREBIL, RICHARD LOUIS
PRESCOTT, EVELYN KATHLEEN
*PRESCOTT, LAURANCE LEIGH
PRESCOTT, RAUSIE LU
*PRESCOTT, VICKI LEE
PRESS, JILL DEBRA
PRETORIUS, KAY PHILLIPS
PREUSS, WENDIE ANN
PRICE, GLENN RUSSELL
PRICE, ROBIN GLENEN
*PRIEST, JOHN BRIAN LESLEY
PRIMMER, CHERYL LOU
PRIMMER, PAMELA RICE
PRISCO, ANNE LOUISE
PRITCHARD, SUZANNE
PRITKIN, NANCI HOLLY
*PRITZKER, EDWARD BRUCE
*PROCH, RUSSELL ALAN
*PROCHASKA, GAIL LYNN
PROCTOR, CHARLES MAIN
*PROCTOR, MICHEAL WILLIAM
PROCTOR, TERESA CAROLYN
PROEFROCK, DAVID WAYNE
*PROJAHN, JUDITH ELAINE
*PROKOP, ROXANNE JOAN
PROKSA, ROSEMARY
PROPST, CHARLES MITCHELL
*PRORAK, STEVEN LEE
PROSEK, ALLEN RICHARD
PROSISE, WILLIAM EDWARD
PROVAN, EVA BETH
PRUETT, RICHARD KEPLEY
PRUNKARD, DONNA ELLEN
PRUZAN, BARBARA ILENE
PRUZAN, KAREN LEE
*PRZYBYLA, CYNTHIA ANN
PRZYBYLSKI, KENNETH STANLEY
*PRZYWARA, KENNETH PAUL
PUCZYNSKI, MARK STANLEY
*PUIG, CARLOS MANUEL
PUKSZTA, FAITH MARIE
PULSFUS, DWIGHT WESLEY
PURCELL, ROBIN RAE
PURVIS, DAVID MICHAEL
*PURVY, ROBERT EDWARD
*PUTNAM, TIMOTHY DUANE
PUTTCAMP, CAROL ELIZABETH
*PYE, STEVEN ROBERT
PYHRR, STUART WALTER
PYLE, DONALD WAYNE, JR.
PYSTER, ARTHUR BRUCE
QUAID, TERESA ANN
QUELLER, KURT J.
*QUINN, ROSEMARY C.

*Quinn, Yvonne Susan
Quirin, Mary Lucinda
Rabin, Alan Jeffrey
Rabin, Linda Sue
Racine, David Paul
*Raczkowski, Andrew Wesley
Radaszewski, Geraldine Mary
*Radell, Jeanne Marie
Radell, Judith Kissell
Rader, Linda Louise
Radin, Robert Samuel
*Radke, Susan Nell
Radkey, William Allen
*Radloff, Stuart Jay
Radtke, Richard Ernest
*Radzevicius, Aldona Terese
Raff, Howard Victor
Rafferty, Patrick Kevin
Ragalie, Glenn Francis
*Rahe, Theresa Joan
Raia, Louis John
Rainboth, Walter John, Jr.
Raino, William Henry
Raisch, Veronica Ann
Raisen, Lynn
Raither, Barbara Poole
Raker, Davie Sue
*Raker, James Curtis
Raker, Rodney Jay
Rallo, Michael James
Ralsky, Stuart Lee
Ramsey, John Walker
*Ramsey, Linda Kay
Ramsey, Patricia Wilson
Ramthun, Edward Jay
Randall, Amy Lee
Randall, Leah Ursula
Randolph, Myra Elizabeth
*Rankin, John Philip
*Rapoport, Alan Bennett
*Rapp, Paul Ernest
Rapp, Stephen Jay
Rarick, Joseph Francis, Jr.
Raslavicius, Jolanta Regina
*Rasmus, James Lee
*Rassi, Gregory Gene
*Rassi, Kathy Annette
*Rathbun, Janet Marlene
Rathbun, Philip Edward
Ratko, Georgeann Estelle
Ratner, Dheena Elaine
*Rattner, Ilene Sue
Raubitschek, William L.
Rauen, Dorothy Jo
Rauh, Eric John
*Rausch, Thomas Jay
Rauschenberger, Carol Jean
*Ray, Randall Parker
Ray, Scott Laury
Read, Kathleen Lois
Read, Marcia Lee
Read, Martin Lewis
Read, Robert Dale
*Reader, John Roderick
Ready, James Francis

Reagan, Bonnie Dee
Reagan, Timothy John
Reardon, Robert Bruce
*Rebitzer, Sandy Joy
Rechel, Kathy Jane
*Rector, Lois Ann
Redard, Thomas Edmund
Redborg, Kurt Eric
Reding, John Joseph
Redmond, Thomas Richard
Redshaw, Michael Dennis
Reed, Patricia Ann
*Reed, Robert Phillip
*Reeder, Guy Scott
Reeder, Kirsten Ruth
Reeder, Rebecca Thompson
Reedy, Colleen Ann
Reeves, Kim Walton
Reeves, Rodney Franklin
Regan, Lucy Lenore
Reichelt, Janis Marie
Reid, Frank Olaf
Reid, John Harvey
*Reifman, William Jay
*Reilley, Ginger Lorene
Reilly, Robert Joseph
Reimann, Dagmar Gudrun
Reimann, John William
*Reimers, Toni Phyllis
*Reinbolt, Kathleen Mary
*Reiner, David Lawrence
*Reinhart, Gregory Duncan
Reinschmidt, Mildred Lackovic
Reis, Deborah Lee
*Reisig, Terri Hobbs
Reisman, Paul Lee
Reisman, Terri Lynne
Rembe, Inge Ambros
Rende, Richard Joseph
Renken, Mary Jane
Renner, Rosina
Renzaglia, Gary John
Repka, Janice Ann
*Resnick, Donald Ira
Resnick, Lynne Karen
*Resnik, Daniel Mark
Resnik, Elena Cinthia
Resnik, Sheri Iris
Retel, Debra Lynn
*Reuben, Gail Beth
*Reuben, Gordon Philip
Reuhl, Nancy Lucille
*Reuler, Peggy Rose
Reuterfors, David
Revak, Joann
*Revord, Sherry Ann
Reynolds, Patrick Timothy
Reynolds, Robert Joseph
Reynolds, Scott Howard
Reynolds, Shelley Patricia
Reynolds, Teri Elaine
*Rheinwald, James George
*Rheinwald, Krystal Luckhart
Rhinehart, Robert Eugene
Rhoads, Dean Bernard

*Rhodes, Beverly Patsky
*Rhodes, Howard Edgar
*Ricci, Ellen Camille
Ricci, Terrence Armand
*Rice, Catherine Nelle
Rice, Davida Nan
Rich, Gary Russell
Richards, Harlan James
*Richards, Laurel Ann
*Richards, Mary Louise
Richards, Steven Craig
*Richardson, Bruce Compton
*Richardson, Carol Ann
Richardson, Elijah
*Richardson, Jean Ann
Richardson, Lucy Jane
Richardson, Michael Jay
*Richardson, Patricia Claire
Richardson, Thomas Lee
Richart, Lanny Ronald
Richert, Janet Elizabeth
Richert, Paul
Richter, Eric Estes
Richter, George Edward
Rickelman, Joseph Grennon
Ricks, Cynthia Sterling
*Riddle, Guy Gregory
Ridgeway, George Ernest, Jr.
*Riedel, Philip Alan
Rieger, Susan Ruth
Riemer, Ladone Gaydos
Rifas, Susan Harriet
Rife, James E.
Rigby, David Benjamin
*Riggins, Virginia Gardner
Riley, Maureen Julia
*Rimdzius, Robert John
Ringl, Karen Kohrt
Rinkenberger, Roger Eric
Rinker, Alan Dale
Riordan, Gavin Patrick
Riordan, Pamela Ann
Rios, Jose Rangel
Rippelmeyer, Lynn Janet
*Rippinger, Debra Lynn
Risik, Robert Alan
Risley, David Earl
Ritacca, Daniel John
*Ritholz, Paula Sue
Ritsert, Laurence Edward
Ritter, Michael Allen
Rittger, Susan Rae
Ritts, Karen Sue
Ritzman, Linda Anne
*Rivera, Marcelo
*Rivers, Gordon Thomas
Rivkin, Andrea Ellen
Rizzi, Dolores
Rizzo, Susanne Frances
Roach, Marcia Frances
Roach, Mary Marguerite
Robben, Allyn Barbara
Robbins, Marc Bradley
*Robbins, Mary Snyder
Robbins, Paula Esther

Robbins, Ralph Norton
*Robbins, Shelley Ruth
Roberson, Garvin Edward
Roberts, Ava Joan
Roberts, Christine Mary
Roberts, Diana Kay
Roberts, Donald Walton
Roberts, Gregory Sinclair
*Roberts, Jeffery Lynn
Roberts, Karen Ann
Roberts, Kathryn Anne
Roberts, Mary Ann
*Roberts, Mary Ann
*Roberts, Patricia Ann
Roberts, Sandra Sue
Roberts, Susan Schuyler
Roberts, Toni Dale
Robertson, Donald U.
*Robertson, Lois Kraft
Robie, Michael Edward
*Robin, Arnold Paul
*Robin, Erwin Lee
Robin, Neil Arnold
*Robins, Karen Eisenstein
Robinson, Alan George
Robinson, Arthur Christopher
*Robinson, Denny Wayne
*Robinson, Gary Edward
Robinson, Guy Cecil
Robinson, Laura Louise
*Robinson, Richard Bruce
*Rock, Jeffrey Blair
*Rockoff, Mark Ronald
*Rockrohr, Lynn Mary
Rockwood, Donald Charles
Roddy, David Joseph
Rodell, Daniel Elias
Roden, Ronald Edward
Roderick, Craig Bryon
Rodgerson, Janet Rae
Rodriquez, Dale Frank
Roeckeman, John David
Roer, Kathleen Marie
Roesch, Susan Rae
Rogers, David Ray
Rogers, Mark Jeffrey
*Rogers, Pamela Ann
Rogers, Rosalie Kay
*Rogge, Paula Ann
Rogowskey, Thomas Allen
Rohde, Douglas John
*Rohde, Janet Gail
*Rohlfing, Michael Bruce
Rohrbach, James Martin
Rohrkaste, Linda Kay
Rokosch, Donald Karl Joseph
*Romain, Paul Lawrence
*Roman, Nan Patrice
Romero, Santiago
Romine, Ross Walter
*Romweber, Susan Thayer
*Ronat, Cheri Rae
Roney, Ellen Elizabeth
*Rook, Karen Sue
Rooker, Lewis William

ROOKER, MAUREEN EVELYN
*ROOS, ADONNA JEAN
*ROOS, CYNTHIA ELAINE
ROSALES, PORFIRIO, JR.
ROSBACH, JAMES HENRY
ROSBOROUGH, MICHAEL JOHN
ROSE, CAROLYN SUE
*ROSE, CYNTHIA JEAN
ROSE, DAVID ALLEN
ROSE, DEBRA MERLE
ROSE, MARK JORDAN
ROSE, WALTER D., JR.
ROSE, WILLIAM HARVEY
ROSE, WILLIAM WARREN
*ROSECRANS, RICHARD KURT
*ROSELLI, RONALD CLIFFORD
*ROSELLINI, ELEANOR FLORENCE
*ROSEN, BARRY STUART
ROSEN, CAROLYN ANNE
ROSEN, ELISSE AMY
ROSEN, HOWARD STEPHEN
*ROSEN, JAMES WILLIAM
ROSENBAUM, ALLEN JEROME
*ROSENBAUM, DAVID NEAL
ROSENBAUM, LINDA JEANNE
*ROSENBAUM, MARY JOY
*ROSENBAUM, RICHARD MORRIS
ROSENBERG, ALAN SCOTT
ROSENBERG, DIANE FLORENCE
*ROSENBERG, JAMES AUGUST
ROSENBERG, KAREN LEE
ROSENBERG, KAREN NADINE
ROSENBERG, MARK RICHARD
ROSENBLUM, DAVID BRIAN
ROSENBLUM, LAURA CATHY
*ROSENBUSH, STUART WILLIAM
ROSENFELD, ALAN LENARO
ROSENFELS, ELLEN
ROSENTHAL, KENNETH LEE
ROSENTHAL, RICHARD HYMAN
*ROSENTRETER, KATHIE ROSE
ROSETT, BONNIE GAIL
ROSINIA, RICHARD WILLIAM
ROSINSKI, KENNETH JOHN
ROSINSKI, LYNN ANN
*ROSMAN, JOSEPH KENNETH
ROSNER, KRISTINE MARIE
ROSS, DAVID MICHAEL
ROSS, DONALD OVINGTON, JR.
ROSS, MARILYN KATHLEEN
ROSS, MARK ALAN
ROSS, MICHAEL EUGENE
*ROSS, ROBIN
*ROSS, SUZANNE
ROSS, WILLIAM ZENON
*ROSSEN, MARJORIE ELIZABETH
ROSTELLO, DONNA JEAN
*ROTFELD, HERBERT JACK
ROTH, BARBARA MYRA
ROTH, EILEEN JOYCE
ROTH, GALE LORRAINE
*ROTH, GARY FRANCIS
*ROTH, GERALD LEE
ROTH, KEVEN SIMONE
ROTH, REBECCA LOUISE

ROTHBAUM, SUSAN ANDREA
ROTHBERG, KATHLEEN MICHELE
*ROTHBLATT, DEBORAH EILEEN
ROTHKOPF, JAMES PAUL
ROTHMAN, HELEN
ROTHROCK, STUART EARL
ROTHROCK, SUSAN RUTH
ROTHSCHILD, BRUCE LEE
ROTMENSCH, JACOB
*ROUFFA, MICHAEL ALAN
ROURKE, TIMOTHY JOHN
ROUSE, RONALD LEE
*ROUSOS, LINDA ANN
ROUTH, REBECCA PAULINE
ROVEL, KATHERINE PARTLOW
ROWE, DAVID DONALD
ROWE, MARIANNE RENEE
ROWE, SUSAN ELAINE
ROWLAND, WILLIAM THOMAS
ROWLEY, THOMAS NATHAN
ROZENSKY, RONALD HOWARD
ROZMARIN, JUDY ANN
*ROZYCKI, CARLA JOANNE
RUBEL, ROBERT CHARLES
RUBERRY, THOMAS MICHAEL
RUBIANO, CONNIE
RUBIN, BERNARD ROSS
*RUBIN, DAVID BERNARD
*RUBIN, DAVID IAN
*RUBIN, DEBORAH RACHEL
*RUBIN, ROSE MILLS
RUBINSTEIN, CHARISSA
RUCH, PEGGIE MARIE
RUDAK, FAYE LINDA
*RUDMAN, SHERWIN MICHAEL
RUDSINSKI, JANICE RUTH
RUEFFER, TERRY CLARENCE
RUEKBERG, MADELEINE
RUFFNER, ROBERT HADSELL
RUFFOLO, LAWRENCE MICHAEL
*RUNDQUIST, BARBARA JANE
*RUNGE, THOMAS FRED
RUPP, MARY
RUSH, ROBERT ALAN
RUSHFORD, KIM ANN
RUSKIN, WILLIAM DAVID
*RUSS, ANN KRISTINE
RUSSELL, MARY DORIA
RUSSELL, SUSAN DIANA
RUTGARD, JEFFREY JAY
*RUTH, DEBORAH ANN
*RUTLEDGE, DAVID ALLAN
*RUTLEDGE, JAMES EDWARD
RUTTENBERG, ALLEN ROBERT
RUTZ, PATRICIA ANN
RUUD, JAMES EDWARD
RUZEVICK, MICHAEL ALAN
RYAN, KATHERINE E.
RYAN, LESLIE PATRICIA
RYAN, MARK RUSS
RYAN, NANCY LORETTA
RYAN, THOMAS PATRICK
RYDING, DAVID GENE
RYHERD, MARCIA JOAN
*RZEPKA, JOYCE ANN

SAAK, MARY TERESE
SABATH, BARRY ALLEN
SABATINO, PAULA JANE
SABIN, CRAIG LEE
SABIN, WENDY
SABITT, MARK NEIL
*SACADAT, STEFFI SUE
SACHISE, THOMAS PAUL
SACHS, JEAN LESLIE
SACHTLEBEN, DALE RICHARD
SACK, SUSAN MARY
*SACKS, NANCY DIANE
SADAUSKAS, JONAS LINAS
SADLER, KARAN DAWN
SAFFOLD, ROSIE M.
*SAFFORD, SHARON ANN
*SAFFRO, RICHARD KENNETH
SAGER, TERRY M.
SAGER, ZOANN JANE
SAILLARD, PATRICIA ANN
SAINDON, ROCHELLE MARIE
SAINSBURY, DAYLE
SAINTEN, CARL BYRON
*SAIPE, GARY SCOTT
SAJDAK, JOANNE MARIE
SAJKEWYCZ, IRENE ANN
SAKAMOTO, DAVID TAKESHI
*SALADINO, JO-ANN CATHERINE
*SALAMINI, ANN SCHEHSCHMIDT
SALETTE, JOSEPH CHARLES, III
SALIAN, SCOTT CHARLES
SALKIN, MARC JEFFREY
*SALOMONE, ANN MARIE
SALS, TERRENCE ARTHUR
SALZMAN, STEVEN RAYMOND
SAMFORD, GARY LEON
SAMMIT, GARY MATTHEW
*SAMPRACOS, ANDREA
*SAMPSON, DIANA J.
SAMPSON, LAWRENCE EDWARD
SAMPSON, SUSAN KAY
SANDER, WILLIAM HENRY, III
SANDERS, DEBORAH SUE
SANDERS, KENNETH STEVEN
SANDERS, MICKEY L.
SANDERS, STEVEN PAUL
SANDERSON, GRETCHEN LEE
*SANDLER, STEVEN ALEX
SANDMAN, CARY STEVEN
SANDROLINI, ELLEN
SANFIELD, LINDA
SANKOWSKY, SUSAN L.
SANTANA, ROSINA
*SANTANDREA, MARY FRANCES
SANTOGROSSI, PATRICIA ANN
SANTORI, MARY-JEANNE
*SANTOSTEFANO, MARIA JEANNE THERESE
*SAPER, CLIFFORD BAIRD
*SARENA, MICHELE LOUISE
SARGENT, MARK EDWARD
SARGENT, WALTER LEE
*SARUK, MICHAEL LOUIS
SARVER, JAY IRWIN
SARVER, PATRICIA DARLENE
SATHRE, JEANNE LEE

*SATTERTHWAITE, MARGARET ANN
SATTERTHWAITE, NEAL R.
SAUER, DAVID LEE
SAUERBRUNN, CHARLOTTE LORRAINE
SAULS, ROBERT JOSEPH
*SAVAGE, BRYAN FRANCIS
*SAVITZKY, DAVID BARRY
SAVULA, NANCY ANN
SAYDEL, KENNETH MICHAEL
SAYRE, ANN JEANETTE
SAYRE, ROBIN ONEIL
SAZUNIC, BERNARDITA MARIA
SCAFURI, RALPH LOUIS
SCALETTA, JOYCE MARIE
SCALETTA, LAWRENCE PHILIP
SCARNATO, MARY SUSAN
*SCHAAR, MARVIN B.
SCHACHT, SUSAN GRETEL
SCHAEFER, GREGORY ROY
SCHAEFER, JAMEY LOU
SCHAEFER, JANE ANN
SCHAEFER, JANE ANN
SCHAEFER, PAUL DANIEL
*SCHAEFFER, RANDY CRAIG
SCHAFER, MARY THERESE
SCHAFFENACKER, GLORIA KAY
*SCHAFFNER, THEODORE MICHAEL
SCHAIBLE, JOHN FREDERICK
SCHALLER, CAROL ANN
*SCHALLHAMMER, DAVID GEORGE
*SCHAPIRO, SUSAN BARBARA
SCHARF, MARY KATHLEEN
SCHATZMAN, LYNN IVY
SCHAUBLE, LINDA KAY
SCHAUM, JOAN LOIS
SCHAVIETELLO, DENNIS CUINO
SCHAYER, LAUREL LEE
SCHECK, DEAN LESLIE
*SCHECKEL, DANIEL PATRICK
SCHECTMAN, JANIS GAIL
SCHEDEEN, GLENN JAMES
SCHEFTER, LINDA RAE
*SCHEIB, MARY A.
SCHEITLER, LAWRENCE EDWARD
*SCHEITLER, MELISSA STOUT
SCHELL, JEFFREY ANTON
SCHELL, LAURA SUSAN
SCHENCK, GEORGE ROBERT
SCHERER, SUSAN CAROL
SCHERMER, WILLIAM HARVEY
*SCHEWE, PHILLIP FRANK
*SCHEWE, STANLEY LOUIS
SCHICK, JAMES B.
SCHIELE, TERESA JOY
*SCHILLING, DAVID ERWIN
SCHILLING, LINDA JOAN
*SCHILLING, MARY WELCH
SCHINDEL, BARBARA ANN
SCHINDLER, FRED HENRY
SCHLAN, JAMES MICHAEL
SCHLAN, LESTER LAWRENCE
SCHLEETER, JANET ELAINE
SCHLEICHER, BARBARA ANN
*SCHLESINGER, MARC LEON
*SCHLESINGER, PAUL KEITH

SCHLESSER, JOSEPH EDWARD
SCHLICHTING, JANAN MARIE
SCHLINK, DAVID VAL
*SCHLOSS, LARRY MARK
SCHLOZ, CAROLE RUTH
SCHLOZ, MARY SUE
SCHLUETER, ROBERT GLEN
SCHMEDAKE, NANCY LEE
SCHMICHER, JUDITH WANDA
SCHMIDT, ARNOLD JEFFREY
*SCHMIDT, BARBARA ANN
SCHMIDT, BARRY LEE
SCHMIDT, BART DAVID
SCHMIDT, CHRISTY KAY
SCHMIDT, CORYNNE ANN
SCHMIDT, DANIEL LEE
SCHMIDT, GAYLA MARIE
*SCHMIDT, GREGORY GLEN
SCHMIDT, LINDA GENE
SCHMIDT, ROBERT KENNETH
SCHMIDT, STEPHEN PETER
*SCHMIEDL, NANCY EILEEN
SCHMITT, ROBERT RICHARD
SCHMITZ, KATHY ANGELA
SCHMITZ, STEVEN MICHAEL
SCHNAYER, MICHELLE CAROL
SCHNEIDER, ANDREA LYNNE
SCHNEIDER, CHARLES MILTON
SCHNEIDER, DANNY LEN
SCHNEIDER, DAVID MICHAEL
SCHNEIDER, DEBRA ANN
*SCHNEIDER, GREGG DAVID
SCHNEIDER, JAMES CHARLES
*SCHNEIDER, PETRA RENATE
*SCHNEIDER, PHYLLIS JEAN
SCHNEIDER, RENEE SUE
*SCHNEIDER, WALTER
*SCHNEIDER, WILLIAM ARTHUR
SCHNEIDMAN, BRUCE ALAN
SCHNIERLE, HAROLD S.
SCHOCH, LINDA SUE
SCHOCK, RICHARD FREDERICK, II
*SCHOENBERG, DANIEL ROBERT
SCHOENEMAN, JANET ELISE
SCHOFIELD, BRUCE EDWARD
SCHOFIELD, CHERIE LYN
SCHOLTENS, LINDA HERRMANN
SCHOONHOVEN, MARGEL JOAN
*SCHOTT, GARY LAWRENCE
SCHOUSBOE, NICOLAI BENEDICT
SCHOY, KENNETH MARTIN
SCHRAMM, CHARLES MARTIN
SCHRAMM, HAROLD LAWRENCE, JR.
SCHRANK, JOHN ARTHUR
SCHRECK, REED CARL
*SCHREIBER, LOREN BENNETT
SCHREINER, VIRGINIA CAROL
*SCHREMSER, VICTORIA CHARLOTTE
SCHRENZEL, NORMA SOFO
*SCHRICKEL, SUSAN MARIE
*SCHRICKEL, THOMAS EDWARD
*SCHRIVER, JANE ELIZABETH
*SCHRIVER, KATHRYN MARIE
SCHROCK, CARL MARSHALL
SCHROEDER, ALAN RANDALL

SCHROEDER, CARL JOHN
SCHROEDER, JERENE CAROL
SCHROEDER, JOYCE KATHERINE
SCHROEDER, LORING WILLIAM
SCHROEDER, THERESA ANNE
SCHROEN, LINDA JEAN
SCHUB, ORA NEHAMA
SCHUB, ZEVA
*SCHUBERT, DONALD KEITH
SCHUBERT, JEFFREY PAUL
SCHUBERT, RICHARD NEAL
SCHUBERT, VIRGINIA SUSAN
*SCHUENGEL, SUSAN RUTH
SCHUETT, LORI JANICE
SCHUETZ, CHRISTINE ANNE
SCHUETZ, DENNIS LEE
*SCHULER, GREGORY GERARD
*SCHULER, SHELLEY SUE
SCHULMAN, STEVEN LEE
*SCHULTZ, CLIFFORD LELAND
SCHULTZ, DAVID WALTER
*SCHULTZ, DIANE MARIE
*SCHULTZ, JANET RAE
SCHULTZ, JOHN M.
*SCHULTZ, RONALD N.
SCHULTZ, SANDRA JANE
SCHULZ, BARBARA ADELAIDE
SCHUMM, GILBERT CONRAD
*SCHUNK, MARCIA ANN
SCHUSTEFF, HELENE
SCHUSTER, RICHARD LELAND
SCHUSTER, SALLY ANN
SCHUTT, ERNEST GEORGE
*SCHUTZ, RONALD WALTER
SCHUVER, ANDREA MICHELLE
*SCHWAB, MICHAEL JOEL
*SCHWAPPACH, KATHLEEN ROSE
*SCHWARTZ, BONNIE HELENE
*SCHWARTZ, BRADFORD SCOTT
SCHWARTZ, CHARLES FREDERICK
*SCHWARTZ, DAVID BRUCE
*SCHWARTZ, JERROLD FREDERICK
SCHWARTZ, LYNN DEE
*SCHWARTZ, SAMUEL CHAIM
*SCHWARTZ, SUSAN MARGARET
SCHWARZKOPF, LINDA JOY
*SCHWEIGHART, SANDRA KAY
SCHWENGEL, BONITA ELLEN
SCHWENGEL, RHONDA SUSAN
SCHWINGL, PAMELA JANE
SCOFIELD, EDRA JONES
SCOGGINS, ELIZABETH ANNE
*SCOTT, BODE COURTNEY
*SCOTT, CAROL ANN
*SCOTT, DON JOE
*SCOTT, GREGORY BRADFORD
SCOTT, JUDITH ANN
SCOTT, KATHRYN JO
*SCOTT, KATHY LYNN
SCOTT, PATRICIA ANN
SCOTT, RICHARD PAUL
*SCOTT, TIMOTHY RALPH
*SCOTT, WILLIAM ROY
SCOTTON, PAUL DOUGLAS
SCUTERI, GLENN ANDREW

SEABOLD, WALTER GARFIELD, JR.
SEABORN, STEVEN EDWARD
SEAMAN, MARGUERITE LAVERNE
*SEAMAN, THOMAS MICHAEL
SEARS, GEORGIA TAYLOR
SEATON, MARY FRANCES
SEBAT, LINDA CHRISTIE
*SEBEK, JAMES JOSEPH
*SEBELA, KAREN MARIE
SEBENIK, MARCIA KATHLEEN
*SECTER, ROBERT HENRY
*SEDERBERG, SCOTT ROBERT
SEDORY, DENIS RICHARD
*SEEGER, MARC ALAN
SEEMAYER, KATHLEEN MARY
*SEFCIK, STEPHAN E., II
SEGLIN, VICKI LYNN
SEHY, DENNIS MARTIN
SEIBERLING, LESLIE KAY
SEIDENBERG, STEVEN
SEIDMAN, CHRISTOPHER
SEIDMAN, MARC BENJAMIN
SEIGEL, DONALD L.
SEIGEL, LYNNE NORMA
SEITZ, HAROLD LEROY
*SEITZ, MICHAEL WILLIAM
*SEKULSKI, JANET MARIE
SELBY, ROSEMARY
*SELBY, SALLY JO
SELFRIDGE, RICHARD JAY
SELIGMAN, LAURIE ANN
SELIN, AUDREY ESTHER
SELLERGREN, KAREN ANN
*SELLERS, LINDA JOY
SELLERS, SUE ANN
SEMENIUK, CATHERINE MYRTLE
SEMLER, LUCINDA JANE
SEMONIN, CECELIA CATHERINE
*SEMPLE, MARGARET ANNE
SENNER, DIANE ANITA
SENNER, WILLIAM LEWIS
*SEPTON, ALLEN MARC
SERBY, KAREN JOYCE
SERCHUK, PETER ROBERT
SERENE, MARILYN KAY
SEROTA, ARNOLD I.
SERVI, MARINA KAY
*SERWINT, NANCY JEAN
SEVCIK, DONALD JAMES
SEVERIN, BLAINE FRANK
SEWELL, CAROLYN HESSE
SEWELL, CHARLES THOMAS
SEXTON, LAURENCE ALLEN
SHABSIN, RICHARD LARRY
SHAE, LAURA HARRIETT
SHAFER, MARTHA JEAN
*SHAFER, STEPHEN CRAIG
*SHAFFER, JANET IRENE
*SHAFTMAN, SARAH MIRIAM
SHALLCROSS, CAROL JEAN
SHALLENBERGER, PAMELA ANN
SHANKS, ROGER D.
SHANNON, EWA MARIE
SHANNON, JOSEPH PATRICK
*SHANNON, KATHLEEN LOUISE

SHANOFF, KENNETH MARK
SHAPERO, BARBARA RUTH
*SHAPIRO, DAVID H.
*SHAPIRO, DEBORAH ARLENE
*SHAPIRO, DENYSE JAN
SHAPIRO, DONALD ALLAN
*SHAPIRO, HELEN DEBORAH
SHAPIRO, IRIS ELLEN
SHAPIRO, JOEL H.
SHAPIRO, MARIYLN DALE
*SHAPIRO, MICHAEL ROBERT
*SHAPIRO, RICHARD ALAN
SHAPIRO, RITA ANNE
SHAPIRO, WAYNE STEWART
SHAPLAND, MARY CHARLOTTE
*SHARP, CAROLYN
SHARP, RANDALL EUGENE
SHAW, BERNARD EVAN
SHAW, CAROLYN JEAN
SHAW, KEITH ALAN
SHEADE, MICHAEL
SHEAGREN, THOMAS GEORGE
SHEAHIN, BARBARA ANNE
SHECHTMAN, STEVEN
*SHEDLOCK, THOMAS EDWARD
SHEETS, ROBERT KENNETH
SHEFFER, CHRISTINE TAYLOR
SHEFFOLD, ARLENE ANN
SHEFNER, JEREMY M.
*SHEFT, JUDITH ANN
SHELANGOUSKI, BEVERLY ANN
*SHELBY, BRUCE DENNIS
SHELTON, PATRICIA JANE
SHENOHA, MARY C.
SHEPARD, ELLEN SUE
SHEPARD, JOAN MADELON
*SHEPARD, LLOYD STANLEY
SHEPARD, TERRY LANCE
SHEPARDSON, SHARON ANN
*SHEPHERD, MELINDA CAROL
SHEPHERD, SALLY VAUGHN
SHERBENOU, JERRE WYN
SHEREOS, VICKI
SHEREY, BRENDA LEE
SHERMAN, BETSY JANE
SHERMAN, CYNTHIA ROSANNE
SHERMAN, DEBORAH NAOMI
SHERMAN, JUDITH FAY
SHERMAN, MARK PHILLIP
SHERMAN, MICHAEL ROSCOE
SHERMAN, PATRICIA ANN
*SHERMAN, PAUL THEODORE
SHERMAN, SCOTT PHILIP
*SHERROD, DANIEL WALLACE
SHERWIN, SCOTT DAVID
*SHICK, JAMES RANDLE
SHIELDS, MICHAEL JOHN
SHIELDS, WAYNE ROBERT
SHIELS, PATRICK LAWRENCE
*SHIFFLETT, LEONARD STEWART
SHIFRIN, CAROL ANN
SHILLING, BONNIE RUTH
SHILLING, LINDA KAY
*SHIMP, KATHLEEN ANNE
SHINDLE, JANE MARIE

108

SHINER, MARCY LYNN
*SHOCKEY, DAVID WILLIAM
SHOLDER, KAREN JUDITH
SHOLDER, MARC STUART
SHOOP, JOHN EVERETT
*SHOR, TOBY IRENE
SHORE, SCOTT ALLEN
*SHORT, BEVERLY JEAN
SHRIVER, JEFFREY LEE
*SHRIVER, REBECCA LOUISE
SHUFTAN, FRANKLIN RAY
SHULRUFF, CHARLES
SHUMATE, MACK HARRICE
SHUMWAY, CONSTANCE MARIE
SHUMWAY, DAVID LUCIUS
SHUMWAY, LINDA LEGNER
*SHURR, MARY JANE
*SHURTLEFF, ROBERT GLEN
*SHUTE, DONALD ALAN
*SHY, CANDICE JANE
SICKS, CAROL JEAN
*SIDO, KEVIN RICHARD
SIEBERT, MARILY ANN
SIEBERT, MELISSA ANN
*SIEBAND, LEONARD BURTON
*SIEGEL, FLORENCE LYNN
SIEGEL, JANET GAIL
SIEGEL, JUDITH ANN
SIEGEL, NED ROGER
SIEGEL, PATRICIA ANN
*SIEGLER, ROBERT STUART
*SIEMER, RICHARD CLEMENS
SIERACKI, NANCY JEAN
SIGNORETTI, LANA MAE
SIKICH, CARROLL EVANS
SIKOROWSKI, LINDA SUE
SILAVIN, SUSAN LAURIE
SILES, STEPHEN MICHAEL
SILKEY, LESLIE FEARN
SILL, KELLY LEE
SILVER, BARRY STEWART
SILVERMAN, ANN ELAINE
*SILVERMAN, CRAIG LYLE
SILVERMAN, IRWIN M.
SILVERMAN, MARLENE JUDITH
SILVERMAN, NANCY JOSEPHS
SILVERMAN, STEVEN ELLIOT
SILVERSTEIN, MARILYN RAE
SIMCOX, PAUL DAVID
*SIMMONS, GEORGE HASKEL, III
SIMMONS, VICTOR HERBERT
*SIMON, CAROL ANN
*SIMON, ERIC EDWARD
*SIMON, JEFFREY MICHAEL
*SIMON, PETER DAVIS
SIMON, ROSALYN WOLF
SIMON, STEVEN ALAN
SIMONS, ROBERT WALTER
*SIMPSON, JOHN ROBERT
SIMS, JOANNE ELIZABETH
*SIMS, SUSAN JANE
SINADINOS, WILLIAM
SINAY, BARBARA JEAN
*SINCLAIR, JAMES STEWART
SINGER, JUDITH LOU

SINGER, THOMAS CLAYTON
SINISE, RICHARD HENRY
SINOW, DAVID MARTIN
SISKIND, SHARON LEE
SISMAN, DENISE ANDREA
SISSORS, DANIEL LELAND
SIT, ELAINE CAROLYN
SIXSMITH, BARBARA ANN
SIXSMITH, NANCY ELIZABETH
SKAPERDAS, CLAIRE
SKELTON, WILLIAM GEORGE
SKILES, BARBARA ANN
SKILES, LANDA SUE
SKLAIR, TERRY LORIS
*SKLANSKY, JEAN
SKLENCAR, MARY BETH
SKOGSBERG, DUNCAN ERIC
SKOGSBERG, KATHY IRENE
SKOLASKI, SANDRA LEE
SKRODZKI, JANE MARY
*SLACK, LAURA SUSAN
SLADE, ROBERT EUGENE
*SLADEN, BERNARD J.
SLAMAR, CHARLES, JR.
SLATER, JOAN CONSTANCE
*SLATTERY, JUDITH ANN
SLATTERY, KATHERINE DIANNE
SLAYMAN, TIMOTHY KENT
SLEDD, GREGORY JAMES
*SLIDER, DARRELL LEE
SLIFE, CHARLES WARREN
SLIGER, MARY LUCILLE
*SLIVE, JACQUELINE DEE
SLIVKEN, BETH JEWEL
*SLIVKEN, ROBERTA ANN
*SLIVON, CHRISTINE ALICE
*SLIVON, LOUISE DORIS
*SLIVON, SYLVIA LOUISE
*SLIZ, DEBORAH VALENTINE
SLOAN, JANE ANN
SLONKOSKY, JANICE BATISTA
*SLOSAR, CATHERINE ANN
SLOTO, JAMES RICHARD
SLOWINSKI, BRUCE EDWARD
*SLUIZER, SUSAN ILENE
*SLUTKIN, GARY
SLUTZ, CRAIG P.
SLY, WAYNE ALAN
*SMALL, ELLEN LYNN
SMALL, SARAH ELLEN
*SMALTER, SUSAN LYNN
SMAW, ALONZO LESTER
SMIETANSKI, ALAN FRANCIS
SMILEY, LINDA SUE
SMISKO, MARSHA JEAN
SMITH, ARLENE FORSLUND
SMITH, ARTHUR FARRELL
SMITH, BARBARA JOAN
*SMITH, BARRY CHARLES
SMITH, BETTY ANN
SMITH, CARL MICHEL
SMITH, CRAIG MELVIN
SMITH, CURTIS DAVID
SMITH, CYNTHIA LOUISE
SMITH, DAVID BRUCE

SMITH, DEBORAH KATHLEEN
*SMITH, DONNA SLIFER
SMITH, DOROTHY HUFF
*SMITH, GARY EDWARD
*SMITH, GERRITT FREDERICK
SMITH, GINGER ANN
*SMITH, GREGORY DEAN
SMITH, GREGORY PAUL
SMITH, JAN ELEANOR
SMITH, JAY ALAN
SMITH, JOANN PATRICIA
*SMITH, KAREN ANDERSON
SMITH. LOWELL VINCENT
SMITH, LUCILLE OLIVIA
SMITH, LUTHER ALLEN, JR.
SMITH, MARCUS GILBERT
SMITH, MARK ANTHONY
SMITH, PATRICIA MARY
SMITH, PAUL RICHARD, JR.
SMITH, PAUL SATTLES
SMITH, RANDY LEMUEL
SMITH, RICHARD SIMPSON, JR.
SMITH, ROBERT ALAN
*SMITH, ROBERT WILLIAM
SMITH, RONALD ROY
SMITH, SHIRLEY ANN
SMITH, STEPHEN ARNOLD
SMITH, SUSAN INEZ
SMITH, TERUKO
*SMITH, TIMOTHY OHREA
*SMITH, TOBY SHARON
*SMITH, WARD WHITLOCK
SMITH, WENDY ANN
SMITH, YOLANDA MARIE
SMITHWICK, THOMAS MICHAEL
*SMOCK, LINDA JAN
*SMOLLER, BARBARA GAIL
SMOOT, LAWRENCE RAY
SNELL, LINDA LEE
SNIDER, LANE S.
*SNIVELY, STEPHEN WAYNE
SNOBLE, KAREL ANTHONY
SNOW, JAMES BRADLEY
*SNOWDEN, CLAUD RANDALL
SNYDER, CYNTHIA JANE
SNYDER, INA RUTH
SNYDER, MARILYN KAY
SNYDER, REBECCA SUE
SOBCZAK, JANE ELLEN
SODERSTROM, JANE ANN
SODIKOFF, ROBERT NOEL
SOER, BARBARA SUE
SOKOL, JUDITH DIANNE
*SOKOL, RONALD JAY
*SOKOL, RONALD P.
SOKOLOWSKI, STEPHEN JOSEPH
SOLOF, MARILYNN ANNETTE
SOLOMON, BARRY ROBERT
SOLOMON, DAVID BARRY
*SOLOMON, JEFFREY PHILIP
SOLOMON, LINDA CAROL
*SOLOMON, ROBERTA HELENE
*SOLON, JUDITH ANN
*SOLOW, SHELDON LOUIS
SOLTER, MARY MARGARET

SOMMER, CHARLES JOSEPH
SOMMERS, RICHARD LEE
SOMMERS, ROBERT JAMES
SONIN, JEFFREY
*SONNA, LINDA GAIL
*SONNEMAKER, MICHAEL WILLIAM
SONNEMAN, TOBY FRIEDL
SONNENBERG, MARK LAWRENCE
SONSINI, FRANK CHARLES
SOONG, JUDY YANG
SORENSEN, BONITA JEAN
SORENSEN, JANET IRENE
SORENSEN, KAREN LYNN
*SORENSEN, MARK WALLEN
SORG, THOMAS J.
SOSDIAN, BRIAN J.
*SOSTRIN, JUDITH SUSAN
SOUKUP, CADY ALLYN
*SOUTHON, EDWARD HENRY
SOVA, JEFFREY LLOYD
SPACEK, DIANE MARIE
SPAGAT, LINDA SUE
SPAGNA, REBECCA SUE
SPARACIO, STEVEN JAMES
*SPARKS, DAVID CHARLES
SPEAR, MICHELLE ENID
SPEAR, THOMAS MICHAEL
*SPEISER, JAMES ROBERT
*SPERLING, MARC LEWIS
SPERLING, PATRICIA ANN
SPEYER, BARBARA KAY
SPIEGEL, DEBORAH LOUISE
*SPIEGLER, ALLAN J.
*SPINNER, GERALD A.
*SPITZ, ALAN JEFFREY
SPITZ, RONALD OTTO
*SPITZE, GLENNA DEAN
*SPITZER, AMY JILL
SPITZER, WILLIAM JOHN
SPIVACK, ANDREW L.
SPOHN, TERRENCE JOSEPH
SPRAGUE, ROSS FREDERICK
*SPRIETSMA, LYNDI ROBIN
*SPRIETSMA, SUZANNE ROBIN
SPRINGER, GREGORY JAMES
SPRINGWATER, DAVID KING
*SPUDIC, MICHAEL WILLIAM
SPUNGEN, CAROL ANN
SPURGETIS, THEODORE DEAN
SQUIER, STEPHEN WINTRINGHAM
SROKA, THOMAS
SRUTOWSKI, NINA MARY
STAAHL, DIANE EDDY
*STAAS, JAMES GREGORY
STABILE, STEPHEN MICHAEL
*STABLER, MARK DOUGLAS
STABOSZ, RAE D'ORAZIO
STABOSZ, WILLIAM LAWRENCE
STACHURSKI, MARY JOSEPHA
STACK, CAROL ANN
*STAGGS, SARAH RUTH
STAGGS, SUE ELLEN
STAHLMAN, DANIEL LEE
STAHLY, LARRY DEAN
STAHNKE, JILL ARDITH

110

STAKE, JEFFREY EVANS
STALEY, DEBORAH PHELPS
STALEY, LAURA LOU
STALLONE, VERNA AUXIER
*STAMERJOHN, DAVID MICHAEL
STAMP, ELAINE RENEE
*STAMP, NANCY HENRIETTE
STANCIK, MARYANN
STANCZAK, MARILYN MARTIN
STANEK, MARILYN VICTORIA
STANKUS, BARBARA MARIE
STANKUS, SYLVIA BIRUT
STANLEY, DANIEL RAY
*STANLEY, LAUREL LOUISE
*STANOWSKI, DANIEL RICHARD
*STANTON, CATHERINE GEORGE
STAPLETON, MAUREEN THERESE
STAR, MERRIE DELPHINE
*STARK, MARILYNN DIANNE
STARK, MARY MARGARET
STARK, RUTH JOAN
*STARKE, DAVID HENRY
*STAROSCIK, JUDY MERIE
STARR, GREGORY ALBERT
*STARR, RANDI
STARR, ROSALYN LERNER
STASINSKI, DAVID DENNIS
STATKUS, FRANCINE MARIE
STAUBER, MARIAN DONALD
STAVER, DAVID ROBERT
STEARNS, SUSAN MARGARET
STED, CHARLES ARTHUR
*STEELE, ROBERT BRUCE
STEER, STEVEN ALLEN
*STEERMAN, CHRISTINE MARIE
STEFANEC, RICHARD JOHN
STEFFEN, DANIEL EUGENE
*STEFFENS, BRUCE CHASE
*STEFFENS, GARY ALAN
STEFFENSEN, JAMES PETER, JR.
*STEGEMEIER, HENRI KAHLERT
STEGER, ROBERTA ANN
STEHMAN, JAMES JOHN
STEICHEN, MICHAEL GEORGE
*STEIN, ALAN
STEIN, ALAN JOSEPH
STEIN, CHERYL IRENE
STEIN, ELIZABETH ANN
STEIN, LINDA HELEN
*STEIN, MARSHA ANNE
STEIN, ROGER DANIEL
STEINBACH, SUSAN MARIE
*STEINBERG, JOEL LARRY
STEINBERG, LILLIAN
*STEINBERG, LOUIS IRA
STEINBERG, NAOMI ANNE
STEINBERG, RICHARD CHARLES
STEINBERG, SARA JEAN
STEINER, MARLENE
STEINER, WILLIAM ERIC
STEINKAMP, LAVERNE LAURA
STEINKAMP, WILLIAM JOSEPH
STEINKEN, DANIEL JAMES
STEINMAN, JANET WONG
STEINMANN, SANDRA JEANNE

STEISKAL, ALISON MARCIA
*STENDER, JERRY HERBERT
STENGER, JOHN FRANCIS
*STEPANEK, DAVID CHARLES
STEPHEN, VALERIE ANN
STEPHENS, JEANETTE ELIZABETH
STEPHENSON, ROBERT MONTELL
STERBA, ANTON WAYNE
STERN, KAREN JOAN
STERN, NANCY ILENE
STERN, PHILIP WINTER
STERN, SHELLEY JOY
STERNAL, JAYNE R.
STERNBERG, FRANCINE CAROL
STERNBERG, LAWRENCE IRA
STERNBERG, SHERYL GAY
*STEUDEL, NANCY LEE
STEURY, CHARLES PETER
*STEVENS, ALICE JEANNE
STEVENS, CAROL LYNN
*STEVENS, ELIZABETH HOOKER
STEVENS, KATHLEEN VALERIE
*STEVENSON, JOHN DAVID
STEVENSON, LINDA DANNENBERG
STEVENSON, SCOTT WAYNE
STEWARD, CAROL DENISE
*STEWART, DEBORAH LYNN
STEWART, DIANE LYNN
STEWART, JOHN HOWARD
STEWART, KATHLEEN MILLARD
STEWART, LINDA SUSAN
STEWART, PATSY EBERHARDT
STIAK, JUDITH KATHLEEN
STICE, SUSAN DEMOSS
*STICHA, PAUL JOEL
*STIEGMAN, GREGORY VAN
STIERMAN, CHARLES FREDERICK
STIFEL, PAUL McDONALD
*STILES, CAROLYN LOUISE
STILES, LANA FRANCINE
STILLI, SUSAN ANN
STILWELL, CAROLYN ELIZABETH
STIPE, MARY ELEANOR
STITT, JAMES STEVEN
STJOHN, GREGORY JOSEPH
STOCK, KATHLEEN JEAN
STOCKBARGER, DANISE ELLEN
STOCKDALE, LAWRENCE EDWARD
STOCKNER, DEBRA FRANK
STOFFREGEN, JOHN VERNON
STOHLE, MICHAEL RALPH
STOJAN, CRAIG THOMAS
STOKES, ALVIN ARDWAY
STOKES, RONNIE JOE
STOKLOSA, CYNTHIA KAY
*STOKOLS, JEFFERY MARK
STOKOLS, MARLEEN SHARON
STOLL, MARIAN MAE
*STOLL, MICHAEL EDWARD
STOLLER, ROBERT CHARLES
STOLMAN, DAVID BRIAN
STOLTENBERG, JOHN JAMES
STOMPANATO, DIA MARIE
*STONE, JOHN ALLAN
*STONE, JOHN BRANDON

STONE, JOHN HARRY
STONE, KENNETH BRUCE
STONEHOUSE, JEANNE MARGARET
STONITSCH, LAURA LYNN
*STOOPS, LORETTA SUSAN
STOTZ, DONNA YAKOS
STRAL, ERIC RICHARD
STRALL, MARGARET ANNE
STRALOW, MARTIN JOHN
STRAND, HELEN MARIE
STRATTON, STEVEN F.
*STRATTON, WILLIAM CLAYTON
*STRAUS, LYNN
STRAUSS, ALAN RICHARD
*STRAUSS, DAVID STEPHEN
STRAUSS, MELINDA NADEL
STRAWBRIDGE, KENNETH RAY
STRAWSER, TERRY LEE
*STREEM, STEVAN BRIAN
STREET, GAIL DENISE
STREID, KATHLEEN ANNE
STRILKY, MIRIAM LORIN
STRINGER, ANN ELIZABETH
*STRITAR, CYNTHIA RUTH
STROHECKER, JERILYN KAY
*STROHL, JANET CHRISTINA
STROHM, DAVID CHARLES
STROM, DEBORAH KAY
STROUD, CURTIS WAYNE
STRUBBE, MARY ANN
STRUBE, DAVID CARL
*STRUTIN, CAROL ROCHEL
*STRYKER, JANE LYNN
STUCKEL, MARILYN ANN
STUCKER, WENDY ELLEN
STUCKMAN, DEBORAH ANN
*STUMPF, DIANE RUTH
STUTZMAN, STACEY LEIGH
SUARDI, MARK WESLEY
SUBECK, SUSAN NACHENBERG
*SUBER, DAVID ALAN
SUCHARD, SUZANNE JO
SUCHY, LINDA SUSAN
*SUDALNIK, ROBERT A.
*SUESS, JUDITH ANNE
SUGARMAN, ANITA FRANCINE
SUGHRUA, MARY SHERYL
SULAK, CLIFFORD NORMAN
SULCESKI, CLAUDIA MARY
SULENSKI, JEFFREY MICHAEL
SULLIVAN, HELEN FRANCES
*SULLIVAN, TIMOTHY EUGENE
SULOWAY, JOHN JEFFREY
SULTAN, STEVEN AARON
SULZER, PAULA JANE
*SUMMER, MARK ALAN
SUMMERS, SCOTT KINGWILL
SUMMITT, ANITA LOUISE
SUMSKI, MICHAEL JAMES
SUNDBERG, KAREN ANN
*SUNDINE, KRISTA EILEEN
SUNDLOF, KENNETH CARR
SUPERFINE, RUSSELL ALAN
SURMA, DIANE
*SURREY, KAREN BARBARA

*SUSLER, JANIS M.
SUSS, LAYNE CHRISTINE
*SUSSMAN, PAUL JOEL
SUTARIK, EDWARD JOHN
SUTFIN, BETTY MAURINE
SUTHERLAND, PAUL WILLIS, JR.
SUTKER, ALLAN NATHAN
SUTKER, WILLIAM LEVIN
SUTOR, MARY ELIZABETH
SUTTLE, MARCIA KAY
SUTTON, KAREN KAY
SUTTON, WILLIAM ROBERT
SUZUKI, ROBERT HAJIME
*SUZUKIDA, IRENE MAE
*SVOBODA, GAIL ELLEN
SWAN, BRENDA FAYE
SWAN, GALE SUZANNE
SWAN, PAMELA JEAN
SWANGER, JAMES CARROLL
SWANSON, CARLA JOAN
SWANSON, JANE ELLEN
SWANSON, JUDITH FINNESTAD
SWANSON, LARRY HOWARD
SWANSON, LAWRENCE CLIFFORD
SWANSON, LESLIE EUGENE
SWARINGEN, ROBERT CALVIN
SWARTZ, BRUCE HOWARD
SWARTZ, PAMELA SUE
SWEDELL, DEDRA LORRAINE
*SWEENEY, ALEXANDRIA
SWEENEY, GAIL MARIE
*SWEENEY, MICHAEL JAMES
SWEET, LYNN DEBRA
SWEETS, HENRY HAYES, III
*SWENGEL, CATHY LYNN
*SWENGEL, STEVEN LLOYD
SWENSON, LORRAINE LYNN
SWETIK, PAUL GEORGE
SWIGERT, THOMAS CRESPA
SWIMMER, GLENN IRA
SWINSON, WILLIAM RICHARD
SYFERT, RODNEY K.
SYLVESTER, RONALD JOHN
SYPNIEWSKI, EDWARD RONALD
SZABO, PAUL
SZARZAK, DANNY ED
SZYDLOWICZ, ROSA
SZYMONIAK, CYNTHIA KAY
TABACHNIK, RENA
TABLER, EDWARD JOHN
TABOR, MARYBETH ANNETTE
TAGGART, JEFFREY CHARLES
*TAGGE, EMILIE DOROTHY
TAKAGISHI, MARK SAMUEL
TAKAMI, LYNNE KIMIYE
TALBOT, DAVID JOHN
TALCOTT, DAVID WAYNE
TALLEY, JEFFREY WAYNE
TALLMAN, LINDA SUE
TALMADGE, BARBARA JEAN
*TALMADGE, PATRICIA ANN
TAMILLO, JOANN CHRISTINE
TANENBERG, MARC THAVIUS
TANNER, ELAINE BLACK
*TANNER, JAMES WILLIAM

112

TANOUYE, RONALD
TANTILLO, PATRICK CARL
TAPHORN, ELLEN CECILIA
*TARDY, HELEN ANN
TARE, NADINE SUSAN
TARTOL, JOHN JOSEPH
TASSLER, PAUL LEWIS
*TATARA, SUSAN MARIE
TATE, LOIS
TATROE, STEPHEN ROBERT
TATZ, ALAN FILIP
TAUB, RICHARD EVAN
*TAUBE, ARNOLD ALBERT
TAYLOR, CHARLES RANDALL
TAYLOR, CYNTHIA KAY
TAYLOR, DONALD PIERCE, JR.
*TAYLOR, DUANE WILLIAMS
*TAYLOR, FREDERICK ROBBINS
TAYLOR, GWENDOL LYNN
TAYLOR, LANCE DOYL
*TAYLOR, MARILYN GAY
TAYLOR, MARY LYNN
*TAYLOR, ROGER LEON
TEAK, JAMES WILLIAM
TEDESCHI, DAREEN ANN
TEEVAN, PEGGY SCOTT
TEICHMAN, JAN WENDY
TEMPLE, CARLA SUE
TEPPER, SHERRY BARBARA
TERP, SUSAN K.
TERRELL, LYNDA LEE
*TERREO, KAREN LYNN
TERRILL, DAVID STANLEY
*TERRILL, MARILYN JEAN
*TERRY, BARBARA ELAINE
*TERRY, JEANNE MARIE
TESSAR, PAUL ALLEN
TESSIER, PHYLLIS ELAINE
*TESTOLIN, RENO BRUCE
TEUSCHER, VIRGINIA HENSEN
*THAIN, JANICE ELIZABETH
THALLER, RETTA ARLENE
THEILKEN, MARK STEVEN
THEOBALD, WILLIAM FRANK
THERIOT, MARILYN FAY
THIBEAU, MARY KATHERINE
*THIEL, CHRISTOPHER WILLIAM
THIEL, DENNIS O'DELL
THIGPEN, CHERLYNNE THERESA
THOLIN, KEITH VICTOR
THOLIN, KENNETH ARTHUR, JR.
THOMA, ARTHUR JOHN, JR.
THOMAS, BECKY SUZANNE
THOMAS, JAMES MARLOW
*THOMAS, JO BERICK
*THOMAS, REBECCA LEAP
*THOMAS, ROSEMARY MORAN
THOMAS, SHARON ANNE
*THOMAS, SHARON ELIZABETH
*THOMAS, STEPHEN MELVIN
THOMAS, SUSANNE KATHERINE
*THOMAS, WANDA FAY
THOMMA, MARK STEVEN
THOMPSON, CAROL SUE
THOMPSON, CAROLYN SUE

THOMPSON, DEBORAH LYNN
THOMPSON, GREGORY JOHN
THOMPSON, JAMES RICHARD
*THOMPSON, JEAN LOUISE
THOMPSON, ROBERTA JILL
THOMPSON, SUSAN MARY
THOMPSON, THOMAS EXCELL
THOMPSON, VICTORIA WOOD
THOMPSON, VIRGINIA CLAIRE
THORNBURG, ROBERTA LEA
*THORNE, MELVIN JAY
THORPE, GREGORY ARTHUR
*THORSEN, PAMELA ANN
THUR, JOHN ROBERT
THVEDT, JOHN ELLIOTT
TIBBS, MICHAEL JOHN
TICHELBAUT, KENNETH MAURICE
*TIEBOUT, HARRY MORGAN
TIELIS, CLIFFORD EDWARD
TIERSKY, DAVID MARK
*TIGERMAN, MARCY HOPE
TIHINEN, PAUL ELWARD
TIMBERLAKE, GEORGE WILLIAM
TIMKO, JOSEPH MICHAEL
TIMKO, PATRICIA O'NEILL
*TIMM, TERRY WILLIAM
*TIMMS, MAX WALTER
TINICH, ANDREW JOSEPH
TINSLEY, SHARON KAY
TINSMAN, DEBORAH ELAINE
*TIPPETTS, JANET SUE
TIPPY, ROGER DEAN
*TIPSWORD, THOMAS NATHAN
TISHER, JEANNETTE ALICE
TITUS, PETER KERN
TJADEN, DEAN ANDERSEN, JR.
TJARKS, JACK ELDON
TOAL, MARGARET LYNN
*TOBEY, TED ALAN
TOBIASZ, FRANCES MARY
TODAS, RICHARD
TODD, GARY LEE
TODD, WILLIAM ROBIN
TOKARCZYK, KAREN
TOKARZ, MARGARET MARY
TOKARZ, MICHAEL THEODORE
TOKAY, SUSAN ANNE
TOLSON, JAMES HENRY
TOM, MARY ELIZABETH
TOMAN, PENELOPE ELOISE
TOMASEK, BRYAN JOSEPH
TOMASEK, JUDITH ALICIA
TOMASKA, DENNIS LEE
TOMBERLIN, JACQUELYN LOUISE
TOMKO, THOMAS NORBERT
*TOMKOVICK, JOHN JAMES
*TOMLINSON, NANCY KAY
*TOMPKINS, DAVID ARTHUR
*TOMPKINS, WILLIAM EARL
TOMPOLES, CONSTANCE
TONELLI, ERNEST JOSEPH, JR.
TONNE, AUGUST RAYMOND
TONYAN, PATRICIA ANN
TOOMEY, JOHN JOSEPH
TOPPE, RICHARD IVEN

113

*Toren, Carolyn Jane
Torgersen, Thomas Lee
Tovian, Steven Michael
Towers, Susan Patricia
Towle, Lynn Marie
*Towle, Ross Albert
Town, Roxanne Jean
Townsend, Mary Ellen
*Trager, Gary Mitchell
Trager, John Charles, III
Tramm, Edwin Capper
Tramm, Martha Ann
Trattler, Ross Alan
Traub, Irene Lucille
Traughber, Arlie Eugene
Traughber, Colleen Marie
Trauscht, John Michael
Trautman, Michael Lewis
Traven, Douglas Allan
Travers, Robert Michael
Travers, Timothy Earl
*Traylor, Samuel James
Trebbe, Susan Elizabeth
*Trefzger, James Edward
Treiman, Susan Kay
Trein, Catherine
Trent, Stephanie Livengood
Trent, Thomas Martin
*Treviranus, Kim Matthew
Tripp, Thomas Alvin, Jr.
*Trogner, Evelyn
*Tronc, Elaine M.
*Trost, Barbara Lee
*Trost, Catherine Anne
Trost, David Ralph
Trotter, Deborah Ann
Trummel, John Eston
Trungale, Linda Kay
Trybus, Thomas William
Tsukuno, Paul Allen
Tull, Caludia Jean
Tumerman, Faith
Tumminello, Monica Louise
Tungate, Susan Ruth
*Tunney, Ann Marie
*Tuomi, Donna Jean
Turbin, Alan Wayne
*Turek, Susan Lee
Turk, Timothy Michael
*Turkowski, Robert Walter
Turman, Stephen Michael
Turnbaugh, Linda Lou
Turnbull, Richard Porter
Turner, Bernard Charles
Turner, John Allan
Turner, Katherine Sue
Turner, Renee Suzanne
Turner, Stephen Gregory
*Tursch, Ilse Marlene
*Turski, Patrick Allan
Tursman, Lucinda Louise
*Tuttle, Betty Trotter
Tuttle, Pamela Jane
Twardy, Ronald David
Twietmeyer, Faith Dorene

Tygret, Susan Vick
Tyler, Jeffrey James
Tymec, Cheryl Marie
Tyrrell, Martha Lee
*Ubell, Joycelyn Anne
Udehn, David Duane
Uebbing, Jane Frances
*Uhl, Adrienne Amy
Ullrich, David Allen
Underwood, Deborah Michele
Underwood, Neal Roger
*Unewitz, Peter Paul
Unger, Michael William
*Uphoff, Carolyn Jean
Urban, Bonnie Jean
Urban, Carol Ann
*Urban, Christina Dona
Urban, Janice Margaret
Urban, John Lawrence
*Urban, Margaret Anne
*Urh, Karen Sue
Urschel, Joseph M.
*Utes, Frank Alan
*Uthoff, Linda Beth
Vaci, Terese Anne
Vaicekonis, Saulius
Valdez, David
*Valenti, Cornelius Dean
Valentine, Arlene Frances
Valentine, Crystal Chase
Valentine, Freida Jean
*Van Arsdale, Janet Louise
Van Buren, David Martin
*Vance, Mary Martha
Van Cleave, Barbara Jean
Vande Berg, Michael James
Vander Laan, Ruth Adrian
Vanderport, Gene Michael
Van Duzor, William M.
Van Dyke, Barbara Rae
Van Dyke, Linda Faye
*Van Eylen, Margaret Mary
Van Hooser, Douglas Paul
Van Huele, Christine Harriet
Van Landeghem, Daryl Julian
*Van Melle, William James
Van Sickle, Catherine Tracy
Van Valkenburg, Charles M.
Van Wassenhove, Joseph Allen
*Van Weringh, Lolkje
Van Zele, Darold Paul
Varga, Anne Kathryn
Varland, David Alan
Vartiak, Gail Ann
Vaseleski, Raymond Charles
Vasilion, Donna
Vavra, Brian Robert
*Vedder, Wolfram
Vehos, Peter
*Velas, Margaret Lynn
Velkovrh, Beverly Ann
Venere, Nancy Carmella
*Venn, Raymond Ernest
*Venos, Kenneth George
*Ventura, Janice Piechocinski

114

*Venturini, Connie Ann
*Vera, Deborah Kolditz
Vercellotti, Gregory Marion
Verhaar, Jean Louise
Verhulst, Robert Maurice
Verma, Raj Bhushan
*Vermilion, Janice Lynn
Vernon, Lydia Jean
Veronda, Marcia Mary
Veronie, Michael
*Vest, Georgiana
*Vetter, Martha Mae
Veverka, Donna Marie
*Vicars, Elizabeth Grace
Vicksta, David John
Vidican, Donald Edward
Villari, Paula
Vincent, Barbara Allison
Vinkler, Gregory Jerome
Vintar, James Stanley
Viravec, Andrea Lorraine
Visin, Deborah Jane
Visk, William George
*Vivona, Louise F.
Voelker, Gary Harold
*Vogel, Patrick Anthony
Vogel, Tyrone Richard
Voget, Antoinette Katherine
Vogt, Larry Alan
Voise, Adrienne Renee
Volchko, Marianne Margaret
Volk, Phyllis Lynn
*Volkmar, Freddie Robert
Vollrath, Jean Marlene
Vonderhaar, Julie Anne
Vonnahme, Mark Conrad
*Vonvogt, Charlotte Ethna
Voorhees, Gregory Dean
Vosen, Victor Vagin
*Vranicar, David Joseph
*Vrhel, Keith Douglas
Vroman, James Arthur
Vucha, Peter Ruhl
Vursell, Stephen Arthur
*Vuylsteke, Leslie Vernon
Vyborny, Glenna
Vyskocil, Jessica Jean
Wachtel, Ira Neil
Waddell, Randy Lee
Wagenbreth, Marge Benedict
*Waggoner, Margaret Anne
Wagley, Elizabeth Louise
Wagner, Gregory Steven
*Wagner, Linda Caryn
*Wagner, Linda Joyce
Wagner, Marilyn Rittenhouse
Wagner, Rebecca Ann
*Wagner, Robert Gene
Wagner, Robert Hewitt
Wagner, Vicki Sue
Wahl, Jane Margaret
Wahlgren, Margaret Lee
Waite, Rebecca De George
Wakat, Rita Anne
*Wakefield, Ann Mary

Wakefield, Connie La Von
*Wakefield, John Frederick
Wakefield, Nancy Jane
Wakeman, Alice Jean
Wald, Sally Ann
Walden, Charles Jesse
Waldon, Ellen Jarvi
Walker, Alice Irene
Walker, Ardis Loretta
Walker, Diane Lynn
Walker, Philip Howard
*Walker, Sherry Lynn
Walker, William Jay
Wall, Bylle Jean
Wall, Jon Thomas
Wallace, Diane Louise
Wallace, Judith Mae
Wallace, Thomas Everett
Wallen, Susan Maureen
*Waller, Cathy Lynn
Wallerstein, Bette Ellen
Wallerstein, Susan
*Wallick, Nancy Eileen
Wallin, Diane Ruth
Wallinder, Janet Lynne
Walrod, Ronald Craig
Walsh, April Kathleen
Walsh, Daniel John
Walsh, Donald Frederick
Walsh, Jane Ellen
Walsh, Janet Marion
Walsh, Patricia Alice
Walsh, Robert Douglas
Walsh, Terrence Michael
Walter, Donald Kim
Walter, Kim Allan
*Walter, Mary Ann
Walter, Steven Louis
Walter, Thomas Charles
Walter, Wendy Marian
*Walters, Sharon Susan
Walters, William Howard
Walther, Margaret Janet
Walton, Clyde Duane
*Walton, Diana Sue
*Waltzek, Jill Marie
Walusek, Robert Alexander
Wangen, Randall Scott
*Wanserski, Janis M.
*Wanserski, Loretta
*Warady, Bradley Alan
*Warady, Monica Sue
Ward, Diane Elizabeth
Ward, Donna
Ward, Kathleen Marie
Ward, Leslie Jeanne
Ward, Michael James
Waren, William T.
Warfel, Michael Ray
Waring, George Robert
*Warma, Kathryn Ann
Warner, Henry Albert
Warnke, Dean Keith
Warren, Linda Lou
Warren, Thomas George

Warshawsky, Sandee Lyn
Washburn, Sharon Sue
Waskelo, Jacqueline Lee
*Wasserman, Julie Beth
Wasserman, Paul Ira
Wastak, Jan Catherine
*Watkins, Judith Marie
Watson, Brenda Jean
*Watson, Craig Allan
Watson, James Lee
Watson, Laura Lee
*Watson, Margaret Mary
Watt, Robert Maur
Watts, Jay Michael
Watts, Kimberlee S.
Waverly, Lynn Lesley
Wax, Saul
Waxler, Robert Dee
*Wear, Thomas George
Weatherhead, Mary Ann
Weaver, Dianne Sue
*Webb, Bruce Ronald
Webb, Melvin
Webb, Roger Alan
Webber, Deborah Lee
Webber, Mary Burrows
*Weber, Barbara Jean
Weber, Charles Scott
Weber, Gretchen Jean
*Weber, Joyce Kay
Weber, Mary Lynn
Weber, Penny Sue
Weber, Raymond Keith
Weber, Raymond Philip
Weber, Warren Russell
Webner, Glen Robert
Webster, Jane Ann
Wedenoja, Linda Ann
*Weeks, Marjorie Estelle
Weeks, Virginia Lueze
Wegloski, Victoria Mary
Wehling, Constance Lee
Wehrle, Judith Lee
Weidner, Mark Donald
Weidner, Nancy Ellen
Weidner, Pamela Inez
Weigel, Linda Clink
*Weil, Margaret Sue
*Weiland, Andrea Lois
*Weinberg, Carol Ann
*Weinberg, Deborah Mary
Weinberg, Nancy S.
Weinecke, Michael Harold
Weiner, Claire
*Weiner, Lee H.
Weiner, Richard Arden
Weingart, Sandra Phyllis
*Weinmeister, Kent Paul
Weinmeister, Patti Jo
Weinstein, Debra Ellen
Weinstein, Leslie Gale
Weinstein, Lynn Ellen
Weinstein, Sandra Lynn
Weinstein, Susan Lynn
*Weintrob, Meda Rebecca

*Weipert, Linda Dianne
*Weisbart, Howard Stanley
*Weisel, Rebecca Lynn
Weisman, Bonnie Paulette
Weisman, Larry Edward
Weisman, Steven Phillip
*Weiss, Barbara Lynn
*Weiss, Barbara Shari
*Weiss, Carey Allen
Weiss, Howard J.
Weiss, Katherine Marie
*Weiss, Kathryn Ann
*Weiss, Sheldon Arnold
*Weissman, Joel S.
Weissman, Susan Joyce
Weissman, Thomas Mark
Weissmann, Karen Lew
Weist, Linda Kay
Weitz, Virginia
Weitzman, Eileen
Welch, Grace Ellen
Welch, Holly Maxine
*Welch, James Robert
Welch, John C.
Welch, Linda Kelley
Welch, Mary
*Welch, Robert Franklin
*Welchko, Gary Louis
*Welker, Peggy Jean
Welker, Weston James
*Welle, Stephen Leo
Weller, Arthur Randall
Weller, Karen Virginia
Wells, Melvin Wesley
Wells, Sara Louise
Welsch, Kathryn Kinnycan
*Welsch, Robert James
*Welsh, John Charles
Wemlinger, Merrie Henshaw
*Wempen, Christine
*Wendel, Martha Ann
Wender, Howard Michael
Wengroff, Cheryl Debbie
Wenzel, Jeanne Marie
Werderits, Donna Jean
Wermers, Gregory Louis
Werner, Dennis Craig
*Werner, Joan Allison
Werner, John Vincent
Werner, Valerie Saikkonen
Wert, Julia Joanne
*Wesley, Glenn David
Wesly, Edward James
Wessel, Paul Spencer
Wessel, Peter Cordell
*Wessely, Robert Paul
West, Crystal Karen
*West, Sandra Swann
West, Stanton R.
Westcott, Janice Ann
Westefer, Robert Alan
Westermeyer, Gretchen
*Weston, Edward Garfield
Weston, Nancy Hochstadter
Westphal, Theodore Michael

116

WEXLER, HOWARD BRUCE
WEXMAN, ERICA GENETTE
WEXMAN, THOMAS JEROME
*WHALIN, KATHLEEN DIANE
WHEELER, GLENN PAUL
WHEELER, HERBERT, III
WHEELER, WILLIAM LEE
WHELPLEY, DOUGLAS PAUL
WHITAKER, JAMES WAYNE
*WHITE, ALAN BRUCE
WHITE, CHARLES ROBERT
WHITE, CHERYL LYNN
WHITE, ERIC BORDERS
WHITE, FABIENE VIOLA
WHITE, FRANCINE JOAN
WHITE, GORDON EUGENE
WHITE, JANET MARGARET
WHITE, MICHAEL JOSEPH
*WHITE, PENELOPE CAROL
WHITE, PHILLIP ANTHONY
WHITE, QUENTIN J.
WHITEE, RITA KAY
*WHITE, ROGER BRADLEY
*WHITE, ROGER LEE
WHITE, STEPHEN THOMAS
WHITE, SUE ELLEN
WHITE, WILLIAM FREDRICK
WHITEHEAD, LINDA DIANN
WHITEHOUSE, CHRISTINA LOUISE
*WHITLOCK, SUE ELLEN
WHITNELL, JANE ELIZABETH
*WHITNEY, JOHN CHARLES
WHITNEY, LINDA HOWLEY
WHITNEY, MARK HAGAN
*WHITNEY, RICHARD STERLING
*WHITSITT, TIMOTHY JOHN
*WHITTEN, PATRICIA LEE
*WHITTINGTON, JOHN WALTER
WHITTINGTON, SUELYN ANN
*WHYTE, ROBERT LLOYD
*WICHTERMAN, KEITH ALLEN
*WICKERT, LYNN EILEEN
*WICKS, EDWARD EUGENE
WICKUM, DAVID PAUL
WIDAMAN, BRIAN LANE
WIDMAR, CANDACE HELENE
WIEBERS, JENNIFER LOUISE
*WIEDLING, JUDITH LYNNE
WIEDUWILT, DAVID MICHAEL
WIEGEL, JEFFREY ALAN
WIEGMAN, DIANE RUTH
*WIEN, PERRY
WIER, KAREN JANE
WIESBROOK, GREGG E.
*WIESLER, WENDY ANNE
WIEZER, JUDITH BARYLSKE
WIGGAM, STEPHANIE ELIZABETH
*WIGODA, KIRA ANN
WIGTON, GREGORY LLOYD
*WIKER, STEVEN LEE
WIKER, TONDA SATTERFIELD
WILBER, HAROLD TALMADGE
WILBER, KAETHE QUITTING
WILBERG, RICHARD WILLARD, JR.
WILBON, CAROLYN DIANE

*WILBRANDT, ROBERT ALBERT
WILCOX, KAREN MARJORIE
*WILDE, DONNA JEAN
WILDER, MARCIA LYNN
WILENSKY, SARA SOLOWEY
WILEY, CHARLOTTE MARIAN
*WILEY, MARY LOUISE
WILEY, PAMELA ELAINE
*WILFORD, LYNNE MARIE
*WILHELM, JOSEPH LEE
WILKERSON, MICHAEL ROBERT
WILKES, MARY LINDA
WILKINSON, CAROLYN JOAN
WILKINSON, JOANNE
WILKINSON, THOMAS HAROLD
*WILKUS, EDWARD FRANK
*WILLAVIZE, SUSAN ANNE
*WILLENBORG, BRIDGETTE ANN
WILLIAMS, CHERYL ANN
*WILLIAMS, DANIEL LEE
*WILLIAMS, DONALD LEE
WILLIAMS, DORIS DIANE
WILLIAMS, HAROLD DEAN
WILLIAMS, HOMER FARRAND
WILLIAMS, INA ASH
WILLIAMS, JILL DIANNE
WILLIAMS, JOSEPH CLAUDE
WILLIAMS, KATHLEEN ANN
WILLIAMS, LIZABETH LYNN
WILLIAMS, MARGARET BETH
WILLIAMS, MARILYNN PURTELL
WILLIAMS, MARK EDWARD
WILLIAMS, MARY DEE
*WILLIAMS, MARYLENE KATHERINE
WILLIAMS, SHARON PARVINE
WILLIAMS, THERESA KATHLEEN
WILLIAMSON, HAROLD ELMER, JR.
*WILLIAMSON, NANCY MARIE
*WILLIS, KATHRYN ANN
WILLIS, LEON M.
WILLMOTT, GAIL ANN
WILLS, ANN CHRISTINE
WILLS, EDWARD LYNN
WILLS, HOWARD WILLIAM
WILLSKEY, ROBERT THOMAS
WILSON, ANNE M.
*WILSON, CORALIE ANN
WILSON, DENNIS WAYNE
WILSON, FREDERIC TERRY
*WILSON, JAMES HUNTER
WILSON, JOHN ROBERT
WILSON, LOREN GAIL
WILSON, SHARON STEARNS
WILT, SUSANNE
WILTON, JAMES HENRY
WILZBACH, MARGARET ANN
WILZBACH, MARTHA FRELS
WINAND, JOHN HERBERT
WINDELBORN, AUGDEN FRED
*WINDLE, PHYLLIS NOELLE
WINDMILLER, JEAN MARGARET
WINKELHAKE, CLAUDIA JEAN
WINKLEBLACK, ROBERT WALTER
*WINKLER, LOUIS MICHAEL
WINLEY, RONALD R.

117

WINN, DOROTHY LILLIAN
*WINSLOW, ANNE MARIE
WINSLOW, CHRISTINE ELIZABETH
WINSTON, LAURA KATHERINE
WINTER, BECKY GAIL
WINTER, CAROLIN LOUISE
WINTER, MICHAEL JEFFREY
WINTERS, CLYDE
WINTHEISER, JOHN GORDON
WISE, CATHY PANTELAKIS
*WISE, KATHLEEN THERESA
WISE, MICHAEL EDWARD
WISE, TRACY LEON
WISEMAN, DEBRA JEAN
WISEMAN, MARCIA LYNN
WISHINSKY, JANET
*WISHNE, BERDINE SHELIA
WISINSKI, LAWRENCE JOSEPH
WISNIEWSKI, MARY FLORENCE
WISNOSKY, MARK GEORGE
*WISS, JAMES ERNEST
WITHAM, DOUGLAS RICHARD
WITORT, HELEN MARIE
WITTE, JENNIFER KAY
WITTERT, CYNTHIA
WITZIG, VIRGINIA NELL
WODETZKI, CYNTHIA SUE
*WOFFORD, FRANCES LYNN
WOJDYGO, LINDA
*WOJEWNIK, KAREN MARIE
WOJNAR, DEBORAH LOUISE
*WOJTAN, LINDA SUE
WOJTOWICZ, PATRICK JOHN
WOLAK, KATHLEEN MARIE
*WOLF, BRENDA JOAN
WOLF, BRUCE RANDY
*WOLF, DANIEL JAY
WOLF, DIANA CHRISTINE
WOLF, GAIL ELLEN
WOLF, JACQUELINE HELENE
WOLF, MARK RICHARD
WOLF, MICHAEL ANDREW
WOLF, PAMELA PIERCE
WOLF, PETER HERMANN
WOLF, WILLIAM ALLEN
WOLFE, HAROLD LESLIE
WOLFE, JAMES ROBERT
WOLFE, MARY JANE
WOLFE, SHEILA FRAN
*WOLFE, SUSAN McHENRY
WOLFF, BEVERLY ANNE
WOLFF, EMERALD J.
WOLFF, GEORGE M.
WOLFF, HENRY PAUL
WOLFF, JEANNE BERNAHL
WOLFF, MARCY PAMELA
WOLFF, MERCEDES MARGARET
*WOLFF, QUENTIN A.
WOLFF, SHARON LEE
WOLFF, TERESA MARIE
WOLFRAM, NONA ELLEN
*WOLFSON, BARBARA JEAN
WOLIN, ROBERT JON
WOLLACK, DEBORAH SUE
WOLOWITZ, DAVID

WOLSKI, CHRISTINE ANN
WOLSKI, WILLIAM JOHN
WOLSTED, SHARON MARIE
WOLSZON, MARSHA ANN
*WONG, HAROLD H.
WONG, ROGER HUNG WAI
*WOO, RUTH MOY
*WOOD, DONALD EUGENE
WOOD, SUSAN CHARLENE
WOOD, WINIFRED JANE
*WOODARD, CAROLYN JEAN
*WOODIN, MARC CRAIG
WOODRICK, MARLA DIANA
*WOODSUM, SUSAN MARY
WOOLMAN, FRANK JAY
*WOOLSEY, THOMAS RICHARD
WORK, ROBERT ORTON
WORM, HOLLY DAWN
WORTH, PENELOPE ANN
WORTHEN, JOHN STUART
WOYWOD, FERDINAND ANTON
WRENN, ROBERT ELIOT
WRIGHT, CARLOTTA HELAINE
WRIGHT, LARRY ALLEN
WRIGHT, MARY KATHERINE
WRIGHT, RONALD GLEN
WRIGHT, SANDRA GOWLER
*WROBEL, BARBARA ANN
WROBLE, KATHRYN SUSAN
WROBLEWSKI, LINDA MAY
WUEBBLES, BARBARA YALEY
WULFF, ALAN GEORGE
*WUORENMA, RUTH ANN
WURST, DOROTHY ANN
*WURTH, GENE RAYMOND
WURTZEL, DOUGLAS MARC
WYATT, DENNIS LEE
WYLDE, ELROY EUGENE
WYLIE, ANNE ELIZABETH
*WYLIE, SCOTT ELWOOD
WYMAN, JOHN FOWLER
WYNN, ALICE LOUISE
WYNN, LOUISE PRATT
WYSOCKI, BERNARD
WYSOCKI, KATHERINE
YAGER, LINDA KAY
*YALEY, BARBARA JOAN
*YANDELL, KAREN L.
YANOV, JOAN MARIE
*YATES, DEBORAH JANE
YATES, JANE AUGUSTA
YATES, PHYLLIS CHRISTENA
YAW, ROBERT RIES
*YEATER, REED LAWRENCE
*YEATS, ELIZABETH HELEN
*YELLIN, LINDA CHERYL
*YELLIN, SANDRA PAULING
*YESINOWSKI, JAMES PAUL
*YEZAVITAS, JAMES PAUL
*YODER, PAMELA RUTH
YOELIN, MICHAEL LEON
YONTZ, RUTH ANN
YOUNG, BARBARA DIANE
*YOUNG, HELEN CHING-HWA
YOUNG, KATHLEEN JOYCE

118

YOUNG, MARK JOHN
YOUNG, MARK STEPHAN
YOUNG, MARY ELIZABETH
YOUNG, MICHAEL BENJAMIN
*YOUNG, MICHAEL JOHN
YOUNG, MICHAEL PHILLIP
YOUNG, RANDY SUE
YOUNG, ROBERT
*YOUNG, STEVEN ROY
YOUNG, VICKIE SUE
YOUNGQUIST, ROBERT RUSSELL
*YOUNGSTRUM, CHRISTINE ANN
*YOUNKIN, SCOTT WILEY
YOUNT, BRUCE GREGORY
YOUNT, MARY BOYD
YUDIN, FREDERICK LEE
YUNG, BERNICE MARJORIE
YURIECI, MARY HELEN
*ZAANDER, MARK CHARLES
ZACHARY, LAWRENCE SAMUEL
ZACK, ANITA MARIE
ZACK, JENNIFER BAKER
ZACK, MARGARET ANN
ZAGOREN, DIANE
ZAHARA, DONNA JEAN
*ZAKAS, JOSEPH CONRAD
*ZAKER, RICHARD ROBERT
ZALCBERG, IRWIN LARY
*ZALE, KENNETH ROBERT
ZALTZMAN, LAUREN SUE
*ZAR, LOREL ELLEN
*ZARET, PHILLIP HARRY
ZARNDT, MICHAEL WAYNE
ZASTERA, JEANNE MARIE
ZAYAS, ROSA MARIA
ZAYNER, NANCY ALLISON
ZEARS, RUSSELL WINFRED
ZEGAR, EDWARD JOSEPH
*ZEIGLER, ROBERT STUART
ZEITZ, EILEEN MOLLIE
*ZELINGER, ALLAN BARNETT
*ZELISKO, SANDRA PEARL
ZELLER, ALISON LOUISE
ZEMAN, CHRISTINE GEORGIANA
ZEMAN, JAMES FRANK
ZENISEK, STEVEN CHARLES
ZENK, THOMAS EDWARD

ZERBEL, STEVEN ROBERT
ZERBENSKI, GLORIA JOAN
ZERWEKH, ROBERT ALAN
ZEVENBERGEN, DONNA JEAN
*ZEVIN, ROBERT JAY
*ZIARKO, MITCHELL JACOB, JR.
ZICH, JANE MARIE
ZIEGLER, CAMILLE KAY
ZIEGLER, MARY ELLEN
*ZIEGLER, NANCY ROSE
ZIELINSKI, ANNA MARGARET
ZIELKE, ELIZABETH ANN
*ZIEMINSKI, GEORGE HENRY
ZIERFUSS, RANDALL WILLIAM
ZIMA, JUDITH AGNES
ZIMMERMAN, FRANK
ZIMMERMAN, JACALYN JOY
*ZIMMERMAN, RICHARD RUSSELL
ZINDELL, STUART MARK
ZINK, SALLY ANN
ZINTL, BRIGITTA MARGARET
ZIOMEK, THERESA ANN
*ZITTER, ROBERT ELLIOT
ZIVIC, JERROLD SIDNEY
*ZLATIN, BARBARA SUSAN
ZOCHERT, DAVID JOHN
*ZOELLICK, MARILYN MARTHA
*ZOELLICK, WILLIAM NORMAN
ZOLDAN, JACK SHELDON
*ZOLLO, PEGGY LEE
ZORDAN, BARBARA ANN
ZOSTAUTAS, BEVERLY ANN
*ZUBINSKI, PAUL KENNETH
ZUCKER, ALAN JEFFREY
*ZUCKER, CYNTHIA ANN
ZUKROWSKI, SOPHIE MARTHA
ZULEGER, JERRILYN ANN
ZUMWALT, PHILIP FRANK
ZUPANCIC, JOANNA
ZUPSICH, STEPHANIE CISEK
ZWART, MICHAEL JOHN
ZWEIBAN, BRUCE E.
ZWIERZYNA, MARYBETH JEAN
ZWILLING, JAMES JULIUS
*ZYCH, MARY ELIZABETH
ZYDEK, CAROLE LYNN
*ZYDOWSKY, MARY ELLEN

## COLLEGE OF PHYSICAL EDUCATION

ADAMS, JOANNE LYNNE
*ADAMS, KATHRYN ANN
ALLEMAN, DEBRA LYNN
ALLEN, PATRICIA ANGELL
ALSIP, JAMES FRANKLIN
ALSIP, RUSSELL HOWARD
ANDERSON, GAIL MARIE
ANDERSON, SIDNEY DWIGHT
ANDREONI, LINDA ANN
ANGELICH, DAVID LAWRENCE
AULT, MARGARET JEAN
BABKA, MARIANN ELIZABETH
BAKER, LOUIS COLIN
*BALLARD, LEXIS SUE
BARBER, CAROLYN

BARGO, KENNITH RAY
BAUGHMAN, SHERRI ANN
BECHLY, CAROLYN JANE
BECKER, CYNTHIA LEE
BECKER, MARILYN EYTH
BECVAR, JUNE SYLVIA
BENBERRY, HERSHEL CLAY
*BERGMAN, JAN ELLEN
BETTS, JAMES FREDRICK
*BIGGS, LAURA LYNN
BIRKNER, JAMES ROY
BITZER, NANCY MARILYN
*BLAHA, SHARALYN ROSE
BLAKEY, HARRY LAST, JR.
BLANKENSHIP, C. B.

119

BOBERT, DAVID LLOYD
*BODANIS, MYRA ANNE
BORCHERT, KATHLEEN ROSE
*BOTTERBUSCH, CORINE ANN
BOTTERON, NORMAN GEORGE, SR.
*BRADY, BONNIE JEAN
BRAUER, KENNETH RUSSELL
*BRAUN, LYNN
BRILL, KATHRYN HOPE
BRILL, WENDY JOYCE
BRIZA, MAUREEN ANN
BROOKS, DAVID JAMES
BROWN, KAREN ANN
BROWN, NANCY GAY
BROWNOLD, ELLEN SUE
BUCHAR, ANN LOUISE
BUCHAR, MERRI JO
BURD, RICHARD LAWRENCE
BURNS, BETH PATRICIA
BURRIS, JUDY LYNN
BUTLER, SHIRLEY WILLENA
BUTTS, JANE PFLEDERER
CANTZLER, KENNETH WAYNE
CARLSEN, DEBORAH LYNN
CARLSON, HILARY LYNNE
CARLSON, MELISSA EILEEN
*CARMACK, MARY ANN
*CERA, MARY JANE
CHEROT, B. ANTONIO
CHOOKASZIAN, DONALD CRAIG
CLARK, MAUREEN THERESA
CLEARY, LEONARD EUGENE, JR.
CLEARY, NANCY ANN
*CLEMENTS, DEBORAH KAY
CLEMENTS, JESSE ANTHONY
CLICKENER, ROBERT RALPH
COHEN, BARBARA JOAN
COLEMAN, BRUCE E.
CONNERS, PATRICIA ANN
COOK, JEFFREY ALLAN
COTTERELL, LOUISE MARY
COX, VADA DIANE
COYNER, KATHLEEN BUTLER
CRAIG, LAWRENCE WILLARD
CRAWFORD, DONNA KAY
CRITTENDEN, BARBARA JEAN
CULLODEN, CAROL ANN
DAHLSTRAND, DONNA DEANE
*DALEY, MARY JOSEPHINE
DANISCH, BRYANT JAMES
DAVIS, NANCY JO
DAY, CHERYL GAY
DEERY, JOANNE DIDIER
DIERCKMAN, VIRGINIA M.
DINSMORE, REBECCA ELLEN
DIORIO, THOMAS JAMES
DIXON, JESSE THOMAS
DIXON, NATHANIEL LORINZO
*DIXON, WESLEY GERALD
DOW, CATHY ANN
DUCHON, CATHI GENTRY
DUFFEY, GEORGE LAWRENCE
DUKE, CAROL ANN
*DUNNAN, MELISSA JO
DYER, CLIFFORD LEE

DYKSTRA, GREGORY LEE
ECKHOUSE, EILEEN SHIRLEY
*EDWARDS, CHARLES GREGORY
EDWARDS, STEPHEN DOUGLAS
EFFLANDT, ALAN LLOYD
ELLENBY, CHERYL INEZ
ELLIOTT, MARGUERITE
ESENTHER, CORT ALLAN
FAJGMAN, LEA SCHULAMIT
FALCONER, JUDITH ANN
FARNEY, JAMES EUGENE
FENCL, KAREN LYNN
FIELDS, BETTY CAROL
FIERKE, CHARLES ALFRED
FOLEY, ANNE
FORD, JUDITH ANNE
GANDOLFI, BOB JAMES
GARRY, PAULA MARIE
GEILS, CORRENCE ELIZABETH
GERULAT, FERNE WINIFRED
GEWEKE, DEBRA LEE
GIERSCH, JACQUELINE JEANNE
GILES, DAVID OMER
GILLESPIE, BECKY LOU
GILMORE, IVY ELLEN
GLENNON, ROBERT EUGENE, JR.
*GRABENHOFER, BONNIE SUZANNE
GRACH, BONNIE TASH
*GRAHAM, CONNIE SUE
GRAYBEAL, JUDITH COLEMAN
GRAYBEAL, RUSSELL OAK
GREAVES, ELLEN CLAIRE
GREEN, CAROL JOYCE
GREEN, LOIS
GREENBERG, MARSHA KAY
GROVE, RICHARD LEROY
GUENZLER, JANE ELLEN
GUIDA, KIM ANN
HAKES, ROBERT L.
HARR, KRISTIN E.
HARTLEY, CATHERINE JANE
HARVEY, EDWARD WILSON
HEATH, KENNETH BRUCE
HILL, MADELINE RUTH
HODGES, WILLIAM JOHN
HOFFMAN, NANCY JANE
HOLIDAY, SHIRLEY M.
HOLMES, BETTY ANN MANKLE
HOLTZMAN, LYNN IRA
HORTON, DAVID MARTIN
HOSKINSON, DIANE BIEDER
HOWARTH, STACEY JEAN
HUBBARD, KATHLEEN GALE
HUBBARD, LINDA DIANE
HUDSON, ANGELINE DENISE
HUISINGA, LARRY RAY
*HULING, KATHLEEN KRYSTON
HUNT, DAVE ELLISON
HYNES, JO LIZABETH
JACKSON, ANITA JOYCE
JAHN, LAWRENCE EDWARD
JAKOSA, RICHARD NEAL
JINKS, CLAUD VINCENT
JOHNSTON, HERBERT SCOTT
JONES, GLENDA GAIL

120

JONES, JAMES HENRY
KARKULA, CYNTHIA HELENE
*KERNER, LINDA JEAN
KETCHAM, SUSANNE HARRIET
*KIEDAISCH, LAURA SUSAN
KIRBY, CATHERINE DOOLIN
KLOMPMAKER, DARCY LOY
*KLUGE, JANICE VAL
KORASEK, BARBARA LYNN
KOSTER, MARK REMI
KRAKOW AMY BETH
KRONENFELD PHILLIP DAVID
KRUEGER, GLORIA RODGERS
KRUGH, JERRY FRANKLIN
KURAS, WILLIAM J.
KYRIAS, MARY KATHERINE
LABRECQUE, BRUCE DOUGLAS
*LANDAUER, KATHLEEN MARIE
LANGE, PEGGY MARIE
LAWLER, SALLIE ANN
LAWRENCE, NANCY FAGIN
*LAYMON, RAE MARIE
LAZ, PEGGY ANN
LAZZARI, ELLEN L.
LESTON, JOAN LORRAINE
LEVANTI, JOHN GREGORY
LEVI, CAROL ELIZABETH
LEWIN, MERLE SUE
LIMERICK, JILL
LOCHNER, FRANK ELMS
LOGIN, JANET SUE
LOVAAS, ANDREA MARGARET
LULICH, DAVID JOHN
LUTHI, WARD EMORY
MACWILLIAMS, SUSAN JOAN
MADENBERG, SHELLEY PAM
MALANY, COLLEEN MAY
MARCHESI, JUDITH ANN
MARCUS, DEBRA ELLEN
MARKSTAHLER, MICHAEL BRUCE
MARSZALEK, CHRISTINE
MAYO, PATRICIA ANN
*McCARREN, LAURENCE ANTHONY, JR.
McCLENAHAN, JOHN STEWART
McCOLGIN, LINDA C.
McCUE, BRIAN JAMES
McFARLAND, MARY ROBERTA
McLELLAN, JEFFREY CREEL
McMULLEN, LINDA SUE
MEHELIC, JANIS MARGARET
MELZER, BEVERLY MARIE
MEYERS, MARY JANE
MIDDLETON, RANDALL LEE
MILKE, SUSAN CAROL
MILLER, BETTY ANN
MILLNS, JAMES GLENFERN, JR.
MINARCIN, KARYN BETH
MINNES, MASON R.
MONKEN, LESLIE JANE
MONTGOMERY, BARBARA
MOODY, DOUGLAS WILLIAM
MOORE, CARL RAYMOND
MOORE, NANCY ANN
MORRIS, CAROLYN SUE
MORRIS, MICHAEL BOWER

MORSCHEISER, JOHN CHARLES
MUELLER, DEBORAH ANN
MUSCH, THOMAS OWEN
NATHANSON, ELLEN SUE
NEKOLA, ILENE MARY
NELLI, R. KEITH
NELSON, RICHARD ALVIN
NELSON, ROBERT MARK
NEVILS, RODNEY LANE
NEW, NASH HARRISON
ODONNELL, BARBARA JEAN
OLESON, CLAUDIA RAE
OROURKE, TERESA ANN
PAGE, PAULA JEAN
PARFITT, LYNN THERESE
PARISI, WILLIAM PATRICK
PAYDON, LINDA JEAN
PECORARO, ROBERT ANTHONY
PESAVENTO, LISA CLAIRE
PETERS, JOYCE MAREE
PETERSON, ERIC KNUTE
PETERSON, REBECKA LYN
*PETRY, TERESA JO
PHILLIPS, KAREN CHRISTINE
*PHILLIPS, LESLIE KAY
PIERCEY, JANET LOUISE
PIPER, RITA LYNN
PLANT, CATHERINE ANN
*PORTER, MARLENE ALICIA
*POTTER, PAMELA SUE
PRATT, GWEN ELIZABETH
PRAY, LINDA WHEELER
PRICE, MICHAEL THOMAS
PURKISER, WILLIAM RUSSELL
QUINN, ROBERT ALLEN
RAAP, LINDA SUSAN
RAMLOW, LINNA D.
*RANDALL, LAUREL WENONAN
RAPIER, MARTHA ELLEN
RAYMOND, EDWARD AUBRE
REGNIER, RACHEL ANN
RIEKE, MARK HARRY
RISTAU, KAREN ANN
ROACH, LINDA JOANN
ROARICK, GREGORY ALAN
ROBERTS, DON C.
ROBINSON, JOHN, JR.
ROEMER, JANICE MARIE
*ROOT, REBECCA LEE
ROSE, JERRY THOMAS
ROSENBERG, SUSAN LOUISE
ROWE, DAVID CHARLES
ROWLAND, SHERYL ANN
*RUBENSTEIN, JOAN BETH
RUDOLPHI, BEVERLY ANN
RUDY, KATHARINA MARIA
RUETER, MARILYN LOUISE
RYAN, KRISTINE RAE
SALAMONE, JOHANNA MARIE
SARMIENTO, JOHN G.
*SAVAGE, LESLIE ANN
SCALETTA, SAMUEL LAWRENCE
SCHAFFER, SARAH GLADD
SCHIKORA, MICHAEL EDWARD
SCHRUMPF, FREDERICK BENJAMIN

121

Schweitzer, Valarie McCann
Schwilk, Donna Lynn
Scott, Anthony Edward
Scott, Judith Wheeler
Scott, Raymond Dale
Scranton, Lynda Kay
Sears, Lynne Marie
Seaton, Marcia Newberg
Seghers, Patricia Anne
Seltzer, Sidney Ann
Semlow, David John
Seyler, Barbara Lynn
Shaw, Gary Earl
Sheets, Judith Ann
Shockley, Glenn Argel
Shultz, Kenneth Lowell
Shupe, Charles Edward, Jr.
Siders, Carol
Siegrist, Beverly Ann
Silberman, Helene Ellen
Slamar, Richard
Smiley, John Milton
*Snuggs, Jean C.
Spangler, Suzanne Pamela
Stahl, Karen Ann
Stanko, Elizabeth Ann
Stein, Juanita Susan
Stern, Laurie Kathryn
Stoller, Robert John
*Stone, Sandra Kay
Strever, Margaret Jean
Swanson, Janet Elizabeth
Swinger, Marla Rae
Syz, Susan Marion
Tadelman, Richard Edward
Taman, Bonnie Carol
*Thomas, Patricia Ann
*Thorpe, Bonnie Jane
Tomczyk, James Lawrence
Trees, Ann Mary
Tucker, Cindy Lee
Turek, Lee Scott
Twist, Michael Scott

Tykvart, Bonnie Jean
Valentine, Karen
Vanhuele, Denise Marguerite
Vanourek, Janet M.
Veverka, Joyce Ann
Vladika, Diane Christine
Vonner, Jackie Lee
Waggoner, Daryl Lee
Walker, Champ Eugene
Walker, Michael Charles
Wancho, Arthur Steven
Warren, Pamela Darley
Washburn, Claudia Krapac
*Webb, Judith Ann
Weedman, Stephen Dale
Weiss, Donna Rae
Weiss, Fanchan Deborah
Wells, Michael Eugene
Wenger, Marilyn
Wenta, David Joseph
White, Katherine Susan
Wiegman, Gloria Gaye
Wilken, Lyndell Kay
Wilson, Deborah Ann
Wilson, Susan Bosan
Wintergreen, Donna Beth
Witkowsky, Beverly Mae
Wittenborn, Charles M., Jr.
Wittler, Cheryl Anne
Wiza, John Francis
Wolf, Marvin Robert, Jr.
Wood, Michael William
Worden, Randy James
Workman, Kendra Kay
Yurtis, Barry Anthony
Zegarski, Christine Mary
Zeinz, Marianne
*Ziebarth, Christine Gail
Zimmerman, Joyce E.
*Zimmerman, Mary Keller
Zito, Hugh John
Zuckerman, Robert Allan
Zweig, Barbara Ann

## COLLEGE OF VETERINARY MEDICINE

Bardelmeier, Dennis Gene
Casper, David Robert
Curtis, Kenneth John
Daly, William Ray
Feldman, Edward Charles
Franklin, Sherwood James
Greenwood, Kenneth Martin
Gutzeit, Diane Lynn
Hepperly, Thomas Ramsay
Hessler, Gertraud Hilde
Hornickel, Daniel Robert
Kellogg, Russell Harding, Jr.
Kreher, Alvin William
Lebeda, Daniel E.
Lindsay, Kay Ellen
MacLellan, John

Martin, Paul Albert
McGrew, Ralph Wayne
Miller, Robert Kenneth
Morris, Kathleen June
Myers, George Douglas
Pask, Alan Joseph
Pavletic, Michael Mark
Reel, Aimee Sue
Ritter, Joseph Herman
Ross, Linda Anne
St. John, Kenneth Alan
Swenson, Richard Brent
Thomas, Michael Parks
VanPoucke, Stephen Mark
Vonderohe, Rebecca Jean
Voss, Phillip Eugene

## SCHOLASTIC HONORARY ORGANIZATIONS

The following is a list of all recognized undergraduate student scholastic honorary organizations at the University of Illinois at Urbana-Champaign.

ALPHA EPSILON (Agricultural Engineering)
ALPHA LAMBDA DELTA (Freshman Women)
ALPHA SIGMA MU (Metallurgical Engineering)
ALPHA ZETA (Agriculture)
BETA GAMMA SIGMA (Commerce and Business Administration)
CHI EPSILON (Civil Engineering)
CHI GAMMA IOTA (Veterans)
DELTA PHI ALPHA (German)
DOBRO SLOVO (Slavic Languages and Literatures)
ETA KAPPA NU (Electrical Engineering)
GAMMA EPSILON (General Engineering)
GAMMA SIGMA DELTA (Agriculture)
GARGOYLE SOCIETY (Architecture)
IOTA SIGMA PI (Women in Chemistry)
KAPPA DELTA PI (Education)
KAPPA TAU ALPHA (Communications)
MORTAR BOARD (Senior Women)
MU PHI EPSILON (Music)
OMICRON DELTA EPSILON (Economics)
OMICRON NU (Home Economics)

ORDER OF ARTUS (OMICRON DELTA EPSILON) (Economics)
PHI ALPHA THETA (History)
PHI BETA KAPPA (Liberal Arts and Sciences)
PHI ETA SIGMA (Freshman Men)
PHI KAPPA PHI (All-University)
PHI LAMBDA BETA (Spanish, Italian, and Portuguese)
PHI LAMBDA UPSILON (Chemistry)
PI ALPHA XI (Floriculture)
PI DELTA PHI (French)
PI MU EPSILON (Mathematics)
PI SIGMA ALPHA (Mechanical Engineering)
PI TAU SIGMA (Mechanical Engineering)
PSI CHI (Psychology)
SIGMA DELTA PI (Spanish)
SIGMA GAMMA TAU (Aeronautical and Astronautical Engineering)
SIGMA IOTA EPSILON (Management)
SIGMA TAU (Engineering)
TAU BETA PI (Engineering)
ZETA PHI ETA (Women in Speech)

# COLLEGE SCHOLASTIC HONORARY ORGANIZATIONS

These students have been elected to membership in the indicated college scholastic honorary organizations.

## ALPHA LAMBDA DELTA (Freshman Women)

ADAMS, VERA ANN
ADLER, JOAN MARIE
ALDERSON, SUSAN K.
ALTER, BARBARA PHYLLIS
ALTSCHUL, MARLA KOLS
APPENZELLER, BILLIE KAY
ARNOLD, LOUANNE K.
ASPER, CHERYL DEONNE
AUBRECHT, KATHRYN ANNE
BABBITT, JEAN HANCOCK
BACCHI, DIANE MARIE
BALLARD, LEXIS SUE
BATTERMAN, KAREN SUE
BEATY, CATHERINE
BECK, BARBARA LOUISE
BECKFELD, MARY CATHARINE
BENNETT, BARBARA ANN
BERMAN, WENDY CAROL
BERNSTEIN, GAIL SANDRA
BERO, CAROL ANN
BERTELSEN, JULIA SUE
BICKLER, MELINDA KAY
BINKIN, GERI SUZANNE
BISHIR, JOAN KATHLEEN
BIZAR, JANET SUSAN
BLUESTONE, ROBIN JOY
BOHL, BETTY JEAN
BORAK, ANDREA JUDITH
BORRE, KRISTEN SUE
BORRENPOHL, LAVONNE
BRAUN, LYNN
BRESNAN, REGINA FRANCES
BRILL, BETTE SUE
BRISKMAN, RANDY JOYCE
BROWN, FRANCES SUSAN
BRUMM, NANCY JOHANSEN
BRUNOEHLER, WANDA LYNN
BUCHSBAUM, YAEL
BUCKHEISTER, BONNIE ELIZABETH
BURMAN, LUAN
BURTNESS, KATHRYN GRACE
BUSH, GAIL LYNN
BYTHELL, CAROL ANN
CANNELL, CAROL A.
CARMACK, MARY ANN
CARRIE, LYNN MARIE
CASSIOPPI, MARIE PAULETTE
CASTLE, ARLENE JOY
CHAUNCEY, JOAN MARGARET
CHEWNING, DIANE SUE
CHRISTOFFERSON, APRIL
CLARK, MARCIA JANE
CLEMENTS, DEBORAH KAY
COHEN, JUDY MAE
COLLINS, SUSAN LEE
CORBETT, PATRICIA LEE

COUGHLIN, COLLEEN DENISE
COURNOYER, ANN KATHRYN
CRESCENZO, MICHAEL
CRITTENDEN, ANITA DELOIS
CUMMINS, DENISE LOUISE
D'AMBROGIO, MARGARET MARY
DANIELS, LESLEY DIANE
DANIS, DANIELLE ROSE
DANNER, MERRY ANN
DAVID, JACQUELINE DEBORAH
DAVIS, DIANE PEARL
DAVIS, MARILYN DEBORAH
DAVIS, RHEA ELLEN
DAVIS, SYLVIA BETH
DAY, CHERYL GAY
DAYTON, KAY ELLEN
DEAN, STACY LILLIAN
DEBOICE, MARY LUCILE
DEL VENTO, CONNIE ANN
DEVACHT, GLORIA LOUISE
DICKMAN, BETTY JANE
DIERSTEIN, JULIE JENE
DIXON, SUSAN LYNN
DONAHUE, FRANCES LEE
DREIFUSS, SUSAN HELEN
DUFFY, KATHLEEN VIRGINIA
DUNNAN, THERESA COLLEEN
EGGERDING, CAROLINE
ELETSON, BRIDGET ANNE
ENGSTROM, KATHY SUSAN
ENNIS, MAUREEN ANN
EOVALDI, PAULA KAY
EPSKY, MARILYN RUTH
ERICKSON, KAREN JANE
ERICKSON, PAMELA IRENE
ESSENFELD, IDYTH
EUSTICE, DEBORAH CLARE
FALTUS, VICKI LYNN
FARLEY, LAURA LYNN
FENBERG, SUSAN LYNN
FONDRIE, BARBARA KAY
FOSS, CATHERINE MARIE
FREDRICKSON, JANE MARIE
FREEDMAN, SHELLEY BETH
FRIEDMAN, JUDITH CHERIE
FRISBIE, ANNE CELESTE
FRYML, KIM GRACE
GAINES, KAY BARRETT
GAMMS, LINDA
GASS, JOANNE MARIE
GAUDIOSO, LYNN MARIE
GAVZER, LAURA NAN
GAYDOS, ANDREA KAY
GERSTEIN, ROESIA HILDY
GLISKER, JANICE LYNN
GOGOLA, PAULINE KAY

GOLD, THERESA
GOLDBERG, JANIS KAY
GOLDBERG, MYRA BERNICE
GOMBERG, BETH MELISSA
GORDON, JANICE S.
GOWLER, VICKI S.
GREGG, KAREN CHRISTINE
GUM, MARY ELAINE
HAAS, MARY CATHERINE
HAFENRICHTER, MARY JEAN
HARR, RHONDA JOY
HASS, JUDITH
HATTIS, CYNTHIA EILEEN
HEARD, BARBARA JO
HEMPEN, CAROLYN JOAN
HENDRIX, PATRICIA ANN
HENDRY, DENISE F.
HICKS, DEBORAH LOUISE
HIRSCH, KAREN IRENE
HO, ELLEN YUAN-CHU
HOCHBERG, GAIL E.
HOCHBERG, SUSAN MYRA
HOEFLER, KATHLEEN THERESE
HOERR, DIANNE MARIE
HOFFMAN, PATRICIA ELEANOR
HOLFORD, BARBARA JEAN
HOLT, JEAN A.
HORWITZ, MARSHA
HOWELL, JAN L.
HUFF, MARTHA ELIZABETH
HUMPHREVILLE, ANNE ELIZABETH
HUNGER, LIANE JEAN
HUTTER, LINDA ANNE
IFFT, NANCY JEAN
ISBELL, SUSAN MARY
JANSSEN, RACHEL LOUISE
JESPERSEN, CAROL ANNE
JOHNSON, CHRISTINA KAY
JOHNSON, CYNTHIA KAY
JOHNSON, LINDA JEAN
JOHNSON, LYNN ANN
JOHNSON, PATRICIA ANN
JONES, DEBORA SUE
KACSH, JUDITH ELLYN
KAISER, MADELEINE MARIE
KANTER, CHARLENE RUTH
KAPLAN, ADALYNN
KASON, BONNIE ANN
KAUFMAN, SHEILA LYNN
KELM, BEVERLY ANN
KENDRICK, MARGARET ANN
KERANS, KAREN SUE
KINCZEWSKI, KATHY ANN
KING, DIANE MARIE
KISTLER, JOAN LOEL
KLEMM, MARGARET ANNE
KLETT, KRISTI LYNN
KLYNSTRA, MELINDA LOU
KOERNER, KAREN SUE
KOPPLIN, JUDITH ANN
KORENGOLD, HELEN L.
KRUEGER, JOYCE LYN
KRUG, KAREN LEE
KUSTON, CASSANDRA ANN

LEFRANCO, ROSALIE ANN
LANG, JANET MARY
LARSON, DEBORAH LYNN
LAUFFENBURGER, SANDRA KAY
LE VINE, BARBARA ANNE
LEVINSON, ROBERTA ANN
LIPSCHULTY, CLAIRE MARCIA
LIPSON, SHELLEY MERLE
LISS, SHEILA RUTH
LITTLE, MARY ELIZABETH
LOESSEL, MARGO SUE
LONG, REBECCA LOUISE
LOSASSO, LEA ANN
LUKEN, BONNIE LOUISE
LUND, CHRISTINE L.
MACKEY, ANN L.
MANGAN, BONNIE FAY
MARCUS, LAURA NAN
MARKWELL, PATRICIA LYNN
MATEK, BETH SAMUEL
MATTHIAS, LINDA KAY
MAXWELL, MARGO JEAN
MCCORMICK, JANICE
MCELROY, BRENDA JOYCE
MCGREAL, DONNA LYNN
MCINTOSH, PATRICIA DORIS
MCKECHNIE, THELMA LOUISE
MEINHEIT, CATHERINE JOANNE
MELER, REBECCA ANN
MERDIAN, JO ANN
MERKEL, LINDA CATHERINE
MICETICH, MARY ANN
MICHELSEN, PEGGY ANNE
MIERNICKI, MARYANN CATHERINE
MIES, VERA JEAN
MIKULA, BARBARA JEAN
MILLER, LINDA ANN
MILLER, JANENE CHRISTINE
MILLER, WENDY MARA
MITCHELL, KAY ANN
MOLDENHAUER, JUDITH ANN
MOLINARI, JANET ELLEN
MOODY, MARY ANN
MOORE, ELIZABETH ANN
MORRISON, MARGARET ELLEN
MOSES, BARGARA SUSAN
MUELLER, MARY JANETTE
MUENCH, JACQELYN RAE
MUHS, JAN LESLIE
MUROWCHICK, LINDA SUE
NADEL, JAN LESLIE
NEPON, JANICE LAURY
NEUNABER, DEBORAH DEE
NIEMANN, JANET KAYE
NISHIMOTO, BARBARA JANE
NORDHEDEN, ANGELENE CARLA
NOTHEISEN, LAURIN DIANE
NUTTING, DEBORAH LANDIS
OERTEL, NANCY MARIE
OGRON, JANET SUE
OLSEN, JANELLEN
OLSON, KAREN HELEN
PACENTA, WENDY LEE
PAMPE, MARCIA LEE

125

PARISH, SYLVIA NELLE
PARK, ALYN SEYMOUR
PARKINSON, ANN NORTH
PARRISH, JANICE BETH
PAUL, DENISE MARIA
PAVIS, VALERIE ANN
PATEK, KATHERINE JANE
PEO, MARGARET LOUISE
PETERS, NANCY
PETERSEN, LINDA RAE
PETTIBONE, JILL ELIZABETH
PHIPPS, KELSEY JANE
PRANGE, CLARICE D.
PRIMMER, CHERYL LOU
PRUZAN, KAREN LEE
QUINN, YVONNE SUSAN
RADZEVICIUS, ALDONA TERESE
REINBOLT, KATHLEEN MARY
REVORD, SHERRY ANN
RICHARDS, MARY LOUISE
RICHARDSON, JEAN ANN
RIPPELMEYER, LYNN JANET
RIZZI, DOLORES
ROGGE, PAULA ANN
ROOK, KAREN SUE
ROSE, ANN DEBRA
ROSENTHAL, JUDITH ILENE
ROWLAND, VIRGINIA ANN
RUBENSTEIN, JOAN BETH
RUBENSTEIN, LOIS MAXINE
RUBIN, DEBORAH RACHEL
RUEBUSH, SARAH JANE
RUNDQUIST, BARBARA JANE
RUSS, ANN KRISTINE
RUTH, DEBORAH ANN
SACKS, NANCY DIANE
SARENA, MICHELE LOUISE
SCHLEICHER, BARBARA ANN
SCHRIVER, KATHRYN MARIE
SCHROEDER, JOYCE KATHERINE
SCHWARTZ, LYNN DEE
SCHWARTZ, SUSAN MARGARET
SCOTT, KATHRYN JO
SCHWARZKOPF, LINDA JOY
SELBY, ROSEMARY
SERWINT, NANCY JEAN
SHAFTMAN, SARAH MIRIAM
SHAPIRO, SUSAN
SHARP, SUSAN MARIE
SHIMP, KATHLEEN ANNE
SHOR, TOBY IRENE
SIEGEL, MICHELLE JO
SIERACKI, NANCY JEAN
SKARZYNSKI, CAROL ANN
SMITH, DEBORA DAWN

SOKOL, JUDITH DIANNE
SOLOMON, ROBERTA HELENE
SOLON, JUDITH ANN
SOSTRIN, CAROL LYNN
SPAK, SUE ELLEN
STAMP, NANCY HENRIETTE
STEIN, CHERYL IRENE
STEIN, MARSHA ANNE
STEVENS, ALICE JEANNE
STEWART, CONNIE ANN
STOMPER, CONNIE MARIE
STROHL, JANET CHRISTINA
SUESS, JUDITH ANNE
SURREY, KAREN BARBARA
SWEET, LYNN DEBRA
TARDY, HELEN ANN
TAYLOR, MARILYN GAY
TERRY, BARBARA ELAINE
TERRY, JEANNE MARIE
THAIN, JANICE ELIZABETH
THOMAS, WANDA FAY
THOMPSON, CAROLYN SUE
TREVILLIAN, CAROL ANN
TROGNER, EVELYN
TULL, CLAUDIA JEAN
TUREK, SUSAN LEE
TURSCH, ILSE MARLENE
URBAN, CHRISTINA DONA
URBAN, MARGARET ANNE
UTHOFF, LINDA BETH
VYBORNY, GLENNA
WAGGONER, MARGARET ANNE
WAKEMAN, ALICE JEAN
WALES, SHERYL EILEEN
WALTER, JOAN ELIZABETH
WALTERS, SHARON SUSAN
WEBER, BARBARA JEAN
WEBBER, DEBORAH LEE
WEINBERG, CAROL ANN
WENDE, KAREN JILL
WHALIN, KATHLEEN DIANE
WHITE, PENELOPE CAROL
WHITTEN, PATRICIA LEE
WIGGAN, STEPHANIE ELIZABETH
WILLIAMS, MARYLENE KATHERINE
WISE, KATHLEEN THERESA
WOLFE, SUSAN MCHENRY
YATES, DEBORAH JANE
YELLIN, LINDA CHERYL
YOUNGSTRUM, CHRISTINE ANN
ZIEBARTH, CHRISTINE GAIL
ZOLLO, PEGGY LEE
ZUCKER, CYNTHIA ANN
ZYCH, MARY ELIZABETH

## ALPHA ZETA (Agriculture)

ALLEN, MARK EATON
ANDERSON, ROSS BYRON
BALKE, NELSON EDWARD
BISCHOFF, THOMAS ARTHUR
BURROW, DANIEL CARL
BUSSE, DONALD FREDERICK
BYERS, RONNIE DEAN

CATLIN, JOHN L.
FOSTER, JAMES STANHOPE
HANES, RICHARD ARTHUR
LAESCH, PHILIP THEADORE
LOY, HAROLD MARVIN
NIGHTINGALE, FRED MARVIN
REETZ, HAROLD F.

126

REEVE, STEWART ANGUS
RINCKER, JAMES DARRELL
SOLON, EDWIN GEORGE
SPILKER, GAYLORD JOHN

STOLLER, JAMES JOSEPH
SVOBODA, WAYNE ETNYRE
TRENT, DAVID ALAN

## GAMMA SIGMA DELTA (Agriculture)

BOLLINGER, DEAN HERMAN
BRIDSON, RANDY GEORGE
DWYER, JAMES FRANCIS
GUENGERICH, FREDERICK PETER
HERBERT, CARL EUGENE
HOLSTINE, WILLIAM JOHN
KITLEY, GARY MICHAEL
LOMAX, LARRY GENE
McGEE, DAVID ALLEN
McMULLEN, PATRICK JOHN

OLSON, GREGORY LYNN
O'NEIL, WILLIAM FRANCIS
RATHGEBER, TERRANCE W.
TALLON, LYLE DUANE
TREES, SCOTT CLYDE
UNDERWOOD, GERALD LEE
WARNER, DAVID ALAN
WEBER, RONALD JOE
WIENRANK, GEORGE DAVID

## GARGOYLE SOCIETY (Architecture)

ADAMS, LARRY LANE
ADAMS, ROBERT DARYL
ANDERSON, RICHARD CLARENCE
BITTNER, SAMUEL PHILLIP
BLANK, WILLIAM CHARLES
CETERA, WILLIAM JOSEPH
CHANG, MICHAEL LOH TIEN
DeVOSS, JOSEPH SHERRILL
EIMER, RONALD WILLIAM
ERBACH, EDWARD ALAN
FISCHER, BRIAN TOM
FREMIN, HERBERT JOSEPH
FUGMAN, ROBERT EDWARD
GOLDENBERG, LEON
GOLDIS, NORMAN Z.
GIUNTOLI, PHILIP ALFRED
GROSSBERG, STEPHEN JAY
HUEHLS, LLOYD BRIAN
JOHNSON, RALPH EVERETT

KELLOGG, JAMES EDWIN
KRESS, CHARLES WILLIAM, JR.
LE, CHI SANH
LERITZ, JAMES PETER
LUEBKEMAN, DAVID JOHN
LUM, GERALD HOONG WUN
MARTIN, JOHN RAYMOND
MESSMAN, GERALD PAUL
MIENER, ROBERT GLEN
MILLETT, MARK LEWIS
PIASKOWY, ANDREW JAMES
PIPER, RICHARD A.
POCIASK, THOMAS JOHN
PROBST, DAVID GLEN
ROSENZWEIG, ALAN DAVID
SEGAL, MARC KALMAN
TRUITT, HENRY
WEEKS, ARTHUR BRUCE
ZECK, WILLIAM JOHN

## KAPPA DELTA PI (Education)

ADEN, VELVI JEAN
ANDREWS, PAMELA LYNN
BANE, MARY ELIZABETH
BANKS, WILSON PALMER
BARBAKOFF, ADRIENNE JOYCE
BARNES, LUANN
BARNHART, PATRICIA R.
BATES, MAVIS ANN
BEAUMONT, KATHERINE SUSAN
BEDLEK, JOHN JOSEPH
BELL, IVAN DON
BERTACCHI, CAROLYN JEAN
BOHREN, JOYCE ELAINE
BOWEN, ROBERT LEE
BRADFORD, JACQUELINE ANN
BRETZLAFF, CELESTE
BROOKS, CONSTANCE JEAN
BROWN, EDWARD E.
BUETTNER, DAVID L.
BURGHARDT, BARBARA
BURRELL, NORMA JANE
CARUTHERS, SHARON LYNNE
CARTER, JOHN FREDERICK

COLEMAN, SUSAN DARE
COLTER, MARGARET C.
COOPER, MARJORIE RHEA
COX, KATHLEEN RAE
CRAIG, BERYL SHIFFMAN
CRAWFORD, BEATRICE P.
CROMBIE, HOWARD FRANKLIN
CURTIS, HIGH FREDRIC
CYBUL, CYNTHIA LOUISE
DADANT, MARY BLISS
DAGUE, MARTHA JO
D'AMICO, JAMES A.
DANIEL, PHILIP TERRIE
DAVIS, ANNA-JANE
DECKER, DONITA INEZ
DEPKE, KATHLEEN ELLEN
DOLIN, JENNIFER SCHAEFFER
DRINKALL, ANITA
EATON, KATHRYN ANN
EDWARDS, GRACE MARY
EDWARDS, JANICE D.
EISENSTEIN, PEGGY CORBIN
ERNSTEIN, KATHLEEN B.

127

EUSTICE, HELEN MARY
EVERHART, BARBARA EILEEN
EWAN, JANE MARIE
FEHR, NANCY BALBACH
FEIGEN, ZANETA B.
FELDMAN, MARILYN PEARL
FILIPPI, CHARLYNE SUE
FINCH, JAMES D.
FINK, NEWTON W.
FINKBEINER, DRUCILLA
FISHMAN, ADRIANNE MAY
FREEMAN, LOUIS G.
FULTON, SUSAN MARIE
GERACI, DIANNE NAPOLITANO
GILCHRIST, JANE MARIA
GILLESPIE, BECKY LOU
GILLMAN, MARGARET MARY
GINGERICH, MARY TERESA
GOLD, MARJORIE LYNN
GRAHAM, MARY JANE
GRAVES, BARBARA LANE
GREGORY, MARK WILLARD
HABLEY, WESLEY RICHARD
HALL, KAREN
HALL, RUTH CONDON
HALL, SHARON DOWERS
HALLER, SUSAN KATHERINE
HAMILTON, WANDA JEAN
HAN, MYUNG-HEE
HANEY, PEGGY HODGE
HEINRICHS, AUDREY STEWART
HELMAN, SUSAN ELAINE
HERTZMAN, LEE
HILST, JAMES JAY
HINES, LINDA S.
HINNERICHS, MARILYNN
HOLT, MARILYN JOHNSON
HOOKER, ELLEN ZIMMERMAN
IMADA, KATHERINE LOU
JEROME, JEROME S.
JOHNSON, HELEN RUTH
KAEDING, IRENE PELLETIER
KAHN, JUDITH DEBORAH
KALLMAN, ARLENE RITA
KARTEN, STEVEN
KEENAN, CHARLES EDWARD
KEMELGOR, BRUCE HOWARD
KENNICUTT, KAREN SUE
KIME, DONNA LOUISE
KIMMEL, E. MARCIA
KIMMEL, ERIC ALAN
KLEIN, BEVERLEY JANIS
KOCH, ROBERT EMIL
KOZIKOWSKI, CONSTANCE ANN
LARSON, KRISTINE LYNN
LARSON, ROBERTA JEANE
LEE, MARJORIE WASHINGTON
LEICHTI, JEAN BETH
LESH, CAROL ANN
LEVICK, LINDA
LEVORA, CHRISTINE FRANCES
LINDAHL, THOMAS J.
LINK, DWIGHT ERIC
LINSKY, NANCY CAROL
LOOMIS, KATHERINE A.

LUTSKY, JUDITH KAY
MADISON, JOHN PAUL
MAGGIO, MATTEW R.
MAHACHEK, DIANE LYNN
MALEK, MARTHA MARY
MALLES, JAMES E.
MANCUSO, JOSEPHINE THERESA
MANN, LAWRENCE ROBERT
MATTEONI, MARSHA
MAY, EUGENE PINKNEY
McDUFFEE, MARY McELROY
McGAUGHEY, JOHN E.
McGILL, ELSIE BARTLETT
McGUIRE, JOSEPH FRANCIS
McNARY, CONSTANCE JANE
McNEIL, DEBORAH KAY
McNETT, MICHAEL EDWARD
MEDDLING, PATRICIA ANN
MELDGIN, LINDA ANN
METZKA, BONITA KAY
METZOW, MARION SELDA
MILLER, MARY LINDA
MOLT, KATHERINE FEIGER
MORIARTY, ANTHONY
MORPURGO, JANE SUSSMAN
MORTVEDT, DONALD F.
MUELLER, MARY LOU
MURPHY, EVA KATHLEEN
NELSON, ROBERT LEWIS
NIEMANN, JEAN MARIE
NOREM, ROXANNE KAY
NOVAK, BARBARA ANN
NOVOSEL, CAROL IRENE
PAALMAN, GRETCHEN
PELZ, ANN ARTHUR
PETERSON, CONNIE JEAN
PLUG, MICHAEL B.
POMERENKE, JUDITH KATHRYN
POWELL, GAYLE CARY
POWELL, THEA JULIANNA
PRATHER, CHERYL LYNN
PROCTER, PATRICIA T.
RAGINS, MARCY BERYL
RASSI, KATHY ANNETTE
REAY, ROSEMARY ANN
REID, FAYE E.
REID, FRANK OLAF
REQUA, SUSAN IRENE
RICH, ROBERTA
RILEY, PATRICIA A.
ROSEN, ELLEN
RUF, PAMALA JOAN
RUNKLE, TERESA NAN
RYOTI, DON EINO
SANDERS, WALTER JOHN
SAVAGE, HELENE SUSAN
SCHNEIDER, MARY THERESE
SCHROEDER, LORING WILLIAM
SCHUMACHER, RUTH DUKES
SEPP, BEVERLY JEAN
SHULER, MARCIA L.
SIEGEL, MARTIN ALAN
SIEGEL, SHERRY JO
SIEGMUND, RALPH C.
SISTER MARY BLAISE GALLOWAY

128

SISTER GRACE LUTHER
SISTER KATHRYN QUINN
SISTER JOAN ROBERTS
SILVERMAN, STUART H.
SIMMONS, MOSBY LINDSAY, III
SIPPEL, WILLIAM H.
SIZE, LINDA EVERS
SMITH, LINDA SUE
SMITH, MADELINE JANES
SMITH, RUTH CORTRIGHT
SPANO, JOLENE A.
STALEY, ELIZABETH KAY
STAMPF, SUSAN MARIE
STAROSTA, ELIZABETH L.
STARK, ROBERT L.
STEWART, IDA SANTOS
STONE, JOHN ALLAN
STROMBERG, SUSAN MARIE
SUMMERVILLE, CAROLE SUE
TALLEY, GERALDINE ELAIN
TAYLOR, DONNA RAE
TEAGUE, PATRICIA ANN
THEISS, CYNTHIA LEA
THOMPSON, ROBERTA JILL

THORNTON, SAM M.
TRAUERNICHT, JO ANN
TRIPLETT, GEORGE H.
TURNER, VIRGINIA KAY
TURSMAN, LUCINDA LOUISE
UCHIDA, RITA J.
UHREN, KAREN KAY
URBANCK, LEILA
van ES, BETTE PERKEL
VAN GILDER, KAY LOUISE
VLAISAVLJEUICH, BETSY J.
VOLAND, MARY ELIZABETH
WALLACE, ROBERT RAY
WASSEL, LYNN GAIL
WENSEL, LOIS P.
WESSELS, BARBARA ANN
WEST, AVERILL ALLEN
WHITESIDE, HELEN ZIEGLER
WIEKHORST, CAROL LARSON
WILKES, MARY LINDA
WILLIAMS, DENNIS ROGER
YELLEN, MARLO ANN
YORK, MARY ELIZABETH
ZAMASTIL, GLEN A.

## KAPPA TAU ALPHA (Communications)

BROTMAN, ERICA
COHEN, SUSAN A.
CUTLER, LEONARD IRA
DALLY, EDWIN PAUL
DANN, MICHAEL HARLEY
DEUTSCH, HELEN
EDWARDS, JOANNA
FASSLER, CYNTHIA BIVINS
GRIFFARD, ROBERT PAUL
JERUTIS, CYNTHIA ANNE
LARSON, DALE BRADLEY

McMILLION, KATHLEEN JOYCE
RATHMAN, CYNTHIA S.
REINHART, CAROL LOUISE
ROBINSON, JAMES MICHAEL
RUGEN, KAREN ANN
SULLIVAN, PATRICIA ANNE
VOREIS, PAMELA WHITING
WILLIAMS, ANNE CELESTE
WINTER, DOUGLAS EARL
ZIV, JAMES KENNETH

## MU PHI EPSILON (Music)

BASH, PATRICIA JO
BERGMAN, SHELLY
BURD, MARY L.
DEHMLOW, NANCY JEAN
DUGINGER, MARILYN MARGARET
KELLY, MARGOT CELESTE

KOCH, LAURIE ANN
LARSON, NANCY C.
OLMSTEAD, SARA LOUISE
RANDALL, DEBORAH SUE
RUETER, ELAINE HELEN
WEINBERG, MARIAN J.

## PHI BETA KAPPA (Liberal Arts and Sciences)

ALLEN, RICHARD BLAIR
ALMGREN, NANCY ANNE
ANSEL, MARC JOEL
ASCHOFF, JOHN GEORGE
BARTON, JAMES MICHAEL
BATKO, KENNETH ALAN
BAUER, STEPHEN MARK
BELSLEY, KATHRYN GENE
BENEDICT, WILLIAM WAITE
BERMAN, STEPHEN ALAN
BERNER, LINDA SUE
BERNSTEIN, LYNN PAULA
BERTOGLIO, MARK RAYMOND
BOIME, SUSAN ILENE
BRATTON, JAY PHILIP

BUSHMAN, MARY ANN
BUSSELL, DIANA BOLZ
CADY, RALPH LOWELL
CAHILL, ANNE LOUISE
CARLSON, BRUCE ELBERT
CARLSON, EVELYN LOUISE
CATTELL, MARY DIANA
COHEN, BRUCE A.
COLBERG, THOMAS PEARSALL
COLE, NANCY SUE
COTTINGHAM, JOHN THEODORE
COX, GRACE ELIZABETH
DAVIS, CAROL BETH
DAY, GREGORY LLOYD
DeGRANDE, GARY GASTON

DUELLO, MARY BETH
DYER, ERIC LEE
EBERSPACHER, EDWARD CHRISTIAN, III
EIMSTAD, WENDY MAE
EISENBERG, MICHAEL J.
ELLIS, JEFFREY JAMES
EPPLIN, JEROME JOSEPH
ESSENPREIS, PATRICIA SUE
EWTON, JOHN HOUSTON
FARRINGTON, THOMAS ARTHUR
FELSENTHAL, STEVEN ALTUS
FIORATO, CATHERINE BACH
FLEISCHMAN, SCOTT CLONICK
FLORA, JANICE ELAINE
FRAZIN, BRUCE EDWARD
FRIEDMAN, GREGORY ANTHONY
GARVEY, NANCY ANN
GEORGE, JOHN MARTIN, JR.
GINDER, GORDON DEAN
GINGERICH, DOROTHY CAROL
GLICK, DONALD LEE
GOLDBERG, MARLENE SUE
GOLDMAN, MYRNA
GOTTFRIED, JOAN M.
GOULKA, JOANNE LYNN
GREDE, MARY ALICE
GUEWTHER, ROBERT KIM
GULLANG, DEBORAH JEAN
GUTHRIE, JANET ELAINE
HAAS, DANIEL DILLON
HALL, SHARON ELIZABETH
HALLSTROM, ARONA HORVITZ
HANKINS, GAIL JACQUELINE
HARMS, JAMES JAY
HARVEY, SCOTT MINER
HAYNES, ROBERT PAUL
HEINZ, KENNETH JOHN
HEITSCH, JANET MARIE
HENDEE, RANDAL JAMES
HERBSTER, BARBARA ANN
HERNANDEZ, DONALD JAMES
HIGGINS, BRYON MARK
HIRSCH, NAOMI
HOHN, MARTHA ALICE
HOHULIN, KEITH RICHARD
HORNKOHL, RHODA GWEN
HOROWITZ, JORDAN JAY
HUDSON, TIGHE F.
HULSEBERG, JUDITH LYNN
INSKEEP, SUSAN LOOMIS
JACOBS, FRED LAWRENCE
JAMIESON, MICHAEL WARREN
JENSEN, JULIE ANNE
JEZIK, MARIE LILETTE
JOHNSEN, LAWRENCE O.
JOHNSEN, TERRENCE O.
JONES, JEFFREY MALDEN
KAMINSKI, MICHAEL JAMES
KANDRAC, KAY POPP
KARLEN, DOUGLAS MELVIN
KASAB, FARIDA
KAZAMA, RODNEY MITSUO
KEARLEY, TIMOTHY GEORGE
KEMP, ALLEN PHILLIP
KENDRICK, LAURA JEAN

KERR, STANLEY PAUL
KLEIN, BEVERLEY JANIS
KOLTUN, PHILIP LOUIS
KOONCE, WAYNE ALLAN
KOZIKOWSKI, CONSTANCE ANN
KRAMER, BARBARA LYNN
KRESCA, LINDA JEAN
KULCZEWSKI, ALAN JOSEPH
KUNZ, GARY LYNN
LABOTKA, RICHARD JOHN
LALISH, GEORGINE RITA
LEONARD, MARGARET MARY
LEPINSKY, SUSAN IRIS
LERNER, EDWARD MARK
LEVIN, ARNOLD LAWRENCE
LEVY, PETER ALEXANDER
LIEBER, DEBORAH LEE
LINDQUIST, JUDITH ANN
LINDQUIST, KENNETH WILLIAM
LOCKMILLER, RICHARD GORDON
LONG, JOHN PERRY
LOOKER, PATRICIA ANN
LOW, TOM WILLIAM
LUNDE, PAULA ANN
MALEK, FRANCINE KAY
MANLEY, MARGARET ANN
MAR, MARY CARLSON
MARINE, PATRICIA ANN
MARTIN, DAVID STUART
MATTIS, HENRY EDWARD
McCANE, CECILIA GAY
McKEOWN, PATRICIA RUTH
McMAHON, LAURIE JO
McNETT, MICHAEL EDWARD
McWILLIAMS, JUDITH MARY
MEYER, SANDRA BRANSEN
MICHAELS, CHERYL MARY
MILLER, GARY J.
MILLER, GERALD JAMES
MILLER, LINDA SUSAN
MIS, BARBARA BERNICE
MOORE, JAMES STRAIGHT
MUNCH, PAUL THOMAS
MYERS, JOHN RILEY
NEEDELMAN, HOWARD WILLIAM
NEIWEEM, BERNARD MICHAEL
NICHOLSON, DEBRA JEAN
NICOL, ARTHUR F.
NORDBERG, DONALD EDWARD
O'CONNELL, SHIRLEY GRAY
OLECK, PATRICIA LYNN
O'LOUGHLIN, MILES WILLIAM, III
PARKS, NOREEN MARY
PARTH, DONALD JAMES
PATCH, ROBERT W.
PATTERSON, SUSAN CAROL
PECK, MICHAEL R.
PERCEFULL, AARON WILLIAM
PETERSON, GEORGE ALLEN
PHILLIPS, BEVERLY RUTH
PLETCHER, W. RANDALL
PODLIPNIK, CAROL JOY
PRUETT, RICHARD KEPLEY
RADELL, JUDITH KISSELL
RADLOFF, STUART JAY

130

RECTOR, LOIS ANN
REID, FRANK OLAF
REUBEN, GAIL BETH
REULER, PEGGY ROSE
RHEINWALD, KRYSTAL LUCKHART
RICHARDS, LAUREL ANN
RIGGINS, VIRGINIA GARDNER
RITHOLZ, PAULA SUE
ROBERTSON, LOIS KRAFT
ROBINSON, RICHARD BRUCE
ROSBOROUGH, TERRILL KENT
ROTHSCHILD, MARILYNN JOYCE
RUDMAN, SHERWIN M.
RUEMMLER, JOHN DAVID
RUNGE, THOMAS FRED
SACKHEIM, RUTH MIRIAM
SCHOENBERG, DANIEL ROBERT
SCHOFIELD, CHERIE LYNN
SCHUNK, MARCIA ANN
SHAPERO, BARBARA R.
SHAPIRO, HELEN DEBORAH
SHIELDS, MICHAEL JOHN
SHIFFLETT, LEONARD STEWART
SHUMWAY, DAVID LUCIAS
SIEDBAND, LEONARD BURTON
SILVER, STEVEN LESLIE
SINCLAIR, JAMES STEWART
SLAVIN, NANCY RABIN
SLIVON, SYLVIA LOUISE
SLUTKIN, GARY
SMOLLER, BARBARA GAIL
SNIVELY, STEPHEN WAYNE
SOCOL, MICHAEL LEE
SONNEMAICER, MICHAEL WILLIAM
SOSTRIN, JUDITH SUSAN

SOUTHON, EDWARD HENRY
STAAS, JAMES GREGORY
STEFFENS, BRUCE CHASE
STEIN, ALAN
STEIN, ARNOLD BRUCE
STICHA, PAUL JOEL
STONE, JOHN ALLAN
STRATTON, WILLIAM CLAYTON
SUTCLIFFEE, LINDA BETH
SUTHERLAND, PAMELA BRUECHKNER
TAKAGISHI, MARK SAMUEL
TAYLOR, ROGER LEON
THOMPSON, JEAN LOUISE
TIPSWORD, THOMAS NATHAN, II
TOMPKINS, CHRISTOPHER WILSON
TOMPKINS, WILLIAM EARL
TROTTER, BETTY MARIE
VAN WERINGH, LOLKJE
VERA, DEBORAH KOLDITZ
VOGET, ANTOINETTE KATHARINE
WEBB, BRUCE RONALD
WEBER, PENNY SUE
WEBSTER, JANE ANN
WENDEL, MARTHA ANN
WESSELY, ROBERT PAUL
WHITMORE, DOUGLAS MICHAEL
WICHTERMAN, KEITH ALLEN
WILLIS, KATHRYN ANN
WINTERBAUER, KAYE PISTORIUS
WOJTAN, LINDA SUE
WOOLSEY, THOMAS RICHARD
WYLIE, LAURENCE TOWNE
ZEITZ, EILEEN MOLLIE
ZIMMERMAN, RICHARD RUSSELL
ZOELLICK, WILLIAM NORMAN

## PHI KAPPA PHI (All-University)

ALLEN, RICHARD BLAIR
ALMGREN, NANCY ANNE
ANSEL, MARC JOEL
ARTHUR, ROBERT BRUCE
BALKE, NELSON EDWARD
BARNARD, MARY KAY
BARNES, MARILYN JOYCE
BARRETT, ANNA KAY
BARTON, JAMES MICHAEL
BEIMAN, ABBIE WILLARD
BERKOWITZ, RHONA SONDRA
BLOEMER, ROBERT WILLIAM
BLOOM, JANET LOUISE
BOWEN, EVELYN ROSE
BRADY, BONNIE JEAN
BRIGHT, PEGGY RENEE
BUCHSBAUM, MARGALIT CLARA
BUSSELL, DIANA BOLZ
CARLSON, EVELYN LOUISE
CLEMENTS, ERNEST VINTON, III
COX, GRACE ELIZABETH
CRANE, RICHARD ALAN
DAGUE, MARTHA JO
DAVIS, CAROL BETH
DOWLING, GLORIA VALBORG
EBERSPACHER, EDWARD CHRISTIAN, III
ESSENPREIS, PATRICIA SUE

EWAN, JANE MARIE
FARK, JANET SUE
FECHTER, ANITA SOPHIE
FEIGER, KATHERINE JOANNE
FELSENTHAL, STEVEN ALTUS
FORD, ROBERT WALTER
FRANCIS, MARY ANN
FUNK, JAMES LORAINE
FYIE, JAY HERBERT
GAMM, AUDREY SUZANNE
GARDNER, PHYLLIS IRENE
GARDNER, VIRGINIA SUSAN
GARVEY, NANCY ANN
GERENSTEIN, JAN LOIS
GINDER, GORDON DEAN
GINGERICH, MARY TERESA
GLICK, DONALD LEE
GOLDBERG, MARLENE
GOTTFRIED, JOAN MAE
GRAZIANO, DAVID CHARLES
GREDE, MARY ALICE
GUENTHER, ROBERT KIM
GULLANG, DEBORAH JEAN
GUTSHALL, ARTHUR ROBERT
HANKINS, GAIL JACQUELINE
HEPPERLY, THOMAS RAMSAY
HIRCHERT, KURT WALTER

131

HIRSCH, AUSTIN LOUIS
HIRSCH, NAOMI
HOLADAY, ALLAN SCOTT
HOUGEN, CARLENE DORAN
HUBER, BRUCE ALAN
HUDSON, TIGHE FRANCIS
IMANAKA, MICHAEL MASARU
JACKSON, ANN LOUISE
JAMES, DAVID CHRISTOPHER
JOHNSEN, LAWRENCE O.
JOHNSEN, TERRENCE O.
JOHNSON, JANICE LYNN
JOHNSON, RICHARD HAROLD
JUNCK, LARRY RICHARD
KAZAMA, RODNEY MITSUO
KEARLEY, TIMOTHY GEORGE
KELMAN, ETHEL BELLA
KEMP, ALLEN PHILLIP
KENDRICK, LAURA JEAN
KESLER, JAMES LESTER
KLEIN, BEVERLY JANIS
KOCH, BEVERLY ANN
KOOI, JOHN H.
KOPECKY, VIRGINIA BLANCHE
LANCASTER, DAVID RUSSELL
LANE, CHARLES RAY
LANE, PHILIP EDWARD
LANGMAN, CHARLES HENRY
LARSON, DALE BRADLEY
LERNER, EDWARD MARK
LEVY, PETER ALEXANDER
LEWIS, MARILYN TOMLINSON
LIEBER, DEBORAH LEE
LINDQUIST, JUDITH ANN
LOMBARDI, MICHELLE JEAN
LOOMIS, SUSAN MARIE
LUNDE, PAULA ANN
MARSHALL, PAUL EDWARD
MARSHALLA, LINDA ROSE
MARTIN, DAVID STUART
MASTERS, MARJORIE LUESE
McCANE, CECILIA GAY
McMAHON, MARY JEANNETTE
McMILLION, KATHLEEN JOYCE
McWILLIAMS, JUDITH MARY
MILES, KATHY ANN
MILLER, LINDA SUSAN
MOORE, FRANCES MAIN

MUNZ, JOHN HARTZELL
MYERS, GEORGE DOUGLAS
NEEDELMAN, HOWARD WILLIAM
NICKELSON, LEE ERNST, JR.
NIELSEN, LINDA LOUISE
NORDBERG, DONALD EDWARD
NULL, NED LYNN
O'HARE, RANDALL SCOTT
OHLSEN, BARBARA JEAN
O'RAVIS, LARRY THOMAS
PETERSON, ROBERT THOMAS
PHILLIPS, BEVERLY RUTH
PISTORIUS, KAYE ELIZABETH
PLETCHER, W. RANDALL
PRUETT, RICHARD KEPLEY
REID, FRANK OLAF
REULER, PEGGY ROSE
ROSS, JOHN DAVID
ROTHSCHILD, MARILYN JOYCE
SACKHEIM, RUTH MIRIAM
SAIKLEY, GILBERT HAVEN
SCHAER, MICHAEL
SCHWEIGHART, SANDRA KAY
SCHWENDEMAN, SUSAN MARIE
SHAFER, STEPHEN CRAIG
SHAPIRO, HELEN DEBORAH
SIEDBAND, LEONARD BURTON
SONNEMAKER, MICHAEL WILLIAM
SPANGLER, SUZANNE PAMELA
STARR, JOYCE ANN
STEFFENS, BRUCE CHASE
STICHA, PAUL JOEL
STOLLER, JAMES JOSEPH
SUDLOW, WILLIAM JOSEPH
TIEMEIER, KATHLEEN JILL
TOMPKINS, CHRISTOPHER
TROTTER, BETTY MARIE
VERA, DEBORAH KOLDITZ
WEBER, PENNY SUE
WEINTROB, MEDA REBECCA
WENDEL, MARTHA ANN
WIENRANK, GEORGE DAVID
WILDE, DONNA JEAN
WILLIS, KATHRYN ANN
WOJTAN, LINDA SUE
WRIGLEY, CAROLE JEAN
WUEBBLES, DONALD JAMES

## SIGMA TAU (Engineering)

ADELT, RICHARD ALLEN
BARTLETT, DONALD LARRY
BELL, MARY ANN
BELTZ, WILLIAM FOARD
BENASSI, JOHN MARIO
BENTON, RONALD LILYARD
BERGER, MICHAEL F.
BERGSTROM, ERIC KENNETH
BERNICKAS, JOHN VICTOR
BERNSEE, FREDERICK RICHARD
BISHAF, PHILLIP CHARLES
BLANDFORD, JAMES BERNARD
BRENNER, MARK A.
BRETZLAFF, ROBERT S.

BROWN, THOMAS GLENN
BUFORD, ROBERT JOHN
BUSH, GARY ALLAN
BUSS, STEPHEN A.
BUTLER, GERALD JOSEPH
CALVETTI, PAMELA JEAN
CHAN, JIMMY SIU-LEUNG
CHAPMAN, EDWARD ALLEN
CHESLEY, PATRICK JOHN
CLEMENTS, ERNEST VINTON, III
COBERLY, GLEN CARTER
COLEMAN, JAMES J.
COOPER, LARRY PHILIP
CULVER, STEVEN RANDALL

DAVIS, H. GLENN
DOMINIK, DANIEL FRANK
EDWARDS, JOHN FRANCIS
ENGLUND, CHARLES JEFFREY
EVANS, WILLIAM THEODORE
FABER, JOHN PIERRE
FEINBERG, STEPHEN JAY
FELDMAN, MARK IRWIN
FIELD, DONALD MARTIN
FOAT, GALEN DELBERT
FOLKERTS, CHARLES HENRY
FONTANA, THOMAS PAUL
FRAILEY, MAX LEE
FRANKLIN, MICHAEL STEVEN
FRANKLIN, SHELDON NORMAN
FRETT, MICHAEL CHARLES
FTACEK, ANDREW PHILIP, JR.
GEHRIG, DOUGLAS BRUCE
GIBSON, TERRENCE LYNN
GISINGER, JACK LORIN
GREENWALD, CARL JOSEPH
GREER, WILBUR CHARLES, JR.
GRIEBENOW, ROBERT RICHARD
GUNNARSSON, THOR
HAAR, THOMAS BERNARD
HALL, DOUGLAS RALPH
HAMMES, ROBERT MATTHEW, JR.
HAMMOND, JOHN B.
HANSON, HOWARD P.
HOPP, RANDOLPH LEE
HOUCK, JOHN DAVID
HUNSINGER, CHARLES RAY, JR.
JOHNSON, JOHN HENRY
KAAR, DAVID RICHARD
KLINE, THOMAS F.
KNELL, CHARLES PINCOFFS
KOSCIK, RICHARD A.
KRAKER, ROBERT GILBERT
LARSON, DOUGLAS ERIK
LEANG, WILLIAM NIM-CHEI
LUDOWISE, MICHAEL JOSEPH
MACKIN, EDMUND FRANCIS
MAK, ALAN SUNG-CHI
MAK, KUI NANG
MANCINI, LOUIS JOSEPH
MARSHALLA, ROBERT ALVIN
MILLER, GLENN HENRY

NELSON, THOMAS E.
NIEHOFF, DENNIS DEAN
O'DONNELL, JOHN PATRICK
O'REILLY, MARGARET MARY
PAGE, ROBERT ALLEN
PECK, KEN R.
PEPPING, RICHARD EDWIN
PFAENDER, THOMAS GEORGE
PIEPER, RICHARD WAYNE
PLATTNER, PAUL FREDRICK
POTT, EDWARD JAMES
POVILUS, DAVID STEPHEN
RAUSCH, PATRICK GLENN
RAYMER, JERRY N.
ROBERTS, LARRY KEITH
ROSBOROUGH, GEORGE WILLIAM
SALM, KURT LEE
SATTERWHITE, DAVID GLENN
SCHLEMBACH, JOHN MICHAEL
SCHNEIDER, RONALD WILBERT
SHEWMAKER, RONALD DEAN
SNODGRASS, KIRK ALLEN
SNOKE, THOMAS EDWIN
SOMMERS, DAVID ARTHUR
SONNEVILLE, STEPHEN THOMAS
SPUDIL, MICHAEL WILLIAM
STAMERJOHN, DAVID MICHAEL
STEFFEN, DAVID EUGENE
STEFFENN, RONALD WAYNE
STOUT, ALAN CAVITT
SWIATOWIEC, FRANK JOHN
TALMADGE, RICHARD NEAL
TESTIN, ROBERT ALAN
TORGERSEN, THOMAS LEE
TRACHTENBARG, DAVID
TREMBLAY, MICHAEL ANTHONY
TUREK, MARK EDWARD
ULVILA, JACOB WALTER
VANBLARICUM, MICHAEL LEE
VANCE, GARY MILES
VANHOOZEN, ALLEN LEE
WILHELM, JOSEPH LEE
WILLIAMS, EARL HARMON
WITTE, BENJAMIN MICHAEL
WONG, KAI SIN
YOUNKER, WILLIS FRED

## BETA GAMMA SIGMA (Commerce and Business Administration)

ANGLES, ROBERT L.
BOLLMAN, TERRY LEE
BROWN, RAYMON MICHAEL
CHENAULT, ORA BRACKETT
CODD, JOHN EDWARD
CRANE, RICHARD ALAN
FICHTER, JOHN KENNETH
FUCHS, MARC ELDON
GAHLON, JAMES MAURITZ
HEGSTAD, SVEN OLAF
HIRSCH, AUSTIN LOUIS
HUSTON, JOHN MATHEW
KARDELL, GARY R.
KOURIS, PAUL ANDREW, JR.
LALEMAN, RICHARD LEE
LERMAN, IRWIN HOWARD

LEWIS, DAVID JOHN
LOEWENSTEIN, RALPH H.
MASKEY, REBECCA SUZANNE
MASTERS, MARJORIE LUESE
MUNZ, JOHN HARTZELL
MURPHY, JAMES PATRICK
O'HARE, RANDALL SCOTT
OSBERG, THOMAS THEODORE
PARVIN, CHARLES LANDON
PIANO, LAWRENCE J.
RUDDELL, BRIAN WAYNE
SHANER, DAN ALLEN
SIKICH, JAMES ANTON
TROMPETER, JEAN E.
WANGER, JAMES P.
WORSHAM, PATRICK MICHAEL

# EDMUND J. JAMES SCHOLARS

The following students are James Scholars in good standing who have cumulative grade averages of 4.5 or better. James Scholars with grade averages below 4.5 are not listed.

ABATE, MARK R.
ABRAMS, MARILYN ADRIAN
ADAMI, PAUL EDWARD
ADAMS, JAY WILLIAM
ADAMS, KATHRYN ANN
ADAMS, MARTHA JEAN
ADAMS, VICKI LYNN
ADKISSON, STANLEY WHITE
ADLER, JOAN MARIE
AGINS, ANN SHERRY
AKULOW, OKSANA ANTOINETTE
ALBRECHT, DAVID WALTE
ALBUN, CARL JEROME
ALLEMONG, JOHN JAY
ALLEN, CAROL ANN
ALLEN, DAVID MICHAEL
ALLEN, KATHERINE GRACE
ALLEN, MARIBETH
ALLEN, RICHARD BLAIR
ALLHANDS, RODGER VERNON
ALMGREN, NANCY ANNE
ALPERN, MICHAEL
ALTER, BARBARA PHYLLIS
ALTON, GUY RICHARD
ALTSCHUL, MARLA KOLS
AMLING, JENNIFER LOUISE
AMORUSO, WILLIAM BRUCE
ANDERSEN, HENRY THOMAS
ANDERSON, ALICE V.
ANDERSON, CAROL L.
ANDERSON, DONALD WAYNE
ANDERSON, GREGORY CHARLES
ANDERSON, KATHLEEN ANN
ANDERSON, KIRK PAUL
ANDERSON, NEAL GEORGE
ANDERSON, PATRICIA LYNNE
ANDERSON, STEVEN GEORGE
ANDREAS, NANCY ELAINE
ANSEL, LESLIE FERN
ANSEL, MARC JOEL
APPENZELLER, BILLIE KAY
ARENSON, SUSAN LESLIE
ARMSTRONG, BENTON LEROY
ARNOLD, SANDRA KAY
ASCHOFF, JOHN GEORGE
ASHER, IRA MANUEL
ASHER, SHARON KAY
ASHLEY, DANIEL JOSEPH
ASHLEY, LANE JOHN
ASPER, GLORIA DEONNE
ATHERTON, JAMES H.
ATKINSON, DAVID EDWIN
ATKINSON, RUSSELL R.
ATLAS, BARRY FOSTER
AUBRECHT, KATHRYN ANNE
AUERBACH, VIVIAN SUE
BABBITT, JEAN HANCOCK
BACCHI, DIANE MARIE

BACE, LYNN ALEXANDRIA
BACKS, WILLIAM MARTIN
BAECHLE, DANIEL ARTHUR
BAEDER, ALICE JOYCE
BAER, ROBERT SCOTT
BAIR, KATHLEEN LOUISE
BAKER, JO ANN
BALBACH, EDITH DEWITT
BALKE, NELSON EDWARD
BALLARD, LEXIS S.
BARBER, KATHLEEN MARIE
BARDELMEIER, DENNIS GENE
BARFIELD, HENRY HARVEY
BARKER, BARBARA
BARNARD, MARY KAY
BARNETT, BENITA KAYE
BARON, DENNIS JOSEPH
BARR, KENNETH HARRY
BARRY, CATHERINE MARY
BARTENSTEIN, JULIE
BARTHOLOMEW, DEBRA KAY
BARTON, CHRISTINE ANN
BARTON, JAMES MICHAEL
BASKIN, CRAIG PAUL
BASSETT, JOHN KAERICHER
BASTIAN, JOHN FREDERIC
BATES, ROBERT JOSEPH, JR.
BATKO, KENNETH ALAN
BATTERMAN, KAREN SUE
BAUER, DAVID CARL
BAUER, STEPHEN MARK
BAUERNFEIND, DEBANEY
BAUSER, JOHN EDWARD
BEAMS, DAVID MICHAEL
BEAVERS, JOHN A.
BECKER, KENNETH MICHAEL
BECKER, WILLIAM BRADLEY
BECKFELD, MARY CATHERINE
BEELER, JOSEPH K.
BEEN, STEVEN ALLAN
BEGOUN, AVIS JOY
BELL, LAIRD ARTHUR
BELTZ, WILLIAM F.
BEND, DONALD DUANE
BENEDICT, WILLIAM WAI
BENNETT, BARBARA ANN
BENTEN, JAMES S.
BENTON, MARK CAMERON
BENTON, RONALD LILYARD
BERG, KENNETH DAVID
BERGER, ARLENE ROSALYN
BERGER, DANIEL BENJAMIN
BERGER, ELLEN ROSE
BERGSTROM, RICHARD LEE
BERKOWICZ, HOWARD HYMAN
BERKOWITZ, RICHARD ALAN
BERKSON, ANDREA JOY
BERLIANT, MARC NORMAN

BERMAN, BONNIE SUE
BERMAN, RONALD CHARLES
BERMAN, WENDY CAROL
BERNARDY, JOHANNA MARY
BERNSEE, ROBERT WILLIAM
BERNSTEIN, ALAN DAVID
BERNSTEIN, AVIS MELIA
BERNSTEIN, HELANE IRIS
BERRY, DAVID PHILIP
BERSHAD, BLAINE D.
BERSON, BRUCE ALAN
BERTELSEN, JULIA SUE
BEST, LARRY V.
BETTNER, ALLEN WAYNE
BEYERS, JOSEPH WAYNE
BIANCALANA, FLORA ERMENIA
BIBLY, KATHERINE
BICEK, MARGARET JANE
BIDNER, MARILYN JEAN
BILLER, CAROL NAOMI
BILLING, MICHAEL GERARD
BILYEU, THOMAS MICHAEL
BINKIN, GERI SUZANNE
BIRSTEIN, KAREN S.
BITZ, DONALD MICHAEL
BJORSETH, KATHLEEN MARIE
BLACK, JANE OLSEN
BLACK, JEAN BAKER
BLAHA, SHARALYN ROSE
BLANC, PETER LEON
BLANK, RUTH ELLEN
BLATH, BARBARA ANN
BLAZEK, JUDITH JEAN
BLOEMER, ROBERT WILLIAM
BLOM, BERNHARD EMILE
BLUESTONE, ROBIN JOY
BLUHM, KAREN L. E.
BLUMENTHAL, HOWARD MICHAEL
BLUMENTHAL, MARC JEFFREY
BODEM, CHARLES RENE
BODLE, MARGERY ANN
BODZNICK, DAVID ALAN
BOHL, BETTY JEAN
BOI, MARTIN T.
BOIME, SUSAN ILENE
BOKSA, KAREN ANN
BOKUNIEWICZ, HENRY JOSEPH
BOLLINGER, DEAN HERMAN
BONNOM, RANDALL CURRY
BONO, BETTE LYNNE
BOONE, LUANN TUCKER
BORAZ, ROYCE ELLEN
BORN, CHRISTOPHER PAUL
BORRE, KRISTEN SUE
BORRENPOHL, LAVONNE
BORRENPOHL, NANCY LEE
BORTH, DAVID EDWARD
BORTZ, SHERI LEE
BOTTERON, MARY ALICE
BOUCEK, CAROL LYNE
BOUDREAU, JAMES KARLE
BOWEN, EVELYN ROSE
BOWEN, ROBERT EVANS
BOYINGTON, BARBARA ANN
BRADBURY, PETER JAMES

BRADLEY, KATIE RACHEL
BRASH, DOUGLAS EDGAR
BRATTON, JAY PHILIP
BRAUER, MARY ALICE
BRAUN, LYNN
BRAVERMAN, MARLA DEE
BRETHAUER, TODD STEVEN
BRETZLASS, ROBERT S.
BREWER, MICHAEL LYNN
BRIGGS, MARTHA LUELLA
BRIGHT, PEGGY RENEE
BRIGHTBILL, FREDERICK ALLEN
BRILL, BETTE SUE
BRINKMANN, CARL ERNEST
BRINKMANN, KENNETH GENE
BRISKMAN, RANDY JOYCE
BRITTAIN, RICHARD GRAY
BRODIN, MARY ELLEN
BRODSKY, MICHAEL AARON
BROOKS, RICHARD LYNN
BROTMAN, ERICA
BROWN, BRUCE T.
BROWN, CHRISTOPHER G.
BROWN, DAVID MARK
BROWN, ROGER MARK
BROWN, STEWART JAY
BROWN, WARREN C.
BRUCE, ROBERT JAMES
BRUMLEVE, CHARLES EVAN
BRUMLEVE, TIMOTHY ROBERT
BRUNO, ELIZABETH ALEXANDRA
BUCHSBAUM, MARGALIT CLARA
BUCHSBAUM, YAEL
BUCK, JAMES WILLIAM
BUCKLIN, ROBERT SCOTT
BUDDE, JANE MARGARET
BUDZ, JEROME THOMAS
BUDZIK, PHILIP MICHAEL
BUDZINSKI, ROBERT LUCUIS
BUESCHER, MELVIN HENRY
BUGOS, DAVID JAMES
BUHAI, BETSY E.
BUNCH, DEBRA JEANNE
BURCH, WILLIAM ALLAN
BURKHOLDER, KATHLEEN LINDA
BURMAN, LUAN
BURTNESS, KATHRYN GRACE
BUSCHBACH, SUSAN KAY
BUSHMAN, MARY ANN
BUTLER, JOHN CHRISTIAN
BYTHELL, CAROL ANN
CACCIATO, DARLENE
CADY, RALPH LOWELL
CAFARELLA, JEAN MARIE
CAMILLO, SUSAN MILDRED
CAMODECA, SILVIO JOSEPH
CAMPANELLA, CARL JOSEPH
CAMPBELL, BILLIE LOUISE
CAMPBELL, CLIVE DOUGLAS
CARAWAY, MYRA SUE
CARDELLA, RICHARD GEORGE
CARDELLI, JAMES ALLEN
CARLEY, STEPHEN EDWARD
CARLSON, ALLEN MARK
CARLSON, JUNE EILEEN

135

Carmack, Mary Ann
Carpenter, Henry A.
Carter, Carolyn Elizabeth
Carter, David Alan
Casagrande, James Bert
Caselton, Marilyn Sue
Cederholm, Fred William
Center, David Steven
Cesarone, Bernard Joseph
Chan, James Lap-Chi
Chan, Wai Kung
Chao, Nancy Shan
Chapman, Lee James
Charney, Wayne Michael
Chauncey, Joan Margaret
Chausow, Alan Martin
Cheek, Charles Edward
Chen, Peter Yale
Chen, Tsun-Huei William
Chesley, Patrick John
Chesrow, George William
Chewning, Diane Sue
Chipman, Jeffrey Thomas
Choi, Tatyin Boniface
Christen, Darryl Karl
Christman, Kathy Lynn
Christoff, Richard Wayne
Christofferson, April Jeanne
Ciemiega, David Jeffrey
Cizmar, Dawn Kathleen
Clancy, Michael John
Clark, Craig Robert
Clark, Linda Jean
Clemens, Michael J.
Clements, Ernest V., II
Cobb, Michael Allan
Coe, Patricia Ann
Cohen, Gerald Arnold
Cohen, Myron Scott
Cohen, Patti Kate
Cohn, Paula Beth
Colbert, Nancy Lynn
Colby, Virginia Gaye
Coleman, Shelley Jean
Collier, Sara Ellen
Collins, Mary Margaret
Collins, Susan Lee
Condon, Susan Joanne
Conroy, Kathleen Randall
Cook, Jeffrey Steven
Cook, Kara Linda
Cook, Martin Leo
Cooper, George Kyle
Corbett, Patricia Lee
Corn, Lila Sarah
Corona, David Anthony
Correale, Michael Gene
Coulias, Dale Christine
Cournoyer, Ann Kathryn
Court, Marcia Louise
Cox, Grace Elizabeth
Crain, Debra Nan
Crain, Martin Ross
Cralley, William E.
Croft, Steven Martin

Crone, Charles L.
Crow, Cynthia Louise
Cunningham, John Tracy
Curtis, Jonathan Ubrey
Cygan, Edward Anthony
Czwornog, Michael
Dachman, Carey Bennett
Dagen, Nancy Elaine
Daley, Mary Josephine
Dalley, Carolyn Ann
Dally, Edwin Paul
D'Ambrogia, Margaret Mary
Damico, Donald Patrick
Daniels, Lesley Diane
Dann, Michael Harley
Daugherity, Kerry Lee
Dauphinais, Jay P.
David, Jacqueline Deborah
David, Myrna Ann
Davidson, James Benjamin
Davidson, Victor Lester
Davis, Carol Beth
Davis, Harry Glenn
Davis, Howard Jay
Davis, Kathryn Ann
Davis, Laura Rebecca
Davis, Marilyn Deborah
Davis, Paula Winsor
Davis, Randall Douglas
Davis, Rhea Ellen
Davis, Robert Wendell
Davis, Sylvia Beth
Davison, Dwight Oran
Dawson, Clyde William
Day, Gregory Lloyd
Day, Richard Joseph
Dayton, Kay Ellen
Dean, Stacy Lillian
Decker, Steven Robert
Decyk, Roxanne Jean
De Decker, Kathleen Ann
Delaney, Carol Jean
Del Vento, Connie Ann
Dennis, Jon Edward
Denny, Jack Warren
Depke, Janet Marie
Destefano, James N.
De Vore, Cynthia Lynne
De Vuono, Mary
Deweese, Joseph E.
Dickey, Katharine Sue
Dickey, Michael Dene
Dickman, Theta Ann
Didech, Dean Michael
Diehl, Randy Lee
Dierstein, Julie Jene
Dietzen, Keith David
Difonzo, Kenneth Wayne
Di Gangi, Claudia A.
Dinges, Clarine Ann
Dodds, Joanne Elizabeth
Dodgson, David Scott
Dodsworth, Clark S., Jr.
Doll, Douglas Christopher
Dominik, Daniel F.

DONOVAN, ERIC BRENT
DOODY, DANIEL PATRICK
DORN, ALAN STUART
DOROGHAZI, PAUL MATTHEW
DOROGHAZI, ROBERT MARK
DOTLICH, DAVID LANDRETH
DOUGLAS, DAVID JOSEPH
DOWDEN, DOUGLAS CALHOUN
DOWLING, GLORIA V.
DRESCH, HENRY J.
DREYER, RICHARD FREDERICK
DRIBIN, MICHELE RENEE
DUBEY, DENNIS ROY
DUBSON, RONALD STEPHEN
DUCOFF, BARBARA ELIZABETH
DUFFIN, JOHN THOMAS
DUFFY, KATHLEEN VIRGINIA
DUGGAN, TIMOTHY EVIN
DUGUID, JOHN ROBINSON
DUNIVENT, AMY ANNE
DUNNAN, MELISSA JO
DUNNE, KATHLEEN THERESA
DUNTEMAN, PAUL LYMAN
DUPUIS, WILLIAM THOMAS
DYKSTRA, CLIFFORD ELLIOT
DYSERT, ALAN R.
EAKLE, CHRISTINE DENISE
EARLY, MICHAEL BRENT
EBERSPACHER, EDWARD CHRISTIAN
ECKSTEIN, BEVERLY JO
EDELMAN, SANDRA LEE
EDGERTON, JAMES ROY
EDSTROM, ROBERT CHARLES
EDWARDS, JANET PATRICIA
EDWARDS, JOANNA
EGAN, MARY ALICE
EGGERDING, CARL LOUIS
EGGERDING, CAROLINE
EISEL, JOHN LESLIE
EISENBERG, CHERI FRAN
EISENBERG, JOHN DAVID
EISENBERG, MICHAEL JAY
EISENSTEIN, ANN RACHEL
EISENSTEIN, MARTIN I.
ELETSON, BRIDGET ANNE
ELLGASS, MICHAEL GREGORY
ELLIOTT, RONALD LEE
ELLIS, DEBRA LYNN
ELLIS, JEFFREY JAMES
ELLIS, RICHARD LYALL
ELLISON, LINDA KAY
ELLSTRAND, NORMAN CARL
EMERY, BARBARA ANN
EMSHOFF, JAMES GORDON
ENDO, DAVID JOJI
ENGELBERG, ALAN LINDS
ENGLE, HOWARD STUART
ENGSTROM, KATHY SUSAN
EPHRON, MARK STEVEN
EPPLIN, JEROME JOSEPH
EPSTEIN, BEVERLY ANN
EPSTEIN, BOB ERIC
EPSTEIN, MARC ALAN
ERDE, MARY ANNE
ERHARDT, PENNY JANE

ERICKSON, KAREN JANE
ERICKSON, PAMELA IRENE
ERICKSON, STEPHEN LEE
ERIN, ROD
ESSENPREIS, PATRICIA
ETZKORN, SHEILA M.
EUSTICE, DEBORAH CLARE
EVANS, ARTHUR H.
EVANS, MARGARET ANN
EWAN, JUDITH ANN
EWERS, THOMAS BEARD
EXNER, BONNIE R.
FALTUS, VICKI LYNN
FARKAS, JACQUES NATHAN
FARMER, ROGER ALAN
FARNER, SUSAN MARIE
FARNHAM, NANCY ELLEN
FARRUGGIA, ROBERT V.
FASSLER, CYNTHIA BIVINS
FAULSTICH, GRETCHEN ANN
FAWCETT, BRADLEY KEVIN
FEINBERG, JOYCE MARILYN
FEINBERG, STEPHEN JAY
FEIST, ELLEN SUE
FELDMAN, ANITA SUSAN
FELL, DAVID ALAN
FELSENTHAL, CAROL GREENBERG
FELSENTHAL, STEVEN ALTUS
FERNALD, STEPHEN CRAIG
FIARMAN, LAWRENCE MORRIS
FIDUK, KENNETH W., JR.
FIELD, DANIEL PLAYFAIR
FIELD, STEVEN DAVID
FIELDS, JACQUELINE ELAINE
FIELDS, SCOTT IRA
FIERSTEIN, IRA
FINE, CAROLE SUE
FINK, MARSHA ANN
FINKE, JEFFREY WAYNE
FINKELSTEIN, MICHAEL WILLIAM
FISCHER, HAROLD ALAN
FISHER, DEBORAH ANN
FISHER, JOY D.
FISHMAN, ADRIANNE MAY
FITZER, SUSAN L.
FJERSTAD, ERIK ALLEN
FLANIGAN, JAMES ROY
FLEABLE, JOHN THOMAS
FLEMING, ELIZABETH CHARLENE
FLENNIKEN, JOHN MICHAEL
FLESSNER, STEPHEN MARK
FOGEL, MAUREEN GAIL
FON, GERALD LEE
FONTANA, THOMAS P.
FOOTE, ROBERT A.
FORAN, PAUL GORDON
FORSBERG, THOMAS WAYNE
FORSE, ROGER JAMES
FOSS, CATHERINE MARIE
FOSTER, CRAIG STEPHEN
FOX, CAROL ILENE
FRANK, CHARLES ROY
FRANK, GERI
FRANK, SHARON LOUISE
FRANKS, WILLIAM DALE

137

Frantz, Larry Thomas
Frederickson, David Lynn
Freedman, Shelley Beth
Freedman, Susan Russe
Freeman, Maynard Lloyd
Freidinger, Joy Lynn
Freireich, Valerie Jane
Friedland, Nancy Ellen
Friedman, Debbie Marsha
Friedman, Deborah Jane
Friedman, Sandra Lee
Friedman, Sheila Karen
Frisbie, Anne Celeste
Fritsch, Kathleen Christine
Frykman, Daniel Paul
Fuchs, Elaine Viola
Fuchs, Nancy Melinda
Fujii, Midori
Fuller, Daniel Leroy
Fuller, Kim Francis
Fulton, Susan Marie
Funk, James Loraine
Funk, Melba Rolf
Fuoss, Dennis Edward
Furlong, Joanne Catherine
Gabriel, Keith Robert
Gaffron, Robert Arthur, Jr.
Gaines, Kay Barrett
Galford, Terese Linda
Gallagher, Daniel Tho
Gams, Linda
Garb, Jeffrey Louis
Gardner, Jane Ellen
Gardner, Phyllis Irene
Garrity, Kim Allison
Garvey, Nancy Ann
Gass, Joanne M.
Gass, Marilyn Atlas
Gates, Joelen Jeri
Gatsis, Karen
Gault, Lonne Kathryn
Gavlin, Suzanne
Gehring, Durward James
Gehrs, Ronald Ferdina
Gehrt, Carl Lee
Geiderman, Joel Martin
George, Donald John
George, Paul Michael
Gerber, Robin Marla
Gerstein, Roesia Hildy
Gerten, Lawrence Joseph
Gibbons, Kathleen Kay
Gibson, Kathleen R.
Giglotto, Joseph Morgan
Gilbert, John Laurence
Giles, John Edwin
Gillespie, Daniel Lester
Gilman, Alan David
Ginsburg, Elliot Kiba
Gitelis, Michael
Gitelis, Steven
Giulietti, Rosalind Virginia
Glazer, Marvin Alan
Glesne, Corrine Elaine
Glick, Donald Lee

Glick, Jeffrey S.
Glick, Roberta P.
Glicker, Joseph Lawrence
Glisker, Janice Lynn
Gloss, Dianne Marie
Gnavi, Walter Michael, Jr.
Goben, Betty Ann
Godar, Mary Kathryn
Gogola, Pauline Kay
Gold, Harriet Lynn
Goldberg, Janis Kay
Goldberg, Marlene Sue
Goldberg, Michael Jerome
Goldberg, Myra Bernice
Goldberg, Susan Carol
Goldberger, Gail Etta
Goldhor, Elizabeth Payne
Goldman, David Eckstein
Goldman, Diane Phyllis
Goldman, Myrna
Goldstein, James Alan
Goldstein, Laurence Jaye
Goodin, Frank Lee
Goodman, Allan L.
Goodwin, Sarah Ann
Gordon, Glenda Gay
Gordon, Janice Susan
Gottfried, Joan Mae
Goundas, Christine Marie
Gowler, Vicki Sue
Grable, Paula
Graham, George Wade
Grandt, Kathleen Ruth
Gray, Charles Hodges
Gray, Georgene Ellen
Gray, Julie Ann
Grazian, Jan Ellen
Greaves, William Walter
Greenfield, Hazel Greta
Greenstein, Sandra June
Greger, Nancy Gay
Gregg, Karen Christine
Gresey, Jennifer Jane
Grieme, Linda Jo
Griffard, Robert Paul
Grman, Michael E.
Gronewold, Marcia Dee
Gross, Allen Frank
Gross, Gary Evan
Grossman, Neil Marc
Guglielmi, Thomas
Gullang, Deborah Jean
Guse, Michael Paul
Gustafson, William Benedetti
Gutenkauf, Linda Ann
Gutierrez, Maria Lisa
Haas, Daniel Dillon
Haas, John Charles
Hadraba, Barbara Jo
Hagan, William Kelly, III
Hagen, Daniel Russell
Hahn, Nancy Ellen
Hahn, Stephen Ray
Hainaut, John Joseph
Halbach, Joseph L.

HALBUR, JOHN DAVID
HALL, MARY JANE
HALLMARK, ROGER ALAN
HALLSTROM, ARONA HARVITZ
HALVORSON, SCOTT ALAN
HAM, ELDON LEE
HAMBY, MARK
HAMILOS, DANIEL LEE
HAMMER, CHARLES RUSH
HANDLER, JOEL F.
HANEY, CYNTHIA K.
HANEY, FORREST LEON
HANKINS, GAIL JACQUELINE
HANNASCH, JAMES DONALD
HANSEN JONATHAN C.
HANSON, JOHN HOLDEN, JR.
HARDUVEL, MARIA CHRIST
HARDY, H. STEPHEN
HARFST, WILLIAM FREDERICK
HARM, THOMAS A.
HARMS, TED E.
HARPER, DENVER
HARPER, SCOTT THOMAS
HARR, RHONDA JOY
HARRISON, WILLIAM HALE
HARSHBARGER, JANICE LEA ACKEBERG
HART, DOUGLAS L.
HARTMANN, KENNETH ORVEL
HARTMANN, PAULA KAREN
HARTWIG, JOHN L.
HARVEY, LYNN
HARVEY, SCOTT MINER
HATTENDORF, TERRY DON
HAVILL, JUANITA RUTH
HAWKINS, THOMAS WAYNE
HAWORTH, ROBERT H.
HAYMAN, SARAH
HAYS, PHILIP GRANVILLE
HEALY, RICHARD WILLIAM
HEDGES, JOAN C.
HEDRICK, JOHN RUSSELL
HEFFLEY, GAY JEAN
HEIL, NANCY JO
HEIMLICH, ESTHER
HEISS, HOWARD EDWARD
HEITSCH, JANET MARIE
HELLMICH, JANET MARIE
HENDEE, RANDAL JAMES
HENDERSON, HARRY GEORGE
HENDERSON, RICHARD CLARK
HENRIKSON, DIANE ELIZABETH
HENSEL, DONALD DEXTER
HEPPERLY, PAUL REED
HEPPERLY, THOMAS RAMS
HERBERGER, GARY RICHARD
HERBSTER, BARBARA ANN
HERBSTMAN, BRYNA GAIL
HERLIEN, ROBERT ALLEN
HERMAN, HOLLY LYNN
HERMAN, PAUL RODNEY
HERSH, ADRIENNE J.
HERSON, ALBERT IRWIN
HESLER, SUSAN DIANA
HEUERTZ, CHARLES MATHIAS
HIGHLAND, WILLIAM R.

HINRICHS, RICHARD L.
HINTON, JAMES EUGENE
HINTON, MARY BETH
HIRCHERT, KURT WALTER
HIRSCH, KAREN IRENE
HISER, MARK WARREN
HIXSON, MARY ALICE
HO, ELLEN YUAN-CHU
HOAG, MARGARET MARY
HOCHBERG, GAIL EILEEN
HOCHBERG, SUSAN MYRA
HOERR, DIANNE MARIE
HOFFMAN, PATRICIA ANN
HOFFMAN, PATRICIA ELEANOR
HOFMANN, ROBERT THOMAS
HOHULIN, KEITH RICHARD
HOLADAY, ALLAN SCOTT
HOLEMAN, TIMOTHY ALAN
HOLLAND, GREGORY
HOLLEYMAN, KIRK BRADFORD
HOLLINGSHEAD, MARK ALAN
HOLTZBLATT, LESTER JOSEPH
HOMER, JEFFREY BARRY
HOPP, RANDOLPH LEE
HORBERG, LAWRENCE KENNETH
HORNER, RICHARD ALLEN
HORNKOHL, RHODA GWEN
HOROWITZ, JORDAN JAY
HORTIN, MARY JANE
HORTON, JENNIFER KAY
HORWITZ, MARSHA
HOSKINS, ANDREW CHARLES
HOSKINS, THOMAS HENRY
HOVEY, MICHAEL CURTISS
HOWELL, SHARON SUE
HOYT, ROGER FRANKLIN
HUBER, BRUCE ALAN
HUCKO, JOSEPHINE THERESA
HUDDLESTON, RODNEY KURT
HUDSON, TIGHE FRANCIS
HUFF, MARTHA ELIZABETH
HUFFMAN, PATRICIA JANE
HUGHES, CAROL ANN
HUMPHREVILLE, ANNE ELIZABETH
HUTCHINSON, ROBERT HAMILTON
HUTSON, MILES AUSTIN
HYKAN, ROBERT ALAN
HYMAN, DAVID BRUCE
HYMEL, SHELLEY CLAIRE
IFFT, NANCY JEAN
INCAPRERO, JOSEPH FRANK
INGRAM, LARRY S.
INGRAM, RICHARD GEORGE
INGRASSIA, LAWRENCE ANDREW
INGRASSIA, PAUL JOSEPH
ISBELL, SUSAN MARY
ISHIDA, LYNN CHERI
JACKSON, ANN LOUISE
JACKSON, DOUGLAS ARTHUR
JACKSON, RICHARD ADRIAN
JACOBI, NEAL HENRY
JACOBS, DEBRA LYNNE
JACOBS, ELLEN
JACOBS, FRED LAWRENCE
JACOBSEN, CARL LAWRENCE

Jacobson, Joanne
Jacobson, Shelley Anne
Jacobus, Charles J.
Jaffe, Austin Jay
Jakes, Dolores Rita
James, David Christopher
Jamieson, Michael Warren
Janes, Elizabeth Ann
Janke, Mark Charles
Jansen, James Howard
Jarman, Priscilla Sue
Jarrell, Ronald Gene
Jauhola, Christine Ann
Jecmen, Robert Milton
Jenik, Robert A.
Jenkins, Rhonda Sue
Jenne, Robert Charles
Jennings, Terese Leslie
Jerutis, Cynthia Anne
Jeske, Susan Ellen
Jespersen, Carol Anne
Johnson, Allan Hale
Johnson, Bruce A.
Johnson, Christina Kay
Johnson, Christine Ann
Johnson, Cynthia Kay
Johnson, Donna Lee
Johnson, Ellen Linnea
Johnson, Gary Burton
Johnson, Gloria Jean
Johnson, John Henry
Johnson, Larry C.
Johnson, Lawrence Lynn
Johnson, Leonard Kurt
Johnson, Lynn Ann
Johnson, Michael Craft
Johnson, Ronald Wayne
Johnston, Susan Duval
Jollie, Malcolm Richard
Jones, Brent Rodney
Jones, Dana Ray
Jones, Debora Sue
Jones, Patricia Ann
Jones, Richard Michael
Judy, Conna Elizabeth
Junck, Larry Richard
Junkus, Joan Cleopha
Jurich, Dale Rade
Jurkin, Gary James
Just, Lawrence Edward
Kaar, David Richard
Kacsh, Judith Ellyn
Kagan, Rosalyn H.
Kahn, Robert Charles
Kahn, Wendy H.
Kahr, Helga
Kaiser, Charles Lee
Kaminski, Thomas Michael
Kammenzind, Richard Henry
Kamowski, Richard Michael
Kampf, Elizabeth
Kamrava, Masoud
Kane, David Arthur
Kant, Renee Judith
Kanter, Charlene Ruth

Kaplan, Adalynn
Kaplan, Daryl
Karabin, Marybeth
Karesh, John W.
Karl, Linda Ann
Karlen, Douglas Melvin
Karps, Paul David
Kasab, Farida
Kass, Irwin Lee
Katerndahl, David Arthur
Katz, Lee David
Katz, Vicki Siegelman
Kaufman, Dale M.
Kaufman, Sheila Lynn
Kawamura, Charlene K.
Kearley, Timothy George
Kearney, James Allen
Keasler, Robert N.
Keck, William Foley
Kendrick, Laura Jean
Kennedy, Larry Ralph
Kepford, Kirby Bernard
Kerr, Stanley Paul
Kesler, James Lester
Kheshgi, Zareena B.
Kiburz, Arnold John, III
Kiedaisch, Laura Susan
Kierig, Paul Nicholas
Kimberley, Wanda Jean
Kimmel, Leslie Ervin
Kimmel, Thomas Allen
Kinczewski, Kathy Ann
King, Arthur Raymond
Kipp, Robert M.
Kirchhofer, Mark Lynn
Kistler, Joan Loel
Kite, Steven B.
Klauke, Diane Marie
Klauke, Sally Ann
Kleckler, Danny Ray
Klein, Charles Allen
Klein, Neal Alan
Klein, Rosemary
Kleiss, Alice Joan
Klemt, Laura Beth Lieberman
Klett, Kristi Lynn
Klocke, Norman Lee
Klotter, Kevin Albert
Kluge, Janice Val
Knapp, Richard Lee
Knight, Charles Daniel
Koch, Beverly Ann
Koehler, Thomas Lee
Koeppen, Bruce Michael
Koerner, Karen Sue
Koester, Connie Kay
Koesterer, Mary Patricia
Kohlmeier, James A.
Kolb, Geoffrey Keith
Kolber, Susan Lynne
Koltun, Philip Louis
Komie, Cynthia Ann
Konopka, Allan Eugene
Koonce, Wayne Allan
Kopp, Marlene Elaine

KOPPLIN, JUDITH ANN
KOREN, NANCY MARIE
KORENGOLD, HELEN LEAH
KOREY, MICHAEL STEVEN
KORNBLATT, IRA BENNETT
KORNBLITH, SANDER JAY
KOSTELNICK, CHARLES JOHN
KOSTER, ELAINE MASSOCK
KOTIN, ANTHONY MARTIN
KOVAL, JOAN BEVERLY
KOWALL, RICHARD J.
KOZLOWSKI, BEATRICE ANNA
KRAKAUER, NEIL JORDAN
KRAMER, JEFFREY
KRAUSE, KENNETH E.
KRAVITZ, KENNETH MICHAEL
KRAVITZ, MARILYN AVIS
KRAZINSKI, JOHN LEO
KREIMEIER, VIRGINIA EDNA
KRIECHBAUM, JEANNE LYNN
KRISCHER, JOEL ERNEST
KRISTEN, CHRISTINE ELAINE
KRON, PRISCILLA LOUISE
KRUGER, KATHRYN DIANE
KRUGER, SARAH LYNN
KUNTZ, JANE ELIZABETH
KUPEC, LYNN MARIE
KURTZ, DONALD LESTER
KUSHNER, MARK STEPHEN
KWIECINSKI, RICHARD ADAM
KWINN, PATRICIA ANNE
LABOTKA, RICHARD JOHN
LABOTKA, THEODORE CHARLES
LACKMAN, SARAH
LACY, STEPHEN R.
LADOLCE, DEBORAH LEE
LAFORCE, NORMAN CHARLES
LAFRANCO, ROSALIE ANN
LAGNADO, DAGMAR MARIA
LAJACK, LEXINE MAGDALENE
LAMBERT, ERNESTINE LEA
LAMORTE, JOSEPHINE
LANCASTER, DAVID RUSSELL
LANE, PHILIP J.
LANG, JANET MARY
LANG, RITA ANN
LARCOMBE, ELSA MARGARET
LARIMER, MARK WILLIAM
LARSON, KRISTINE GARMAGER
LASH, RALPH M.
LATOS, LINDA ANN
LAUDE, JOHN WILLIAM
LAUF, ROBERT JOHN
LAUGAL, PATTI LEE
LAUNSPACH, JEAN ANNE
LAVINE, RONALD MARK
LAWICKI, JOY MARIE
LEAHY, KATHRYN MARY
LEAVITT, ILONA SUE
LEE, REBECCA ANN
LEHMANN, JAY ALLAN
LEHMANN, RANDALL EARL
LEHNEN, DAVID CHARLES
LEIBACH, STEVEN JAY
LEIBSON, PAUL JOSEPH

LEMAN, MARCUS L.
LEMAN, MARVIN GENE
LEMEIN, GREGG DOUGLAS
LEOPOLD, WILBUR RICHARD, III
LEPPERD, THOMAS EDWIN, III
LERITZ, JAMES PETER
LERNER, EDWARD MARK
LESK, HELENE
LESKE, DEBORAH ANN
LESSARIS, CONSTANCE ANDREA
LEVIE, MARK ROBERT
LEVIN, MARK HOWARD
LEVIN, SHELLEY
LEVINE, BARBARA ANNE
LEVINSON, ROBERTA ANN
LEVIT, SHARON IDALIE
LEVY, PETER ALEXANDER
LEWIS, EDWARD RUSSELL
LEWIS, ROBERT WATKINS
LIEBOVITZ, SUSAN GAIL
LIECHTY, RICHARD DAVID
LINARD, RITA ANN
LIND, RICHARD ELLIS
LINDER, DAVID CHARLES
LINDER, SHARON MARIE
LINGQUIST, KENNETH WILLIAM
LIPKIN, DAVID MICHAEL
LIPPOLD, KATHRYN GAE
LIPSCHULTZ, CLAIRE MARCIA
LISS, PAUL LLOYD
LISSAK, DEBRA JO
LITTLE, DANIEL EASTMAN
LIU, WING KI
LOB, CLIFFORD G.
LOCKMILLER, RICHARD GORDON
LOEHMAN, WILLIAM CHARLES
LOHMANN, WALTER E.
LOMBARDI, MICHELLE JEAN
LOMPERIS, LINDA SUSAN
LONDON, DEBORAH
LONG, JOHN PERRY
LONG, REBECCA LOUISE
LORBER, MARC I.
LORD, ROBERT JOHN
LOSASSO, LEA ANN
LOTTES, STEVEN ARTHUR
LOVELACE, DAVID BRYAN
LOW, TOM WILLIAM
LOWE, JOHN CHEUNG
LOWRY, MICHAEL MURDOCK
LUBIEN, RAYMOND BERNARD
LUBIN, STUART FREDRIC
LUDOWISE, MICHAEL J.
LUKEN, BONNIE LOUISE
LUNDBERG, JEAN MARIE
LUNDFELT, JEAN KATHLEEN
LUTZ, PATRICIA DIANE
LUXION, DENNIS WAYNE
LYNCH, DENNIS EUGENE
LYNGAAS, MICHAEL EDWARD
MACGREGOR, STEVEN WILLIAMS
MACK, TOM E.
MACKEY, SHEILA KAY
MACRANDER, ALBERT TIEMEN
MADER, SANDRA LANCE

141

MADSEN, ELIZABETH CHRISTINE
MAGNER, JAMES ARTHUR
MAJCHROWICZ, DENNIS MICHAEL
MAJKO, RICHARD MICHAEL
MALLICOAT, HERMAN ALLEN
MALLIN, THOMAS WAYNE
MALLORY, ROBERT MARK
MALLOY, ROBERT GERALD
MAN, DIANE GAIL
MAN, NORMAN LEE
MANCINI, LOUIS JOSEPH
MANDEL, MIRIAM SHARON
MANDELL, MICHAEL STEVEN
MANGEL, MARC STEVEN
MANLEY, MARGARET ANN
MANN, SHELDON H.
MANN, STEWART RALPH
MARCHIANDO, ALBERT WILLIAM
MARCUS, LAURA NAN
MARCUS, LINDA ELLEN
MARCUS, RICHARD JAY
MARDER, ROBERT JOEL
MARION, BRAD ALLAN
MARION, RAYMOND H.
MARK, JEFFREY SCOTT
MARKWELL, PATRICIA LYNN
MARSHALLA, LINDA ROSE
MARSHALLA, ROBERT ALVIN
MARTENS, KATHRYN IRENE
MARTIN, DIANE MARIE
MARTIN, ELLEN MYRTLE
MARTINEK, STEPHEN JOHN
MARZEC, MARIANNE MARGARET
MASLOVITZ, ROCHELLE CELIA
MASSINGILL, MARSHA ELAINE
MASTERS, CURTIS BRIAN
MASTERS, MARJORIE LUESE
MATEJCAK, RAYMOND JOSEPH
MATEK, BETH S.
MATTHEWS, SHELDON HAROLD
MATTHIAS, LINDA KAY
MATTIS, HENRY EDWARD
MATTSON, RICHARD LEONARD
MAUTZ, CARL DAVID
MAXWELL, MARGO JEAN
MAXWELL, MICHAEL B.
MAZZONE, THEODORE
MCCAMY, RAYMOND WINFIELD
MCCANN, PHYLLIS RUTH
MCCARTHY, GAIL KATHLEEN
MCCLARY, ELMER RAY
MCCLELLAND, GARY MILES
MCCORMICK, JANICE
MCCOY, ROBERT GEORGE
MCCULLOCH, ELLEN ANN
MCDERMOTT, PATRICK WILLIAM
MCELLIGOTT, MARY ELLEN THERESE
MCELROY, BRENDA JOYCE
MCEWAN, BETTE E.
MCFARLAND, PATRICK ARTHUR
MCGETRICK, JOHN JOSEPH
MCKNIGHT, RICHARD SAMUEL, JR.
MCKOWN, RUSSELL CARL
MCLEAN, CHRISTINE ROSE
MCLEVIGE, WILLIAM VICTOR

MCMILLIN, KIM IRVING
MCQUEEN, CHARLES RAY
MEACHUM, JANET RAE
MEADE, CYNTHIA ANN
MEARA, JAMES LEWIS
MEIER, DUANE EDWARD
MEINKE, LINDA MARION
MEISS, HARRIETTE LEONA
MEISTER, SUSAN JOY
MELCHER, RICHARD EARL
MELDI, DOMINIC MATTHEW
MELVIN, TYRONE RAY
MENEGHINI, ROBERT
MENG, RONALD LESLIE
MERKEL, LINDA CATHERINE
MERNIN, CATHERINE SUE
MERRION, PAUL ROBERT
MERRITT, LORENCE H.
METCALF, ROBERT ALAN
METRICK, SCOTT ALAN
METZ, RUSSELL ALLEN
MEYER, JOAN ELLEN
MICHAELS, DEBBIE LYNN
MIERNICKI, MARYANN CATHERINE
MIKULA, BARBARA J.
MILES, DONALD EUGENE
MILES, LINDA MARIE
MILLER, BRUCE NATHAN
MILLER, JANENE CHRISTINE
MILLER, JOHN E.
MILLER, KAREN LEAH
MILLER, LARRY EVAN
MILLER, LINDA SUSAN
MILLER, MELISSA GAY
MILLER, RONALD DWIGHT
MILLER, SANDRA
MILTON, PENNY MARIE
MINER, DONALD LEE
MINNICK, CRAIG ALAN
MINTON, MARK ALLEN
MIS, BARBARA BERNICE
MITCHELL, JAMES WHITNEY
MITCHELL, KAY ANN
MITCHELL, STANLEY E.
MNISZEWSKI, MALVINA THERESA
MOELLER, RAYMOND JOSEPH, JR.
MOGILL, MICHAEL ALAN
MOLDENHAUER, JUDITH ANN
MOLINARI, JANET ELLEN
MOLL, DANIEL WILLARD
MONYPENNY, ALICE
MOODY, MARY ANN
MOORE, DIANE ELAINE
MOORE, PATRICK JAMES
MORRIS, CLIFFORD T.
MORRISON, JANICE ELAINE
MORROW, DWIGHT WAYNE
MOSER, ELIZABETH ANN
MOTENKO, GAIL LYNN
MOY, AUDREY LYNN
MOYE, CHARLES EDWARD
MULCAHEY, ROBERT WILLIAM
MULCH, ROBERT F., JR.
MULLER, RICKI SUE
MULLIGAN, PATRICIA ANN

142

MUNDT, GORDON KENNETH
MUNZ, JOHN HARTZELL
MURIN, CAROL JEAN
MUROWCHICK, LINDA SUE
MURPHY, JANIS I.
MURRAY, CHRISTOPHER CAMERON
MUSE, JOHN EDWARD
MYERS, JOHN RILEY
NAAB, ELISABETH MARIA
NADEL, JAN LESLIE
NAFSHUN, MAXINE LOU
NAKASHIMA, CATHY YURI
NASH, ROBERT N.
NAZIMEK, LARRY E.
NEAL, PHILLIP GRANT
NEEDELMAN, HOWARD WILLIAM
NELSON, RICHARD HERBERT
NELSON, RUSSELL WILLIAM
NESHEIM, SANDRA LYNN
NEWELL, LARRY MICHAEL
NICHOLSON, DEBRA JEAN
NICHOLSON, PETER ALLEN
NICKELSON, LEE ERNST
NICKESON, HOLLY KAY
NICKOLLS, JOHN RICHARD
NICOL, ARTHUR DUEY
NIEBRUGGE, DANIEL JOSEPH
NIGHTINGALE, FRED M.
NIPPA, DOUGLAS LAWRENCE
NISHIMOTO, BARBARA JANE
NOBLE, SCOTT WILLIAM
NORDBERG, DONALD EDWARD
NORDGREN, CAROL ANN
NORDHEDEN, ANGELENE CARLA
NOREM, JOLENE FERN
NOSEK, RICHARD DOUGLAS
NOVAK, GREGORY C.
NOVARIA, ROBERT JOHN
NOWAK, EDWARD DANIEL
NUMRICH, PAUL DAVID
NUSBAUM, MARK EDWARD
NUSINOW, ALAN IRA
NUTTING, DEBORAH LANDIS
NYMAN, EMILY ADELE
NYSTROM, HALVARD EDWARD
OBENAUF, CARL DEAN
OBYRNE, STEPHEN MICHAEL
O'CONNELL, SHIRLEY GRAY
O'DONNELL, KATHLEEN MARIE
OGRON, JANET SUE
O'HARE, RANDALL SCOTT
OHMAN, SANDRA MAE
OLECK, PATRICIA LYNN
OLMSTEAD, SARAH LOUISE
OLSEN, CRAIG ALAN
OLTMAN, NORMA YOUNG
ORAM, RICHARD WHITE
ORAVIS, LARRY T.
OSTREICHER, JEFFREY IAN
OVITSKY, DENNIS JAY
OZYURT, YILDIZ GULER
PACHOLKE, JANE TOMISEK
PAINE, THEODORE EDWARD
PALMER, BARBARA JANE
PALMER, RICHARD ALLEN

PALMIERI, VINCENT LEO
PAMPE, MARCIA LEE
PARISH, JAMES MICHAEL
PARK, ALYN SEYMOUR
PARK, STEPHEN MICHAEL
PARKS, DAVID MOORE
PARKS, JOHN ROBERT
PARKS, PAUL BROWNLEE
PATCH, ROBERT WARNER
PATEK, KATHERINE JANE
PATINKIN, LYNN DIANE
PATINKIN, TERRY ALLAN
PATTERSON, CHARLES STEWART
PATTERSON, GWENDOLYN MARIE
PAVIS, VALERIE ANN
PAYNE, JAMES GREGORY
PAZERO, JOSEPH EDWARD, JR.
PEARCE, MARTHA MORRIS
PEARD, BEVERLY ADELE
PEARLMAN, BARBARA RUTH
PEARSON, WILLIAM RAYMOND
PECK, MICHAEL ROBERT
PELC, PAULETTE AYN
PEMPER, MARY JANET
PENCE, ROBERT J.
PEO, CAROL KANT
PEO, MARGARET LOUISE
PEPPER, DANIEL
PERCIACH, SUSAN JANE
PERLMAN, BRUCE STEPHEN
PERRY, THOMAS JAY
PETERSEN, NANCY MARIAN
PETERSON, CHRISTOPHER MERLE
PETERSON, GEORGE ALLEN
PETERSON, LARRY DEAN
PETERSON, ROBERT THOMAS
PETITT, KATHY ALENE
PETRY, TERESA JO
PETTIBONE, JILL ELIZABETH
PETTITT, KENNETH DALE
PFAENDER, THOMAS G.
PHILLIPS, JOHN VINCENT
PHILLIPS, LESLIE K.
PHILLIPS, ROBERT EDWIN
PHIPPS, KELSEY JANE
PICKERING, JOHN
PICL, FRANK MATTHEW
PIENKOS, PHILIP THOMAS
PIEPER, RICHARD WAYNE
PISCHKE, KEITH MARTIN
PLASS, JANE PAULA
PLONDKE, JAMES CHARLES
PODELL, JUDITH SUE
PODLIPNIK, CAROL JOY
POEHLER, DAVID WAYNE
POKER, DAVID BRIAN
POLK, JANINE LYN
POLLACK, MICHAEL DORN
POMRENKE, BONNIE J.
PONOROFF, CAROL RUTH
PORTER, DARCY ANN
PORTER, ROBERT L.
PORTER, STEVEN MICHAEL
POST, WARREN MICHAEL
POTTER, PAMELA SUE

POWLESS, JAMES KENNETH
PRANCE, CLARICE DIANE
PRENTICE, KIM DONALD
PRIEST, JOHN BRYAN
PRITKIN, NANCI HOLLY
PRIZER, STEPHEN E.
PROCHASKA, GAIL LYNN
PRUZAN, KAREN L.
PRZYWARA, KENNETH PAUL
PURVY, ROBERT EDWARD
QUINN, ROSEMARY C.
QUINN, YVONNE SUSAN
RABIN, DONNA LEE
RACZKOWSKI, ANDREW WESLEY
RADKE, SUSAN NELL
RADLOFF, STUART JAY
RAISEN, LYNN
RALSTON, ALAN LYNN
RANDALL, LAUREL W.
RAPP, PAUL ERNEST
RASMUS, JAMES LEE
RASSI, GREGORY GENE
RATH, GALEN DONALD
RATHBUN, JANET MARLENE
RAUSCH, PATRICK GLENN
RAY, ALAN BENJAMIN
REBITZER, SANDY JOY
REED, RICHARD CHARLES
REEDER, GUY SCOTT
REEM, DENISE ELAINE
REIFMAN, WILLIAM JAY
REILLEY, GINGER LORENE
REINBOLT, KATHLEEN MARY
REINER, DAVID LAWRENCE
REINHART, CAROL LOUISE
REISIG, TERRI LEE HOBBS
RESNICK, DONALD IRA
RESNIK, DANIEL MARK
REUBEN, GAIL BETH
REUBEN, GORDON PHILIP
REULER, PEGGY ROSE
REVORD, SHERRY ANN
RHOTON, JUNE ELIZABETH
RICE, CATHERINE NELLE
RICHARDS, LAUREL ANN
RICHARDSON, CAROL ANN
RICHARDSON, JEAN ANN
RICHARDSON, PATRICIA CLAIRE
RICKER, RANDALL EDWARD
RIDDLE, GUY GREGORY
RIEDEL, PHILIP ALAN
RIEDELL, CAROLYN BETH
RIEGER, RODNEY WALTER
RIGGINS, VIRGINIA SUSAN
RIMDZIUS, ROBERT JOHN
RINKENBERGER, KENNETH WAYNE
RITHOLZ, MARCIA BETH
ROBBINS, SHELLEY RUTH
ROBINSON, GARY EDWARD
ROBINSON, RICHARD BRUCE
RODGERS, JANICE ELAINE
ROGERS, PAMELA ANN
ROGGE, PAULA ANN
ROHDE, JANET GAIL
ROMAN, NAN PATRICE

RONAT, CHERI RAE
ROOF, JULIA GENE
ROOSE, THOMAS ROBERT
ROSE, CYNTHIA JEAN
ROSELLI, RONALD CLIFFORD
ROSEN, BARRY STUART
ROSENBAUM, DAVID NEAL
ROSENBERG, JAMES AUGUST
ROSENBLUM, DAVID BRIAN
ROSENBUSH, STUART WILLIAM
ROSENFELD, MARLA JOY
ROSENTHAL, JUDITH ILENE
ROSS, DONNA JEAN
ROSS, MARGARET ELIZABETH
ROSS, ROBIN
ROSS, SUSAN ELIZABETH
ROSZKOWSKI, MARK EDWARD
ROTH, GARY FRANCIS
ROTH, WILLIAM H.
ROTHBLATT, DEBORAH EILEEN
ROTTMAN, DAVID BRUCE
ROUFFA, MICHAEL ALAN
ROUSOS, LINDA ANN
ROZYCKI, CARLA JOANNE
RUBENSTEIN, JOAN B.
RUBIN, DAVID BERNARD
RUBIN, DAVID IAN
RUBIN, DEBORAH RACHEL
RUBIN, ROSE JOAN MILLS
RUBINSTEIN, CHARLOTTE
RUBY, ROBERT A.
RUCH, PHILLIP LEE
RUDDELL, BRIAN WAYNE
RUNDELL, KATHRYN LOUISE LUTZ
RUNDQUIST, BARBARA JANE
RUNGE, THOMAS FRED
RUSS, ANN KRISTINE
RUTH, DEBORAH ANN
RUTLEDGE, DAVID ALLAN
RUTLEDGE, JAMES EDWARD
SACADAT, STEFFI SUE
SACKS, NANCY DIANE
SAFFORD, JAMES M.
SAFFORD, SHARON ANN
SAFFRO, RICHARD KENNETH
SAGAN, CAROLE
SAKOL, BARRE M.
SALADINO, JO-ANN CATHERINE
SALLER, RICHARD PAUL
SALOMONE, ANN MARIE
SAMARAS, KATHRYN THEODORA
SAMMANN, ERNEST ALBERT
SAMPRACOS, ANDREA
SANDLER, STEVEN A.
SANDROLINI, LAURA
SANTOSTEFANO, MARIA J.
SAPER, CLIFFORD BAIRD
SARENA, MICHELE LOUISE
SARUK, MICHAEL LOUIS
SAVAGE, BRYAN FRANCIS
SAVAGE, LESLIE A.
SAVITZKY, DAVID BARRY
SAYLES, MELANIE SUSAN
SCHAEFFER, RANDY CRAIG
SCHALLER, MICHAEL JAY

144

SCHAPIRO, SUSAN BARBARA
SCHATZMAN, LYNN IVY
SCHEITLER, MELISSA STOUT
SCHERMERHORN, ROY DEWAIN
SCHEWE, STANLEY LOUIS
SCHIAVONI, ROGER MICHAEL
SCHICK, JAMES BENJAMIN
SCHILLING, DAVID E.
SCHLESINGER, PAUL KEITH
SCHMID, BENJAMIN D.
SCHMIDT, ARNOLD J.
SCHMIDT, CHERYL LYNN
SCHMIDT, GREGORY GLEN
SCHMIDT, JOHN WILLIAM
SCHMIEDL, NANCY EILEEN
SCHNEIDER, DAVID RAY
SCHNEIDER, GREGG DAVID
SCHNEIDER, JAMES C.
SCHNEIDER, RONALD WILBERT
SCHNEIDER, WALTER
SCHOENBERG, DANIEL ROBERT
SCHOENBERG KURT F.
SCHOTTMAN, FREDERICK JOSEPH
SCHRAM, RICHARD MICHAEL
SCHRANZ, NORBERT JOHANNES
SCHRICKEL, THOMAS EDWARD
SCHRINER, MARILYN GEORGIA
SCHROEDER, WILLIAM JOHN
SCHUENGEL, SUSAN RUTH
SCHULER, GREGORY GERARD
SCHULER, SHELLEY SUE
SCHULTZ, RONALD NORMAN
SCHUMAKER, CAROL ANN
SCHUTZ, RONALD WALTER
SCHWAB, MICHAEL JOEL
SCHWARTZ, BONNIE HELENE
SCHWARTZ, BRADFORD S.
SCHWARTZ, DAVID BRUCE
SCHWARTZ, SAMUEL CHAIM
SCHWARTZ, SUSAN MARGARET
SCHWEITZER, ERIC ALLIN
SCOTT, CAROL ANN
SCOTT, DON JOE
SCOTT, GREGORY BRADFORD
SCOTT, WILLIAM ROY
SEBEK, JAMES JOSEPH
SEDERBERG, SCOTT ROBERT
SEEGER, MARC ALAN
SEITZ, MICHAEL WILLIAM
SEKULSKI, JANET MARIE
SELANDER, JOHN M.
SEMPLE, MARGARET ANNE
SEPTON, ALLEN MARC
SERWINT, NANCY J.
SEVERIN, WARREN DONALD
SHAPIRO, DEBORAH SUSAN
SHAPIRO, DENYSE JAN
SHAPIRO, MICHAEL ROBERT
SHAPIRO, RICHARD ALAN
SHARP, CAROLYN
SHEFT, JUDITH ANN
SHEPARD, LLOYD STANLEY
SHEPHERD, MELINDA CAROL
SHEWMAKER, RONALD D.
SHICK, JAMES RANDLE

SHIFFLETT, LEONARD STEWART
SHIMOJIMA, ANNE LANI
SHIMP, KATHLEEN ANNE
SHOCKEY, DAVID WILLIAM
SHOR, TOBY IRENE
SHORT, BEVERLY JEAN
SHURR, MARY JANE
SHURTLEFF, ROBERT G.
SHUTA, JAMES MICHAEL
SHY, CANDICE JANE
SIDO, KEVIN RICHARD
SIEBERT, CATHERINE R.
SIEDBAND, LEONARD BURTON
SIEGEL, FLORENCE LYNN
SIEGEL, MICHELLE JOY
SIEMER, RICHARD CLEMENS
SIEU, BENNY LOU
SILVA, GAIL ROBIN
SILVERMAN, CRAIG LYLE
SIMON, CAROL ANN
SIMON, ERIC EDWARD
SIMON, JEFFREY MICHAEL
SIMON, PETER DAVIS
SIMS, SUSAN JANE
SIMS, WAYNE RICHARD
SKAGER, PAUL STEVEN
SKLANSKY, JEAN
SKWERES, MARYANN
SLACK, LAURA SUSAN
SLADEN, BERNARD J.
SLATTERY, JUDITH ANN
SLIDER, DARRELL LEE
SLIVON, LOUISE DORIS
SLIVON, SYLVIA LOUISE
SLOAN, EUGENE DENNIS
SLOSAR, CATHERINE ANN
SLUIZER, SUSAN F.
SLUTKIN, GARY
SMALL, ELLEN L.
SMELCER, WILMA JEAN
SMITH, BARRY CHARLES
SMITH, DANIEL SHEPHERD
SMITH, GARY EDWARDS
SMITH, JAMES LEE
SMITH, JOHN BRUCE
SMITH, KEITH LON
SMITH, MARK STEVEN
SMITH, ROBERT WILLIAM
SMITH, SUSAN DIANE
SMITH, TRACY
SMOLLER, BARBARA GAIL
SNEARLY, CYNTHIA LEE
SNIVELY, STEPHEN WAYNE
SNODGRASS, JOYCE LYNN
SNUGGS, JEAN CHRISTINE
SNYDER, TERRY LEE
SOCOL, ROBERT SCOTT
SOKOL, JUDITH DIANNE
SOKOL, RONALD JAY
SOKOL, RONALD PAUL
SOLOMON, ROBERTA HELEN
SOLON, JUDITH ANN
SOLOW, SHELDON LOUIS
SOMENZI, CANDACE JOYCE ANNE
SOMMER, HENRY JOSEPH, III

145

SONNA, LINDA G.
SONNEMAKER, MICHAEL WILLIAM
SOROSKY, LAURA JEAN
SOSTRIN, JUDITH SUSAN
SOUTHON, EDWARD HENRY
SPAGAT, LINDA SUE
SPERLING, MARC LEWIS
SPICER, DAVID ALAN
SPIEGEL, SUZANNE
SPIEGLER, ALLAN JAY
SPILKER, ROBERT LEONARD
SPUDIC, MICHAEL WILLIAM
STAMERJOHN, DAVID MICHAEL
STAMP, NANCY HENRIETTE
STANLEY, GALEN WARD
STANLEY, LAUREL LOUISE
STANTON, CATHERINE GEORGE
STARK, MARILYNN DIANN
STARKE, DAVID HENRY
STARR, JOYCE ANN
STARR, RANDI
STEERMAN, CHRISTINE MARIE
STEFFENS, BRUCE CHASE
STEFFENS, GARY ALAN
STEGEMEIER, HENRI KAHLERT
STEIN, ALAN
STEINBERG, LOUIS IRA
STENDER, JERRY HERBERT
STEPANEK, DAVID CHARLES
STEPNICKA, CRAIG DOUGLAS
STERN, FRANCINE
STERN, GARY MICHAEL
STERN, ROBERT STEVEN
STERNBERG, LAWRENCE I.
STEVENS, ALICE JEANNE
STEVENSON, JOHN DAVID
STEVENSON, TERESA GAIL
STEWART, DEBORAH LYNN
STICHA, PAUL JOEL
STILES, CAROLYN LOUISE
STOKOLS, JEFFERY MARK
STOLL, MICHAEL EDWARD
STOLLER, JAMES JOSEPH
STOMPER, CONNIE MARIE
STONE, JOHN BRANDON
STRANG, AUDREY LYNN
STRAUSS, DAVID STEPHEN
STRAUSS, JAMES BARTLEY
STREEM, STEVAN BRIAN
STROHL, JANET CHRISTINA
STROTHMANN, NANCY C.
STRUBBE, MARY ANN
SUDLOW, WILLIAM JOSEPH
SUGARMAN, BARRETT
SULLIVAN, TIMOTHY EUGENE
SUMMER, MARK ALAN
SUNDINE, KRISTA EILEEN
SURREY, KAREN BARBARA
SVOBODA, GAIL ELLEN
SWAIN, PAULA C.
SWANSON, BARBARA JEAN
SWANSON, KURT ROBERT
SWEENEY, MICHAEL JAMES
SWEET, LYNN DEBRA
SWENGEL, STEVEN LLOYD

SZYDLOWICZ, ROSA
SZYMANSKI, CATHERINE BEATRICE LINGANE
TAGGE, EMILIE DOROTHY
TALMADGE, RICHARD NEAL
TARABORI, JAMES ALLEN
TARDY, HELEN ANN
TATELBAME, ILEANE FAY
TAUB, RICHARD E.
TAUBE, ARNOLD ALBERT
TAYLOR, BRADLEY ALAN
TAYLOR, DUANE WILLIAMS
TAYLOR, FREDERICK ROBBINS
TAYLOR, MARILYN GAY
TAYLOR, ROGER LEON
TEMPLETON, HELENA LENORE
TERLIZZI, ERIC L.
TERRILL, MARILYN JEAN
TERRY, BARBARA ELAINE
TERRY, JEANNE MARIE
TESTOLIN, RENO BRUCE
THAIN, JANICE ELIZABETH
THIEL, CHRISTOPHER WILLIAM
THIEL, ERIC GEORGE
THOMAN, GARY EDWARD
THOMAS, DEBRA LOUISE
THOMAS, MICHAEL PARKS
THOMAS, REBECCA LEAP
THOMAS, ROSEMARY M.
THOMPSON, JEAN LOUISE
THOMPSON, ROBERT RAY
THORNE, MELVIN JAY
THORPE, BONNIE JANE
THORSEN, PAMELA ANN
THUN, NANCY LEE
TIMMS, MAX WALTER
TIPSWORD, THOMAS NATHAN
TOBEY, TED ALAN
TOKAY, SUSAN ANNE
TOLLIVER, MARK E.
TOMBAUGH, LARRY WILLIAM
TOMKOVICK, JOHN JAMES
TOMLINSON, CAROLE ANN
TOMLINSON, NANCY KAY
TOMPKINS, DAVID ARTHUR
TOWLE, ROSS ALBERT
TOY, ALBERT VICTOR
TRAGER, GARY MITCHELL
TRAYLOR, SAMUEL JAMES
TREFZGER, JAMES EDWARD
TREVILLIAN, CAROL ANN
TRIPLETT, KEVIN TIMOTHY
TROGNER, EVELYN
TROJAN, WILLIAM THOMAS
TROST, CATHERINE ANN
TRYBA, HOLLY ANNE
TRYTTEN, STEVEN EARL
TUREK, SUSAN LEE
TURNER, BRYCE E.
TURSCH, ILSE MARLENE
TUTTLE, BETTY MARIE TROTTER
UBELL, FRANKLIN DAVID
UBELL, JOYCELYN ANNE
UHL, ADRIENNE AMY
ULLRICH, DAVID ALLEN
UPHOFF, CAROLYN JEAN

URBAN, MARGARET ANNE
VALENTINE, CATHY LOUISE
VANARSDALE, JANET LOUISE
VANBLARICUM, MICHAEL
VANCE, MARY MARTHA
VANEYLEN, MARGARET MARY
VANLANDINGHAM, JOHN THOMAS
VANMELLE, WILLIAM JAMES
VANWASSENHOVE, JOSEPH ALLEN
VARSHNEY, PRAMOD K.
VENEZIA, KENNETH RAY
VENOS, KENNETH GEORGE
VEST, GEORGIANA
VICARS, ELIZABETH GRACE
VOLK, RHEA MARIE
VOREIS, PAMELA SUE W.
VRANICAR, DAVID JOSEPH
VUYLSTEKE, LESLIE VERNON
WAGGONER, MARGARET ANNE
WAGHER, BONNIE LYNN NELSON
WAGNER, JERRY A.
WAGNER, LINDA JOYCE
WAGNER, RICHARD MARK
WAIT, JAY JENNER
WAKEFIELD, JOHN FREDERICK
WALDROP, PARK D.
WALES, SHERYL EILEEN
WALL, PAMELA ANN
WALLER, CATHY LYNN
WALTER, MARY ANN
WALTERS, SHARON SUSAN
WALTON, DIANA SUE
WANSERSKI, LORETTA
WARADY, MONICA SUE
WARMA, KATHRYN ANN
WARMAN, ROBIN SHERYL
WASSERMAN, JULIE BETH
WASSERMAN, LOUIS
WATKINS, JUDITH MARIE
WATSON, CRAIG ALLAN
WEATHERHEAD, PAUL D.
WEBER, BARBARA JEAN
WEBER, CHARLES RICHARD
WEEKS, MARJORIE ESTELLE
WEIK, RICHARD DALE
WEIKART, GEORGE SCOTT
WEIL, MARGARET SUE
WEILAND, ANDREA LOIS
WEINBERG, DEBORAH MARY
WEINER, CLAIRE
WEINER, LEE H.
WEINMEISTER, KENT PAUL
WEINMEISTER, PATTI JO
WEINZIERL, THOMAS A.
WEISEL, REBECCA LYNN
WEISHAR, MICHAEL CHARLES
WEISMAN, STEVEN PHILLIP
WEISS, BARBARA SHARI
WEISS, CAREY ALLEN
WEISS, KATHRYN ANN
WEISS, SHELDON ARNOLD
WEISSMAN, SANDRA THEA
WELLE, STEPHEN LEO
WELSCH, KATHRYN ANNE
WELSCH, ROBERT JAMES

WEMPEN, CHRISTINE
WENDE, KAREN JILL
WERNER, JOAN ALLISON
WESSELY, ROBERT PAUL
WESTON, EDWARD GARFIELD
WEYGANDT, STEVEN LEE
WEYRAUCH, JOHN BENJAMIN
WEYRAUCH, JOHN ROBERT
WHALIN, KATHLEEN DIANE
WHITE, ALAN BRUCE
WHITE, ANDREW BURTON
WHITE, PENELOPE CAROL
WHITE, ROGER BRADLEY
WHITNEY, JOHN CHARLES
WHITTEN, PATRICIA LEE
WHYTE, ROBERT LLOYD
WICKERT, LYNN EILLEEN
WICKS, EDWARD EUGENE
WIEDLING, JUDITH LYNNE
WIELAND, DONALD L.
WIEN, PERRY
WIESLER, WENDY ANNE
WIGODA, KIRA ANN
WIKER, STEVEN LEE
WILBRANDT, LAURENCE A.
WILBRANDT, ROBERT A.
WILFORD, LYNNE MARIE
WILHELM, JOSEPH LEE
WILKEN, GARY A.
WILKENS, TERRY LELAND
WILKUS, EDWARD FRANK
WILLIAMS, ANNE CELESTE
WILLIAMS, EARL HARMON
WILLIAMS, JOHN JAY
WILLIAMS, ROBERT KIM
WILLS, HOWARD WILLIAM
WILSON, DONALD EUGENE
WILSON, JAMES HUNTER
WILSON, JOHN ROBERT
WINKLER, LOUIS MICHAEL
WINTER, CAROLIN LOUISE
WINTER, DOUGLAS EARL
WINTER, LARRY ALAN
WINTER, MICHAEL JEFFREY
WINTER, STEPHEN M.
WINTERGREEN, DONNA BETH
WISE, KATHLEEN THERESA
WISHNE, BERDINE SHELIA
WISNIEWSKI, CHARMAINE LYNN
WISS, JAMES ERNEST
WITSCHY, CARL EDWARD
WOJEWNIK, KAREN MARIE
WOJTAN, LINDA SUE
WOLF, BRENDA JOAN
WOLFE, SUSAN MCHENRY
WOLFSON, BARBARA JEAN
WOLINETZ, MIRIAM LYNN
WONG, HAROLD H.
WOOD, DONALD EUGENE
WOOLSEY, THOMAS RICHARD
WORSHAM, PATRICK MICHAEL
WROBEL, BARBARA ANN
WUBBEN, ROBERT C.
WUELLNER, WILLIAM WALTER
WUORENMA, RUTH ANN

147

WURTH, GENE RAYMOND
WUTTKE, STEPHEN ANTHONY
YEATER, REED LAWRENCE
YEATS, ELIZABETH H.
YESINOWSKI, JAMES PAUL
YOUNG, MICHAEL JOHN
YOUNGSTRUM, CHRISTINE ANN
YOUNKER, WILLIS F.
YOUNKIN, SCOTT WILEY
ZAANDER, MARK C.
ZACK, GREGORY WILLIAM
ZAKER, RICHARD ROBERT
ZALE, KENNETH ROBERT
ZANCHO, DEBORAH HARTMAN
ZAR, LOREL ELLEN
ZEIGLER, ROBERT STUART

ZELINGER, ALLAN BARNETT
ZELISKO, SANDRA PEARL
ZEVIN, ROBERT JAY
ZIEBARTH, CHRISTINE GAIL
ZIELINSKI, EDWARD LEE
ZIMMERMAN, RICHARD RUSSELL
ZITTER, ROBERT ELLIOT
ZIV, JAMES KENNETH
ZLATIN, BARBARA SUSAN
ZOELLICK, MARILYN MARTHA
ZOELLICK, WILLIAM NORMAN
ZOLLO, PEGGY LEE
ZUBAK, BARBARA ANN
ZUBINSKI, PAUL KENNETH
ZUCKER, CYNTHIA ANN
ZYCH, MARY ELIZABETH

## SOCIAL ORGANIZATIONS

Social organizations, whether national or local, and all organized houses which, for the two semesters preceding the Honors Day Convocation, have an average of twenty hundredths (.20) of a point above the two-semester all-undergraduate average for that period, are entitled to the privilege of being named in the Honors Day program. The following organizations met this requirement this year.

### FRATERNITIES

Alpha Epsilon Pi
Delta Kappa Epsilon
Farmhouse
Pi Lambda Phi
Sigma Alpha Mu

Tau Delta Phi
Tau Epsilon Phi
Triangle
Zeta Beta Tau

### SORORITIES

Alpha Chi Omega
Alpha Delta Pi
Alpha Epsilon Phi
Alpha Gamma Delta
Chi Omega
Delta Delta Delta
Delta Gamma
Gamma Phi Beta

Iota Alpha Pi
Kappa Alpha Theta
Kappa Delta
Kappa Kappa Gamma
Phi Sigma Sigma
Pi Beta Phi
Sigma Delta Tau
Zeta Tau Alpha

# PRIZES AND AWARDS GIVEN THROUGH
# THE UNIVERSITY TO UNDERGRADUATE STUDENTS

AIR CONDITIONING, REFRIGERATION, AND HEATING AWARD (Engineering)
KATZ, STUART MARC   Senior   April, 1971

ELLIOTT RITCHIE ALEXANDER AWARD (Chemistry and Chemical Engineering)
KLOTTER, KEVIN ALBERT   Sophomore   April, 1971

ALLERTON AMERICAN TRAVELING SCHOLARSHIP (Architecture)
GIUNTOLI, PHILIP ALFRED   Senior   April, 1970
OLSON, BENJAMIN HARRY   Junior   April, 1970
ALTERNATES
ROSENBLUM, MARTIN JAY   Senior   April, 1970
WEST, MICHAEL GORDON   Senior   April, 1970

ALPHA CHI SIGMA PLAQUE (Chemistry and Chemical Engineering)
MELDI, DOMINIC M.   Freshman   April, 1971

ALPHA LAMBDA DELTA PRIZE (Senior Book)
LEPPER, CAROLYN SUE   Senior   May, 1970
WILLIS, KATHRYN A.   Senior   May, 1970

ALPHA RHO CHI MEDAL (Architecture)
HULT, ROBERT JARMAN   Senior   April, 1970

ALPHA ZETA PLAQUE (Agriculture)
CRONE, RICHARD CHARLES   Freshman   October, 1970

ALSCHULER AWARD (Architecture)
LINK, JOAN M.   Senior   April, 1970

AMERICAN INSTITUTE OF AERONAUTICS AND ASTRONAUTICS AWARD (Engineering)
CHESLEY, PATRICK JOHN   Senior   April, 1971
McCLEISH, JOHN LAWRENCE   Senior   February, 1971

AMERICAN INSTITUTE OF ARCHITECTS PRIZES (Architecture)
BULLMAN, BRUCE DAVID   Senior   April, 1970
THOMSON, RODERIC LAIRD   Senior   April, 1970

AMERICAN INSTITUTE OF CHEMICAL ENGINEERS SCHOLARSHIP AWARD
WILHELM, JOSEPH LEE   Junior   April, 1971

AMERICAN INSTITUTE OF CHEMISTS STUDENT AWARD
LEOPOLD, WILLIAM RICHARD, III   Senior   April, 1971
RACZKOWSKI, ANDRES WESLEY   Senior   April, 1971

AMERICAN INSTITUTE OF INDUSTRIAL ENGINEERS AWARD
FELDMAN, MARK IRWIN   Senior   April, 1971

AMERICAN SOCIETY OF AGRICULTURAL ENGINEERS HONOR AWARDS
KLOCKE, NORMAN LEE   Senior   April, 1971
WAIT, JAY JENNER   Senior   April, 1971

AMERICAN SOCIETY OF AGRICULTURAL ENGINEERS HONOR AWARDS
SCHNEIDER, RONALD W.   Junior   April, 1971

AMERICAN SOCIETY OF CIVIL ENGINEERS AWARDS
OLSEN, CRAIG ALAN   Senior   April, 1971
WILKEN, GARY A.   Senior   April, 1971
WUELLNER, WILLIAM WALTER   Senior   April, 1971

**AMERICAN SOCIETY OF LANDSCAPE ARCHITECTS AWARD**
RAIMAN, RANDALL GRANT                    Senior              May, 1970

**AMERICAN SOCIETY OF MECHANICAL ENGINEERS PRIZES**
LEHMAN, JOHN HAROLD                      Senior              April, 1970

**IRA O. BAKER, PRIZES AND PLAQUE (Civil Engineering)**
OLSEN, CRAIG ALAN                        Senior              April, 1971
TAYLOR, WILLIAM MICHAEL                  Senior              February, 1971

**MARTHA BELLE BARRETT PRIZES IN HISTORY**
GEORGE, JOHN MARTIN, JR.                 Senior              June, 1970
HARKONEN, JAMES S.                       Senior              June, 1970
STEIN, ARNOLD BRUCE                      Senior              June, 1970

**BORDEN AWARD**
AGRICULTURE
MARSHALL, PAUL EDWARD                    Senior              September, 1970
HOME ECONOMICS
KOCH, BEVERLY ANN                        Senior              October, 1970

**BRADLEY AND BRADLEY AWARD (Architecture)**
ELIAS, JOHN C.                           Senior              February, 1971

**H. R. BRAHANA PRIZE (Mathematics)**
JAMIESON, MICHAEL W.                     Senior              March, 1971
REINER, DAVID L.                         Senior              March, 1971

**CHEMICAL RUBBER COMPANY ACHIEVEMENT AWARD**
MOORE, DEBRA LEE                         Freshman            April, 1971

**COMMUNICATIONS ALUMNI MEMORIAL AWARD**
BROTMAN, ERICA                           Senior              May, 1971

**WILBUR H. COULTAS MEMORIAL AWARD (Agriculture)**
CANTLIN, JOHN LAWRENCE                   Senior              May, 1970

**DANFORTH AWARDS**
AGRICULTURE
TOMBAUGH, LARRY W.                       Freshman            May, 1970
HOME ECONOMICS
SIMMONS, BRENDA LOU                      Freshman            May, 1970

**DEETER-RITCHEY AWARD (Fontainebleau Scholarship)**
LERITZ, JAMES PETER                      Junior              April, 1970
ALTERNATE
JOHNSON, RALPH EVERETT                   Junior              April, 1970

**DELTA SIGMA PI KEY (Commerce and Business Administration)**
CHAN, JAMES LAP-CHI                      Senior              May, 1971

**DONALD W. DOERSCHER MEMORIAL AWARD (Philosophy)**
LITTLE, DANIEL EASTMAN                   Senior              March, 1971

**M. T. DURAL UNDERGRADUATE RESEARCH PRIZE**
WENNER, THOMAS JOHN                      Senior              April, 1971

EDWARD C. EARL PRIZE (Architectural Study of Design, Theory and Drawing)
FREEHAND DRAWING

| | | |
|---|---|---|
| GOLDENBERG, LEON | Junior | April, 1970 |
| KUBALA, THOMAS A. | Sophomore | April, 1970 |
| SARGENT, STEVEN LESLIE | Sophomore | April, 1970 |
| WALKER, STEVEN CHARLES | Sophomore | April, 1970 |

SUMMER EXPERIENCE

| | | |
|---|---|---|
| DAVIS, BRUCE WARREN | Senior | January, 1971 |
| GIUNTOLI, PHILIP ARTHUR | Senior | January, 1971 |

ARCHITECTURE 132

| | | |
|---|---|---|
| DEPIETRO, RUSSELL J. | Junior | February, 1971 |
| JONES, JAKE A., III | Sophomore | May, 1970 |
| LUEBKE, CHARLES M. | Sophomore | May, 1970 |
| MEATTE, MARK C. | Sophomore | February, 1971 |
| PAXTON, THOMAS C. | Sophomore | May, 1970 |
| REYNOLDS, DALLAS KENT | Junior | February, 1971 |

ARCHITECTURE 234

| | | |
|---|---|---|
| TROSKY, GEORGE ALBERT | Junior | February, 1970 |

ARCHITECTURE 235, 236, 337

| | | |
|---|---|---|
| BROWN, GERALD W. | Senior | February, 1971 |
| CRNKOVICH, CHARLES M. | Senior | February, 1971 |
| FARNSWORTH, GEOFFREY LEE | Senior | February, 1971 |
| GOLDENBERG, LEON | Senior | February, 1971 |
| GIUNTOLI, PHILIP A. | Senior | February, 1971 |
| KUMNICK, RICHARD J. | Senior | February, 1971 |
| LAVOT, ALAIN | Senior | February, 1971 |
| LE, CHI-SANH | Senior | February, 1971 |
| LUEBKEMAN, DAVID J. | Junior | February, 1971 |
| MOK, LEWIS STEPHEN | Junior | February, 1971 |
| MOLINARO, MICHAEL J. | Junior | February, 1971 |
| PEPPER, ALAN M. | Senior | February, 1971 |
| SKELTON, JAMES D. | Senior | February, 1971 |
| WEEKS, ARTHUR BRUCE | Senior | February, 1971 |

ARCHITECTURE 338

| | | |
|---|---|---|
| ELIAS, JOHN CHARLES | Senior | February, 1971 |

ENGINEERING OPTION

| | | |
|---|---|---|
| JOHNSON, RONALD BERT | Senior | April, 1970 |
| THEIS, ALAN ROBERT | Senior | April, 1970 |
| THEISS, MICHAEL JOHN | Senior | April, 1970 |

C. J. ELLIOTT MEMORIAL AWARD (Agriculture)

| | | |
|---|---|---|
| OLSON, GREGORY LYNN | Senior | May, 1970 |

ABRAHAM EPSTEIN MEMORIAL SCHOLARSHIP (Architecture)

| | | |
|---|---|---|
| ADAMS, ROBERT DARYL | Junior | April, 1970 |

ETA KAPPA NU AWARD (Electrical Engineering)

| | | |
|---|---|---|
| ZACK, GREGORY WILLIAM | Senior | December, 1970 |

FIELDS, GOLDMAN AND MAGEE SCHOLARSHIP (Architecture)

| | | |
|---|---|---|
| PAAPE, JOHN CONRAD | Junior | April, 1970 |

OLAF FJELDE ALPHA RHO CHI AWARD (Architecture)

| | | |
|---|---|---|
| ANDERSON, WILLIAM LIPPINCOTT, JR. | Sophomore | April, 1970 |

DR. LESTER E. FISHER AWARD (Veterinary Medicine)

| | | |
|---|---|---|
| GREENFIELD, JONATHAN WAINWRIGHT | Senior | April, 1971 |

EDWARD S. FRASER AWARD

| | | |
|---|---|---|
| HUBER, BRUCE ALAN | Senior | April, 1971 |

**REYNOLD CLAYTON FUSON AWARD (Chemistry or Chemical Engineering)**

| | | |
|---|---|---|
| Damon, David Anthony | Senior | April, 1971 |

**GAMMA SIGMA DELTA PLAQUE (Agriculture)**

| | | |
|---|---|---|
| Guengerich, Frederick Peter | Senior | April, 1970 |

**GARGOYLE PLAQUE (Architecture)**

| | | |
|---|---|---|
| Novickas, Algis J. | Freshman | April, 1970 |
| Summers, James Douglas | Sophomore | April, 1970 |

**GENERAL ENGINEERING PROJECT DESIGN AWARD**

| | | |
|---|---|---|
| Fellman, Charles Walter | Senior | April, 1971 |
| Rutger, Ronald Russell | Senior | April, 1971 |
| Turner, John Alger | Senior | April, 1971 |

**GEOLOGY ALUMNI ASSOCIATION SENIOR AWARD**

| | | |
|---|---|---|
| Smith, Stephen Arnold | Senior | May, 1970 |

**A. A. HARDING AWARD (Bands)**

| | | |
|---|---|---|
| Glover, John Franklin | Senior | June, 1970 |
| Patton, John McDowell, III | Graduate | June, 1970 |
| Tasa, David Wayne | Senior | June, 1970 |
| Tessin, Kathryn O. | Graduate | June, 1970 |

**HASKINS AND SELLS FOUNDATION AWARD (Accountancy)**

| | | |
|---|---|---|
| Munz, John Hartzell | Junior | July, 1970 |

**RANDOLPH P. HOELSCHER AWARD (General Engineering)**

| | | |
|---|---|---|
| Mancini, Louis J. | Junior | April, 1971 |

**HOME ECONOMICS CLUB AWARD**

| | | |
|---|---|---|
| Park, Alyn S. | Sophomore | September, 1970 |

**HONEYWELL AWARD**

| | | |
|---|---|---|
| Barr, Kenneth Harry | Junior | April, 1971 |

**DR. H. PRESTON HOSKINS AWARD (Veterinary Medicine)**

| | | |
|---|---|---|
| Geiser, Dennis Richard | Junior | April, 1971 |

**GEORGE HUFF CERTIFICATE**

| | | |
|---|---|---|
| Anderson, Robert Alan | Graduate | March, 1971 |
| Barr, Kenneth Harry | Junior | March, 1971 |
| Beck, Bruce Allen | Junior | March, 1971 |
| Benberry, Herschel Clay | Senior | March, 1971 |
| Bluhm, Ronald Ray | Senior | March, 1971 |
| Bobert, David Lloyd | Senior | March, 1971 |
| Bucklin, Robert Scott | Junior | March, 1971 |
| Burgener, David Brian | Sophomore | March, 1971 |
| Butts, Larry John | Senior | March, 1971 |
| Cheriot, B. Antonio | Senior | March, 1971 |
| Christensen, Gary Marvin | Junior | March, 1971 |
| Clements, Ernest Vinton, III | Senior | March, 1971 |
| Collier, Glenn Haven | Junior | March, 1971 |
| Cook, Jeffrey Allan | Senior | March, 1971 |
| Dixon, Wesley Gerald | Junior | March, 1971 |
| Dunlap, Thomas Donald | Senior | March, 1971 |
| Durkin, John Francis | Senior | March, 1971 |
| Dykstra, Gregory Lee | Senior | March, 1971 |
| Fregeau, John Charles | Senior | March, 1971 |
| Gardner, Robert Edward | Senior | March, 1971 |
| Gibala, Nicholas John | Sophomore | March, 1971 |
| Howard, Joseph Omar | Senior | March, 1971 |

| | | |
|---|---|---|
| HOWAT, CLAUDE RICHARD | Senior | March, 1971 |
| HOWLAND, DENNIS RAY | Senior | March, 1971 |
| HOWSE, KENNETH RAYMOND | Senior | March, 1971 |
| JOHNSON, STEVEN | Senior | March, 1971 |
| KAISER, JOHN | Senior | March, 1971 |
| KALIN, GENE STUART | Junior | March, 1971 |
| KELLY, JOHN PAUL | Senior | March, 1971 |
| KIRKPATRICK, BRUCE LEONARD | Graduate | March, 1971 |
| KOSTER, MARK REMI | Senior | March, 1971 |
| KRONENFELD, PHILLIP DAVID | Junior | March, 1971 |
| KUEHN, CLYDE LOUIS | Senior | March, 1971 |
| LEVINE, ROBERT MILES | Senior | March, 1971 |
| MAJERCIK, LARRY DENNIS | Senior | March, 1971 |
| MANGO, ROBERT JOSEPH | Sophomore | March, 1971 |
| MATTEN, BRADLEY KARL | Senior | March, 1971 |
| MAXWELL, BARRY SCOTT | Junior | March, 1971 |
| McNABB, LOUIS JOSEPH | Junior | March, 1971 |
| OBERROTMAN, ALAN MAURICE | Junior | March, 1971 |
| PECK, KENNETH E. | Senior | March, 1971 |
| PEGORARO, ROBERT ANTHONY | Senior | March, 1971 |
| POST, WARREN MICHAEL | Senior | March, 1971 |
| PRICE, MICHAEL THOMAS | Senior | March, 1971 |
| RAYMOND, EDWARD AUBREY | Graduate | March, 1971 |
| SCHWARTZ, LAWRENCE BARRY | Senior | March, 1971 |
| SMITH, GEORGE KENT | Senior | March, 1971 |
| STEFFENSEN, JAMES PETER | Freshman | March, 1971 |
| STERBA, ANTON WAYNE | Sophomore | March, 1971 |
| TJADEN, DEAN ANDERSEN | Senior | March, 1971 |
| TROBE, PETER MICHAEL | Senior | March, 1971 |
| WOLFF, QUENTIN A. | Senior | March, 1971 |
| YURTIS, BARRY ANTHONY | Senior | March, 1971 |

ILLINOIS MOTHER'S ASSOCIATION BOOK AWARD

| | | |
|---|---|---|
| ADAMS, MARTHA JEAN | Freshman | February, 1971 |
| ADKISSON, STANLEY WHITE | Freshman | February, 1971 |
| ALBANO, DEBORAH LINN | Freshman | February, 1971 |
| ALBRECHT, CAROL JEAN | Freshman | February, 1971 |
| ALI, SAFYED MOHAMMED | Freshman | February, 1971 |
| ARNOLD, SANDRA KAY | Freshman | February, 1971 |
| ASHER, IRA MANUEL | Freshman | February, 1971 |
| ASHLEY, LANE JOHN | Freshman | February, 1971 |
| ATKINSON, DAVID EDWIN | Freshman | February, 1971 |
| BASS, STEVEN ALLEN | Freshman | February, 1971 |
| BENDER, DANIEL EUGENE | Freshman | February, 1971 |
| BENTHAUS, JULIE LYNN | Freshman | February, 1971 |
| BERGER, CATHY MICHELE | Freshman | February, 1971 |
| BERNARDY, JOHANNA MARY | Freshman | February, 1971 |
| BERNSTEIN, HELANE IRIS | Freshman | February, 1971 |
| BEYERS, JOSEPH WAYNE | Freshman | February, 1971 |
| BJORSETH, KATHLEEN MARIE | Freshman | February, 1971 |
| BLACK, ELLEN JEAN | Freshman | February, 1971 |
| BLAZEK, JUDITH JEAN | Freshman | February, 1971 |
| BLUNIER, DORIS ELAINE | Freshman | February, 1971 |
| BORTH, DAVID EDWARD | Freshman | February, 1971 |
| BREWER, MICHAEL LYNN | Freshman | February, 1971 |
| BRIGGS, MARTHA LUELLA | Freshman | February, 1971 |
| BRODERICK, THOMAS F. | Freshman | February, 1971 |
| BROWN, JAMES MICHAEL | Freshman | February, 1971 |
| BUDZIK, PHILIP MARTIN | Freshman | February, 1971 |
| BUTLER, DEBORAH KATHRYN | Freshman | February, 1971 |
| BUTTINGER, PAUL RICHARD | Freshman | February, 1971 |
| CARDELLA, RICHARD GEORGE | Freshman | February, 1971 |
| CARLEY, STEPHEN EDWARD | Freshman | February, 1971 |
| CATTELL, RODERIC GEOFFREY | Freshman | February, 1971 |
| CEDAR, ROBERT BRUCE | Freshman | February, 1971 |

| | | |
|---|---|---|
| CHAO, NANCY SHAN | Freshman | February, 1971 |
| CLARK, LINDA JEAN | Freshman | February, 1971 |
| CONDON, SUSAN JOANNE | Freshman | February, 1971 |
| CONROY, KATHLEEN RANDALL | Freshman | February, 1971 |
| COOPER, RICHARD ALLEN | Freshman | February, 1971 |
| COUGHLIN, RICHARD TODD | Freshman | February, 1971 |
| COURT, MARCIA LOUISE | Freshman | February, 1971 |
| CRENSHAW, SARAH LOUISE | Freshman | February, 1971 |
| CROMBIE, PETER BLYTH | Freshman | February, 1971 |
| CUTLER, DEBORAH SUSAN | Freshman | February, 1971 |
| CUTLER, ROBERT BRIAN | Freshman | February, 1971 |
| DECHSEL, JEANNE ANN | Freshman | February, 1971 |
| DON, MARCIA | Freshman | February, 1971 |
| DORN, ALAN STUART | Freshman | February, 1971 |
| DOTY, JANE LOUISE | Freshman | February, 1971 |
| DOWNEY, TIMOTHY WILL | Freshman | February, 1971 |
| DUCHON, JANE KATHLEEN | Freshman | February, 1971 |
| FUFFIN, JOHN THOMAS | Freshman | February, 1971 |
| DUKES, ROBERT REYNOLDS | Freshman | February, 1971 |
| DUNIVENT, AMY ANNE | Freshman | February, 1971 |
| DYREK, EDWARD LEWIS | Freshman | February, 1971 |
| EARP, LAWRENCE MARSHBURN | Freshman | February, 1971 |
| ELLENBY, CHERYL INEZ | Freshman | February, 1971 |
| ELLSTRAND, NORMAN CARL | Freshman | February, 1971 |
| EMSHOFF, JAMES GORDON | Freshman | February, 1971 |
| EWAN, JUDITH ANN | Freshman | February, 1971 |
| EWANIC, DEBRA EVON | Freshman | February, 1971 |
| FAWCETT, BRADLY KEVIN | Freshman | February, 1971 |
| FAY, JOSEPH WILLIAM | Freshman | February, 1971 |
| FEINBERG, JOYCE MARILYN | Freshman | February, 1971 |
| FLINT, PATRICIA ANN | Freshman | February, 1971 |
| FOSTER, CRAIG STEPHEN | Freshman | February, 1971 |
| FOX, JANET ELAINE | Freshman | February, 1971 |
| FRANK, SHARON LOUISE | Freshman | February, 1971 |
| FRASER, SUSAN ELIZABETH | Freshman | February, 1971 |
| FRIEDMAN, CARYN BETH | Freshman | February, 1971 |
| FRIEDMAN, DEBBIE MARSHA | Freshman | February, 1971 |
| FRIEDMAN, DEBORAH JANE | Freshman | February, 1971 |
| FRIEDMAN, LEE | Freshman | February, 1971 |
| GARRY, PAULA MARIE | Freshman | February, 1971 |
| GASS, JEROME HENRY | Freshman | February, 1971 |
| GASSMAN, MARSHA ANN | Freshman | February, 1971 |
| GEHRING, DURWARD JAMES | Freshman | February, 1971 |
| GEORGE, PAUL MICHAEL | Freshman | February, 1971 |
| GITMAN, DAVID | Freshman | February, 1971 |
| GNAVI, WALTER MICHAEL, JR. | Freshman | February, 1971 |
| GOLDMAN, LINDA | Freshman | February, 1971 |
| GOLDSTEIN, JAY LAWRENCE | Freshman | February, 1971 |
| GOLDSTEIN, LAURENCE JAYE | Freshman | February, 1971 |
| GOODMAN, ALLAN LEE | Freshman | February, 1971 |
| GOODMAN, BETH FRANCINE | Freshman | February, 1971 |
| GRAY, DAVID PAUL | Freshman | February, 1971 |
| GRAY, JULIE ANN | Freshman | February, 1971 |
| GRISOLANO, JAMES MARTIN, JR. | Freshman | February, 1971 |
| GUIDO, DIANE CHRISTINE | Freshman | February, 1971 |
| HAGEN, DANIEL RUSSELL | Freshman | February, 1971 |
| HAGEN, DAVID LOUIS | Freshman | February, 1971 |
| HALEY, DELORES ANN | Freshman | February, 1971 |
| HALPERIN, DEBRA SUE | Freshman | February, 1971 |
| HARPER, SCOTT THOMAS | Freshman | February, 1971 |
| HARRIS, HARLENE DEBRA | Freshman | February, 1971 |
| HARRIS, ILA | Freshman | February, 1971 |
| HELSPER, NORMA JANE | Freshman | February, 1971 |
| HENRIKSON, DIANE ELIZABETH | Freshman | February, 1971 |
| HIRSCHTICK, ROBERT EDWARD | Freshman | February, 1971 |

| | | |
|---|---|---|
| HORTIN, MARY JANE | Freshman | February, 1971 |
| HOVEY, MICHAEL CURTISS | Freshman | February, 1971 |
| HUCKO, JOSEPHINE THERESA | Freshman | February, 1971 |
| HYKAN, ROBERT ALAN | Freshman | February, 1971 |
| INGRASSIA, LAWRENCE ANDREW | Freshman | February, 1971 |
| JACKSON, JUANITA MARLENE | Freshman | February, 1971 |
| JACOBI, NEAL HENRY | Freshman | February, 1971 |
| JOHNSON, GARY BURTON | Freshman | February, 1971 |
| JONES, RICHARD MICHAEL | Freshman | February, 1971 |
| KANTER, JANICE | Freshman | February, 1971 |
| KANTER, JOANNE | Freshman | February, 1971 |
| KAVITT, BARBARA JOY | Freshman | February, 1971 |
| KEHOE, DANEA M. | Freshman | February, 1971 |
| KEMP, NANCY MARIE | Freshman | February, 1971 |
| KENIS, LINDA JOY | Freshman | February, 1971 |
| KHESHGI, ZAREENA D. | Freshman | February, 1971 |
| KIES, KARLA KLARE | Freshman | February, 1971 |
| KIMMEL, THOMAS ALLEN | Freshman | February, 1971 |
| KINNEY, CAROLYN MARGARET | Freshman | February, 1971 |
| KNIGHT, CHARLES DANIEL | Freshman | February, 1971 |
| KOBYLECKY, JUDITH KATERINE | Freshman | February, 1971 |
| KOLBER, SUSAN LYNNE | Freshman | February, 1971 |
| KONRAD, WILLIAM KURTIS | Freshman | February, 1971 |
| KOPERA, ANNE THERESE | Freshman | February, 1971 |
| KUHLI, SARA EDITH | Freshman | February, 1971 |
| LAMB, MICHELLE EVA | Freshman | February, 1971 |
| LANGLEY, DEBORAH ANN | Freshman | February, 1971 |
| LANTZ, PATRICK EUGENE | Freshman | February, 1971 |
| LAUDE, JOHN WILLIAM | Freshman | February, 1971 |
| LEAHY, KATHRYN MARY | Freshman | February, 1971 |
| LEE, REBECCA ANN | Freshman | February, 1971 |
| LENAHAN, JOHN THOMAS | Freshman | February, 1971 |
| LEUTLOFF, CYNTHIA ANNE | Freshman | February, 1971 |
| LISSAK, DEBRA JO | Freshman | February, 1971 |
| LOMPERIS, LINDA SUSAN | Freshman | February, 1971 |
| LUXION, DENNIS WAYNE | Freshman | February, 1971 |
| MACKOWIAK, MARILYN IRENE | Freshman | February, 1971 |
| MADSEN, ELIZABETH CHRISTINE | Freshman | February, 1971 |
| MAJCHROWICZ, DENNIS MICHAEL | Freshman | February, 1971 |
| MALLIN, THOMAS WAYNE | Freshman | February, 1971 |
| MARZEC, MARIANNE MARGARET | Freshman | February, 1971 |
| MCATEE, ELEANOR ANN | Freshman | February, 1971 |
| MCCLARY, ELMER RAY | Freshman | February, 1971 |
| MCGETRICK, JOHN JOSEPH | Freshman | February, 1971 |
| MCKAHAN, KATHLEEN HELEN | Freshman | February, 1971 |
| MCLEAN, SANDRA | Freshman | February, 1971 |
| MEACHUM, JANET RAE | Freshman | February, 1971 |
| MEISTER, SUSAN FOY | Freshman | February, 1971 |
| MELDI, DOMINIC MATTHEW | Freshman | February, 1971 |
| MELVIN, TYRONE RAY | Freshman | February, 1971 |
| MENDELL, MICHAEL STEVEN | Freshman | February, 1971 |
| MICHAELS, DEBBIE LYNN | Freshman | February, 1971 |
| MILLER, KAREN LEAH | Freshman | February, 1971 |
| MILLER, SHAYLE | Freshman | February, 1971 |
| MOHR, DEBORAH L. | Freshman | February, 1971 |
| MOORE, DEBRA LEE | Freshman | February, 1971 |
| MORROW, DWIGHT WAYNE | Freshman | February, 1971 |
| MOYE, CHARLES EDWARD | Freshman | February, 1971 |
| MURASKI, MARY JEAN | Freshman | February, 1971 |
| MYERS, DONNA LYNNE | Freshman | February, 1971 |
| NAATZ, KENNETH ALLEN | Freshman | February, 1971 |
| NESVIG, KRISTIN LOUISE | Freshman | February, 1971 |
| NEWELL, LARRY MICHAEL | Freshman | February, 1971 |
| NOBEL, SCOTT WILLIAM | Freshman | February, 1971 |
| NOLAN, MARGARET MARY | Freshman | February, 1971 |

| | | |
|---|---|---|
| NUMRICH, PAUL DAVID | Freshman | February, 1971 |
| PALEY, DEBORAH KAY | Freshman | February, 1971 |
| PARKS, JOHN ROBERT | Freshman | February, 1971 |
| PIENKOS, PHILIP THOMAS | Freshman | February, 1971 |
| PIERCE, KENNETH REID | Freshman | February, 1971 |
| PITZEN, TRACY JAMES | Freshman | February, 1971 |
| PLASS, JANE PAULA | Freshman | February, 1971 |
| POLK, JANINE LYN | Freshman | February, 1971 |
| POWELL, LENORA ANN | Freshman | February, 1971 |
| PRESS, JILL DEBORA | Freshman | February, 1971 |
| PURTLE, GEORGE ALAN | Freshman | February, 1971 |
| RANDALL, ANNE CAMELIA | Freshman | February, 1971 |
| RICKER, RANDALL EDWARD | Freshman | February, 1971 |
| RITHOLZ, MARCIA BETH | Freshman | February, 1971 |
| RODGERS, JANICE ELAINE | Freshman | February, 1971 |
| ROOSE, THOMAS ROBERT | Freshman | February, 1971 |
| ROSE, MARK JORDAN | Freshman | February, 1971 |
| ROSEN, BARRY STUART | Freshman | February 1971 |
| ROUSOS, LINDA ANN | Freshman | February, 1971 |
| ROZYCKI, CARLA JOANNE | Freshman | February, 1971 |
| RUBIN, GLORIA M. | Freshman | February, 1971 |
| RUBINSTEIN, CHARLOTTE | Freshman | February, 1971 |
| SMALLER, RICHARD PAUL | Freshman | February, 1971 |
| SALOMONE, ANN MARIE | Freshman | February, 1971 |
| SANDROLINI, LAURA | Freshman | February, 1971 |
| SANTOSTEFANO, MARIA JO | Freshman | February, 1971 |
| SARTORE, STEPHAN JOHN | Freshman | February, 1971 |
| SAULS, ROBERT JOSEPH | Freshman | February, 1971 |
| SCHATZMAN, LYNN IVY | Freshman | February, 1971 |
| SCHMIEDL, NANCY EILEEN | Freshman | February, 1971 |
| SCHUBERT, RICHARD NEAL | Freshman | February, 1971 |
| SCHWARTZ, BRADFORD SCOTT | Freshman | February, 1971 |
| SCHWARTZ, STEVEN | Freshman | February, 1971 |
| SEMPLE, MARGARET ANNE | Freshman | February, 1971 |
| SHAPIRO, DEBORAH SUSAN | Freshman | February, 1971 |
| SHERMAN, JUDITH FAY | Freshman | February, 1971 |
| SHORT, BEVERLY JEAN | Freshman | February, 1971 |
| SLATER, ANNE ELIZABETH | Freshman | February, 1971 |
| SMITH, GARY EDWARDS | Freshman | February, 1971 |
| SMITH, MARK STEVEN | Freshman | February, 1971 |
| SOMMER, HENRY JOSEPH, III | Freshman | February, 1971 |
| STAR, MERRIE DELPHINE | Freshman | February, 1971 |
| STARR, RANDI | Freshman | February, 1971 |
| STILES, CAROLYN LOUISE | Freshman | February, 1971 |
| STOKOLS, JEFFERY MARK | Freshman | February, 1971 |
| TOMKOVICK, JOHN JAMES | Freshman | February, 1971 |
| TOMPOLES, CONSTANCE | Freshman | February, 1971 |
| TRANQUILLI, RITA MARIE | Freshman | February, 1971 |
| TRIPLETT, KEVIN TIMOTHY | Freshman | February, 1971 |
| TROST, CATHERINE ANNE | Freshman | February, 1971 |
| VALENTINE, CATHY LOUISE | Freshman | February, 1971 |
| VANDERLEAN, RUTH ANN ADRIAN | Freshman | February, 1971 |
| VANMELLE, WILLIAM JAMES | Freshman | February, 1971 |
| VICARS, ELIZABETH GRACE | Freshman | February, 1971 |
| VLADIKA, DIANE CHRISTINE | Freshman | February, 1971 |
| VOLK, RHEA MARIE | Freshman | February, 1971 |
| WAKEFIELD, JOHN FREDERICK | Freshman | February, 1971 |
| WEISS, CAREY ALLEN | Freshman | February, 1971 |
| WESSEL, PETER CORDELL | Freshman | February, 1971 |
| WHITE, ROGER BRADLEY | Freshman | February, 1971 |
| WHYTE, ROBERT LLOYD | Freshman | February, 1971 |
| WIGODA, KIRA ANN | Freshman | February, 1971 |
| WILBRANDT, LAWRENCE ARTHUR | Freshman | February, 1971 |
| WINTER, MICHAEL JEFFREY | Freshman | February, 1971 |
| WINTERGREEN, DONNA BETH | Freshman | February, 1971 |

| WISHNE, BERDINE SHEILA | Freshman | February, 1971 |
|---|---|---|
| WITSCHY, CARL EDWARD | Freshman | February, 1971 |
| WOLFSON, MARK ALAN | Freshman | February, 1971 |
| WORTHEM, DENNIS WAYNE | Freshman | February, 1971 |
| WROBEL, BARBARA ANN | Freshman | February, 1971 |
| WUORENMA, RUTH ANN | Freshman | February, 1971 |
| ZAKER, RICHARD ROBERT | Freshman | February, 1971 |
| ZITTER, ROBERT ELLIOT | Freshman | February, 1971 |
| ZLATIN, BARBARA SUSAN | Freshman | February, 1971 |
| ZUBAK, BARBARA ANN | Freshman | February, 1971 |

### ILLINOIS RACING BOARD SCHOLARSHIP (Veterinary Medicine)

| EMIG, CHARLES DAVID | Junior | April, 1971 |
|---|---|---|
| NATHANSON, ALAN HOWARD | Junior | April, 1971 |

### ILLINOIS STATE VETERINARY MEDICAL ASSOCIATION AWARD

| DZIEN, WALTER PAUL | Senior | April, 1971 |
|---|---|---|

### ILLINOIS VETERINARY MEDICAL ALUMNI ASSOCIATION AWARD

| HUGI, ROSS EDWARD | Senior | April, 1971 |
|---|---|---|

### ILLINOIS VETERINARY MEDICAL ALUMNI ASSOCIATION EDITORIAL AWARDS

| LINDSAY, KAY E. | Sophomore | April, 1971 |
|---|---|---|
| O'KEEFE, COLLEEN M. | Freshman | April, 1971 |
| RIMAS, AL A. | Freshman | April, 1971 |
| SHAPIRO, SARAH BETH | Sophomore | April, 1971 |

### INTERCOLLEGIATE CONFERENCE MEDAL (Physical Education)

| SCHWARTZ, LAWRENCE BARRY | Senior | May, 1970 |
|---|---|---|

### MIMI JEHLE AWARD (German)

| WILBER, KATHE QUITTING | Senior | May, 1970 |
|---|---|---|

### HARVEY H. JORDAN AWARD (Engineering)

| SUDLOW, WILLIAM JOSEPH | Senior | April, 1971 |
|---|---|---|
| ZACK, GREGORY WILLIAM | Senior | April, 1971 |

### KAPPA DELTA PI AWARD (Education)

| HOUGHTON, LINDA ANN | Senior | May, 1971 |
|---|---|---|

### KENDALL AWARD (Chemistry)

| LEOPOLD, WILBUR RICHARD, III | Senior | April, 1971 |
|---|---|---|
| KESLER, JAMES LESTER | Senior | April, 1971 |

### DR. EDWARD C. KHUEN AWARD (Veterinary Medicine)

| FETZER, LARRY LEE | Senior | April, 1971 |
|---|---|---|

### KIVETT AND MYERS TRAVELING FELLOWSHIP AWARD (Architecture)

| KOHNEN, DANIEL J. | Junior | April, 1970 |
|---|---|---|

### AGNES SLOAN LARSON AWARD (Chemistry and Chemical Engineering)

| FINKELSTEIN, MICHAEL | Sophomore | January, 1971 |
|---|---|---|
| HANEY, CYNTHIA KAY | Sophomore | January, 1971 |
| JONES, DEBORA S. | Sophomore | January, 1971 |
| KLOTTER, KEVIN A. | Sophomore | January, 1971 |
| LIND, RICHARD E. | Sophomore | January, 1971 |

### E. W. LEHMANN AWARD

| KLOCKE, NORMAN LEE | Senior | April, 1971 |
|---|---|---|
| TEIJIDO, JOSEPH A. | Senior | April, 1971 |
| WAIT, JAY JENNER | Senior | April, 1971 |

**O. A. LEUTWILER AWARD (Mechanical and Industrial Engineering)**
LANCASTER, DAVID RUSSELL            Senior          April, 1971
WILSON, DONALD EUGENE            Senior          April, 1971

**KARL BAPTISTE LOHMANN AWARD (Urban Planning)**
ROTTMAN, DAVID BRUCE            Senior          May, 1971

**FRANK S. AND JENNIE M. LONG TRAVELING SCHOLARSHIP AWARD (Architecture)**
LERITZ, JAMES PETER            Junior          April, 1970
LOOK, DAVID WALTER            Junior          April, 1970

**MACHINERY AWARD (Mechanical Engineering)**
ANDERSON, DONALD WAYNE            Senior          April, 1971

**H. L. MARCUS-L. B. PHILLIPS AWARD (Engineering)**
NELSON, DANNY LEE            Senior          April, 1971

**WERNER MARX AWARD (German)**
MUNCH, PAUL THOMAS            Senior          May, 1970

**DUDLEY McALLISTER MEMORIAL AWARD (Communications)**
BLANKENSHIP, BONNIE LEE            Senior          May, 1971

**CARRIE McGREEVY AWARD (Veterinary Medicine)**
DUPUIS, ROGER ALAN            Senior          April, 1971

**MERCK AWARD (Chemistry or Chemical Engineering)**
SCHOENBERG, DANIEL ROBERT            Senior          April, 1971
VASELESKI, RAYMOND CHARLES            Senior          April, 1971

**CHARLES E. MERRIAM ESSAY AND SCHOLARSHIP AWARD (Political Science)**
MYERS, JOHN RILEY            Senior          April, 1971
NICOL, ARTHUR DUEY            Senior          April, 1971
PETRY, JANET KAY            Junior          April, 1971
SOLOW, SHELDON L.            Junior          April, 1971

**MORROW AWARD PLAQUE (Civil Engineering)**
HOLLINGSHEAD, MARK A.            Sophomore          April, 1971

**MOTOROLA INCORPORATED AWARD (Industrial Design)**
LODUHA, PAUL            Sophomore          May, 1970
WENNER, GERRY            Junior          May, 1970
WITTKAMP, JON            Junior          May, 1970

**MU PHI EPSILON AWARD (Music)**
LEVORA, CHRISTINE F.            Senior          May, 1970

**MUELLER COMPANY AWARD (Engineering)**
LEMAN, MARVIN G.            Junior          April, 1971

**OMICRON NU PLAQUE (Home Economics)**
KOCH, BEVERLY ANN            Senior          February, 1971
PARK, ALYN S.            Sophomore          February, 1971

**PHI BETA KAPPA SCHOLARSHIP AWARD (Liberal Arts and Sciences)**
GULLAND, DEBORAH JEAN            Junior          May, 1970
LUNDE, PAULA ANN            Junior          May, 1970

**PHI KAPPA PHI AWARDS (All-University)**
GARVEY, NANCY ANN            Senior          May, 1970
KESLER, JAMES LESTER            Junior          May, 1970

**PHI LAMBDA UPSILON CUP (Chemistry or, Chemical Engineering)**

| | | |
|---|---|---|
| Brethauer, Todd Steven | Sophomore | April, 1971 |
| Klotter, Kevin Albert | Sophomore | April, 1971 |
| Lind, Richard Ellis | Sophomore | April, 1971 |

**PI KAPPA LAMBDA AWARD (Music)**

| | | |
|---|---|---|
| Hallmark, Roger Alan | Junior | May, 1970 |
| Munakata, Yoko Hirasa | Senior | May, 1970 |

**PI TAU SIGMA AWARD (Mechanical Engineering)**

| | | |
|---|---|---|
| Frederickson, David L. | Sophomore | April, 1971 |

**STANLEY H. PIERCE AWARD (Engineering)**

| | | |
|---|---|---|
| Lancaster, David Russell | Senior | April, 1971 |

**PLYM PRIZES**

| | | |
|---|---|---|
| Graham, Gary Linn | Senior | April, 1970 |
| Johnson, Robert Wayne | Senior | April, 1970 |
| Roecker, James Allen | Senior | April, 1970 |

SUMMER SKETCHES

| | | |
|---|---|---|
| Armon, Robert Andrew | Senior | January, 1971 |

**W. H. RAYNER SURVEYING AWARD**

| | | |
|---|---|---|
| Riggins, Robert Eldon | Senior | April, 1971 |

**ERNEST A. REID OPEN HOUSE AWARD (Engineering)**

| | | |
|---|---|---|
| Battle, Francis Lyman, Jr. | Junior | April, 1971 |

**RICKER PRIZES (History of Architecture)**

| | | |
|---|---|---|
| Goldenberg, Leon | Junior | April, 1970 |
| McCue, Thomas Edward | Junior | April, 1970 |

HONORABLE MENTION:

| | | |
|---|---|---|
| Jurgemeyer, Clark Richard | Junior | April, 1970 |
| Meyers, Russell William | Junior | April, 1970 |

**WORTH HUFF RODEBUSH AWARD (Chemistry)**

| | | |
|---|---|---|
| Yesinowski, James Paul | Senior | April, 1971 |

**HAROLD G. ROETTGER MEMORIAL AWARD (Communications)**

| | | |
|---|---|---|
| Larson, Dale Bradley | Senior | May, 1971 |
| Winter, Douglas Earl | Senior | May, 1971 |

**LISLE ABBOTT ROSE MEMORIAL AWARD (Engineering)**

| | | |
|---|---|---|
| Ubell, Franklin David | Senior | April, 1971 |

**PETER F. ROSSITER SCHOLARSHIP AWARD (Political Science)**

| | | |
|---|---|---|
| Bindenagle, James B. | Senior | April, 1971 |
| Sokol, Ronald P. | Junior | April, 1971 |

**EDWARD L. RYERSON TRAVELING FELLOWSHIP IN LANDSCAPE ARCHITECTURE**

| | | |
|---|---|---|
| Ries, Terry Allen | Senior | May, 1970 |

**DR. JESSE SAMPSON AWARD (Veterinary Medicine)**

| | | |
|---|---|---|
| Johnson, Richard A. | Junior | April, 1971 |

**SCARAB MEDAL (Architectural Design, Site Planning and Housing)**

| | | |
|---|---|---|
| Gibson, Michael A. | Sophomore | April, 1970 |
| Trosky, George Albert | Junior | April, 1970 |

**FRED B. SEELY AWARD (Engineering Mechanics)**

| | | |
|---|---|---|
| Parks, David Moore | Senior | April, 1971 |

**SIGMA ALPHA IOTA AWARD (Music)**

| | | |
|---|---|---|
| WILSON, MICHAEL W. | Junior | March, 1971 |

**TAU BETA PI OUTSTANDING FRESHMAN AWARD (Engineering)**

| | | |
|---|---|---|
| DAVIS, HARRY GLENN | Sophomore | April, 1971 |

**A. L. THOMAS AWARD (Civil Engineering)**

| | | |
|---|---|---|
| REED, RICHARD C. | Senior | April, 1971 |
| TOMLINSON, CAROLE A. | Junior | April, 1971 |

**UPJOHN COMPANY PRIZE (Veterinary Medicine)**

| | | |
|---|---|---|
| BENSON, GORDON JOHN | Senior | April, 1971 |
| GREENFIELD, JONATHAN WAINWRIGHT | Senior | April, 1971 |

**JAMES M. WHITE MEMORIAL PRIZES (Construction and Materials)**

ARCHITECTURE 141, 142, 241, and 242

| | | |
|---|---|---|
| LERITZ, JAMES PETER | Junior | April, 1970 |
| ROECKER, FREDERICK JOHN | Senior | April, 1970 |

ARCHITECTURE 245, 246, 247, and 257

| | | |
|---|---|---|
| ABRAMSON, DAVID VICTOR | Senior | April, 1970 |
| BULLMAN, BRUCE DAVID | Senior | April, 1970 |

ARCHITECTURE 344

| | | |
|---|---|---|
| COLE, CLAYTON CAMMETT, JR. | Junior | April, 1970 |
| HAWKINSON, WILLIAM WALTON | Junior | April, 1970 |
| WILLIAMS, TERRY LEE | Junior | April, 1970 |

**C. C. WILEY TRAVELING AWARD (Highway Engineering)**

| | | |
|---|---|---|
| WILKEN, GARY ALLEN | Senior | April, 1971 |

**WOMEN'S AUXILIARY OF THE AMERICAN VETERINARY MEDICAL ASSOCIATION**

| | | |
|---|---|---|
| RODEN, PATRICK HARLAND | Senior | April, 1971 |

**XI SIGMA PI OUTSTANDING FRESHMAN AWARD (Agriculture)**

| | | |
|---|---|---|
| PALLARDY, STEPHEN GERARD | Sophomore | April, 1971 |

# GENERAL SENATE RULES FOR RECOGNITION OF HONOR STUDENTS

### HONORS DAY RECOGNITION

In the spring of each year, the University holds a convocation of students and members of the faculty, with an address by a distinguished speaker, to give public recognition to its superior students. The printed program is designated by the Honors Day Book and contains the names of all students receiving University recognition, as well as the names of the current recipients of prizes and awards for undergraduates. Also listed are students currently elected to college scholastic honorary societies.

Students whose names are printed in the Honors Day Book as receiving University recognition are those who have been on the Dean's List (see following page) of their college for any semester in which they were enrolled in the University since the last Honors Day Convocation. This recognition is recorded on the Student's University transcript as "Honors Day Recognition (year)."

### UNIVERSITY HONORS PROGRAMS

Successful performance for one year as an Edmund J. James Scholar is recognized by the University Faculty Honors Council, Urbana. This recognition is made by an appropriate typographical sign beside the student's name in the Honors Day Book, and is recorded on the student's University transcript as "Edmund J. James Scholar (year)."

### UNIVERSITY HONORS: THE BRONZE TABLET

Sustained academic achievement is recognized by inscribing the student's name on the Bronze Tablet which hangs on the walls of the main Library. To be eligible, a student must:

(1) Have at least a 4.5 cumulative grade average for all work taken at the University through the semester prior to his graduation, excluding grades in required service courses in physical education.

(2) Rank, on the basis of his cumulative average, in the top three per cent of the students in his college who will graduate when he does.

If the student is a transfer, he must:

(1) Have earned forty or more semester hours at the University of Illinois prior to the semester of his graduation.

(2) Have a University of Illinois cumulative average and a total cumulative average as high as the lowest one listed for eligible students in his college who have completed all of their work at the University of Illinois.

## THE DEAN'S LIST

The name of every full-time student (as defined under "Rules") who has achieved a grade average of 4.0 or better for a given semester is placed on a list prepared for the dean of his college. This list is publicized within the University and is sent to the Office of Public Information for distribution to news agencies throughout the state. Names of James Scholars are preceded by an appropriate typographical sign.

## HONORS DAY RULES OF PROCEDURE

(1) Averages are computed to three decimal places by the Office of Admissions and Records. Grades considered for honors are those earned in semesters of residence as follows: (a) second semester previous year; (b) first semester current year; (c) Bronze Tablet candidates are based upon all semesters prior to the one in which they graduate. Grades used in determining honors for students are those on file in the Office of Admissions and Records.

(2) Only those students are considered who have earned in courses at least fourteen hours of academic credit during each semester under consideration and have maintained a 4.0 or better semester grade-point average (excluding basic service courses in physical education).

(3) Unclassified students are not considered.

(4) Special examinations are disregarded in computing the status of students for honors.

(5) Minor changes may be made from time to time as occasion demands in these Rules of Procedure by the University Faculty Honors Council Committee on Honors (Urbana) without specific reference to the University Senate.

CPSIA information can be obtained
at www.ICGtesting.com
Printed in the USA
BVHW041001180119
538188BV00006B/93/P